"A GLORIOUS PAGE IN OUR HISTORY"

The Battle of MIDWAY
4-6 June 1942

Adm. Chester Nimitz, 1942

CARRIERS, PACIFIC FLEET

FROM	COMINCH				
TO (Action)	ALL TASK FORCE COMMANDERS PACIFIC FLEET	DATE 9 JUNE 42	SUP.	CWO	RELEASE
TO (Info.)					
HEADING					

THE NAVY MARINE CORPS AND COAST GUARD JOIN IN ADMIRATION FOR THE AMERICAN NAVAL MARINE AND ARMY FORCES WHO HAVE SO GALLANTLY AND EFFECTIVELY REPELLED THE ENEMY ADVANCE ON MIDWAY AND ARE CONFIDENT THAT THEIR COMRADES IN ARMS WILL CONTINUE TO MAKE THE ENEMY REALIZE THAT WAR IS HELL " UNQUOTE CINCPAC HEARTILY JOINS IN THE SENTIMENTS EXPRESSED"

USS Enterprise—5-11-42—50M.

WRITTEN UP ON MID WATCH JUNE 9 GCT.

"A GLORIOUS PAGE IN OUR HISTORY"

The Battle of MIDWAY
4-6 June 1942

Adm. Chester Nimitz, 1942

Contributors:

Robert J. Cressman   Steve Ewing   Barrett Tillman   Mark Horan   Clark Reynolds   Stan Cohen

LIBRARY OF CONGRESS CATALOG CARD NO. 90-63323

ISBN 0-929521-40-4

First Printing November 1990

PRINTED IN U.S.A.

Typography: Arrow Graphics & Typography
Missoula, Montana

Cover Design: Mike Egeler
Layout: Stan Cohen & Robert J. Cressman

Cover Painting: Robert L. Rasmussen.

Title Page Painting:
"The Turning Point, Midway, June 1942" by R.G. Smith

PICTORIAL HISTORIES PUBLISHING COMPANY
107 South Third West, Missoula, Montana 59801

INTRODUCTION

· · · · · · · · · · · · · · · · · · · ·

*T*he genesis of this book lies in the gathering of historians at Pensacola, Florida, for the May 1988 symposium hosted jointly by the United States Naval Institute and the Naval Aviation Museum Foundation, on the Battle of Midway. This gathering produced the conviction among the contributors to this volume that even with all of the books that have been written—Samuel Eliot Morison's *Coral Sea, Midway and Submarine Actions* (1949); Mitsuo Fuchida and Masatake Okumiya's *Midway: The Battle That Doomed Japan* (1955); Walter Lord's *Incredible Victory* (1968); Gordon W. Prange's *Miracle at Midway* (1982) and John B. Lundstrom's *The First Team* (1984), the battle still continues to interest a new generation of historians. It also spawned the conviction that what was really needed was a pictorial history of the battle, a veritable portable exhibit.

Some of the contributors to this book had already written about the Battle of Midway—Clark Reynolds in Time-Life's *The Carrier War,* Steve Ewing in *USS Enterprise (CV-6): The Most Decorated Ship of World War II,* Barrett Tillman in his histories of the Grumman "Wildcat" and Douglas "Dauntless," and Bob Cressman in *That Gallant Ship: USS Yorktown (CV-5)*; only Mark Horan, an aggressive and dauntless (no pun intended) researcher, had not had anything published on the battle. His in depth research will be most evident in the chapters he had a major hand in.

The most obvious question heard was "Why *another* book on the Battle of Midway?" Every author, one suspects, when looking over other publications in the field, has said to himself at one time or another, "I wouldn't have written a book on that subject in that way," so it is, no less, here.

Books on the Battle of Midway often begin with only a sketchy outline of the background of the island itself. While one does not necessarily need to hear a dissertation on watch-making to be able to determine intelligently what time it is, we felt that all too often Midway's story had been relegated to a mere appendix. Herein, what occurred on Midway before 1935 is given its own chapter, as is what occurred between the coming of Pan American Airways and incipient Navy interest in the mid-1930s and the start of World War II. Likewise, Midway's first battle with the Japanese, on 7 December 1941, is given its proper place.

Taking advantage of recent scholarship on the Pacific War—some of which has been based on hitherto unavailable Japanese sources—as well as primary records (action reports, translated Japanese records, war diaries, interviews, etc.), and interviews with participants, what follows herein should give the reader an idea of exactly what Midway—both the place and the Battle—is.

Central to this book, though, are the photographs contained herein, gathered from public and private sources. These photographs, whether they be of people or places, ships or planes, represent moments frozen in time: the desolation of Midway and its smallness when compared to the size of the ocean in which it lies; the devastation wrought by shell, bomb, or torpedo; the power and grace of the warships involved in the battle, or the workmanlike and purposeful lines of the vital auxiliaries without which the modern fleet could not function. The faces of men like Cannon, Fleming, Henderson, Ramsey, Fletcher, Nimitz, Spruance, McClusky, Gallaher, Lindsey, Massey, Waldron, Leslie, Best or Short; the pilots of the three torpedo squadrons who perished attacking the Japanese Fleet and their adversaries: Yamamoto, Nagumo, Yamaguchi, Kobayashi and Tomonaga. All were men doing their duty, keeping their minds on the task at hand, fighting a war, doing their best to destroy the enemy and at the same time remain alive themselves.

Inevitably, at the start of a project, people seem to be just names. In time, however, one has the good fortune of sitting down with some of them, sometimes trying to envision them in the cramped cockpits of Grummans or Douglases, trying to imagine what it must have been like locked in aerial combat or diving on a hostile deck ringed with anti aircraft guns; in each case coming away filled with a sense of awe and respect. We are in their debt, for they pass along to another generation what they have seen; what they have learned. It is a privilege to know them, and to call them friends; they have written, boldly, "a glorious page in our history."

ROBERT J. CRESSMAN
STEVE EWING

ACKNOWLEDGEMENTS

. . . .

As usual with a work of this nature, thanks are due to many individuals for their help. Understanding wives have helped, and many thanks to Linda Cressman and Rose Horan for their patience while their respective husbands worked long into the night, and to Christine and Robert Cressman Jr., for their patience with their daddy.

The list of individuals, friends and colleagues at the Naval Historical Center must necessarily begin with the Center's Director, Dr. Dean C. Allard, whose asking me to contribute to the planning for the "staff ride" on the Battle of Midway in June 1988 provided a necessary challenge, and intellectual and professional stimulation at a time when it was most needed; to the Operational Archives Branch's excellent staff, most especially Mike Walker, Mrs. Kathy Lloyd and Ms. Regina Akers; to Roy Grossnick and MAJ John M. Elliott, USMC (ret.) of the Aviation History Branch; Mark Weber of the Curator Branch's Photographic Section; and to Raymond A. Mann, James L. Mooney, and John C. Reilly Jr., of the Ships' History Branch, my friend and car-the Contemporary History branch, my friend and carpooler who endured more verbalizing about the Battle of Midway than he probably cared to in countless trips to work and back!

Special thanks, too, for their encouragement, to Mike Wenger, Jim Sawruk, John Lundstrom, Bob Lawson, Dave Lucabaugh and Dr. Thomas C. Hone.

RJC

A NOTE ON THE PHOTOGRAPHS

. . . .

We have attempted to compile a nearly comprehensive pictorial account of the Battle of Midway. While we would like to have pictured all the people involved in the battle, the sheer number of individuals, on both sides, obviously precludes this from being done. As a compromise, we have tried to include as many "people pictures" as possible, to give the reader an idea of what some of the individuals mentioned in the text looked like — to put faces on men who often appear as only mere names. Those readers seeing many *Yorktown*-related photographs will no doubt recognize them from *That Gallant Ship: USS Yorktown (CV-5)* but this is unavoidable as she had at least two photographers active that day and much action centered around her during the battle. Likewise, *Astoria* and *Portland* each had active photographers, as did *Pensacola*. While readers may recognize certain views that have been seen in countless Midway-related articles or books (this, too, cannot be helped), they should note that the captions provided herein in many cases correct previous captioning errors and add new information wherever possible.

A unique feature of the Battle of Midway was the fact that the noted New York designer Norman Bel Geddes set up reconstructions or dioramas of certain portions of the battle and photographed them. These provide the reader with a good picture of the action that went unphotographed between 3 and 6 June, often from an aerial perspective. They have been used throughout the text along with photographs taken during the battle itself. Photos with contributor's names after them are from private collections; those with the A.C. suffix are available from the National Air and Space Museum; NH-numbered photos are from the Naval Historical Center and 19-N- and 80-G-numbered photos are from the National Archives' Still Pictures branch. PAA-marked photographs are from the collection of Pan American Airways. Any individual wishing to order any of the publicly available photography should do so by first contacting the agency in question to determine availability and price, particularly the latter, since these are subject to change.

CONTENTS

Introduction v

Acknowledgments vi

A Note on the Photographs vi

Glossary viii

USN and Japanese Aircraft Names ix

Chapter One: *"A Very Desolate Island"* 1

Chapter Two: *"Second in Importance Only to Pearl Harbor"* 9

Chapter Three: *"The Sentry for Hawaii"* 19

Chapter Four: *"Time is Everything"* 31

Chapter Five: *"We Will Do The Best We Can With What We Have"* 43

Chapter Six: *"Midway . . . Had a Good Fight on its Hands"* 57

Chapter Seven: *"No Bomber is a Match for a Bunch of Fighters"* 69

Chapter Eight: *"Well, Murray, This is it."* 83

Chapter Nine: *"Skipper, There's a Zero on My Tail"* 91

Chapter Ten: *"Like a Haystack in Flames"* 101

Chapter Eleven: *"Incontestible Mastery of the Air"* 113

Chapter Twelve: *"I Will Do What You Pilots Want"* 141

Chapter Thirteen: *"As Easy as Shooting Ducks in a Rainbarrel"* 153

Chapter Fourteen: *"A Grim and Terrible Business"* 167

Chapter Fifteen: *"A More Pleasant Place"* 179

Appendix I: *Personalties and Perspectives* 187

Appendix II: *Tribute* 195

Appendix III: *American and Japanese Carriers at Midway* 202

Appendix IV: *American and Japanese Aircraft at Midway* 206

Appendix V: *The Truth About Miles Browning* 214

Bibliography 218

Index 222

GLOSSARY

Miscellaneous Terms and Abbreviations
A-V(N) aviation officer USNR holding the designation as naval aviator, qualified for general duty afloat or ashore
BuNo Bureau Number
CAP Combat Air Patrol
CARDIV Carrier Division
CEAG Commander, *Enterprise* Air Group
CEC Civil Engineering Corps
CHAG Commander, *Hornet* Air Group
ChC Chaplain Corps
CINCPAC Commander in Chief, Pacific Fleet
CO Commanding Officer
COM 14 Commandant, 14th Naval District
CP Command Post
CTF Commander, Task Force
CXAM Air Search Radar
CXAM-1 Air Search Radar
CYAG Commander, *Yorktown* Air Group
DFC Distinguished Flying Cross
DSM Distinguished Service Medal
D-V(G) USNR officer qualified for general duty, afloat or ashore
Kido Butai "Carrier Striking Force" (Japanese Navy)
LSO Landing Signal Officer
MAD Marine Aircraft Detachment
MAG Marine Aircraft Group
MC Medical Corps
mm. millimeter
MTBRON Motor Torpedo Boat Squadron
NAP Naval Aviation Pilot
NAS Naval Air Station
OPNAV Office of the Chief of Naval Operations
SC Signal Corps (US Army), Supply Corps (US Navy)
TF Task Force
T.H. Territory of Hawaii
USA United States Army
USAAC United States Army Air Corps
USCGC United States Coast Guard Cutter
USMC United States Marine Corps
USMCR United States Marine Corps Reserve
USN United States Navy
USNR United States Naval Reserve
XO Executive Officer
YE Homing Signal Transmitter
ZB Homing Signal Receiver

Ranks and Rates
ADM Admiral
AMM1c/2c/3c Aviation Machinist's Mate 1st/2d/3d Class
AOM1c/2c/3c Aviation Ordnanceman 1st/2d/3d Class
ACRM Aviation Chief Radioman

ARM1c/2c/3c Aviation Radioman 1st/2d/3d Class
BGEN Brigadier General
CAPT Captain (USN, USMC, USAAC & Japanese Navy)
CDR Commander
CP Chief Photographer
COX Coxswain
CPL Corporal
ENS Ensign
F3c Fireman 3d Class
FPO1c/2c/3c Flight Petty Officer 1st/2d/3d Class (Japanese Navy)
LCDR Lieutenant Commander
LGEN Lieutenant General
LT Lieutenant
LT(jg) Lieutenant (Junior Grade)
MGEN Major General
MM2C Motor Machinist's Mate 2d Class
MTSGT Master Technical Sergeant
PhM1c Pharmacist's Mate 1st Class
PO1c/2c/3c Petty Officer 1st/2d/3d Class (Japanese Navy)
PVT Private
RADM Rear Admiral
SC2c Ship's Cook 2d Class
SEA1c/2c/3c Seaman 1st/2d/3d Class
SGT Sergeant
S2c Steward 2d Class
TM2c Torpedoman 2d Class
TSGT Technical Sergeant
VADM Vice Admiral
WO Warrant Officer (Japanese Navy Aviation Rate)

Ship Types
AK Cargo Ship
AM Minesweeper
AO Fleet Oiler
AOG Gasoline Tanker
APV Transport and Aircraft Ferry
AS Submarine Tender
AT Fleet Tug
AV Seaplane Tender
AVD Seaplane Tender (Destroyer)
BB Battleship
CA Heavy Cruiser
CL Light Cruiser
CV Aircraft Carrier
DD Destroyer
PT Motor Torpedo Boat
SS Submarine
YP District Patrol Vessel

Squadrons
VB Bombing Squadron
VCS Cruiser Scouting Squadron
VF Fighting Squadron
VMF Marine Fighting Squadron
VMSB Marine Scout-Bombing Squadron
VO Observation Squadron
VP Patrol Squadron
VS Scouting Squadron
VT Torpedo Squadron

NOTE: Unless otherwise specified, all USN ship names will be understood as being preceded by USS (United States Ship); a USN ship's hull number will only be used the first time it appears in the text. The Battle of Midway presents a headache to anyone attempting to write about it, in that it took place back and forth across the international date line and in different time zones. Even in reporting the action, the American ships utilized two different time zones in their after-action reports! For the ease of the reader, all times have been converted into the time observed by Midway itself, since it was around this atoll that all of the attention centered between 4 and 6 June 1942. All times, unless otherwise specified (particularly the first chapter, since the action therein took place largely before the acceptance of "military time") will be reckoned in "military time"—i.e., 0100 is one'clock in the morning and 1300 is one o'clock in the afternoon.

USN Aircraft Names
Brewster F2A-3 "Buffalo"
Grumman F4F-3/-4 "Wildcat"
Consolidated PB2Y-2 "Coronado"
Consolidated PBY-5/-5A/-5B "Catalina"
Douglas R4D-1 "Skytrain"
Douglas SBD-2/-3 "Dauntless"
Vought SB2U-3 "Vindicator"
Curtiss SOC-3 "Seagull"
Douglas TBD-1 "Devastator"
Grumman TBF-1 "Avenger"

USAAC Aircraft Names
Boeing B-17E/F "Flying Fortress"
Martin B-26 "Marauder"
Douglas C-53 "Skytrain"
Curtiss P-40E "Kittyhawk"

Japanese Naval Aircraft Names
Aichi D3A1 Type 99 Carrier Bomber (*kanbaku*) ("Val")
Aichi E13A1 Type 00 Reconnaissance Floatplane ("Jake")
Kawanishi E7K2 Type 94 Reconnaissance Floatplane ("Alf")
Mitsubishi A6M2 Type 00 Carrier Fighter (*kansen*) ("Zero")
Mitsubishi G4M1 Type 1 Land Attack Plane ("Betty")
Nakajima B5N2 Type 97 Carrier Attack Plane (*kanko*) ("Kate")
Nakajima E8N2 Type 95 Reconnaissance Floatplane ("Dave")
Yokosuka D3Y1 Type 13 Experimental Carrier Bomber ("Judy")

DEDICATION
. . . .

To the Memory of Those Who Fought in the Battle of
Midway, and to Their Families

and to
Verna J. Ewing (1920-1988)
Mildred M. Cressman (1918-1988)
Mark W. Cressman (1985-1988).

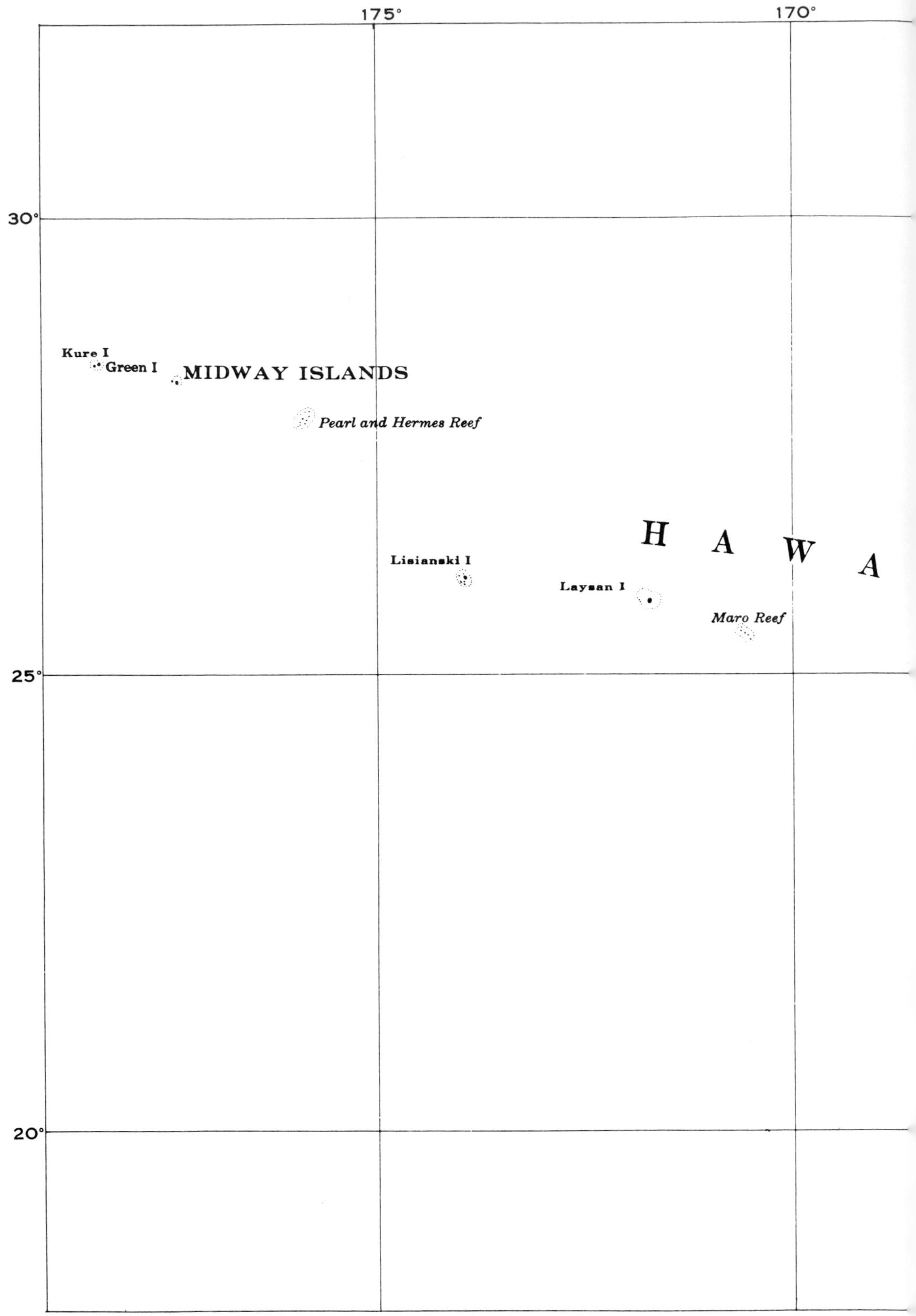

175°   170°

30°

Kure I
 ·.· Green I   .·MIDWAY ISLANDS

                  .· Pearl and Hermes Reef

                                          H   A   W   A

              Lisianski I
                   .·   Laysan I
                                    ·.·   A

                                        Maro Reef
                                           .·.

25°

20°

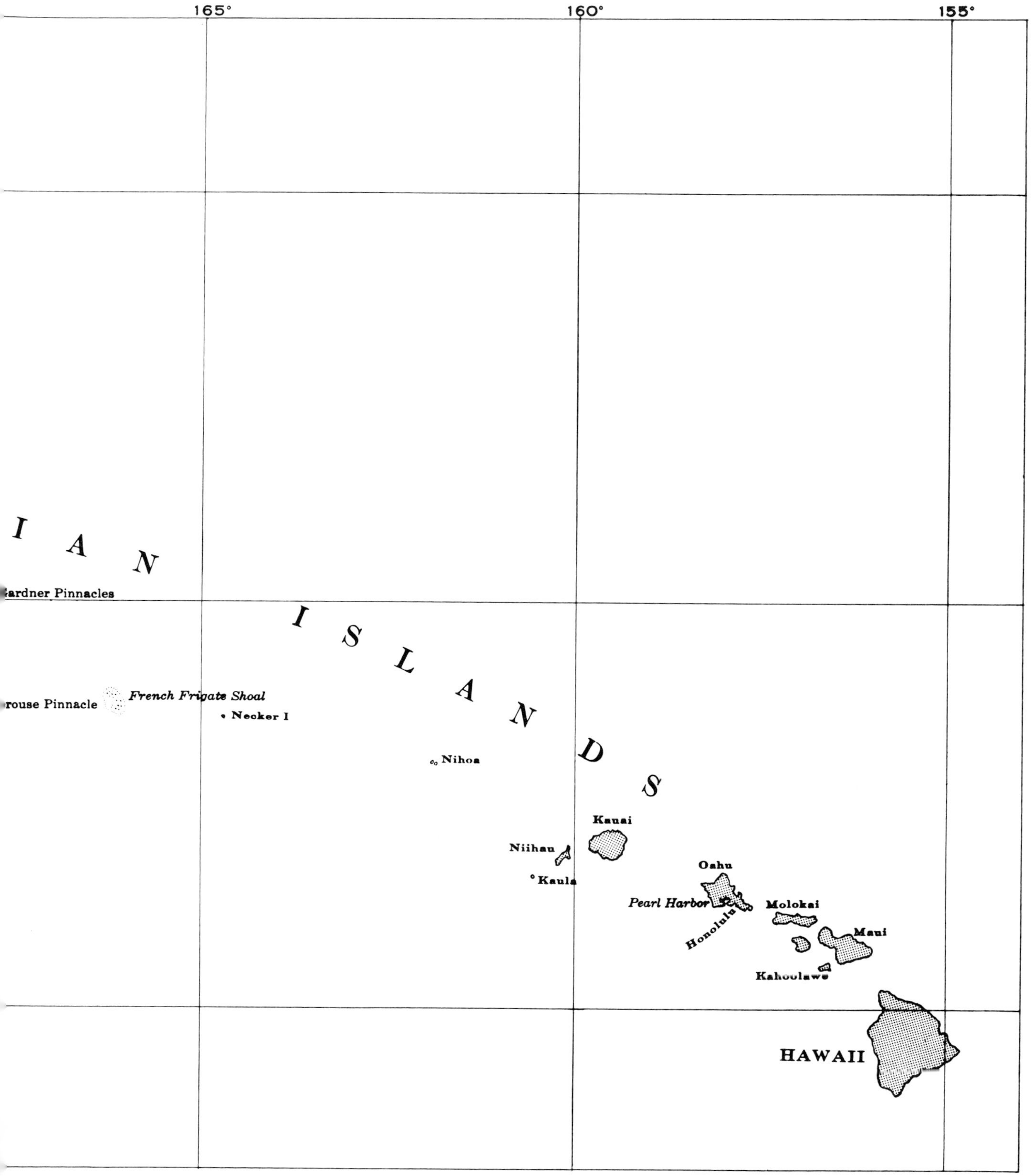
165°
160°
155°
I A N
ardner Pinnacles
I S L A N D S
rouse Pinnacle
French Frigate Shoal
Necker I
Nihoa
Kauai
Niihau
Kaula
Oahu
Pearl Harbor
Honolulu
Molokai
Maui
Kahoolawe
HAWAII

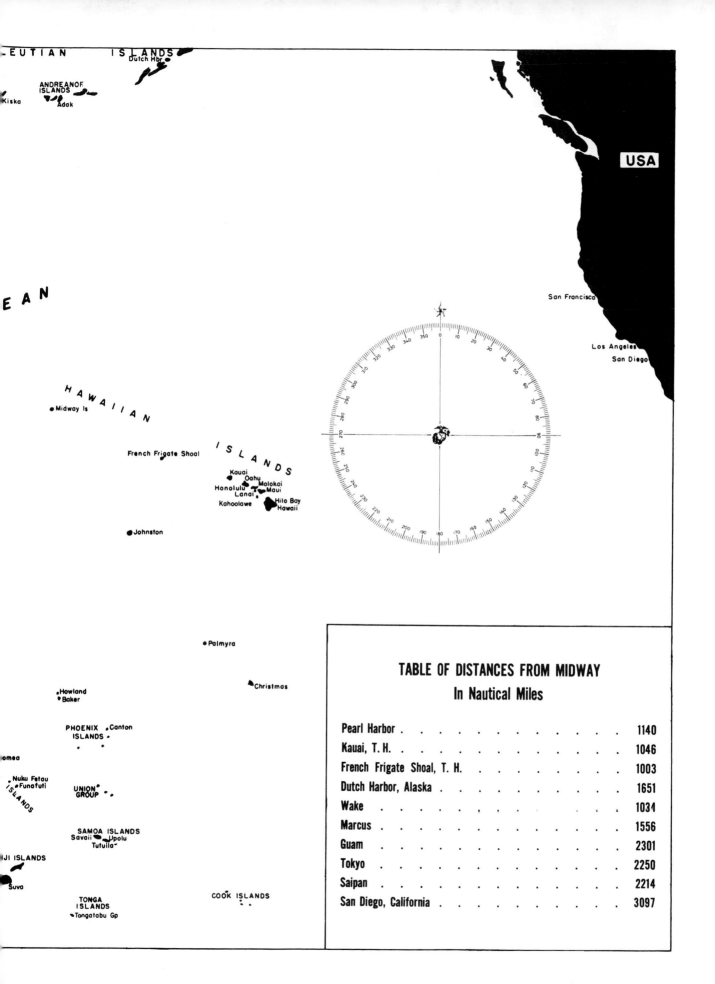

LEUTIAN   ISLANDS
Dutch Hbr

ANDREANOF
ISLANDS
Kiska   Adak

USA

E A N

San Francisco

Los Angeles
San Diego

H A W A I I A N
Midway Is

French Frigate Shoal   I S L A N D S

Kauai
Oahu   Molokai
Honolulu   Lanai   Maui
Kahoolawe   Hilo Bay
Hawaii

Johnston

Palmyra

Christmas

Howland
Baker

PHOENIX   Canton
ISLANDS

omea

Nuku Fetau
Funafuti
ISLANDS   UNION
GROUP

SAMOA ISLANDS
Savaii   Upolu
Tutuila

JI ISLANDS

Suva

TONGA   COOK ISLANDS
ISLANDS
Tongatabu Gp

TABLE OF DISTANCES FROM MIDWAY
In Nautical Miles

Pearl Harbor	1140
Kauai, T. H.	1046
French Frigate Shoal, T. H.	1003
Dutch Harbor, Alaska	1651
Wake	1034
Marcus	1556
Guam	2301
Tokyo	2250
Saipan	2214
San Diego, California	3097

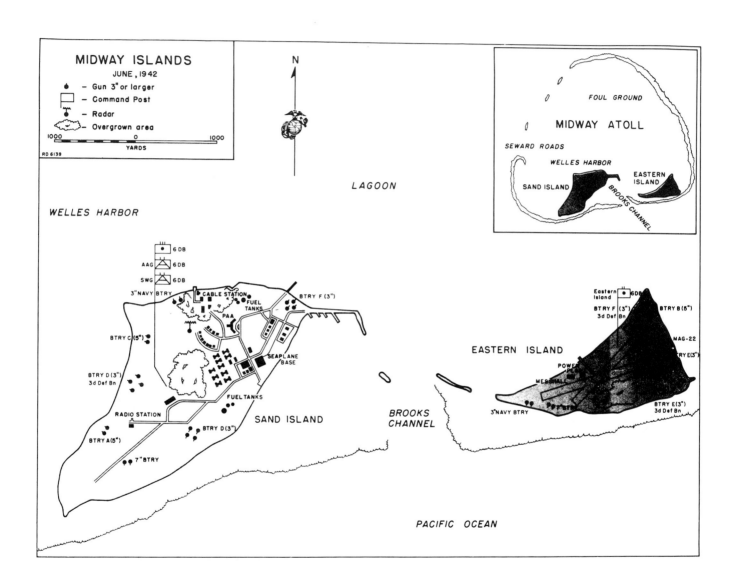

MIDWAY ISLANDS

JUNE, 1942

- Gun 3" or larger
- Command Post
- Radar
- Overgrown area

1000   0   1000
YARDS

RD 6139

N

LAGOON

WELLES HARBOR

MIDWAY ATOLL

FOUL GROUND

SEWARD ROADS

WELLES HARBOR

SAND ISLAND

EASTERN ISLAND

BROOKS CHANNEL

6 DB

AAG   6 DB

SWG   6 DB

3" NAVY BTRY

CABLE STATION

FUEL TANKS

BTRY F (3")

PAA

BTRY C (5")

SEAPLANE BASE

BTRY D (3")
3d Def Bn

FUEL TANKS

RADIO STATION

SAND ISLAND

BTRY A (5")

BTRY D (3")

7" BTRY

Eastern
Island   6 DB

BTRY F (3")   BTRY B (5")
3d Def Bn

MAG-22

EASTERN ISLAND

BTRY E (3")

POWER

MESS HALL

3" NAVY BTRY

BTRY E (3")
3d Def Bn

BROOKS CHANNEL

PACIFIC OCEAN

CHAPTER ONE

. . . .

"A Very Desolate Island..."

Since the dawn of recorded time, intrepid seafarers have sailed the Pacific on voyages of exploration and trade. Vessels manned by hardy New England Yankees in search of whales began plying that ocean as early as 1791. *Balaena*, of New Bedford, and *Equator*, of Nantucket, killed a whale off Kealakekua Bay in September 1819, and became the first of many such ships to touch at Honolulu. Within a little over 25 years, some 400 whalers—"no more ungraceful or lumbering ships ever outfitted"—called at Honolulu in the course of voyages that took them to Japan and to the Kurile Islands, and to the South Pacific.

As they hunted, one or more of these sturdy, bluff-bowed ships may have chanced upon the little atoll located in mid-Pacific at latitude 28 degrees, 12 minutes north, longitude 177 degrees, 22 minutes west, but if they did, no extant chronicle records it. On 5 July 1859, however, the Hawaiian bark *Gambia* hove-to there, and the ship's enterprising American master, CAPT N.B. Brooks, claimed that remote circular atoll some six miles in diameter in the name of the United States, under the "Guano Islands Act" of 1856. That law authorized Americans to occupy, temporarily, unclaimed islands in the Pacific to obtain guano (the droppings of seafowl) which had been found to be valuable as fertilizer. *Gambia's* master named his discovery "Middlebrooks." "Middle..." for its location between the west coast of the United States and Japan, and "...brooks" for himself.

Brooks extolled the virtues of his find when he reached Oahu. "With the exception of Honolulu," one writer declared upon hearing Brooks' report, "these Islands possess advantages for a coaling depot far superior to any other place on the line from California to China." The Pacific Mail Steamship Co.—which would pioneer

regular trans-Pacific passenger service in 1867—urged the United States Navy Department to gather more information on "Middlebrooks."

From 1861 to 1865, however, the American Civil War prompted the Navy to place its priorities on dealing with blockade-runners and commerce raiders, not on voyages of exploration. Once the conflict had ended, though, Secretary of the Navy Gideon Welles revived interest in Brooks' island. On 28 May 1867, he directed RADM Henry K. Thatcher, commander of the North Pacific Squadron, to send the sloop of war *Lackawanna* or "some other suitable and available vessel . . . without unavoidable delay" to search for the island that Brooks had reported, and, if they found it, to "take possession of it in the name of the United States, and to make as accurate and complete a survey of it as possible." Thatcher consequently ordered CAPT William Reynolds, commanding *Lackawanna*—a ship that had been cruising among the Hawaiian Islands, a region recognized as being of great and increasing interest and importance to the United States—to formally take possession of Brooks' islands. Reynolds, no stranger to voyages of discovery and exploration, had, as a passed midshipman, served in the Wilkes Expedition of 1838-1842.

CAPT William Reynolds (1815-1879) is seen here as a commander, CO of *New Hampshire*, in a photograph by Samuel A. Cooley of Savannah, Ga., circa 1864. NH 47138

On 28 August 1867, soon after *Lackawanna's* arrival there, CAPT Reynolds "took formal possession of Brooks Island, and reefs, for the United States." Having erected a "suitable flag-staff," Reynolds landed that day with all of the officers who could be spared from the ship, and six boats of armed men. After a 21-gun salute, the warship's captain hoisted the stars and stripes to the cheers of all assembled, while an agent of the Pacific Mail Steamship Co., a CAPT Burdette, looked on. Reynolds then exercised his men at howitzer and small arms practice, and the ship's marine detachment conducted target practice. After procuring "an abundant supply of fish," *Lackawanna's* men then cooked their dinner ashore, and spent the rest of the day, "pleasantly, pic-nic fashion, upon the island."

"It is exceedingly gratifying to me," Reynolds later reported, "to have been thus concerned in taking possession of the first island ever added to the dominion of the United States, beyond our own shores." He hoped that "this instance will by no means be the last of our insular annexations . . ." He then informed the Department that he had named the harbor for Secretary of the Navy Welles and the roadstead for Secretary of State William H. Seward.

By January 1869, Welles had provided the Senate Naval Affairs Committee with "documents and charts" pertaining to a place then called simply the "Midway Islands..." Soon thereafter, the committee recommended that a naval station be established on "Midway." While the commercial possibilities of a coaling station there, however, were not lost upon the legislators, neither was the political aspect. Recalling how Nassau, a British possession, had harbored the Confederate cruisers *Alabama* and *Florida* during the Civil War prompted the legislators to desire to retain Midway under the Stars and Stripes. They wanted no repetition of the *Alabama* and *Florida* incidents, which had proved costly to Yankee trade.

Two months later, on 1 March 1869, Congress appropriated $50,000 "for deepening the entrance to the harbor of Midway Islands...to afford a safe rendezvous and port of refuge and resort for the naval and merchant vessels of the United States." Learning of this comparative pittance allocated to such an ambitious undertaking, the *Honolulu Advertiser* editorialized on 10 April 1869: "To parties residing in these islands knowing the facts regarding their (Midway Islands') character, it seems strange that a reasonable man could suggest, and urge an appropriation of $50,000, for the improvement of the mouth of a lagoon in a low coral island."

Soon thereafter, the Navy detailed the sidewheel gunboat *Saginaw*, LCDR Montgomery Sicard, commanding, to proceed to Midway and carry out the dredging operation; and chartered the schooner *Kate Piper* to carry supplies and men from Honolulu. *Saginaw* arrived at the islands on 24 March 1870, and work began almost immediately, initially utilizing the Pacific Mail scow found there. By the summer, Sicard could see that formidable natural obstacles needed to be overcome; on 21 July, in his third progress report, he reflected: "I cannot help thinking that the amount of time and work required to make this canal were never properly appreciated. . . ."

Some would have had little trouble seconding Sicard's statement. The contractors toiled at their task, often hampered by bad weather, into the autumn of 1870. Success, however, did not smile upon the endeavor, and

The wooden-hulled sidewheel gunboat *Saginaw*, at about the time of her loss in 1870. NH 20212

LCDR Montgomery Sicard (1836-1900), "one of the most able, upright, and conscientious officers of the service . . . whose courage, calmness and presence of mind in time of danger...were proverbial and unquestioned." NH 2013

this compelled Sicard, the task unfinished and the appropriation expended, to admit defeat. On 28 October 1870, *Saginaw* embarked the contractor's party and as much equipment as it wished to carry with it, and departed.

Sicard charted a course for Ocean (later Kure) Island, to provide aid to shipwrecked mariners, if any happened to be in that remote spot, before he would return to Honolulu. At about three o'clock in the morning on 29 October, however, *Saginaw* ran aground on the reef surrounding Ocean Island. After all on board had reached shore safely with small stocks of provisions and what could be salvaged from the ship, Sicard, exhibiting "the high personal qualities which characterize him as an officer," immediately took steps to prepare for any eventuality. Choosing the fittest boat for the task, the ship's executive officer, LT John G. Talbot, COX William Halford and three other men, all volunteers, sailed for Honolulu for help. Sicard, meanwhile, put the men left on Ocean Island to work building a schooner with material salvaged from *Saginaw's* wreck.

The full story of the voyage of *Saginaw's* gig falls beyond the scope of this work, but suffice it to say the five men suffered much hardship on their 31-day voyage before reaching the island of Kauai; tragically, the gig overturned in the surf and four of the weakened men drowned. Only Halford survived to carry Sicard's dispatch ashore. Help was soon on the way and *Saginaw's* men, and the contractors—their schooner nearly finished—were rescued. Halford received the Medal of Honor.

After Congress turned down further appropriations for work at the atoll, Midway remained largely uninhabited for the next 15 years, the buildings constructed by the contractors brought out by *Saginaw* remaining empty and the place once more taken over by flocks of seabirds. On the night of 15 November 1886, however, the schooner *General Siegel*, en route back to Honolulu after a shark-fishing voyage, foundered on the reef in a storm. Strange and sinister happenings then followed.

One man, J.A. Jorgenson, was suspected of murdering some of his shipwrecked companions, prompting the rest to sail to the Marshalls and safety. For six months, Jorgenson lived alone, with only the birds for company. His deliverance in January 1888, when the British bark *Wandering Minstrel* put into Welles Harbor, proved short-lived, as a storm wrecked that ship, too, marooning her people along with Jorgenson. Later Jorgenson, along with the mate from *Wandering Minstrel*, and a Chinese boy from the crew, sailed for the Marshalls and reached safety at Jaluit. For over a year, the other castaways lived on Midway until rescued by the

British bark *Norma* on 26 March 1889, and landed at Honolulu on 7 April.

Wandering Minstrel's master, CAPT F.D. Walker, returned subsequently to Midway in 1891 with two scientists from the Rothschild Expedition. One expedition member, George A. Munro, recording his impressions of Midway in his diary, noted Sand Island as being "almost a mile long, low and sandy, with a few mounds 12 feet high covered with large scrub at one end; at the other end is a patch of grass. . . . It is a very desolate island with a great extent of low-lying sandy ground, which seems to be swept by heavy seas during heavy weather. . . . There is something melancholy about this desolate place," he wrote in his diary on 12 July 1891, "the sigh of the wind 'round the house, the wail of the petrel, at any time melancholy, seems even more so . . . a feeling of depression comes over one. . . ."

Soon thereafter, the Pacific Mail line seems to have shelved its plans for making Midway a coaling station, and the Hawaiian government ignored a request by the Pacific Phosphate and Guano Co. to obtain a guano lease there. Fortunately, after the only major attempt to develop the atoll had failed, burgeoning interest in transpacific cable communications saved Midway from becoming a "dainty . . . 'white elephant' " on the United States' hands. In April 1896, the Senate Foreign Relations Committee took up the idea.

While competing companies vied for the franchise to lay the cable, none seemed to want to go through Midway, preferring instead to go through the Marshall Islands, which were then a German mandate. The Marshalls, proponents of that idea pointed out, possessed inhabitants and existing port facilities; Midway had neither. The United States government, however, wanted an "All-American" cable, and awarded the contract to the Pacific Commercial Cable Company, that had been formed expressly for the job.

In the spring of 1900, the Navy sent the tug *Iroquois* to Midway, to take soundings. Upon their arrival on 26 May, the Americans discovered Japanese poachers killing the sea birds on the islands for their plumage. The United States government consequently lodged a protest with the Japanese, stating that it would not regard that colonization "as affording any basis for a claim to the islands by the Japanese government."

Work on the cable, meanwhile, proceeded apace over the next two years. On 15 December 1902, the cable ship *Silverton* began laying cable at San Francisco, and finished at Honolulu on Christmas Day. On New Year's Day 1903, congratulatory messages went out unimpeded, and commercial use of the cable linking the west coast of the United States with Hawaii began the next day.

In the meantime, mounting complaints about Japanese poachers and squatters prompted President Theodore Roosevelt to put Midway under Navy Department control on 20 January 1903, in Executive Order 199-A. On 29 April 1903, the steamship *Hanalki* arrived with the initial increment of cable company workers, and found the Japanese schooner *Yeiju Maru* anchored in the lagoon, her crew busily engaged ashore in killing birds. The Americans warned the Japanese to stop the slaughter and to bury those they had already killed. That done, the Cable Company people erected temporary buildings and pitched tents.

The converted tug *Iroquois* at the U.S. Naval Station, Honolulu, circa 1903. Acquired by the Navy in 1898 during the war with Spain, she was assigned to the Naval Station at Honolulu in 1899, and operated in the Hawaiian chain until 1910.
NH 102107, MARTIN FENNE COLLECTION

On 3 June 1903, *Iroquois*, LCDR Hugh Rodman, commanding, arrived at Midway to find a Japanese schooner there and her people slaughtering sea birds. *Iroquois'* captain ordered them to stop the killing, and gave them 48 hours to depart. The Japanese captain, however, objected to Rodman's orders and questioned his authority. Rodman whereupon told him that he had, in effect, violated many laws, not the least of which was "working foreigners on American soil in violation of the alien contract law." Unwilling to discuss the matter further, Rodman shortened the time he would give the Japanese to 24 hours, instead of 48, and threatened to

tow the schooner to Honolulu where formal charges would be preferred against her captain. That night, the schooner sailed for home under cover of darkness. Before *Iroquois* left, Rodman appointed Mr. Benjamin W. Colley, of the Cable Co., as "naval custodian" of the islands (and justice of the peace), adjuring him to prevent "the wanton destruction of birds that breed at Midway, and not let them be disturbed or killed except for purposes of food supply."

Work on the laying of cable, meanwhile, progressed well. At 4 p.m. on the afternoon of 27 June 1903, the cable ship *Colonia* put ashore the end of the Guam to

Cable station buildings on Sand Island, circa 1905. Note buildings and well-kept grounds. NH 102085

General view of cable station grounds on Sand Island, circa 1905, showing grasses planted to cut down soil erosion; Note twin windmills. NH 102088

Gardens planted on Sand Island for the cable station employees to raise their own produce. Note barrier formed by the trees surrounding the plots, and the grasses in the background. NH 102087

Midway cable; within a few days, the cable ship *Anglia*, en route to Honolulu from Midway, had put ashore the last portion of the cable at Waikiki beach at 1 p.m. on 3 July. Workmen spliced the cables together to effect a global hook-up in time for President Roosevelt to send an Independence Day message. By the end of August, the Cable Station boasted quarters for the operators and the supporting people, a cable house, mess room, kitchen and storeroom—all temporary buildings of rough, unpainted lumber.

Supplying that isolated possession involved long distances, and unloading the necessary provisions and stores proved difficult and dangerous—no piers existed at Midway. On 22 October 1903, the chartered schooner *Julia E. Whalen* foundered; the provisions she had brought from Honolulu were a total loss. Fortunately for the cable company people attempting to "tame" the islands, the Navy provided *Iroquois* to bring supplies and food out. These frequent supply runs proved invaluable, such as three years later when the Pacific Mail's SS *Mongolia* ran aground, forcing the cable station employees to host over 600 people until the vessel, her cargo temporarily removed, was refloated.

The Pacific Commercial Cable Co., meanwhile, had sought government assistance for its operation at Midway, requesting an appropriation for blasting a channel through the coral into the lagoon and for making the latter a suitable harbor; the placement of buoys and construction of a lighthouse and landing facilities; and the assignment of "Marines or guards of some character to maintain order and enforce the laws of the islands." The Navy provided buoys and "simple channel markers," and erected a lighthouse, but the cable company had to build its own dock.

To protect the station, a Marine detachment (one officer and 20 enlisted men) disembarked from the storeship *Supply* on 2 May 1904 and set up camp north of the center of Sand Island. This addition of a Marine "garrison" under 2dLT Clarence S. Owen, USMC, brought the population of Midway to approximately 100—contractor's employees, Marines, and cable station people. The latter ultimately became, for at least a time, Midway's sole residents; the Marines being withdrawn to the continental United States on 19 March 1908. By 3 February 1905, more permanent cable quarters (what eventually became Navy buildings 619, 623, 628 and 643) were completed and occupied. Between 1903 and 1930, United States naval vessels visited Midway sporadically—*Iroquois*, for example, was among those that brought in supplies and supplemented the cruises of the Cable Company's *Flaurence E. Ward*, which made monthly trips between Honolulu and Midway.

Hints of the advance of the modern age, and of Midway's future importance in defense matters, first appeared in the autumn of 1920. On 10 October, Midway's first recorded airplane flight occurred, when the patrol craft *Eagle No. 40* (PE-40) arrived at 0700. The *Eagle* hoisted the plane, that she had brought out from Oahu, into the water and it took off for a survey flight, the observer taking photographs for charting purposes. The plane developed engine trouble, however, and had to return to the ship before she completed the assigned mission. Early the following morning, *Eagle No. 40* sailed for Oahu.

On 9 August 1921, the tanker *Patoka* (AO-9) arrived to fuel a group of destroyers, inaugurating Midway's use as a way station for Navy ships on transpacific voyages. "Convoying of torpedo boat destroyers across Pacific both east and west [is]," the cable station diary recounts, "to be a regular thing, with Midway as a rendezvous for fueling. [This] will mean seven or eight vessels visiting . . . three or four times a year."

During 1923 — the same year in which the Attorney General of the Territory of Hawaii acknowledged direct ownership of Midway by the United States — the minesweeper *Tanager* (AM-5) visited the atoll as part of an expedition in the Hawaiian chain, and on 30 April 1924, the minesweeper-seaplane tender *Pelican* (AM-27), LCDR John Rodgers, commanding, arrived with two planes to survey it; these flew around the atoll, while a party from the ship surveyed and took photographs. Three months later, *Seagull* (AM-30) ar-

rived at Midway along with eight submarines, which operated in the vicinity and then returned to Oahu.

With the coming of the 1930s, growth of world aviation meant another new stage in the atoll's life, while Japan's renunciation in 1934 of the 1922 Washington Treaty posed a threat to it, as the nearest Japanese possessions lay only 1,500 miles away. In March 1935, Pan American Airways (PAA) announced its intention to route passenger and freight-carrying aircraft from San Francisco to the Philippines with Midway earmarked to be one of the way stations. On 12 April 1935, the PAA expedition ship *North Haven* arrived at Midway, royally welcomed by the cable company people, who eagerly pitched in to land supplies ranging from tractors to refrigerators, and enough equipment to maintain an airport.

The following month, the Navy held maneuvers in the vicinity of Midway, as a part of that year's major fleet exercise, Fleet Problem XVI. At one point, 21 naval vessels anchored near the islands, which were the scene of great activity. On 11 May, covered by a smoke screen, 750 Marines, transported in the auxiliary *Utah* (AG-16), landed on Sand Island, and established their camp by 1500. Upon the conclusion of the exercises, though, they returned to *Utah* and sailed for Hawaii. Peace and quiet, punctuated only by the occasional visit of ship or clipper, returned to Midway.

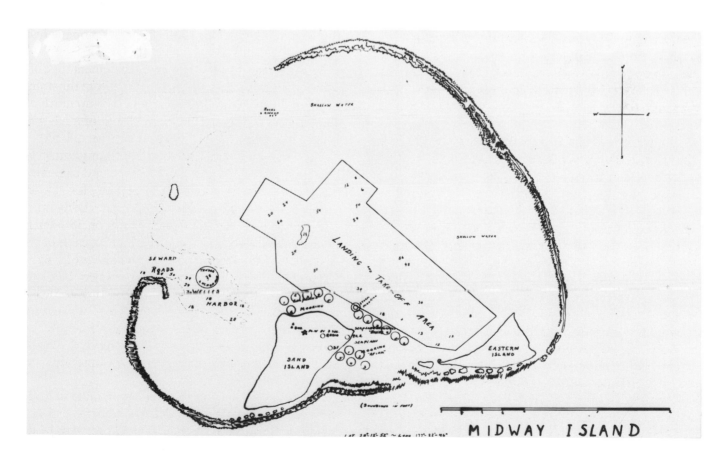

MIDWAY ISLAND

The *Philippine Clipper* approaches the mooring barge in the lagoon at Midway, circa 1936. Note PAA flag (L) and member of the *Clipper*'s crew in the bow hatch, preparing to moor the flying boat. PAA

PAA passengers dine during a stopover at Midway, circa 1936. A House Naval Affairs subcommittee, staying here as PAA's guests on 30 September-1 October 1940, found the hotel very comfortable and well-equipped. PAA

CHAPTER TWO

....

"Second In Importance Only to Pearl Harbor..."

While an occasional visit of warships, auxiliaries, or airplanes to Midway was one thing, establishing a permanent naval presence was another. The dredging of a channel through the southern reef between Eastern and Sand Islands confronted the Navy with its first big task in realizing that goal. Open to storms and unsafe, Welles Harbor presented little prospect for a good base for naval aviation operations. The Cable Company, to

clear an entrance for the cable, had blasted a hole in the south reef in 1923. Although the Army Corps of Engineers had surveyed the area in April 1936, work proved slow in getting underway, and it was not until the spring of 1938 that it began in earnest, a little less than two years after Pan American *Clippers* had begun flying across the Pacific. On 19 May 1938, the submarine tender *Beaver* (AS-5) and minelayer *Oglala* (CM-4) arrived at Midway to support the work of the Hawaiian Dredging Co.

Just two days before, Congress had authorized Secretary of the Navy Claude A. Swanson to appoint "a board of not less than five officers to investigate and report upon the need, for purposes of national defense, of additional submarine, destroyer, mine, and naval air bases on the coasts of the United States, its Territories, and possessions..." Swanson duly appointed this board, and placed it under RADM Arthur J. Hepburn, a former CINCUS and then the commandant of the 12th Naval District. Even before completion of the southeast channel entrance at Midway, the Hepburn Board's report, published on 3 January 1939, provided further impetus for the construction of a base there.

The Board found that "from a strategic point of view, an air base at Midway Island is second in importance only to Pearl Harbor." It considered the "scope of the present project and, in particular, the depth and width of the channel," inadequate, declaring that the completed channel "should be sufficient to accommodate a large tender or tanker." Further, it urged continuing the development of Midway to enable a base there to fully maintain two patrol plane squadrons, but with shops

The Hepburn Board (left to right): CAPT Arthur L. Bristol Jr., RADM Edward J. Marquart, RADM Arthur J. Hepburn, CAPT James S. Woods, CAPT Ralph Whitman (CEC) and LCDR William E. Hilbert (recorder), in Washington, DC, 15 July 1938. NH 50780

necessary only for "minor repair and overhaul work," and stressed the "major importance" of an "adequate storage of plane fuel." Hand in hand with the projected air base, and on the grounds that Midway "as an operating base for both air and submarines, is not second in importance to any other location recommended," Hepburn urged that accommodations for two divisions of submarines, operating without a tender, be provided.

Spurred on by the Hepburn Board's work, construction of Midway's facilities proceeded apace. On 4 March 1940, the small seaplane tender *Swan* (AVP-5) navigated the recently finished channel. On 21 March, the cargo ship *Sirius* (AK-15), the equipment-laden dump scow *YD-69* in tow, sailed from Pearl Harbor, and arrived at Midway on the 27th, with men and materials for the construction of a Naval Air Station (NAS); the work to be done by an association of three firms—the Hawaiian Dredging Co., the Raymond Concrete Pile Co., and the Turner Construction Co.—known as Contractors, Pacific Naval Air Bases (CPNAB). The Navy's overseer of the project, LT D.B. Ventres (CEC), simultaneously relieved the Cable Co. superintendent as naval custodian of Midway. Work commenced on the Navy dock in May and continued into the summer,

the contractors finding it necessary at one point to sink piles down 70 feet before finding solid ground.

That summer, Midway served as a stopover point for Patrol Squadron (VP) 26, when it arrived on 4 June 1940, as it was ferrying newly overhauled PBYs out to the Philippines. Upon arrival, the planes fueled from either a steel barge moored in the harbor, a PAA gassing barge, or from the small seaplane tender *Childs* (AVD-1), while *Childs* provided the off-watch men with berthing and messing facilities. Taking off on the 5th for Wake, Guam, and, ultimately, Cavite, VP-26's pilots and crew, bringing back VP-21's older PBYs, retraced their route and paid a return call to Midway on 19-20 June, taking off at sunrise on the latter date for Pearl Harbor. That same day (20 June), the cable ship *Dickerson* entered Midway lagoon via the newly completed entrance, helping to "usher in a new era in Midway's history."

The incipient base came in for high-level attention soon thereafter, as 14 Navy ships arrived there on 18 July 1940; flag officers making an informal inspection included VADM Adolphus Andrews, RADM Gilbert J. Rowcliff, RADM Milo F. Draemel, RADM John H. Newton, and one whose name would be forever linked

Sirius (AK-15), working cargo at Pearl Harbor, 14 March 1940. Atop No. 1 hatch lie pilings for the cofferdam that will be necessary for construction of the ramp that will be built for seaplanes at Midway, atop No. 2 lie steel sheet piles, a 40-ton lighter, two small tugs, and six portable refrigerator boxes. NH 96599

Sirius, with dump scow *YD-69* in tow, passes Diamond Head as she sails for Midway, 21 March 1940. NH 96602

Sirius edges away from the Navy pier at Sand Island, 3 September 1940, while civilian contractors look on and a district tug (YT) stands ready to assist. NH 96596

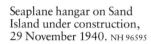

Seaplane hangar on Sand Island under construction, 29 November 1940. NH 96595

The north side of the permanent barracks on Sand Island, 29 November 1940, soon after completion. NH 96604

to Midway's, RADM Frank Jack Fletcher. Shown about the cable station grounds, and observing the state of the construction programs, the visitors came away impressed with "the beautiful garden spot that is now the Cable Station."

By 1 September 1940, a year after World War II had started with Hitler's invasion of Poland, the Navy pier stood complete. *Sirius* arrived that day to the "blowing of horns and waving of flags," accorded the honor of being the first vessel to moor there. "The ability to land materials directly without use of lighters," one observer stated, would "materially facilitate the work being carried on" at Midway.

Later that same month, on 30 September, the House Naval Affairs subcommittee, appointed to inspect naval facilities at Pearl Harbor and Pacific islands, left Pearl by air for Midway, Johnston, and Palmyra. Congressmen Colgate W. Darden Jr., W.S. Jacobsen, A.B. Jenks, John Z. Anderson, and Robert H. Harper (clerk), accompanied by VADM William F. Halsey Jr. (COMAIRBATFOR and COMCARDIV 2) and RADM Aubrey W. Fitch (COMCARDIV 1), reached their destination late on the afternoon of the same day, and immediately commenced their work of inspection. After spending the night at the PAA hotel, the subcommittee moved on to Johnston the next morning. By that point, Midway's base facilities were only 25 percent complete; nonaviation fuel and diesel oil storage, defense, and additional aviation shore facilities only 5 percent.

Intended initially as only a seaplane base—construction of a hangar and temporary living quarters on Eastern Island, and power houses, hangars, seaplane ramps, utility shops, family quarters, BOQs and a dispensary on Sand Island were well underway—Midway soon came under scrutiny for use as a land-plane base as well. An additional contract was let, with the five CPNAB companies being incorporated to build a suitable base on Eastern Island, to improve Sand Island's facilities, to do additional dredging to widen and deepen the channel, and to reclaim and fill-in the land areas near the longer runways. In April 1941, the Officer-in-Charge, Completed Naval Installations, visited Midway and conducted an inspection of the projects then underway. The number of birds on Eastern Island worried him, and he reported that the numerous fowl rendered landings extremely dangerous, and recommended eliminating the threat entirely.

Establishment of defensive positions, to be manned by Marines, meanwhile, proceeded ahead. A survey by COL Harry K. Pickett, USMC, assisted by CAPT Alfred R. Pefley, USMC, had, in 1939, outlined the requirements for a defense plan for the island. The 3d Defense Battalion—initially formed at Parris Island, S.C., on 10 October 1939 as an element of the 1st Marine Brigade, Fleet Marine Force, and redesignated as the 3d Defense Battalion on 1 December of that year—provided an advanced unit of seven officers and 138 enlisted men under MAJ Harold C. Roberts, USMC, which reached Midway in *Sirius* and two high-speed minesweepers on 26 September 1940. Ultimately, the rest of the battalion—LTCOL Robert H. Pepper, USMC, commanding—embarked in the general stores issue ship *Antares* (AKS-3) and the light cruisers *Brooklyn* (CL-40), *Philadelphia* (CL-41) and *Savannah* (CL-43), and sailed from Pearl Harbor on 10 February 1941. Task Force (TF) 3, as it was designated, proceeded uneventfully, the three cruisers and one auxiliary vessel traveling darkened at night, with a destroyer screen, and arrived on the 13th, disembarking the Marines the following day.

Over the months that followed, the leathernecks

Philadelphia (CL-41)—seen here at New York City, April 1939—transported elements of the 3d Defense Battalion to Midway as a unit of Cruiser Division EIGHT, February 1941.

Antares (AKS-3), circa 1940, painted in the pre-war No. 5 Navy gray, took part in the lift of men and equipment of the 3d Defense Battalion to Midway in February 1941.

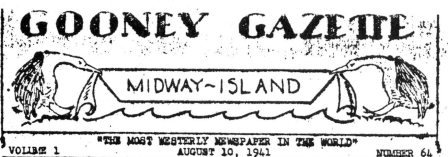

GOONEY GAZETTE
MIDWAY~ISLAND

"THE MOST WESTERLY NEWSPAPER IN THE WORLD"

VOLUME 1   AUGUST 10, 1941   NUMBER 64

TONIGHT'S CONCERT

Depending upon the weather, the special 'Pop' Concert will be held either in the Stadium or in the Auditorium at 7:30 tonight. Announcement will be made at dinner tonight.

WORLD NEWS

CLEVELAND, OHIO

Chas. Lindbergh charged tonight the Nation was operating under a policy of government by subterfuge leading to war. "I fully realize that the charge of subterfuge is serious in the extreme", he said in an address prepared for an America first rally, "but let me recall to your mind a few facts that lie behind it". First, he asserted, Americans were told repeal of arms embargo would be the surest way to keep out of war; next he added, the country was told that to sell arms on a "cash and carry" basis would insure victory for the Allies. "They were emphatic in saying no one asked us to lend money or to send troops abroad", he continued. "The hypocrisy and subterfuge that surrounds us comes out in every statement of the war party", he asserted.

"When we demand that our Government listed to the 80 percent of the people who oppose war, they shout that we are causing disunity. The same groups, who call on us to defend Democracy and Freedom abroad, demand that we kill Democracy and Freedom at home by forcing four-fifths of our people into war against their will".

RYE, N.Y.

"TOMORROW'S NEWS TODAY"

VICHY

Fernand De Brinon, envoy of the Vichy Government in occupied France, declared today in an interview in Paris (made public in Vichy tonight) that France has decided to accept the German version of the new world order as opposed to that of Britain and the U.S.

As the interview was made public there was considerable speculation on results of the daylong conference here among Chief of State Marshall Potain, Jean Darlan, General Weygand and Defense Minister General Huntziger on the future of the French empire.

Informed sources in London maintained a non-committal attitude toward Vichy and reports of possible French-German collaboration were subordinated to word that Weygand was still proving the biggest stumbling block to the pro-Axis element of the French Government.

WASHINGTON D.C.

The manufacture of white sidewall auto tires was prohibited, effective midnight August 23, by the office of production management in a move designed to conserve rubber. Cessation would save more than 6000 tons of crude rubber a year. It takes about two pounds more crude rubber to make a white sidewall tire than ordinary black one.

ANKARA, TURKEY

The British are preparing to take vigorous direct action in Iran

The front page of the 10 August 1941 (Vol. I, No. 64) issue of the *Gooney Gazette*, the paper billing itself as the "Most Westerly Newspaper in the World."

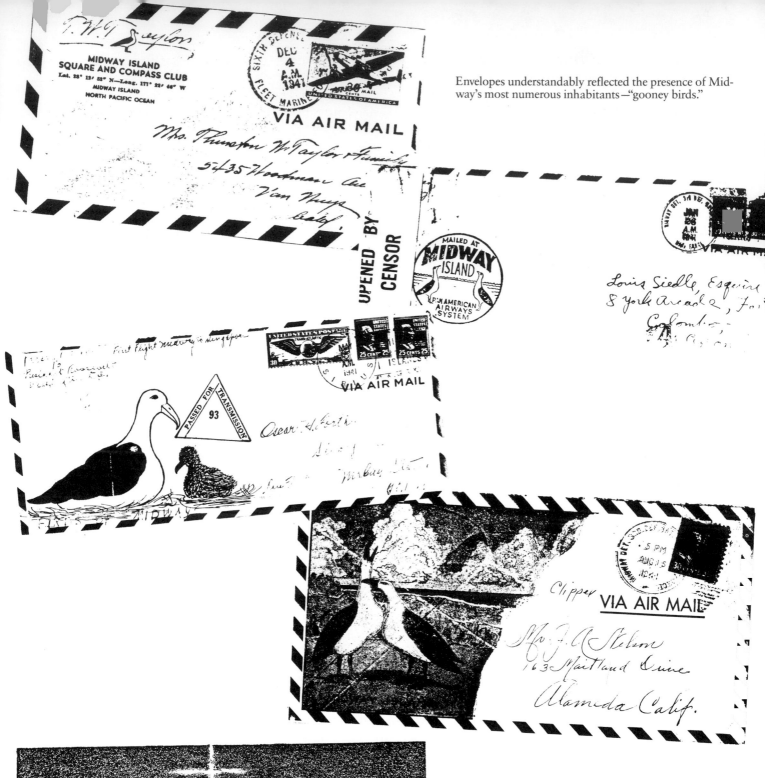

Envelopes understandably reflected the presence of Midway's most numerous inhabitants—"gooney birds."

Midway's Christmas Card, 1941.

toiled ceaselessly to emplace the seacoast and antiaircraft guns and fire control equipment, as well as the requisite shelters and magazines. Not only did they perform arduous construction work—principally with only hand tools—but served, as the occasion demanded, as "stevedores and longshoremen" for ships touching at the atoll.

At the outset, living conditions left much to be desired: inadequate facilities, enormous numbers of flies, and the noise of mating gooney birds that often continued throughout the night. Bedbugs infested the existing barracks and billets inherited from the Army Engineers. Ultimately, after the arrival of the main body of Marines in February, contractors and Marines made great strides in improving living conditions. The men found that the atoll's white sand induced eyestrain and reflected heat; the light-textured sand frequently found its way into one's shoes, and high humidity resulted in a great number of cases of "prickly heat and other annoying skin ailments." Those with allergies to bird feathers also found themselves suffering, too.

The threats posed to aircraft by the local population of fowl notwithstanding, on 1 August 1941, NAS Midway was placed in commission, and 17 days later, CDR Cyril T. Simard assumed command. By this time, surfaced roads had been completed, street lights erected, and a telephone system placed in operation. Eastern Island possessed the airstrips, and Sand the married officers' quarters, shops, and administration buildings.

At about the same time, elements of the 6th Defense Battalion began arriving at Midway to relieve the 3d. On 11 August, the advance echelon of the 6th, under LTCOL Harold D. Shannon, USMC, XO of the unit, reached the atoll in the heavy cruiser *Chester* (CA-27) and light cruiser *Nashville* (CL-43). One month later, the remainder of the battalion, under its commander, COL Raphael Griffin, USMC, arrived to take over the defense duties from the 3d Battalion.

Such construction of both aviation facilities and defense installations as had been finished was completed none too soon, for as the year 1941 drew on, prospects of accord between the United States and Japan over Far Eastern matters dimmed as the shadow of war lengthened across the Pacific basin.

In late October, with the reinforcement of the Philippines proceeding apace, the Army staged 26 Boeing B-17s of the 19th Bombardment Group through Midway. As MAJ David R. Gibbs, CO of the 19th Bombardment Group, later reported, Eastern Island possessed an excellent all-weather, hard-surfaced field, with parking areas of crushed, graded coral that could support an airplane in any weather. Up to three planes could be fueled at one time, and "ample" accommodations existed for 25 crews. Officers stayed at NAS Midway for $1.00 a day; enlisted men with the Marine detachment for 60 cents a day.

Within two weeks of the departure of the last "Flying Fortress," Midway received an important visitor. On 9 November, the PAA Boeing 314 *Clipper* carrying special envoy Saburo Kurusu and his secretary, Yuki, arrived. Kurusu, a British courier on board the *Clipper* surmised, was en route to Washington to check Ambassador Kichasaburo Nomura's reports that the United States was not bluffing in its attitude toward Japan's moves in the Far East, and to find signs of weakness in the American stance to exploit in the negotiations that dealt with the situation in the Far East.[1]

Engine trouble, however, necessitated a three-day layover. Having been forewarned of Kurusu's arrival, and the nature of his diplomatic mission, CDR Simard and LTCOL Shannon (who had relieved COL Griffin shortly before as CO, 6th Defense Battalion), agreed to "arrange a reception calculated to impress [Kurusu] with the alertness and strength...of the Midway garrison." During some discussion of the proposed reception for the Japanese envoy, someone even had offered the suggestion that all available PBYs be flown overhead! Precise timing enabled the diplomat to step on land from the boat that had brought him to shore from the *Clipper* at the moment when a seemingly endless line of Marines, in light marching order, began filing past. A squadron of PBYs, easily visible from the PAA dock, was drawn up on the seaplane apron on Sand Island.

After being greeted by CDR Simard and LTCOL Shannon, and ushered into CDR Simard's car, Kurusu was driven to the PAA Hotel. As they drove by the grim, marching Marines, Shannon nonchalantly explained this to be merely a maneuver by a "small part of the command." In truth, the "small part of the command" was actually "every available man (cooks and messmen included) scraped together to make a single line long enough so that Kurusu could not see how pitifully few" Midway's defenders were.

CDR Simard, for his part, apologized for not rendering the honors normally accorded a diplomat of Kurusu's stature, but explained that circumstances dictated that every available moment be spent in training, and hoped that Kurusu would understand. Also during the envoy's stopover, he heard plenty of firing practice by the 3-inch batteries located near the PAA hotel. If the gunfire did not visibly bother the Japanese diplomat, neither did a little precipitation, for at one point in his stay, Kurusu was attending a movie on Sand

----

1. The United States and Japan had been at odds over the situation in the Far East for several years, but most specifically since July 1937, when Japan invaded China, and September 1940, when Japan commenced its occupation of French Indochina.

Midway, 24 November 1941. Eastern Island lies in the foreground with the airstrip; Sand Island lies at the top.
80-G-451086

Island when raindrops started falling; those who attended saw neither LTCOL Shannon nor his guest leave their seats until the show was over!

Kurusu left Midway on the 12th, and the training and preparations for war continued apace. The day after the Japanese diplomat had departed, CDR Simard ordered all outgoing cables censored. Within a month's time, the most serious problem confronting the Cable Co. was the disappearance of turkeys from the company's yard areas. The superintendent suspected Marines of the theft.

More serious problems than the disappearance of turkeys, however, were soon demanding attention. An "unusually tense situation" confronted ADM Husband E. Kimmel, CINCUS/CINCPAC, in late November and early December. Relations between the United States and Japan were worsening almost daily, and to bolster America's defensive perimeter in the Pacific, Kimmel decided to send planes to both Wake and Midway. Wake was to receive fighters—12 Grumman F4F-3s of VMF-211; Midway, scout-bombers from VMSB-231. The former were to be transported in *Enterprise*, which departed Pearl on 28 November in TF 8 under VADM Halsey, and the latter in *Lexington* (CV-2) in TF 12, under RADM John H. Newton.

Midway, meanwhile, stood ready to receive the planes allocated it. While PBYs operated from there, to cover the advance of the two task forces, the seaplane tender *Wright* (AV-1) arrived on 4 December, bringing 2dLT Loren D. Everton, USMCR, 20 enlisted men, and approximately 20 tons of equipment and gear—the advance element of the expected aviation units slated to arrive at the atoll a few days hence. On the 5th, TF 12 sailed from Pearl; off Oahu, 18 Vought SB2U-3 "Vindicators" from VMSB-231, under MAJ Clarence J. "Buddy" Chappell, USMC, landed on board *Lexington*, along with "Lady Lex's" air group. Planes having been recovered, the force set course for Midway. Two submarines, meanwhile, reached their assigned stations off the atoll, as part of a simulated war patrol: *Trout* (SS-202) on 2 December and *Argonaut* (SS-166) on the 3rd.

Unbeknownst to ADM Kimmel, the "unusually tense situation" was about to explode. A Japanese task force, formed around six carriers, was nearing Oahu. Its mission: to destroy the U.S. Pacific Fleet in its base at Pearl Harbor. War was about to engulf the Pacific, and with it, Midway.

Wright (AV-1) at Pearl Harbor, circa late 1941.

Argonaut (SS-166) underway off Oahu at 1100 hours, 4 January 1939. 38021 A.C.

The Japanese destroyers *Ushio* (left) and *Akebono* (right), in pre-war exercises. *Ushio*, along with another sistership, *Sazanami*, shelled Midway on the night of 7 December 1941. NH73047

CHAPTER THREE

· · · · · · · · · · · · · · · · ·

"*The Sentry for Hawaii...*"

*A*s dawn broke on 7 December, *Argonaut*, LCDR Stephen Barchet commanding, continued her submerged patrol off Midway, her watch noting the "usual" weather: "partly cloudy, gentle winds, calm sea, with long rollers." She remained on station throughout the day.

Five PBYs from VP-21, meanwhile, had taken off on patrol; two took off to rendezvous with the expected SB2U-3s from VMSB-231; five more sat on the ramp on Sand Island, each armed with a pair of 500-pound bombs. Two more PBYs, flown by Consolidated Aircraft crews, had taken off for Wake Island, on the next leg of their delivery flight, bound, ultimately, for Batavia in the Netherlands East Indies.

At 0630, an Army Signal Corps operator, a member of the five-man Army detachment under 1stLT Henry E. Mattingly, (SC), USA, on Midway for communication work with the staging of B-17s to the Philippines, received a message telling of the bombing of Hickam Field. He immediately telephoned LTCOL Shannon's command post and that of the commander of defense forces on Eastern Island, CAPT Hoyt D. McMillen, USMC. Soon, another transmission told of an air raid on Pearl Harbor; a dispatch from the commandant of the 14th Naval District then arrived verifying the fact that Japanese planes had attacked airfields on Oahu. A half hour later, at 0700, one of the two submarines deployed off Midway, *Trout*, which had extended her radio receiver antenna hourly in the course of her patrol, picked up the word that "Hostilities with Japan commenced..."

In the 6th Defense Battalion's officers' mess, CAPT Jean H. Buckner, USMC, was having breakfast with the other officers when 2dLT William R. Dorr Jr., USMC, the duty officer, entered and told those assem-

bled of the Japanese attack upon Oahu. All hands thought he was joking and wasted no time in telling him so. Dorr, though, stuck to his guns, and said he had even awakened LTCOL Shannon with the word. As if to underscore the authenticity of Dorr's tidings, Shannon himself soon arrived and confirmed it, and told all battery commanders to put their men on alert and have them ready to man their battle stations within the hour. Buckner and nearly everyone else, though, remained unconvinced; they felt that this was a "realistic war game"—nothing more.

"War game" or not, VP-21's five standby PBYs on the ramp were soon in the water and getting aloft for patrol. Soon thereafter, OPNAV ordered the execution of War Plan 46 against Japan; at 0918, LTCOL Shannon called the 6th Defense Battalion to arms and by 0945, all hands stood on the alert. CDR Simard, meanwhile, immediately ordered the recall of the two Dutch "Catalinas." VP-21 commandeered them upon their return.

In the meantime, as lookouts anxiously watched the horizon, all hands carried out preparations for blackout, and extinguished lights on navigational aids. Five civilians, showing "suspicious attitudes, statements, or actions," soon found themselves confined on CDR Simard's order—there would be no "fifth column" on Midway.

Late that afternoon, VP-21's "Catalinas" lumbered in from their patrols. All returned between 1530 and dusk; the last landed at 1745. At least one returning "Catalina" earlier that day had occasioned a "false alarm," rudely interrupting CAPT Buckner's noon meal of fricasseed chicken! All PBYs—except the Dutch ones, which had no mounts for them—were then armed with bombs and machine guns. A dispatch received shortly before the planes began returning directed that a dawn search be undertaken the following day, between Midway and Johnston Island.

Argonaut, oblivious to events, surfaced around sunset to recharge her batteries, and for the first time learned of the Japanese attack on Pearl Harbor, when some of her chief petty officers, sitting around their radio, heard the news. At 1715, the ship received a message from CINCPAC "announcing commencement of hostilities with JAPAN." In order to reduce her silhouette against the bright moon, LCDR Barchet kept *Argonaut* cruising east and west.

At 1828 on 7 December, Midway's radar picked up a target bearing 360 degrees, 14,000 yards distant. Less than 15 minutes later, a Marine lookout reported a flashing light bearing 221 degrees, 10,000 yards away. Almost three hours elapsed before lookouts suddenly reported gun flashes from the west at 2130; the "Midway Neutralization Unit"—the destroyers *Sazanami* and

Ushio, under CAPT Konishi Kaname—had arrived "to bombard and neutralize the air base at Midway, thus ensuring a safe return" for the Pearl Harbor attack force, "and to divert American attention by decoying reconnaissance flights. . . ."

At that time, as LTCOL Shannon later described it, Midway lay bathed in bright moonlight. "All the new construction glistened...the reflection of the moon on the white buildings, the window glass, and on the black-and-white squares of the water tower must have been visible for miles at sea. The sand looked like snow and the breakers on the reef clearly outlined the island area. It was an ideal night" for an attack.

CAPT Buckner's "D" battery was ready; Condition III permitted half of the Marines at the batteries to sleep in the gun or range section pits, ready for action within one minute. At 2130, the lookout's report of "flashes on the horizon" to the southwest prompted Buckner to assume that "A" battery (5-inch guns) had opened fire on a target to the west. Thinking that the flashes close to the beach emanated from "A" battery's guns, and that the distant flashes were "projectiles striking the water and exploding," Buckner continued watching, "amused by the antics of 'A' battery," and remarked to that effect to 2dLT Dorr. Buckner and many of his men climbed atop the parapet to afford themselves a better view.

Suddenly, "several guns flashed relatively close to the island . . . but at great enough range not to be mistaken for 'A' battery." "In addition," Buckner later recounted, "my illusions and those of the entire battery were further shattered when something that sounded like a freight train passed immediately over our heads, followed by explosions in the vicinity of the powerhouse. The tops of the parapets were deserted without order."

Frank E. Settle, a civil engineering draftsman employed by one of the contractors at Midway, had just seated himself on the edge of his bunk and was removing his shoes when he heard the sound of gunfire. Knowing that the barracks would be in the line of fire due to its proximity to the hangar and the powerplant, Settle quickly set off for the high ground.

Sighting what appeared to be gun flashes, *Argonaut* changed course to investigate. As she headed west, she picked up two successive radio transmissions from Midway, the first telling of enemy ships south of the reef and the second of direct shelling of the island. *Trout*, on the surface, 10 miles to the northeast of Midway when the firing started, proceeded toward the western channel entrance at top speed.

As *Argonaut* approached the scene from the west, shells splashed between the reef and the beach—the first of 108 fired by *Ushio* and 193 by *Sazanami*—but that firing ceased after four minutes and the two destroyers

1stLT George H. Cannon, USMC. Commissioned 2dLT, 25 June 1938, he ultimately joined Battery "H," 2d Defense Battalion, 16 February 1941. He sailed for Pearl Harbor in July and reached Midway on 7 September 1941. USMC

altered course to close. Reopening fire at 2148, *Sazanami* and *Ushio* were soon spotted, standing 2,500 yards off the southwestern point of Sand Island at 2153, close enough that several Marines could see "a large Japanese flag...plainly visible flying from the foremast" of one of the ships. Two minutes later, the Marines having been given the order to open fire on "all appropriate targets," a searchlight struck arc and pinpointed *Sazanami*; one 3-inch battery soon claimed three hits (of 13 fired) on the lead ship, two in the superstructure and one on her forecastle, near the waterline. *Ushio* came under fire from a 5-inch battery, which claimed two hits (of nine fired) near the waterline, forward.

One enemy 5-inch shell, however, entered the air port of Battery "H's" CP, on Sand Island, where it exploded, mortally wounding 1stLT George H. Cannon, USMC. His pelvis crushed, losing blood rapidly, Cannon nevertheless remained conscious and, refusing evacuation, directed the efforts to get his CP back in operation. Among the other men hurt was CPL Harold R. Hazelwood, USMC, the switchboard operator. Although wounded by fragments from the same shell that had felled 1stLT Cannon, Hazelwood immediately set up the switchboard again and re-established communications. Only at that point was the mortally wounded officer forcibly removed. For his selfless gallantry, Cannon—who died soon after being taken from his CP—would be awarded the Medal of Honor, posthumously, the first given to a Marine in World War II; Hazelwood would receive the Navy Cross.

Another Marine in the 6th Defense Battalion who would earn a Navy Cross was CPL Dale L. Peters, USMC, who had begun the battle in the tower atop the seaplane hangar on Sand Island. A bursting shell blew him through a window and deposited him some 14 feet below. Despite his understandably dazed condition, Peters was soon at work assisting sailors in the hangar, removing bombs from the burning building.

LT(jg) John M. Eaton Jr., D-V(G), one of the ground officers with VP-21 on temporary duty on Midway, was also assisting in the recovery of material in the hangar area. Among the items of equipment damaged or demolished by the hangar fire was a PBY-3 whose tanks held 1,500 gallons of gasoline, and under whose wings had hung two fused 500-pound bombs. With the normal equipment used in the launching of the PBYs destroyed by fire, Eaton, on his own initiative, organized a civilian work crew and "succeeded in launching such of these heavily overloaded Catalina aircraft as were capable of flight." Stripped to his underwear and working solely by the flickering light cast by the burning hangar, Eaton toiled bravely in the cold lagoon, and around the parking area and ramp, in water flooded with volatile aviation fuel. Knowing that a slight shift in wind direction, a chance spark, or a resumption of firing by the Japanese ships would undoubtedly have meant his (and his men's) doom, he unswervingly continued his work. His "having organized and directed an untrained and untried group of civilians into an efficient working crew, in having accomplished a prosaic

and purely technical operation, and in having done so under danger of imminent destruction from enemy gunfire, gasoline explosion . . . without possibility of retaliation or succor," Eaton had displayed "extreme courage, ability, and fortitude." He, too, was awarded the Navy Cross.

At 2158, a Japanese shell put the searchlight out of action, but the enemy destroyers ceased fire and made smoke, retiring out of range. *Trout* reached the western channel entrance after the firing had stopped and hove to, not having sighted anything nor seen in which direction the enemy ships retired. *Argonaut*, meanwhile, made out two "good-sized destroyers or small cruisers" heading northwest, about three miles distant. Reasoning that a full moon militated against his being able to attack unseen, Barchet took *Argonaut* down to make a sound approach. The Japanese ships, however, apparently sighted her, as they changed course to pass down her port side, and *Argonaut* could not bring her tubes to bear. Soon thereafter, she heard "pinging," as if the Japanese were hunting her, but these noises died out soon thereafter, and she found herself again alone.

While *Argonaut's* approach had been frustrated, Midway's seacoast defenses may have drawn blood. A short time after the Japanese had departed, eluding *Argonaut* as they did so, CAPT John H. Hamilton, flying the PAA Martin 130 *Philippine Clipper* en route to Midway, with a crew of eight and 26 civilian evacuees from Wake, saw two ships heading away from their destination; one appeared to be afire.

In their brief visit, however, the two Japanese ships had wreaked considerable havoc: six shells hit the seaplane hangar; the roof burned completely, although the structure remained largely intact. One PBY lay demolished in the hangar; another, while deemed repairable,

A 5-inch shell, one of 301 fired by *Ushio* and *Sazanami* during bombardment on the night of 7 December 1941, which failed to explode.
80-G-2022

Hastily camouflaged hangar on Sand Island, probably photographed on 8 December 1941. Note that while the structure appears intact, the roof has been burned. At right lies the nose section of a gutted PBY-3 (BuNo 0824).
80-G-2019

Gutted nose section of the Consolidated PBY-3 (BuNo 0824) demolished in the shelling of 7 December 1941, lies near the seaplane hangar on Sand Island. This aircraft was the first production PBY-3. 80-G-2299

Laundry building on Sand Island, 8 December 1941, showing the hole in the roof from a Japanese 5-inch shell. In the background, to left of center, lie the fuel tanks that would eventually be destroyed on 4 June.
80-G-2292

lay nearby, riddled with shrapnel, as was one of the commandeered Dutch PBYs. A shell destroyed one corner of the torpedo and bomb sight building, three or four hit the walls and roof of the powerhouse, while one, ricocheting off the laundry building, hit the powerhouse, too. One shell hit the parachute loft and utility building; shrapnel damaged the upper part of the structure. Further, the Japanese shells had demolished six of the eight PAA radio direction finder masts.

As several civilians had served alongside LT(jg) Eaton in his work with the PBYs, several more volunteered to help gun crews during the action; the following day, the 5th Artillery Civilian Defense organization, consisting of 36 civilians "who will give assistance to Marine gun crews" was established. Frank Settle, the draftsman, who had had previous military service, soldiered among them.

At 2234, a little over a half hour after the Japanese retired, the first PBY—enabled in large part to do so thanks to LT(jg) Eaton and his civilian work crews—took off, followed at intervals by others. One hit a buoy in the dark, though, and, having suffered damage, returned. Another hit a buoy head and sank. One officer, ENS Donald A. Kraker, A-V(N), died in the mishap; several men suffered injuries.

At 2316, the *Philippine Clipper*, which had been holed 16 times during the attack on Wake that morning, "slipped into Pan American's blacked-out Midway base as though it had been broad daylight..." CAPT Hamilton told CDR Simard of the Japanese ships heading away from Midway a short time before, and of his experiences at Wake. The following morning, the *Philippine Clipper* took off for Pearl Harbor.

Argonaut, surfacing to recharge her batteries the next morning, had a run-in with a utility plane from Midway (perhaps the J2F "Duck" assigned to the NAS), before resuming her submerged patrol. "If there is another attack at moonrise tonight," Barchet wrote in his patrol report, "we will be there...luck can't be against us all the time..." He had never seen a crew so transformed by imminent action: "The snap and precision is wonderful to see," *Argonaut's* captain recounted, ". . . they are using their heads and thinking." That night, *Argonaut* received orders to "execute unrestricted submarine warfare against Japan." Unwilling to trust "friendly" planes after their experience on the 8th, Barchet kept his submarine on submerged patrol during daylight. Eventually, having no more run-ins with American forces, *Argonaut* wound up her patrol and returned to Pearl Harbor, as did *Trout*.

Over the next few days, meanwhile, Midway readied itself for war. The prominent white buildings received hasty camouflage; CDR Simard ordered civilians

(whether contractor or PAA) exhibiting "suspicious or demoralizing attitude, statements or actions" confined. PBY patrols over Pearl and Hermes Reef and Kure Island disclosed "nothing of import." One contractor, confined on 7 December, was put on a water diet with the warning that "he would not eat until he agreed to work." His "fast" lasted from 13 to 15 December, when he consented to return to work and was released.

In the meantime, the exigencies of war had prevented the squadron earmarked for Midway, VMSB-231, from carrying out its assigned mission. Retained on board *Lexington* as TF 12 patrolled the Johnston-Midway-Palmyra triangle, it eventually returned to Oahu on 10 December. Less than a week later, the decision was made to fly the SB2U-3s directly from Oahu to Midway. Flight crews and ground crews turned-to with a will; on short notice, all toiled almost continuously for 24 hours, checking engines and making the necessary repairs to planes for which there were only meager spares. Ultimately, at 0630 on 17 December 1941, 17 SB2U-3s (one had suffered engine failure and had to be left behind) took off for Midway from Hickam, as Ewa Mooring Mast Field had been deemed too short for the "Vindicators," which were fully laden with fuel for the trip. For nine hours and 45 minutes the Marines flew in formation over the Pacific; no plane guards steamed below in case any had to "ditch." Only 21-P-1, the PBY flown by LCDR George T. Mundorff, VP-21's CO, accompanied them.

In advance of the arrival of VMSB-231's aircraft, men of the CPNAB construction crews removed the tar barrel obstructions from one of the three runways that they had blocked to prevent their use if an enemy landing had been attempted. Shortly before 1600, the "Vindicators" droned into view, and as they let down to land, men of the defense battalion stood atop their gun emplacements and cheered; as then-1stLT David Silvey, USMC, would later recall, "They [VMSB-231's planes] represented a real Christmas present." At 1550, the first of the SB2U-3s landed. The 1,137-mile flight came to a successful conclusion when all planes landed on Eastern Island after the longest overwater flight by single-engined land planes in aviation history up to that point. MAJ William H. Benson, USMC, commanding the elements of the 6th Defense Battalion on Eastern Island, and 2dLT Everton, greeted Chappell and his men.

The following day, VMSB-231 began routine patrols, CDR Simard placing in MAJ Chappell's hands the responsibility for the air protection of Midway.[1] Simard

---

1. A mishap befell the newly arrived VMSB-231 during the night alert, though, and the squadron suffered its first accident at its new advanced base, when 1stLT Randolph C. Berkeley's SB2U-3 (BuNo 2069) crashed on takeoff from the Eastern Island strip. Dazed by the impact and suffering facial lacerations, Berkeley remained, stunned, in the cockpit as the "Vindicator" caught fire. His radio-gunner, SGT Carl T. Hickman, clambered unhurt from the after cockpit and assisted Berkeley from the burning bomber, thus saving his life.

also entrusted Chappell with the task of directing "the employment of aviation based on Eastern Island so that the maximum use and training...should be scheduled commensurate with the problems at hand and the limitation of the aircraft..." That same day, the Dutch PBY riddled on 7 December made a successful test flight, repaired with over 334 patches by the "combined efforts of PAA, contractors and U.S. Navy."

The following morning, LCDR Mundorff (in 21-P-1) led a flight of two aircraft (his own and one of the repaired Dutch PBYs) off, heading back to Pearl Harbor. That afternoon, a PBY arrived from Pearl with guard mail for Wake Island.

On the 19th, a PBY took off for Wake Island at 0618, and returned the following evening bringing MAJ Walter L.J. Bayler, USMC, for duty with VMSB-231, the "Last Man Off Wake Island." The men in the PBY crew brought back grim accounts of conditions on that atoll. A few days later, on 23 December 1941, Midway received "unconfirmed reports"—later proved true—of the fall of Wake.

Around Christmas, substantial reinforcements began arriving at Midway, as "defense preparations continued." On 24 December, the same day upon which VMSB-231 began regular patrols, Wright, escorted by Porter (DD-356), reached Midway at 0820 with Batteries "A" and "C," 4th Defense Battalion, USMC, with 7-inch and 3-inch guns and equipment, the first to be installed on Eastern Island. Unloading proceeded into the night under dimmed blue lights. At 0900 on Christmas Day,

Marines embark in Tangier (AV-8) at Pearl Harbor, 15 December 1941, earmarked for the relief of Wake. Some of these men, however, would disembark at Midway after the Japanese overran Wake on the 23rd. Rifles carried appear to be a mix of Garands and Springfields.
80-G-266632

Tangier (AV-8) (right) unloads equipment originally destined for Wake Island, 26 December 1941; *Ralph Talbot* (DD-390) and *Blue* (DD-387), her escorts, lie at left; *Tamaha* (YN-44) is at the end of the pier.
80-G-266631

Contractors, Pacific Naval Air Bases, on board the non self-propelled stevedoring barge *YS-88* after disembarking from *Tangier* (AV-8), at Pearl Harbor, 31 December 1941, after their voyage from Midway. The tug *Milioi* is in the background. 80-G-266635

14 Brewster F2A-3 "Buffalo" fighters of VMF-221 under MAJ Verne J. McCaul, USMC, originally earmarked for the relief of Wake (which had fallen on 23 December), flew in from *Saratoga* (CV-3) after having been launched 100 miles out. That same day, CDR Simard ordered a contractor, who had refused to work because his contract had expired that day, confined on a "water diet."

The following day, 26 December, the seaplane tender *Tangier* (AV-8)—also originally allocated to the Wake Island relief expedition—arrived at 1002, less than two hours after the departure of *Wright* and *Porter*, bearing Battery "B," 4th Defense Battalion; .50-caliber machine guns of the Special Weapons Group of that unit; the ground echelon of VMF-221, aviation supplies, and radar sets, as well as equipment desperately needed by the 6th Defense Battalion. *Wright* had sailed with 203 contractors embarked (including four as prisoners), as well as two cable company employees, two PAA employees, a Civil Aeronautics Administration official, and the eight Consolidated Aircraft employees who had flown the Dutch PBY-5s to Midway before the commencement of hostilities.

Unloading *Tangier* proceeded, like the unloading of *Wright*, throughout the night, under blue lamps. *Tangier* left a portable radar set (originally earmarked for Wake), for use with aviation activities on Midway, and took on board a load of PBY parts salvaged from the losses of 7 December. She also embarked 597 contractors' employees (including the one confined on a water diet on 24 December), 50 PAA employees, two cable company men, and the small Army detachment under 1stLT Mattingly, whose equipment had been left on Eastern

Island for the Marines to use. Her mission completed, *Tangier* sailed for Oahu at 0905 on 27 December.

On 9 January 1942, MAJ William J. Wallace, USMC, arrived at Midway via a Consolidated PB2Y-2, to command the Marine Aviation Detachment (MAD) of MAG-21. Accompanying the "Coronado" had been the 18th VMSB-231 "Vindicator," flown by 2dLT Richard L. Blain, USMCR, whose engine had failed to start the morning the squadron departed Hickam Field shortly before Christmas.

"Buddy" Chappell and "Mac" McCaul met Wallace at the dock soon after the big flying boat had arrived, and immediately began going over the aviation picture. Although, as Wallace later reported, the "set-up" looked good, and the defense plan sound, Chappell and McCaul complained about the contractors—promises but no action. The newly arrived commander of the MAD looked over the situation and, having been told by "Si" Simard that he could have what he wanted, made known his wants. The contractors attempted to talk Wallace out of individual bunkers for his planes, but he "stuck to his guns." "Since Si said I could have anything available," he later wrote, "they [the contractors] gave up and got two built that day." More would follow.

Training proceeded apace. By later January, Wallace was planning for the "Vindicator" pilots to get in bombing practice with 100-pound water-filled ordnance on targets in the lagoon, and noted how VMF-221 "wants to fire their guns." By that point, while VMF-221 pilots were making dummy runs on each other, they understandably wanted "a little more confidence in their ability to hit a red disc."

Over the next several weeks, the war continued to go badly for the United States and its Allies, as the Japanese tide of conquest continued to rise in the Far East and South Pacific. Midway, meanwhile, maintained its readiness, continuing regular local air patrols from Eastern Island. Occasionally, a Japanese submarine would appear to enliven the existence of Midway's men; on 25 January 1942, *I-173* shelled the atoll. To give the aviators some insight into how submarines operated, Bill Wallace invited LCDR Waldeman N. Christensen, captain of *Cachalot* (SS-170)—which had pulled into Midway on the 22d—to talk to his pilots. The indoctrination lecture took place on the 27th.

On the evening of 8 February, *I-69* surfaced and commenced firing at 1805, lobbing three shells at Sand Island. One landed on the southeastern beach, one in the open area northeast of the radio towers, and one on the steps of the inert magazine close to those same towers. Damage proved very slight and no one got hurt; "A" battery (5-inch) lobbed two shells in the direction of the sub, which submerged. Two days later, another submarine attack occurred, but the enemy managed to get only two rounds off before two "Buffaloes" pounced on her, dropping 100-pound bombs that forced her down only 48 seconds after surfacing. The waning light of day did not permit an assessment of any damage. Wallace's pilots must have been listening carefully to the lecture on submarine tactics!

Trading shells with submarines was one thing; intercepting inbound aircraft was another. On 9 March, LCDR Joseph J. Rochefort, head of the communications intelligence unit at Pearl Harbor (Station "Hypo"), recommended to COM 14 that a dispatch be sent to Midway, warning that enemy flying boats could possibly attack that night or the next. Soon, Bill Wallace had a test of the fighter pilots' "ability to hit a red disc."

At 1037 on 10 March, Midway's radar picked up a "target" bearing 260 degrees, 43 miles distant. One minute later, the air alert sounded. According to standard doctrine, all planes cleared the field—13 F2A-3s by 1043 and 15 SB2U-3s by 1045. Soon after they had gotten airborne, VMF-221 was split into two patrols (high and low) to "await orders." Wallace, who had arrived at the CP at 1039, directed his fighters to orbit on the 280 bearing, 20 miles out; continued reports from the radar indicated the stranger was coming in on the 280-285 degree bearing.

The "bogey" had been picked up at 43 miles, but changed course several times, opening out as far as 73 miles before coming in to 50 miles again, where the island's aviation radar picked him up at 1101, indicating the target at possibly 7,000 feet. Wallace detached one division of four F2A-3s and vectored them out to intercept.

CAPTAIN NEEFUS' DIVISION

PLANE NO. (BuNo)	PILOT
221-MF-1 (BuNo 01537)	CAPT James L. Neefus
221-MF-12 (BuNo 01542)	2dLT Francis P. McCarthy
221-MF-4 (BuNo 01548)	1stLT Charles W. Somers
221-MF-9 (BuNo 01524)	MARGUN (NAP) Robert L. Dickey

Neefus, VMF-221's XO, acknowledged the orders and proceeded as directed, while the SB2U-3s had reached their station 20 miles from Midway on the 100 degree bearing. At 1110, Neefus, with 2dLT McCarthy flying on his right wing, reported a "bogey" five miles away at 9,000 feet, and transmitted "Tallyho!" Wallace ordered Neefus to attack. Up to that point, all had assumed this to be merely a drill.

Above 3,000 feet, visibility was excellent, with broken cumulus clouds that extended in some places from 3,000 feet down to 800 feet; down to the water in others. Small scattered rain showers rendered it impossible to see more than two miles or so beneath the constantly changing cloud formations. The strange aircraft proved to be one never before encountered in combat: one of the two prototype Kawanishi H8K1 Type 2 flying boats ("Emily") large, four-motored aircraft with splendid speed and range. Two of these planes, fueling from a submarine in Operation "K," had attempted to bomb Pearl Harbor just six days before, but had only succeeded in dropping their ordnance on Mt. Tantalus or in the water off the entrance to Pearl Harbor. One of these two planes was now nearing Midway; the other, Johnston Island. LT Toshio Hashizume, one of the most accomplished flying boat pilots in the Imperial Japanese Navy, flew the one which the Marines sought.

Neefus climbed and turned toward the flying boat, which, upon apparently sighting him, turned right, away from him. The Marine found the enemy aircraft to be very fast, and could get little distance on him. Hashizume put the big flying boat into a 30-degree glide; Neefus, with McCarthy now about 225 yards astern, immediately pushed over into a high-side attack. His .50-caliber fire apparently set the outboard engines afire, as they began to emit trails of black and gray smoke.

The flying boat continued in its dive, trailing smoke, as McCarthy attempted, with some difficulty, to overtake it. At approximately 3,500 feet, McCarthy crossed over and slightly astern of the Kawanishi, which now lumbered along 300 feet beneath him, to make an approach from out of the sun. Beginning his above rear approach, the lieutenant suddenly noticed another "Buffalo" closing in.

The pilot McCarthy saw was Dickey, who, having become separated from his section leader, was, like his comrades, having considerable trouble catching the flying boat, even using maximum power in high blower. Slowly closing the range, though, the enlisted pilot saw the Kawanishi near a layer of heavy overcast, obviously seeking to evade the Marines. "I knew if I didn't get it then," Dickey later said, "I'd lose it. I went after it. It was necessary to keep close to the ship to see it in those clouds." Apparently unaware of McCarthy's presence above, Dickey pressed home his attack, coming up close astern on the right side of the aircraft and firing. McCarthy managed to get off 50 rounds "in the proximity of the gunner's blister on the upper part of the fuselage" just before the Kawanishi, drifting down to the left with the enlisted pilot sticking with him, entered the thick overcast. Dickey turned sharply to the right to get on the tail of the flying boat, but at that moment, his "Buffalo" took seven hits: one passed through the tail wheel bearing, three penetrated the skin of the aircraft, one passed through no. 7 cylinder; one passed through the firewall between two cylinders, and one holed the left side panel of the windshield, that bullet breaking his left arm above the elbow. Soon realizing that his left arm was useless, he made a diving turn, coming out at 500 feet above the Pacific. Having neither "movement or sensation" in his hurt arm, he picked it up with his right hand and placed it across his lap, and began to try and figure out how to get back to Midway.

1stLT Somers, having seen the other three planes carry out their attacks, and Dickey "breaking away very sharply"—undoubtedly the moment the wounded enlisted pilot had disengaged—pressed home his attack as the flying boat emerged from a small cloud. The Kawanishi continued his steep dive, Somers following. He made a high-side approach from the left, and closed the range until about 100 yards away. Seeing the flying boat enter another cloud, Somers pulled away to avoid a collision.

McCarthy, meanwhile, had spotted the Kawanishi emerging from the clouds some 2,000 feet below, in a steep vertical bank to the left, shortly before it disappeared once more into the overcast. For five minutes, McCarthy circled the area at 5,000 feet, but due to the heavy cloud cover never sighted the enemy again.

Neefus, in the meantime, had come around again for a second pass, seeing one of the planes from his division tailing the flying boat and firing at it, and made his second approach as the flying boat emerged from a cloud. Recovering above the overcast, Neefus found himself alone. For three minutes, he flew along at the same heading the Kawanishi had been on when last seen before he reversed course and dove below the clouds, hoping to pick up his wingman and the second section. Looking below, he saw a large fire in the water, emitting black smoke. For four minutes Neefus flew around

the circle of fire on the ocean, but could not see with any certainty what was burning, only debris floating on the surface. At 1125, Neefus transmitted his report of the fire in the water. At that time, having lost contact with the rest of his division, he feared it marked the loss of one of his men.

As all of this was transpiring, MARGUN Dickey had been taking stock of his situation. Other than the engine running rough and his windshield being covered with oil, "everything else," he later wrote, "seemed satisfactory." His initial course took him to Kure, an atoll that "closely resembles Midway in both formation and appearance." He realized his mistake, however, and made the necessary correction. At that juncture (1128), he reported that he was returning to base. The CP radioed him soon thereafter and asked him to report his position, which he did.

At 1142, CAPT Neefus reported that he had, by that point, joined up with McCarthy and Somers and was heading back to Midway. Dickey, meanwhile, reported in at 1148 that he was five miles out and "coming in direct." He then appended the request to notify the shore batteries to hold their fire. Five minutes later, a "Buffalo," its engine noisily showing evidence of having been hit (LTCOL Wallace noted a "spitting or backfiring" noise as the F2A-3 came in) descended for the landing on Eastern Island, Dickey requesting that an ambulance be sent to the runway. As he recounted later, it had been "pretty tough" returning with his one good arm. "Every time I'd let go of the stick to handle the switches," he said, "we'd jump all over the sky."

Ultimately, all planes, including the VMSB sections and the fighters, landed back at Eastern by 1415. A flight surgeon later removed a 7.7-mm. bullet from Dickey's left arm, and the gunner was recommended for a DFC, as were Somers and McCarthy; Neefus, for his part in leading the division, was put in for the Navy Cross, all pilots' citations recognizing their pressing home a "determined, aggressive, and effective" attack "under most difficult flying conditions."[2]

The attempted reconnaissance by one flying boat, however, seemed to reflect growing Japanese interest in Midway—the atoll which VADM Nagumo regarded as "the sentry for Hawaii"—for around that time (the first week of March 1942) planners in the Combined Fleet began thinking of Midway as a future objective.

Japanese forces had already cut off the Philippines, swept down onto Singapore and the Dutch East Indies, driving all before them, and had devastated Darwin, in northern Australia. A carrier task force was slated

---

2. BGEN Ira L. Kimes, USMC (Ret), writing on 20 January 1948, recalled that LTCOL Wallace and his staff provided another "reward" to the victorious pilots—a bottle of bourbon!

Poor quality, but nonetheless significant, photograph of VMF-221's pilots, Eastern Island, circa late January or early February 1942. Front row (left to right): 1stLT Charles J. Quilter, 2dLT Robert E. Curtin, MAJ Verne J. McCaul (CO), CAPT Harold W. Bauer (XO until 8 February), MTSGT Robert L. Dickey, 2dLT Marion E. Carl. Middle row: 2dLT Henry A. Ellis, 2dLT Philip R. White, USMCR, 1stLT Robert R. Burns, 2dLT Loren D. Everton (had come out in *Wright* just before Pearl Harbor), CAPT James L. Neefus (w/goatee), 1stLT Frederick R. Payne Jr., 2dLT David W. Pinkerton, USMCR. Rear row: 2dLT John F. Carey, 1stLT John R. Alvord, 1stLT Charles W. Somers Jr., CAPT John L. Smith, CAPT Robert M. Haynes, 2dLT Herbert T. Merrill, 2dLT Francis P. McCarthy, USMCR, CAPT John F. Dobbin, 2dLT William C. Humberd. Of these pilots, two, Bauer and Smith, would earn the Medal of Honor during World War II, and one, Carl, would become one of the leading USMC "aces" of the conflict. SOMERS

to move into the Indian Ocean, to seek out and destroy the small British fleet in that area, and to attack Ceylon and thereby isolate India.

In time, Japanese forces were to intensify operations to cut off Australia and drive her from the war; assault and occupy Fiji and New Caledonia—setting up advance bases for aircraft and submarines there—and assault Samoa, destroying the facilities there but withdrawing upon the conclusion of the work of destruction, thereby severing the lines of supply and communication between the United States and Australia.

Nor was that all. Also included in the "second phase" operations was the assault on, and occupation of, Midway, supported by a diversionary strike into the Aleutians, to prevent any surprise attacks on the Japanese home islands. American raids on the Marshalls, Gilberts, and Wake Island were one thing, but on Marcus Island, only 1,000 miles from Japan proper, on 4 March 1942—that was the proverbial last straw. The Japanese desired to destroy the American capability for conducting the surprise raids it feared (and that had proved such an embarrassment to the Navy) and to use submarine and air power to whittle down American fleet strength

in the classic strategy of attrition.

ADM Yamamoto's staff prepared a plan of attack that called for seizure of Midway and some islands in the Aleutians in early June. After the decisive battle with the American fleet—which, they felt, would not allow the occupation of Midway to go unchallenged—advanced bases would be seized at Johnston in August 1942, and assaults on Hawaii in October 1942 and on Oahu in April 1943, would follow, specifically to destroy American air power there. From there, surprise attacks could be carried out on the west coast of the United States.

At Midway, meanwhile, the atoll maintained its usual defensive posture; on 28 March, the seaplane tender *Curtiss* (AV-4) arrived and unloaded eight Brewster F2A-3s for VMF-221 and four SB2U-3s for VMSB-231 (which unit would soon be redesignated as VMSB-241), as well as disembarked pilots to man them. Within less than a fortnight, on 7 April 1942, the cable connecting Midway with Guam was severed at the reef to preclude possible "subversive communication." The Midway-to-Hawaii cable, however, was retained intact, a valuable link that permitted in-clear communication free from enemy eavesdroppers.

While Midway was maintaining its defensive posture, initially oblivious to plans being laid for its fate, Yamamoto approved the plan his staff had drafted, on 1 April, and had it submitted to the Naval General Staff. Objections to the plan within that body having been overcome by Yamamoto's threat to resign from his post as CINC, Combined Fleet, the chief of the Naval General Staff, ADM Osami Nagano, presented it to the Emperor on 16 April 1942.

Throughout the period of the plan's gestation, from early March into mid-April, the Navy's opposite numbers in the Army had let their objections be known. A showdown over Midway would undoubtedly have occurred had not American bombs fallen on Tokyo exactly two days later. On 18 April, 16 North American B-25 medium bombers, flying from the aircraft carrier *Hornet* (CV-8) and led by LTCOL James Doolittle, bombed military targets at Tokyo and other Japanese cities. Furthermore, the task force whence the B-25s had come, centered around *Hornet* and *Enterprise*, retired unscathed—a humiliation for the Japanese Navy, whose hitherto undefeated might was supposed to have rendered the sacred soil of the homeland secure from the depredations of a handful of American bombers!

The Japanese had estimated that three American carriers were definitely in the Pacific—*Enterprise, Hornet* and *Saratoga*—but despite suspicions that she was under repairs on the west coast, they believed *Lexington* sunk off Oahu on 11 January, and that the Americans had lost another carrier off Rabaul on 20 February. For the United States, the operations of its carriers had been a bright star in an otherwise dismal firmament in early 1942: VADM William F. Halsey's task force had hit the Marshalls, Wake and Marcus; VADM Wilson Brown's had raided Lae and Salamaua. In reality, no American carriers had been lost, only *Saratoga* (not *Lexington*) had been damaged by a submarine torpedo; the carrier "sunk" off Rabaul was wishful thinking. The Japanese held American aircrew in low esteem, and rated American aerial torpedo attack capability as "almost nil."

Ironically, Yamamoto himself had foreseen the possibility of an American strike on Japan, and, determined to prevent a repetition of the Halsey-Doolittle Raid, decided to go ahead at once with plans for the operations against Midway. Whatever doubts had existed in the Japanese Navy about the efficacy of striking at Midway and the Aleutians vanished as the result of the Halsey-Doolittle Raid. The raid had its effect on the Army, too, which had hitherto refused allotting any troops to the endeavor. The Army General Staff offered its cooperation and the Navy accepted it eagerly. Planning proceeded apace, and draft copies were distributed for comment on 28 April. Soon, "the sentry for Hawaii" would be challenged.

MGUN (NAP) Robert L. Dickey, his left arm in a cast, receives his DFC from RADM Wilhelm L. Friedell, commandant, Mare Island Navy Yard, at the Naval Hospital, Mare Island, 16 May 1942, while COL M.C. Shearer, USMC, CO of the Marine Barracks, Mare Island, looks on. DICKEY

ADM Nimitz awards a Navy Cross to CAPT James L. Neefus, 2 May 1942, for his part in shooting down the Kawanishi H8K1 Type 2 flying boat on 10 March 1942. To right of center is LTCOL Ira L. Kimes, CO, MAG-22; LTCOL Omar Pfeiffer, CINCPAC's fleet Marine officer, who drafted the citations for the decorations Nimitz is awarding, is behind and to Kimes' right. NH 62745

After awarding him the DFC for his part in shooting down the Type 2 flying boat on 10 March, ADM Nimitz congratulates 2dLT Francis P. McCarthy, USMCR, who, unbeknownst to either man, had only one month and two days left to live. CDR Cyril T. Simard stands second from right, wearing sunglasses and a steel helmet. 80-G-6170

ADM Nimitz, accompanied by LTCOL Kimes (L) and CDR Simard (R), inspects Midway, 2 May 1942. NH 62743

ADM Nimitz congratulates LTCOL Shannon (L), on the latter's spot promotion to colonel on 2 May 1942. RADM Bellinger stands third from right.

CHAPTER FOUR

·················

"Time Is Everything."

While the Japanese were making plans to add Midway to their timetable, ADM Nimitz had added the atoll to his itinerary, too, following his conference with ADM Ernest J. King, COMINCH, at San Francisco in late April. Intelligence information, gained from reading the Japanese Navy's message traffic, had hinted strongly at enemy movements in the South Pacific, toward Port Moresby. Since nothing appeared to be headed for Hawaii, Nimitz had planned to concentrate his four carriers to meet the Japanese Navy's movement toward the Coral Sea. Stripping the Hawaiian chain of carrier protection, however, had bothered King, who had expressed particular concern over the security of Midway. As a result, Nimitz had decided to pay the atoll a personal visit.

On 2 May, CINCPAC, accompanied by RADM Patrick N.L. Bellinger, COMPATWING TWO, arrived at Eastern Island at 1325 in a VP-51 PBY-5A, "to present awards and make [an] informal inspection." During the ceremony, Nimitz expressed pleasure at being able to visit that command, which had demonstrated such ample "alertness and ability to resist enemy attack." Among those the CINCPAC decorated were two of the pilots (Neefus and McCarthy) who had participated in shooting down the Japanese flying boat on 10 March. In addition, he conferred spot promotions to captain for CDR Simard and to colonel for LTCOL Shannon. He then conducted a vigorous and energetic "informal" inspection (one Marine noted later that at day's end, only the admiral and COL Shannon appeared "still full of energy"), and upon the conclusion of it, appeared "highly pleased with what he had seen."

Afterwards, Nimitz conferred with Simard and Shannon in the former's quarters, questioning the latter at length as to what he needed if the Japanese decided to hurl an attack against the atoll. "If I get you all these things," Nimitz asked, "then you can hold Midway against an amphibious assault?" Shannon responded unequivocally and confidently, "Yes, sir." The manner in which the colonel, a veteran of fighting in France with the 6th Marines in World War I, responded, elicited a smile from the admiral. Nimitz then told Shannon to list his needs. He promised that if it was available, Midway would get it. Nimitz—feeling that Midway could withstand a "moderate attack"—cleared the atoll at 0600 on 3 May, departing the same way he had come.

When he returned to Oahu, Nimitz notified COMINCH that he intended to send the antiaircraft units of the 3d Defense Battalion, consisting of 12 3-inch antiaircraft guns, eight 37-mm. antiaircraft, and 12 twin 20-mm. mounts, to Midway. He also urgently requested more men to fill up the 3d Battalion. Reflecting Nimitz's plans to reinforce Midway, the CINCPAC Graybook notes, with considerable understatement: "This important outpost has been given considerable thought."

Well that it should have—especially in view of what the Japanese were contemplating. At that time, the strength of the Midway garrison stood at about 1,300 men. The 6th Defense Battalion manned five 5-inch/.51-caliber guns, four 3-inch anti-boat guns, and 12 3-inch antiaircraft guns, in addition to 48 .50-caliber machine guns and 36 .30-caliber. Against that, the Japanese planned to hurl 5,000 men—both Special Landing Force (SLF) (sailors trained to fight on land, similar in mission to U.S. Marines) and Army troops.Their plans called for a three-day pre-landing bombardment by planes from their carriers. The *Ichiki Detachment* (Army) was to land from the south on Eastern Island, while the 2d Combined SLF was to come ashore simultaneously from the south on Sand. Alternately, landings were to be made from the north across the beaches on the lagoon. The Navy would control the island once captured, and the two Navy pioneer (construction) battalions would return the air facilities (expected to be heavily damaged in the pre-invasion bombardment) to operational status.

While those plans were gathering momentum, the projected Japanese thrust toward Port Moresby took place. TF 17, however, centered around *Yorktown* and *Lexington*, stopped it in the Battle of the Coral Sea, but at a heavy cost: *Yorktown* had suffered damage and *Lexington* had had to be sunk by friendly forces. The battle, however, had decimated *Zuikaku's* air group and rendered her sistership *Shokaku* incapable of operating aircraft. TF 16—formed around *Enterprise* and *Hornet*—sent from Pearl to support TF 17, arrived too late to take part in the battle but played a major supporting role in the unfolding drama as it was spotted by the Japanese in the South Pacific theater, far from Hawaii.

In the Battle of the Coral Sea, the first in history where neither side's ships saw the other, the Japanese achieved a tactical victory, in that *Lexington* (CV-2) had to be sunk by friendly forces. In this photo, she is seen from one of her accompanying ships on 8 May 1942, as fires burn fiercely throughout her length. However, the air groups from *Lexington* and *Yorktown* achieved a different kind of triumph, as they inflicted heavy losses on *Zuikaku*'s air group and scored damage to *Shokaku* that limited her ability to operate planes. The damage suffered by *Yorktown* was not irreparable. Such was Japanese overconfidence that the planners of the Midway operation deemed four fleet carriers in the striking force to be sufficient. NH 51382

CAPT (then-LCDR) Joseph J. Rochefort led the codebreakers at station HYPO that gave the Americans the intelligence edge that allowed them to be ready to meet the Japanese at Midway. He ultimately received a belated DSM for this work in 1985. NH 84826, Pineau

Gathering, from his intelligence information, that the Japanese had apparently postponed the Port Moresby operation indefinitely, on 9 May ADM Nimitz ordered *Yorktown* brought back from Tongatabu, to which Fletcher had repaired after Coral Sea, knowing that "any carrier which is not 100 percent effective" operated at a "grave disadvantage in the duels which usually result when forces containing carriers oppose each other." Damaging your opponent, he reasoned, did not compensate "for being sunk yourself." Besides damage and plane losses, *Yorktown*, outside of two brief periods spent at anchor at Tongatabu, had been at sea almost continuously for three months.

On 5 May, the Navy Section of Imperial General Headquarters had ordered ADM Yamamoto to carry out operations aimed at capturing Midway and strategic places in the Aleutians. On 12 May, Yamamoto issued his operation plan for the assault on Midway. By the 14th, indications are that Joe Rochefort's cryptanalysts, as the plan made its way to various addressees in the Imperial Navy, had discovered "several significant indications of future enemy action:" (1) an attack on the Midway-Oahu line in force about the first week of June; (2) a simultaneous attack on the Aleutian chain and Alaska; (3) the occupation of Ocean and Nauru Islands about 17 May, and (4) reinforcement of the New Britain-New Guinea force to strike to the southeast "at any time" between 25 May and 15 June.

On 15 May, ADM Nimitz reviewed his options. "It was evident" to CINCPAC that "if estimates of the enemy's strength and intentions were true, that the situation was most serious." Midway could only support an air group the size of that operated by an aircraft carrier. Having already recalled TF 17 "for rest and replenishment," Nimitz on 17 May (18 May west of the International Date Line) directed Halsey to "expedite" his return to Pearl.

Presaging Midway's build-up, four VP-23 PBY-5s

Scouting SIX SBDs (foreground, one LSO stripe on fin) and, just beyond, VB-6 SBDs, on the flight deck of *Enterprise*, 11 May 1942. S-4, an SBD-3 (BuNo 03206) was flown on 4 June by LT Charles R. Ware. Note VF-6 F4F-4 which retains the old-style red-centered star (foreground). *Sabine* (AO-25) approaches in the background. 80-G-14115

Grumman F4F-4s of VF-6 and VS-6 SBDs on board *Enterprise*, 18 May 1942, the day VADM Halsey received orders to "expedite return." 80-G-14120

under LT Howard P. Ady Jr., arrived on 15 May to search for a Curtiss SOC from the light cruiser *Nashville* (CL-43) that had disappeared during a scouting flight a short time before. The searches, conducted over the next several days, all proved negative.

On 17 May, messages from COMINCH to CINC-PAC and CINCPAC to COMINCH crossed paths, each estimating future Japanese intentions. King urged Nimitz to concentrate a strong force in Hawaiian waters, and to chiefly employ "strong attrition tactics," not allowing American forces to "accept such decisive action as would be likely to incur heavy losses in our carriers and cruisers." He also urged the creation of a North-ern Pacific Force, drawn from Northwest and Western Sea Frontier forces, as well as whatever fleet units Nimitz could send. Nimitz promised to watch the Pacific situation closely. Furthermore, CINCPAC indicated that *Yorktown's* damage was within the capacity of the navy yard at Pearl to repair, and that he would retain the carrier's air group in readiness for active operations upon completion of the ship's repairs.

Around mid-May, meanwhile, Joe Rochefort's cryptanalysts' tireless monitoring of Japanese communications had yielded information pointing to the assembly, in the Marianas, at Guam and Saipan, of an occupation force for a "forthcoming campaign." Another message hinted at one ship embarking an air base unit, proceeding to Saipan, and thence to a place designated only as "AF." Fragmentary messages had led Rochefort and LCDR Edwin T. Layton, Nimitz's intelligence officer, to assume that "AF" stood for Midway, but those two officers knew that only the Japanese could provide the definitive proof that Nimitz sought: whether or not "AF" stood for Midway. Rochefort proposed that Midway receive orders to transmit an urgent, plain-language—but *bogus*—message reporting a serious casualty to the fresh water system. Layton took the idea to Nimitz, who approved it heartily. The order to transmit the fake message went out via the cable connecting Oahu with Midway.

In the meantime, while Nimitz continued to consider his options, he wanted everything possible to be ready by 25 May. On the 18th, the admiral reached tentative decisions to (1) reinforce Midway with part of a raider battalion, (2) station four submarines off the atoll, (3) operate Army bombers from Midway to enable them to strike enemy carriers, (4) conduct searches with a dozen PBYs, (5) employ *Yorktown*, if ready, in support of TF 16, (6) move TF 1 (battleships) along with *Saratoga*, (7) form the North Pacific Force—TF 8—and dispatch it to Alaskan waters and (8) expedite repairs to all ships then lying in the navy yard.

The Japanese, meanwhile, as hoped, snapped at the bait dangled before them in Rochefort's bogus message. On 18 May, NAS Midway dutifully reported its water casualty and the following day, a Japanese message indicated how "AF" was having trouble with its fresh water distillation system. On 20 May, Rochefort's group "broke" the Japanese dispatch, thus providing Nimitz with his proof. Armed with this knowledge, CINCPAC immediately set to work forming the North Pacific Force, to be commanded by RADM Robert A. Theobald. That same day (20 May), COM14 (RADM David W. Bagley), by dispatch, warned CAPT Simard to expect an attack "sometime after 25 May . . . by planes from as many as 4 carriers supported by cruisers, destroyers, and possibly battleships." Promising more information to be forthcoming, Bagley informed Simard that CINCPAC was reinforcing him. Furthermore, a squadron of PT boats would be sent out from Pearl, slated to arrive on 25 May, for use as a striking force at Simard's discretion, as well as four district patrol craft (YPs) and a converted yacht (PY) for patrol duty, scheduled to arrive on the 26th. Bagley urged dispersal of foodstuffs, storage and dispersal of potable water, and dispersal of ammunition, while keeping it accessible. "The Commander-in-Chief in his recent visit . . . was very much impressed with the fine spirit of the personnel," Bagley concluded, "and has expressed his extreme confidence in their ability to hold the Island. Both he and I charge you to give them hell."

Also around 20 May, all ships assigned to the second "K" operation—an aerial reconnaissance of Pearl Harbor supported by refueling submarines—sailed for their assigned stations. The previous day, 19 May, representatives of the 24th Air Flotilla and the 6th Fleet met at Kwajalein and concluded an agreement for the operation. The 24th Air Flotilla would contribute two Type 2 flying boats ("Emily"), and the 6th Fleet would provide the 13th Submarine Division and part of the 3d to the operation that was planned for 31 May. The plan allowed for a postponement, but if the flight could not be carried out by 3 June, it was to be called off. Three of the submarines were to serve as refueling ships, to linger at French Frigate Shoal to refuel the flying boats when they arrived. One was designated as a beacon ship, one a rescue ship to cruise in the waters southwest of Pearl Harbor in the event of an emergency landing. The last was to lie in a position southwest of Oahu to provide weather data.

On 22 May 1942, MAG-22 went on the alert, and LTCOL Ira L. Kimes and his staff began planning how to deploy the available resources. As was standard practice, they decided that when Midway's radar picked up an incoming raid, all operable planes would clear the field; VMF-221 would be vectored out to intercept the enemy before it reached Midway. Under Verne McCaul and, after 17 April, MAJ Floyd B. "Red" Parks, VMF-221 had worked to reduce the time it took to get airborne; the time to get together in the air. Following radioed instructions from the fighter director, the fighters had practiced interceptions on any inbound planes, such as PBYs from Oahu. Kimes would later call VMF-221 "a cracker-jack good fighter squadron." Another contemporary observer called VMF-221 "the smoothest flying gang" he had ever seen. "Their formations, airdrome technique, and fighter tactics looked perfect."

The scout-bombers, once they had cleared the field, would rendezvous at a point 20 miles from Eastern Island and await further word, "prepared to proceed immediately to attack enemy carriers or to track enemy aircraft back to their carriers and attack." MAJ Lofton R. Henderson, who had relieved "Buddy" Chappell in command of VMSB-241 on 17 April 1942, stepped up the training, reorganizing the squadron and instituting tactics using 19 planes: four boxes of four aircraft apiece, with the lead element consisting of the commanding officer and two wingmen.

That same day (22 May), however, an unforeseen disaster occurred which drastically affected Midway's ability to operate aircraft; at 0900, an error in the final hookup of an electrical system led to an explosion which rocked the atoll as 375,000 gallons of gasoline went up in smoke; fuel was lost in 16 out of 31 tanks. Informed of the disaster, ADM Nimitz immediately ordered the dispatch of gasoline, in drums, to the station.

Also that same day, six PBY-5As from VP-44 arrived to begin their patrols and assist VP-23 in carrying out the important search flights from the atoll. Over the days that followed, VP-23's PBY-5s droned over the Pacific in the vicinity of the reefs and islands within a 400-mile radius of Midway. VP-44's "Catalinas," starting on the 27th, would search out to 600 miles in a fan-shaped arc, ranging from the northwest to the southwest.

Nimitz's staff, meanwhile, wrestled with the logistics of defending Midway. On 23 May, Nimitz told his chief of staff, RADM Milo F. Draemel, to have CAPT Arthur C. Davis, his aviation officer, and RADM Bellinger, discuss Midway's defense with MGEN Clarence L. Tinker, Commanding General of the 7th Air Force. Nimitz outlined the problem confronting them as getting the "maximum of effect from the Army and Navy air strength in the Hawaiian Islands in defeating Japanese attacks on Midway and/or any of the main islands of the Hawaiian Group—without exposing our carriers to [the] danger of destruction out of proportion to the damage they can inflict. We must calculate the risk," he informed Draemel, "and must accept the danger when our prospects of frustrating or destroying enemy carriers are sufficiently good." He ordered an immediate and careful survey of available air assets, afloat and ashore, to counter what stood to be five Japanese carriers arrayed against Midway. "Our air force—both Army and Navy," posited Nimitz, "must be employed with the maximum skill and such attacks as we attempt must be carried out with the greatest determination." Nimitz stressed the need to expedite matters, so that the findings of Bellinger, Davis, and Tinker would be available when Halsey arrived in a few days with TF 16. "Time," the admiral emphasized, "is everything." Before the day was out, the estimates of the situation, and comments upon them, had been made.

CAPT Simard's promised PT boats were soon on their way, to proceed under their own power in convoy with the seaplane tender *Ballard* (AVD-10). At 1415 on 25 May 1942, that ship sailed from Pearl Harbor. As she stood down the channel, a motor launch overtook her, and transferred two men to her. One, a 6-foot-two-inch redhead ("as Irish as Paddy's pig") was familiar to many in the motion picture world—CDR John Ford, USNR. He had been called only a short time before by ADM Nimitz, who had told him to "throw a bag together and come out here and see me." He had then been directed

to report to RADM Bagley, who in turn had had him taken out to that ship. Ford did not have the slightest idea of either where he was bound or what he was doing when he stepped on board the seaplane tender, but he soon found out that his destination was Midway. John A. MacKenzie, PhoM2c, whose father had been a cinematographer at Twentieth Century Fox, accompanied the veteran director.

Also on the 25th, the light cruiser *St.Louis* (CL-49), escorted by the destroyer *Case* (DD-370), arrived at Midway, at 0800, the former with Companies "C" and "D," 2d Raider Battalion—which had completed its basic training in mid-April—embarked. The two companies were assigned to the 6th Defense Battalion; one was assigned to Eastern Island and the other to Sand. The ships that had brought the "raiders" did not linger long; they sailed at 1730.

St. Louis (CL-49) stands out of Pearl Harbor, 22 May 1942, with Companies "C" and "D" of the 2d Marine Raider Battalion, "Carlson's Raiders," embarked. NH 50796

On 26 May, VMSB-241 practiced glide-bombing and strafing, as well as squadron tactics. That same afternoon, MGEN Tinker arrived on Midway via a B-17; with him rode MAJ Jo K. Warner, slated to serve as liaison officer between the Army Air Corps and the naval establishment. The two airmen went into conference with CAPT Simard and LTCOL Kimes shortly after they arrived at Sand Island.

Later that day, the aircraft ferry *Kitty Hawk* (APV-1), escorted by *Gwin* (DD-433), arrived from Hawaii with 19 Douglas SBD-2s for VMSB-241 and seven Grumman F4F-3s for VMF-221, as well as 21 new pilots (17 of them fresh from flight training) for the two squadrons, and 35 enlisted men. Among the older pilots was 35-year-old MAJ Benjamin W. Norris, USMCR, VMSB-241's new XO. While some of the old hands in 241 joked that the new arrivals were "just in time for the party," MAJ Henderson's telling them the next morning that "the Japs were overdue" caused the newcomers to do "a little more thinking on the matter." *Kitty Hawk* also unloaded a platoon of eight light tanks for use in the ground defense of the island.

That same day (27 May west of the Date Line), the Japanese striking force sailed from the Inland Sea. "Navy Day" in Japan found the Imperial Navy feted grandly. The *Japan Times and Advertiser* declared that Navy Day 1942 was a time to hail Japan's new world position and rededicate the Navy's resources to set up and protect a "new world order which will enable the peoples of East Asia to develop their own destinies free from the shackles of Anglo-American exploitation." Navy Day 1942, boasted the *Advertiser*, "is the climax for which all Navy Days of the past years have been a preparation." A junior officer in the battleship *Haruna* summed up this feeling of excitement that day when he wrote in his diary: "To the attack!"

Up to that point in the war, the Japanese had done well. After the *Kido Butai* had returned to home waters, following the Indian Ocean operations, though, there followed a period of rest and refit. Contrary to popular belief, the cutting edge of Nagumo's sword was not nearly as sharp as it had been when the blow had fallen upon Pearl Harbor. Nagumo's ships had sailed, however, with a large number of new pilots embarked; due to a "considerable turn-over in personnel, practically no one got beyond the point of basic training. Even the experienced fliers," Nagumo would later note, "barely got to the point where they could make daytime landings on the carriers...even some of the more seasoned fliers had lost some of their skill."

During mid-May, the torpedo bomber pilots had been put through their paces, and did not perform well. "The records during these tests," Nagumo complained, "were so disappointing that some were moved to comment that it was almost a mystery how men with such poor ability could have obtained such brilliant results in the Coral Sea . . ." Level-bombing leaders had conducted practices against the target ship *Settsu* in the Inland Sea, obtaining a "fair degree of skill," while the dive bomber pilots could not carry out more than one drill a day due to the distance they had to fly to utilize the services provided by *Settsu*. "Even this minimum practice," the *Kido Butai's* commander lamented, "could not be conducted satisfactorily because the men were kept busy with maintenance work."

The ships themselves had spent repair and maintenance periods, with only *Kaga* being available for carrier qualifications. Nagumo would later admit that the combat efficiency of the carriers "had been greatly lowered" before the *Kido Butai* sailed for Midway. Coupled to that, as Nagumo would later admit: "We had practically no intelligence [information] concerning the enemy...we participated in this operation with meager training and without knowing the enemy..."

Kitty Hawk (APV-1)—"a strange and wonderful ship," wrote one Marine afterward, as she arrived with aircraft reinforcements—moored alongside Ford Island in March 1942, with *Enterprise* in background (L). *Kitty Hawk* proved invaluable in transporting "new" planes to VMSB-241 and VMF-221, as well as new pilots, to Midway on the eve of the battle. 80-G-16756 via Wenger

As seen from the ramp on Ford Island, *Hornet* (CV-8) returns to Pearl Harbor, 26 May 1942. The large tractors in the foreground were used to tow flying boats ashore. Note sandbagged machine gun emplacement at right. 80-G-66132

On the day the *Kido Butai* sailed, ADM Nimitz and his staff were evaluating their own carrier situation. They noted that *Yorktown* had suffered damage at Coral Sea, and that she required replacement planes. They theorized that she could perhaps be placed in service within four days, but that if the yard force could not effect the necessary repairs she would have to be sent immediately to the Puget Sound Navy Yard. Her disposition would have to be determined by 28 May if she were to play a role in the battle that lay ahead. To be sure that all hands were on the alert, meanwhile, ADM Nimitz suspended all leaves and liberty—for all except the men of TF 16 and TF 17. They had been at sea for a long time, Nimitz reasoned, and could use some diversion before going back into the fray.

TF 16 arrived back at Pearl on 26 May having accomplished its mission of worrying the Japanese, but with its commander, VADM Halsey, suffering from painful worries of his own—dermatitis. Unable to command TF 16 at that critical juncture, the ailing admiral recommended unhesitatingly that RADM Raymond A. Spruance--who had commanded the cruisers that had screened *Enterprise* since the day the war began—be given the task. Nimitz agreed and Spruance got TF 16. The latter took his own flag lieutenant but inherited Halsey's staff, headed by the brilliant but temperamental CDR Miles R. Browning.[1]

The following day, the 27th, MGEN Tinker left Midway at 0715 to fly back to Hawaii. That day, MAJ Warner continued getting acquainted with the naval aviation end of Midway; after spending the morning

looking over the communications facilities on Eastern Island; he then spent much of the rest of the day with LTCOL Kimes and MAJ McCaul, MAG-22's operations officer, discussing plans. Later that afternoon, LCDR Robert C. Brixner, VP-44's CO, took the airman on a radar flight in a PBY-5A, educating him on the subjects of bearings and homing.

The "new" SBD-2s were brought over to Eastern Island, meanwhile, after *Kitty Hawk* had unloaded them, under the direction of the newly promoted MAJ Leo R. Smith, USMC, in one of his last actions as VMSB-241's XO. After placing them in commission and bore-sighting the guns, the Marines began familiarizing themselves with the SBD-2s. Given the exigencies of the situation (particularly the fuel problem) proper training for combat was, of necessity, rather limited. By the 27th, routine patrols for 241 were confined to a one hour nightly flight between 1840 and 1940.

At Pearl Harbor on the 27th, all hands who could do so turned out to cheer *Yorktown's* arrival. She had launched her 42 flyable aircraft at 1026, and stood into Pearl's channel at 1352. Her crew mustered in whites on her flight deck in the bright Hawaiian sunshine, while oil from her leaking tanks mingled with her wake. After rounding Ford Island, *Yorktown* eased into the repair basin, berth 16, so that the exact extent of her damage could be ascertained.

Also that day, ADM Nimitz summoned GEN Delos Emmons, Commanding General of the Hawaiian Department, and MGEN Robert C. Richardson, Jr., Director of the War Department's Bureau of Public Relations, for a conference. Present, too, was RADM Spruance. "While nothing new was brought out," one ob-

---

1. See the essay by Clark Reynolds later in this volume.

ADM Nimitz pins a DFC on the blouse of LT(jg) Cleo J. Dobson, for the latter's performance of duty in the Marshalls, on board *Enterprise* on 27 May 1942. A few days later, some of the pilots Nimitz decorated here would have the opportunity to win further laurels in combat. 80-G-80433

server noted, "all hands expressed views," and ADM Nimitz clearly explained the existing problems. During the course of the meeting, GEN Emmons, noting how many B-17s were to be sent to Midway under Nimitz' OpPlan 29-42, complained that he hadn't "anywhere near enough planes to defend Oahu." That was, Nimitz's war diarist commented wryly, "of course, nothing new."

Promulgated at 1800 on 27 May 1942, CINCPAC's Op-Plan 29-42 detailed how Nimitz expected to fight the Battle of Midway.[2] He organized his striking forces into three groups: TF 16, under RADM Spruance, around *Enterprise* and *Hornet*; TF 17, under RADM Fletcher, around *Yorktown*; and TF 11, under RADM Aubrey W. Fitch, around *Saratoga*. Each task force contained sufficient cruisers and destroyers for a screen. Nimitz grouped his submarines into TF 7, under RADM Robert H. English, based at Pearl Harbor. He allocated 12 submarines (as opposed to the four originally envisioned) to the Midway patrol; others to a "support" patrol.

Believing that an attack on Midway could be preceded by an attack on Oahu, Nimitz estimated that the enemy thrust was designed to capture Midway and use it as a base for strikes against the Hawaiian area. Beginning

2. According to then-COL Omar T. Pfeiffer, USMC, who was then CINCPAC Fleet Marine Officer and Assistant War Plans Officer, the actual Op-Plan 29-42 was drafted by CAPT Lynde D. McCormick, CINCPAC's War Plans Officer.

In a view similar to prewar Tai Sing Loo views, *Astoria* (CA-34) returns to Pearl Harbor, 27 May 1942, photographed by T.E. Collins, P3c, USN. 80-G-66118

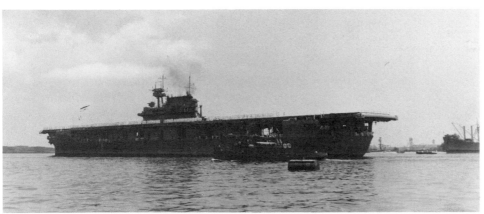

Yorktown (CV-5) arrives at Pearl, 27 May 1942, her crew at quarters on the flight deck in dress whites. A mute reminder of the Japanese attack of 7 December lies visible beyond the carrier's stern: the mainmast of the battleship *Arizona* (BB-39). The tug *Hoga* (YT-146) is in the foreground. 80-G-21931

as soon as 30 May, CINCPAC informed his addressees, Japanese submarines would probably reconnoiter; submarine-fueled patrol planes could carry out a diversionary bombing raid against Oahu; carriers would approach Midway at high speed; carrier aircraft, coming from a northwesterly bearing, would carry out air strikes on Midway that would begin at daylight and last as long as it took to eliminate the atoll as an American base. Additional carrier groups, in addition to fast battleships, would cover the attacking carriers by striking American surface ships.

A landing would probably be made at night, the estimates declared, featuring the "usual attempts at infiltration and extreme resolution on the part of the individual enemy soldier." Gas and incendiary bombs could be employed. The Japanese would immediately occupy the island and establish an air base and a motor torpedo boat base. Enemy submarines would attempt to intercept supporting American forces and destroy them. "It is probable," Nimitz concluded, "that if our carriers are sighted early in the operation, they will become the primary object of the Japanese carriers."

So relatively complete was American knowledge of the Japanese plan, and so secret was the source of the information, an officer on board *Enterprise* marveled that "our man in Tokyo is worth every cent we pay him!" At Midway, Ira Kimes noted that the composition of the forces bearing down on the atoll appeared to "include everything but Hirohito with an outboard motor on his bathtub."

At the time Op-Plan 29-42 was issued, only TF 16's availability for battle was a "given" in the equation. Fitch's TF 11, ready to depart the west coast on 5 June, would proceed immediately to Oahu. TF 17 was an unknown factor because of the undetermined condition of *Yorktown*; if she were unable to participate in the action, she would be sent to Puget Sound Navy Yard and her screening ships would be apportioned where they could do the most good. Nimitz also included TF 8 in his plans, deploying it to be ready for the expected enemy thrust into the Aleutians. A separate order, Op-Plan 28-42, had already been promulgated on 21 May for the forces defending the Aleutians.

"Hold Midway and inflict maximum damage on the enemy by strong attrition tactics," Nimitz had stated. He charged the striking forces to "inflict maximum damage," through "attrition tactics," but to not accept "decisive action as would be likely to incur heavy losses in our carriers and cruisers." To guide Fletcher and Spruance, Nimitz issued a "letter of instruction," which instructed them to be "governed by the principle of calculated risk," which he defined as "the avoidance of exposure of your force to attack by superior enemy forces

without good prospect of inflicting, as the result of such exposure, greater damage to the enemy."

The striking forces, Nimitz continued, would operate to the northeast of Midway at the outset, to seize the opportunity to surprise the enemy. He ordered the establishment of air search in the sector to the northeast of Midway. TF 16 would depart Pearl on 28 May; other forces would join TF 16 "as directed."

Nimitz charged TF 7 with inflicting "maximum damage" to the enemy, assigning priorities to carriers, battleships, transports, cruisers and auxiliaries, in that order. As soon as available, his submarines would take their stations. When they received information as to the enemy's location, they were to proceed to that objective regardless of area assignment. He also desired that the submarines transmit "such information as does not interfere with the primary task of attack." The submarines in the "support patrol" were to take station and be ready to support the striking force if circumstances compelled it to retire.

Patrol planes were to operate from Midway and Johnston, under the COs of the respective air stations. COMPATWINGs was also to station a seaplane tender at French Frigate Shoals to deny its use to Japanese submarines. *Thornton* (AVD-12), a sister ship of *Ballard*, drew that duty, and arrived in time to frustrate Japanese plans.

Nimitz charged the Midway local defense forces with the simply stated task — easier in the stating than in the doing — of holding the atoll. He ordered daily searches to the maximum practicable radius from Midway, covering, daily, the "maximum arc possible with the number of planes available." He urged CAPT Simard to "take every precaution against [his aircraft] being destroyed on the ground or water." To avoid such destruction, land-based long-range aircraft were authorized to retire to Oahu; patrol planes could refuel from small seaplane tenders (AVD) at French Frigate Shoals, if necessary.

CINCPAC ordered the local defense forces to have patrol craft watching the approaches to the atoll, and to have them exploit favorable opportunities to attack carriers, battleships, transports and auxiliaries; they were to observe Kure, as well as Pearl and Hermes Reef. They were to give "prompt warning" of the approach of any enemy forces. The local defense commander was to keep CINCPAC informed of the air searches and other air operations and also report the weather encountered by the search planes. Forces at Johnston were to conduct daily searches, while the island patrols would furnish gasoline and other assistance "as may be required."

Nimitz did not neglect the Army's supporting role in the drama. The Hawaiian Department was to provide, as directed, a striking force of "long-range bombers and torpedo carrying aircraft" to operate under CO, NAS Midway, and would hold long-range bombers in readiness in the Oahu-Kauai area to strike enemy forces attacking Midway.

Enemy submarines, Nimitz concluded, were not important objectives, and must be positively identified before they were attacked. The Hawaiian Department's bombers were not to attack submarines in certain specified areas. Recognition of friendly forces, CINCPAC noted, "is vital." CINCPAC would inform all task force commanders at sea of all attacks ordered by shore-based aircraft.

The following morning (28 May), tugs assisted *Yorktown* into Dry Dock No. 1, where ADM Nimitz personally inspected her damaged hull soon thereafter. "We must have this ship back within three days," he told the inspecting party. One could almost sense the relief which greeted the determination that *Yorktown's* damage was not "enough to prevent operations on the evening of the 29th."

Elsewhere in Pearl Harbor that day, TF 16, formed around *Enterprise* and *Hornet*, put to sea before noon, bringing on board their respective air groups several hours out at sea. *Enterprise's* came from Ford Island; *Hornet's* from Ewa Mooring Mast Field. One VS-8 pilot, LT William J. "Gus" Widhelm, one of the squadron's more colorful characters, found himself cursed with a "Dauntless" that would not start. He left the plane behind and "hitched" a ride in one of VT-8's TBDs.

Misfortune, though, marred the recovery of *Enterprise's* air group. At 1608 on 28 May, LCDR Eugene E. Lindsey, CO of VT-6, the first to come on board,

made a bad landing; his TBD-1 hit the ramp and then caromed over the port side into the water. Lindsey suffered internal chest injuries in the crash but, along with his two passengers, managed to escape from the plane. *Monaghan* (DD-354), the plane guard destroyer, picked up the three men and kept them on board until ultimately transferring them back to the carrier on the afternoon of the 31st.

That same day (28 May), *Ballard* reached Lisianski, and rendezvoused with the four district patrol craft (former purse seiners and tuna boats) then lying at anchor with drummed fuel for the PT boats. *Ballard* refueled two of the PTs and then stood out to serve as an antisubmarine screen while the four "Yippie" boats fueled the remainder. The whole evolution consumed a little less than seven hours, with the refueling completed by 1710. Underway for Midway at that point, the little flotilla continued on its voyage, and, delayed only briefly by repairs to the fuel strainer on board *PT-24*, reached their destination at 1000 on 29 May. An engine casualty in *PT-25* forced the tender to take her in tow; other than that, all boats reached Midway under their own power.

Thornton's arrival at French Frigate Shoals soon had its desired effects on the enemy. When *I-123* reached French Frigate Shoal on 29 May, she found that the Americans had gotten there first. Upon receiving word of *I-123's* findings, the Commander of the 24th Air Flotilla postponed the operations until 31 May.

Soon after *Ballard* moored at Midway she disembarked John Ford and Jack MacKenzie at 1045. Ford took in his surroundings with his trained director's eye for detail, and was soon quite busy. With his hand-held

LCDR Eugene E. Lindsey's TBD-1 (BuNo 0370)—the first plane to land upon the return of the air group from Ford Island—sinks astern of *Enterprise* after hitting the ramp at 1608 on 28 May 1942. The plane guard, *Monaghan* (DD-354) is in the background. 80-G-7744

16-mm. movie camera he filmed the comic antics of the aptly named "gooney birds," that existed in such great numbers on Midway. The PT boats, too, fascinated him ever since his trip in *Ballard*. Having "nothing but admir-ation" for that "wonderful group of boys," he filmed them, too. The impending action? "If it did come," he disclosed later, "I didn't think it would touch us."

The 77-foot ELCO motor torpedo boat *PT-20*, July 1941, in peacetime No. 5 Navy gray with white hull number shadowed in black. Note the boat's two .50-caliber machine gun turrets, and canvas-covered 21-inch torpedo tubes. NH 44481

CDR John Ford, USNR, relaxes in England, 1944. The noted film director, born in Cape Elizabeth, Maine, 1 February 1895, had been given a USNR commission in 1934. He reported for active duty in September 1941, shortly after he had finished directing the motion picture "How Green Was My Valley," and was promoted to LCDR., USNR, in October 1941. 222-FPL-P-71

Two Vought SB2U-3s take off on a tactics hop shortly before the Battle of Midway, during the feverish training taking place for the new pilots of VMSB-241, between 27 May and 3 June. Plane no. 6, in foreground, was BuNo 2045. Flown on 4 June by 2dLT James H. Marmande, USMCR (one of the new arrivals on Midway via *Kitty Hawk*), this aircraft was lost on 4 June when it and its crew (Marmande and his radio-gunner, PFC Edby Colvin) disappeared about 10 miles from Midway. USN

CAPT Logan C. Ramsey, reading his orders assigning him command of *Block Island* (CVE-21) in March 1943, served as CAPT Simard's operations officer on Midway in June 1942. Luce, via Lawson

CHAPTER FIVE

· · · · · · · · · · · · · · · · ·

"We Will Do The Best We Can With What We Have."

The 29th of May proved a busy day for some. While TF 16 continued on its way to "Point Luck," VF-6's diarist wrote: "No flying all day for us—they are 'saving' us. We are to butch up a Jap attack on Midway. . . ."

In order to provide more of the necessary lifeblood of the planes operating from the atoll—aviation fuel—Nimitz that day dispatched the gasoline tanker *Kaloli* (AOG-13), with the minesweeper *Vireo* (AM-52) as escort, to sail for Midway with a cargo of avgas. At that same juncture, *Kitty Hawk*, having delivered and un-loaded her important cargo expeditiously, sailed for Pearl at 0500, escorted by *Gwin* and *Sicard* (DM-21).

How best to "butch up" the "Jap attack" had been the object of considerable attention by a great number of individuals. More of the tools to do the required "butching" began arriving at Midway on the 29th. Four sleek Martin B-26 "Marauders" from the 18th Recon-naissance Squadron arrived from Oahu at 1315 on 29 May; at Ford Island, their crews had been given a crash course in torpedo-dropping by men from VT-6.

To direct the work of the planes operating from NAS Midway, meanwhile, RADM Bellinger sent CAPT Logan C. Ramsey out to the atoll in a PBY-5 from VP-11, along with a small staff of four officers and four enlisted radiomen. They arrived, along with three other VP-11 "Catalinas," at 1400 on the 29th, a half hour after *Ballard* cleared Midway to return to Pearl Harbor. Ramsey's presence freed Simard to concentrate on ad-ministration and logistics, handling the influx of men and materiel. A half hour after Ramsey's PBYs had arrived, eight more "Catalinas"—from VP-23—reached Midway to bring the squadron up to full strength. Each of the 12 flying boats that reached the atoll that day carried one torpedo.

Still later that day, the four promised "Yippie" boats (YPs) arrived at Midway: *YP-284, YP-290, YP-345* and *YP-350,* each a converted tuna boat requisitioned to perform local patrol and escort duties. Simard soon allocated *YP-284* to Lisianski, *YP-290* to Laysan;

YP-345 to Gardner's Pinnacles; and *YP-350* to Necker Island.

The training for VMSB-241, meanwhile, continued. Because of the different operating characteristics of the squadron's planes, Henderson divided it into two units: one consisting of 19 SBD-2s and the other of 12 SB2U-3s. He would command the first, grouping the SBDs as he had done the SB2U-3s a few days before; Ben Norris, the new XO, would command the second, that would operate independently of the SBDs in three "boxes" of four planes.

His new pilots needed much training: two ground-loops on the 27th had cost VMSB-241 two SB2U-3s, but the half-dozen Voughts retained as spares took care of such contingencies. On 29 May, 2dLT Sumner H. Whitten inadvertently raised the landing gear of one of the SBDs (while waiting to take off) and put it out of commission. On the 30th, VMSB-241 conducted practice formation flights for groups of four SBDs and the SB2U-3 unit, while the pilots in the SB2Us (for the most part fresh from flight school) practiced glide-bombing.

The land-based Marines, meanwhile, had not been idle—they strengthened existing dug-in positions, with all the new units dug-in or underground. Anti-boat obstacles—steel pickets and cables—surrounded Eastern and Sand Islands; anti-personnel mines, sown on both sides of barbed wire, could be detonated by electricity of by rifle fire. Marines improvised "Molotov (or 'Vic-tory') cocktails" for use against Japanese tanks, and placed anti-boat mines fashioned from TNT-filled sewer pipes, wired for electric detonation, at points deemed most strategic.

Company "C" of the Raider battalion, on Sand Island, under the "energetic and resourceful" direction of CAPT H.K. Throneson and CPL C.E. Knight, manufactured 1,500 anti-tank mines. Further, the men emplaced all machine guns and sited them so that they could do dou-ble duty—against planes and against landing craft. With

Marines wearing World War I-vintage steel helmets man a .50-caliber Browning water-cooled machine gun at Ewa Mooring Mast Field, circa 1942. Marines at Midway were equipped with such weapons as part of the antiaircraft battery.
USMC 145167

all of the barbed wire strung, additional obstacles, consisting of iron screw pickets, were planted in rows eight to 12 deep. Jury-rigged machine gun mounts were placed on PT boats and tugs.

Back at Pearl, *Yorktown* lay in drydock, swarming with yard workmen and ship's company making her battleworthy.[1] Afterward, an inspection asserted that "all essential watertight boundaries on (the) second deck and below" had been "restored." *Yorktown's* underwater damage had been determined to be "light" and she would thus be able to leave on the 30th with TF 17. That, CINCPAC's war diarist recounts, gave the Americans "a much better chance to be successful at Midway the first week of June."

While *Yorktown* teemed with repair work, an air group to fly from her deck was being formed. Of the original group of four squadrons with which she had started the war, only VB-5, its ranks comparatively intact (VS-5 had suffered heavy losses at Coral Sea), was retained, and was temporarily redesignated as "Scouting" FIVE.

The others came from *Saratoga's* group. Of those squadrons, VF-3 had its own unique problems, as its new Grumman F4F-4s outnumbered its pilots; *Yorktown's* VF-42 furnished 16 combat-seasoned aviators who would leaven the new men fresh from the Advanced Carrier Training Group, the squadron under the command of LCDR John S. "Jimmy" Thach, who had seen combat off *Lexington* in February and March 1942. LCDR Donald A. Lovelace, who had served under Thach in VF-3, but who'd been slated to return to the west coast and take over his own squadron, volunteered to served as Thach's XO and train the new men in the "beam defense" tactic Thach had pioneered. Thach

readily accepted Lovelace's offer.

Torpedo THREE was slated to receive new Grumman TBF-1s, but was still flying the Douglas TBD-1 "Devastator." The squadron CO, though, LCDR Lance E. Massey, who had assumed command of VT-3 on 24 May, had seen combat in the Marshalls as VT-6's XO. While his squadron had trained intensely out of Kaneohe, most of the men had never operated from a carrier before. Bombing THREE, another ex-*Saratoga* squadron, under LCDR Maxwell F. Leslie, had seen limited service at sea, when it had spelled VS-6 during *Enterprise's* operations in April, when it had not been at Kaneohe.

As has been seen, questions had existed about *Yorktown's* fitness for the fight that lay ahead. Nor was that all; ADM King doubted RADM Fletcher's competence to handle TF 17 for the battle in the offing. To allay King's fears and to determine for himself Fletcher's fitness for the task, ADM Nimitz summoned the admiral to account for his actions as CTF 17. Fletcher did so so convincingly that, on 29 May, Nimitz informed King that "matters [pertinent to Fletcher] had been cleared up" to his [Nimitz'] satisfaction. Fletcher (an "excellent, seagoing, fighting naval officer"), CINCPAC wrote, had done a "fine job" and exercised "superior judgement." Fletcher would remain at the helm of TF 17. Then, noting *Yorktown's* repairs and her being given a full complement of planes, Nimitz declared that that ship would "in all respects be ready to give a good account of herself" when she sailed from Pearl on the 30th. "We are actively preparing," he continued, "to greet our expected visitors with the kind of reception they deserve." Furthermore, Nimitz promised King: "We will do the best we can with what we have."

At 0730 on 30 May, TF 17 got underway, when the first of the six destroyers assigned to that force slipped

---

1. For details on the repairs, see Robert J. Cressman, *That Gallant Ship: USS Yorktown (CV-5)*.

While salvage work proceeds in the background on the battleships damaged in the Japanese raid of 7 December 1941, *Yorktown* lies in Dry Dock No.1 at Pearl Harbor Navy Yard, 29 May 1942. Her CXAM radar is turned at a 90-degree angle to the camera, while the scaffolding indicates that repairs to her external degaussing cable are underway. Note her fouled hull below the waterline, indicative of the long time it had been since her last drydocking; the two 20-mm. mounts in a "tub" below the bow ramp, and the boxcars of stores visible at left, foreground. Armed Marines, some wearing Hawley helmets, stand guard atop them. 80-G-13065

LTCOL Walter C. Sweeney Jr., USAAC, around the time of the Battle of Midway.

her moorings and stood out. *Yorktown* brought up the rear, her band sprightly rendering "California, Here I Come." On board was a British naval observer — CDR Michael B. Laing, who'd been XO of the carrier HMS *Furious*; he had finally prevailed upon ADM Nimitz to send him to sea in an American carrier. Beneath a clear sky, Fletcher's ships headed northwesterly in a fresh breeze. Tragedy visited *Yorktown* during the recovery of her air group that afternoon, though, when VF-3's XO, Don Lovelace, was killed in a landing accident. Men observing the plane recoveries from the screening ships as interested spectators could see that this seemed to be an inexperienced air group. LCDR Harry B. Jarrett, *Morris'* captain, thought that the pilots looked definitely "green."

That same afternoon, as *Yorktown* and her consorts steamed northwestward, ADM Nimitz was speaking at Memorial Day exercises at Pearl Harbor. Knowing what he did, that perhaps the course of the war would be determined in events of the next few days, Nimitz hinted that "long periods of intensive preparation, arduous labor, and even danger — perhaps future disappointments . . ." lay ahead before the United States could achieve ultimate victory in the conflict. Only the comparative few who had been privy to all of the work in getting Midway, and the forces now at sea supporting it, ready to meet the Japanese thrust, could have known how close to the truth Nimitz was.

On 30 May, four PBY-5s were detached to Johnston Island, while the first eight B-17Es arrived on Eastern Island, led by LTCOL Walter C. Sweeney Jr., a man who possessed (in the eyes of one naval officer who had worked with him) qualities of "unusual leadership, initiative, cooperation and sound judgement" — a fortunate

choice in this cooperative Army-Navy venture at that time. The planes were drawn from the 431st Bombardment Squadron, 11th Group, as well as the 394th, 31st and 72d Squadrons, 5th Group. Nimitz had readily acknowledged the difficulty in protecting the B-17s on the ground, but was willing to take the risk in view of the stakes involved. One of the eight bore ground crews to help service the "Flying Fortresses" at their Midway base; another carried BGEN Willis H. Hale, MGEN Tinker's deputy, who was to inspect the facilities at the atoll.

As sufficient planes became available, searches out to 700 miles went out from Midway daily, covering the ocean that lay in the sector roughly from the north-northeast to the south-southwest; they maintained this coverage from 30 May on, except in the generally northwesterly direction where low visibility conditions prevented the planes from searching the maximum distance.

Inevitably, with men from one side seeking to know the other's movements, contacts between the two were bound to occur. And, occur they did, the first one on 30 May. While VP-23 and VP-44 had been carrying out their operations from Midway, augmented from time to time by planes from other squadrons, the Japanese had not been idle, either. The Midway Expeditionary Force, under CAPT Chisato Morita, operated 10 Mitsubishi Type 1 land attack planes from Jaluit. On the 30th, one Midway-based PBY-5A from VP-44 reported a contact with an enemy twin-engined bomber, 450 miles west by south of Midway, at about 0945; at about 1008, another PBY reported encountering a Type 1, 480 miles roughly southwest by south of Midway. Several men had been injured and both "Catalinas"

Boeing B-17E "Flying Fortresses" of the 431st Bomb Squadron take off from Eastern Island to conduct a long-range search for the Japanese on the afternoon of 31 May 1942. Aircraft at center is a Boeing B-17E-BO (Serial 41-2397), with an early-model Bendix ball turret, flown by 1stLT Kinney, USAAC. Sand and dark green paint have been added to break up the olive drab upper surface finish. 22635 A.C.

damaged in those short, sharp encounters which, to Logan Ramsey, only accentuated the "Catalina's" weakness as a search plane; as he observed: "*Any* type of Japanese plane could, and did, assume the offensive against the PBY."

Given the increasing tempo of operations, and the imminent arrival of the Japanese, it was perhaps natural for men's thoughts to turn to what lay ahead, and to the possibility that each day a man lived would be his last. On 30 May, CAPT Richard E. Fleming, USMCR—a dark-eyed, slender young man of 24—wrote a letter and reflected on fond memories of a young lady, and of their relationship. From the tenor of the letter, it is apparent that Fleming, in his innermost thoughts, perhaps did not expect to survive the battle that lay ahead. "Letters like this should not be morbid nor maudlin," he wrote to Peggy Crooks, a special friend, "suffice it to say that I've been prepared for this rendezvous for some time . . . this is something that comes once for all of us; we can only bow before it." He then tenderly wrote his goodbye, and gave the sealed letter to LT Charles R. Forrester, MC, USN, VMSB-241's flight surgeon, to be mailed.

Nine more B-17Es arrived at Midway on the 31st, along with two PBY-5As earmarked as replacements for the "Catalinas" damaged the previous day, and a Consolidated PB2Y-2 "Coronado" flown by LCDR William N. Nation, CO of VP-13; the big flying boat bore four replacement crews for the PBYs that had been flying the grueling searches. For the Marines, practice with their older aircraft (SB2U-3s) continued apace on the 31st, but the severe fuel shortage curtailed the SBDs' use—the PBYs and B-17s operating from Midway had put a "heavy drag on the fuel supply"—the situation had been acute since the inadvertent explosion of the mine-field on 22 May. The more experienced VMSB-241 pilots needed to transition to the SBD-2s; familiarization flights took priority over tactics hops.

CAPT Simard dispatched 15 B-17s to proceed to the expected Japanese fleet rendezvous, that same day, 700 miles to the west of Midway. The bombers—each fitted with a long-range gas tank and four 600-pound bombs—lumbered skyward between 1330 and 1350 but found nothing. LTCOL Sweeney had had to bring his plane home due to a fuel problem, returning at 2000, the first back. Homing the B-17s proved difficult ("inferior flight and communication discipline," Logan Ramsey observed) and they straggled in between 2000 and 0330.

Unbeknownst to the defenders, unseen eyes watched them. The recently overhauled *I-168*, which had departed Kure on 23 May, had reached her station off Midway on the 31st. She scouted Sand Island at the outset, gathering intelligence information to transmit back to the advancing Japanese fleet.

As BGEN Hale meanwhile took part in the defense planning and observed things at Midway, he grew increasingly concerned over how Ira Kimes was holding up under the strain. Kimes, a man of somewhat nervous temperament anyway, did not appear to be weathering the stress well. His XO, MAJ. L.B. Stedman Jr., his tour over, had been detached and left Midway in *Kitty Hawk* on 29 May, with no relief having been provided. Kimes' operations officer, Verne McCaul, tried to step in and take up the slack left by Stedman's departure but already "out on his feet" from overwork, lacked adequate rest.

"I tried to lighten his burden," Kimes explained later, "by performing some of the duties...myself, but neither [CAPT Robert R.] Burns (assistant operations officer) nor I were in noticeably better condition for the same reason." Availing themselves of the Army Air Corps MAJ Warner's "capabilities and willingness," Kimes assigned the airman the work of an assistant XO and assistant operations officer. "Not only did he do an outstanding job in that capacity," Kimes continued, "but before many days, we practically made a Marine out of him."

At Pearl Harbor that day (31 May), LT Harold H. Larsen, commanding the VT-8 detachment at Ford Island, received orders to pick enough men to man six TBFs and "report to Commander Base Air Defense for temporary duty . . ." All of "Swede" Larsen's men volunteered, so he had no trouble making up six crews. To command the detachment, Larsen selected 32-year-old LT Langdon K. Fieberling; to help them reach Midway (the pilots had never made a flight of this length before), ENSs Jack W. Wilke and Joseph M. Hissem, A-V(N), from VP-24, volunteered to navigate, one in each three-plane section: Wilke would go with Fieberling, Hissem with ENS Oswald J. ("Os") Gaynier, A-V(N).

The ebb and flow of aircraft at Midway, meanwhile, continued; on 1 June an Army B-17 arrived with spare parts, taking off again the same day; another pair of PBY-5As arrived, and six new Grumman TBF-1 "Avengers" from VT-8, the latter after an uneventful eight-hour flight. The men from VT-8 noted "tension in the air" at Midway, and "seemed exhilarated about the prospect of meeting the enemy." That same day, CAPT Simard dispatched one PBY-5A back to Pearl for further repairs. BGEN Hale was to fly back to Hickam, but his B-17 blew a tire while taking off, and he remained on Midway until the next morning.

Also on 1 June, LCDR Yudachi Tanabe, commanding *I-168*, made his first report concerning Midway, noting the "incessant aerial patrol...day and night...and

LTCOL Ira L. Kimes, USMC, CO, MAG 22, outside of his scaveola-camouflaged CP on Eastern Island, holding a Hawley helmet. A graduate of the USNA Class of 1923, Kimes was later awarded the DSM for his meritorious service at Midway. USMC

MGEN Willis H. Hale, USAAC, (seen here at Eniwetok, 4 June 1944) was serving as deputy commander of the 7th Air Force at the time of the battle. 80-G-254968, cropped

[the] strict security measures...being taken." Tanabe also noted the one patrol boat in the waters south of Sand Island, the many cranes installed on land, and the apparent expansion of facilities underway. He surmised ". . . from the fact that a patrol plane was seen about 600 nautical miles southwest of Midway Island...the enemy is conducting extensive aerial patrols..." Tanabe would continue his work off Midway, reporting meteorological conditions, until 3 June.

The "extensive patrols," of course, involved the "Catalina" flying boats. By 2 June, some disturbing practices had come to the attention of VP-44's skipper. He had heard that plane crews had been making adjustments to their guns which had not only been made incorrectly, but had resulted in the guns not functioning when they needed them most—in combat!

Brixner reminded his men that "a thoroughly reliable picked crew of ordnancemen" had been assigned to "service, adjust, and re-arm" the guns, who put them in excellent condition prior to each take off. *"Leave them that way,"* he admonished the plane crews. Each man who serviced the guns knew his job and "would give his bottom dollar for a place in your flight crew..." After giving his men some pointers about when to test guns (not within 10 miles of any ships or island), the am-

munition load, not making internal adjustments to the guns at any time, not refilling magazines unless instructed to do so properly, and handling guns and sights with care so that they would work when they were supposed to, Brixner added "Disregard any of the above, [it] might well be a matter of life and death to you and your shipmates."

Back at Ewa Mooring Mast Field, near Barbers Point, on Oahu, COL Claude Larkin, CO of MAG-21, had a different kind of problem. While he had rejoiced in getting two brand-new Douglas R4D-1s ("Navy DC-3s") on 30 May, fresh from the factory at Santa Monica, he privately worried about using them. "I hope we do not have to..." Larkin confided to MGEN Ross E. Rowell, Commander of the 2d Marine Aircraft Wing, on 1 June, since, with no guns for protection, "they haven't a chance against attack."

That very afternoon, however, RADM Bellinger asked Larkin if the Marines could undertake an "emergency flight to Midway." VMJ-252's new R4D-1s looked like the planes that could deliver a cargo of pneumatic tailwheels for VMF-221's F2A-3s and .50-caliber machine gun ammunition for MAG-22—as well as carry more relief crews for the PBYs.

Rumors had been rippling through Ewa ever since

CAPT Albert S. Munsch, USMC, VMJ-52, January 1942. "Gunner" Munsch was typical of the Marine Naval Aviation Pilots (NAPs) who made up the backbone of the Corps' aviation units at the start of the war. Munsch

Douglas R4D-1 (BuNo 3143) at Ewa Mooring Mast Field, T.H., on the day of its arrival from the mainland, 30 May 1942. Shortly thereafter, it would see service operationally for the first time in the Marine Corps, on a flight from Ewa to Midway. Munsch

the pair of planes had landed on the 30th. CAPT Albert S. Munsch, who had flown one of them (BuNo 3143) from the west coast, and who had earned a DFC flying DeHavilland DH-4s in Nicaragua in 1927, volunteered to take one of the new "DC-3s" to Midway. Known as a courageous and skilled pilot, he had survived the Japanese attack on Ewa field on 7 December 1941; like so many others, he was eager to have a hand in squaring some accounts with the enemy.

Barely clearing the eight-foot fence which surrounded Ewa, Munsch's heavily loaded R4D lifted off the field at 0210 on 2 June. In the course of the flight, worried sailors aft in the cabin came forward from time to time, anxiously pointing out "Japanese planes" that proved to be only twinkling stars. Munsch finally instructed his flight engineer, MTSGT Maynard E. Julson, to sit by the door and keep the jittery sailors out of the cockpit!

Ahead, at Midway, an Army C-53 (the Army version of the DC-3 and equivalent to the R4D-1) landed at 0625 with an engine for a B-17 and some Navy freight. It stayed on Eastern Island less than two hours, departing at 0820 to return to Oahu.

In the prevailing good weather over that stretch of the Pacific, meanwhile, Munsch and his co-pilot/navigator, TSGT (NAP) Paul Baker, flew along the rhumb-line track from Barking Sands, on the northwest corner of Kauai, along a line of volcanic rocks, small uninhabited isles and reefs to Pearl and Hermes Reef, a small upthrust of coral near Midway. When about 300 miles from their destination, Munsch took the Douglas down to 100 feet, figuring that the Japanese, if they were nearby, would have a harder time finding him.

At 1050 on 2 June, the R4D touched down on Eastern Island, and Munsch and his crew disembarked to stretch their legs and found the place bustling with activity. To Paul Baker, it looked as if "every type of airplane flying in the Pacific" jammed the airstrip. Ira Kimes, well aware of the congestion, greeted them with: "We want you out of here as soon as possible. When can you leave?" Having just completed the over eight-hour flight from Oahu, Munsch asked for a couple of hours sleep and a pre-sundown departure. Kimes assented to letting the R4D crew—Munsch, Baker, Julson, and their radio operator, SGT Charles L. Mullins—sleep in a dugout near the airstrip. After they had slumbered, they grabbed a quick meal in the mess hall.

Munsch saw evidence of a hot reception being prepared for the advancing Japanese; as he recounted later: "You could really tell that something was in the air, defense preparations were going on like mad. Planes were being checked over, and all around the field, men were digging foxholes and . . . extra machine gun pits around the runways. . . . They knew the Japs were coming. . . ."

CAPT Simard summoned Munsch to his CP on Sand Island, and entrusted him with dispatches to be hand-delivered to ADM Nimitz on Oahu. Before departure, the Marine sensed an air of desperate determination at Midway. It seemed "like every unit commander had some important dispatches to send back . . . I also had two of the largest mail sacks I ever saw. [I] guess everyone wanted to get a last letter out."[2] At 1430 on 2 June, Munsch and his crew re-embarked in the R4D-1 and took off, flying at 100 feet for the first 300 miles. Ultimately reaching Ewa at 2315, Munsch found himself met by a jeep conveying an officer and two armed Marines. Driven over blacked-out roads to CINCPAC headquarters, the pilot was debriefed by a member of ADM Nimitz' staff, among others, who asked "a million and one questions about everything in the book about what I saw at Midway. . . ."

Of the material Munsch had taken out, 1,200 of the 5,000 rounds of ammunition went to VP-44, for its free guns in its PBY-5As; the rest went to VMF-221, whose ordnancemen and armorers belted it and loaded it into the gun bays of the F4F-3s and F2A-3s. The relief crew went to VP-23, whose men were almost at the point of exhaustion.

Exhaustion was a subject elsewhere, too. BGEN Hale's departure on the morning of 2 June eased Logan Ramsey's mind. Hale had not been pleased when he had left; he protested that too much was being demanded of the B-17 crews, and threatened "that upon his arrival at Pearl Harbor he would make strong representations to that effect." Ramsey admitted that the Army crews were being "pushed to the limit" but "no more than the crews of the patrol planes whose cheerful devotion to duty provided a refreshing contrast to the attitude" generally exhibited by the Army. Interestingly enough, after Hale's departure, neither CAPT Simard nor CDR Ramsey received any Army complaints about how they were treated. LTCOL Sweeney, on the other hand, effusively praised the Navy and Marine Corps.

While the problem with Hale, as far as Midway was concerned, may have gone when the general left, as soon as he returned to Oahu he immediately informed ADM Nimitz that Kimes' stood "on the verge of collapse from nervous strain and overwork." Hale's report, by Kimes' later admission, hit pretty close to the mark, but sufficiently alarmed by the tidings Hale brought back from Midway, CAPT Davis, Nimitz's aviation officer, called COL Larkin and told him what Hale had said.

2. The fate of Wake Island was still fresh in the Marines' minds.

Larkin then spoke, in succession, with Hale, RADM Bellinger and ADM Nimitz. Nimitz told Larkin he had better send Kimes "a little help." The admiral turned down Larkin's offer to send himself, since Larkin would have outranked both Simard and Shannon and it would not do to insert someone of higher rank with a major battle in the offing. Larkin then considered Bill Wallace, who had been at Midway in command of the aviation detachment there, but demurred when that would have meant relieving Kimes without giving him a fighting chance. Finally, the colonel offered MAJ Raymond C. Scollin, who was familiar with "the installations, weather, operations, personnel and equipment." Larkin then told Nimitz, Bellinger and Davis that Kimes was "O.K.," explained Kimes' temperament, and added that he did not feel Hale to be "capable of passing judgement on an officer he had seen only once, and then only for a few hours." To give Kimes a hand, though, Larkin sent Scollin to Midway in the next available PBY. As soon as he arrived, Kimes "immediately" handed him "enough work for six men."

On the same day that Hale had departed (2 June), CDR R. Massie Hughes, skipper of VP-23, asked John Ford if he wanted to go for a ride in a PBY the next day. "It looks like there is going to be a little trouble out there," Hughes drawled. "You and I are too damned old for this war anyway, so we'[d] better take the easy dog leg."

Kaloli, meanwhile, reached Midway on 2 June, mooring to a dock at Sand Island at 1724; she commenced pumping her liquid cargo ashore at 1800. A little over 24 hours later, she made all preparations for getting underway, "having been ordered to get clear of Midway Island due to expected attack by enemy forces . . ." Underway at 1855, she set sail for a point on the ocean five miles east of Pearl and Hermes Reef to "await further orders," accompanied by *Vireo*.

That day (3 June), John Ford got his PBY flight. "We . . . didn't see anything for a very long time," Ford recounted later, due to the "very, very cloudy weather." The plane's radar picked up something, however, ("we presumed it was one of our task forces," Ford recalled) and through a rift in the clouds, some 60 miles off, spotted some ships. Seeing some cruiser planes approaching, however, prompted Hughes to do a "quick bank." Eventually running out of clouds for cover, Hughes took the big "Catalina" down nearly to the water and headed for Midway. "It's too bad we just saw the task force for a moment," Ford lamented later, "it was so far away, otherwise I would have gotten a good picture of the disposition . . ." Given the sector searched by Hughes that day, the ships Ford saw were most probably TF 16 or TF 17, and the "cruiser planes" Curtiss SOCs from

-50-

the screen's heavy cruisers!

That night, CAPT Simard summoned Ford as plans were being made for the morrow. It soon became evident he was not merely being tapped to take pictures: "Well now, Ford," Simard began, "you are pretty senior here . . . how about getting up top of the power house, the power station, where the phones are? Do you mind?" Ford, acclaimed in the motion picture world for his "distinct flair in his use of the camera," and his memorizing camera angles before he even shot a picture, responded that he did not mind in the least: "It's a good place to take pictures."

Simard, however, told him to "forget the pictures" and give him a blow-by-blow account of the attack as it developed, so he could see the size of the incoming strike. The captain then told him to go out and do the best he could, and to lay out his phone lines. "We expect to be attacked tomorrow," Simard said. As Ford later recounted, Simard and Ramsey had sent him up to the power house because he was "a motion picture man and naturally should have a photographic eye, so I made a pretty good choice, because I knew what to do and that was to count planes . . ." Used to "that sort of thing, reporting, taking battle scenes and mob scenes and notice every detail . . . that's why I probably would notice a lot more than the layman..."

While the men on Midway had been preparing for battle and planes from her lagoon and runways were conducting searches, the task forces steaming to its defense had not been idle, either. Planes from TF 16 had been flying searches to augment those from Midway and Johnston, and provide security for the task force as it passed beyond the areas covered by Oahu-based planes. During the course of flight operations on the 29th, *Hornet* had lost one of her SBDs, when ENS Richard D. Milliman, A-V(N), crashed some 15 miles from the ship while on inner air patrol. *Maury* (DD-401) was detached to search the area thoroughly, but found no trace of Milliman or his radio-gunner, Tony Pleto, ARM3c. *Hornet* planes covered the search during the forenoon watch on 1 June—the same day that TF 17 fueled from the oilers *Cimarron* (AO-22) and *Platte* (AO-24)—but fog cancelled the afternoon one.

That same day, RADM Spruance warned his force of the impending Japanese attack, and of the approximate composition of the enemy force. If the Americans remained undetected by the Japanese, Spruance posited, "we should be able to make surprise flank attacks on enemy carriers from positions northeast of Midway." Should *Enterprise* and *Hornet* become separated during enemy air attacks, Spruance continued, "they will endeavor to remain within visual touch." He laconically gave his men some inkling of the importance of their mission, too, as he informed TF 16 that "the successful conclusion of the operations now commencing will be of great value to our country."

On 2 June, *Enterprise's* planes had the duty, but poor visibility conditions and a 100-foot ceiling compelled their early return, causing VF-6's diarist to observe: "Cold and wet as hell so the first we'll probably hear of the Japs will be on the Midway radar." Rain and fog again cancelled the afternoon scouting missions. That afternoon, Fletcher's ships rendezvoused with TF 16 and the admiral assumed tactical command of the strike force as it prowled the Pacific north of Midway, steering courses designed to keep "well clear of the Hawaiian

His face bearing the recent scars of his ditching on the 28th, LCDR Gene Lindsey enters a breeches buoy on board *Monaghan* around 1035 on 31 May, to return to *Enterprise*. Behind Lindsey is Charles T. Granat, ARM1c, USN, who, like his CO, would die in the battle a few days hence. Thomas E. Scheaffer, CAP(PA), hands-in-pockets, the third crew member of Lindsey's TBD, awaits his turn. 80-G-7748

chain" and to avoid Japanese submarine activity. Nimitz's timely dispatch of Fletcher's and Spruance's task forces found them well at sea by the time the Japanese submarines, deployed as pickets across the projected path of the American ships for just that purpose, in the event that submarine-supported flying boats could not reconnoiter Pearl Harbor, could arrive on station.

ENS James P.O. Lyle, A-V(N), who'd been a chemist in civilian life, patrolling to the southwest of Midway, on 3 June, was over four hours into his patrol that morning when he spotted something on the ocean below. He transmitted a report to Midway at 0843: "Investigating suspicious vessel." He took the PBY down, and got closer; soon thereafter, at 0904, Lyle transmitted another message, that he had spotted two Japanese converted minesweepers, 470 miles from Midway to the west southwest—the first surface contact report with Japanese ships. The ships were *Tama Maru No. 3* and *Tama Maru No. 5*, half of the Minesweeping Group allotted the Midway operation. They had sailed from Wake Island at 2000 on 31 May. Shortly thereafter, however, another sighting would overshadow Lyle's.

While members of *Monaghan*'s crew look on, Charles T. Granat returns to *Enterprise* on 31 May via breeches buoy. The canvas-covered object between the destroyer's stacks is a 5-inch drill gun, used to develop gun crew proficiency.
80-G-7747

Yorktown underway at sea en route to "Point Luck," as seen from *Portland*, circa 31 May 1942. 80-G-32585

ENS James Palmer O'Neil Lyle, A-V(N), the pilot who first reported *Tama Maru*'s *No.3* and *No.5* approaching Midway on 3 June, and who later tracked enemy ships on the 5th. Awarded a DFC for the latter, Lyle died in a plane crash in San Diego Bay on 5 April 1945.

Bel Geddes' depiction of the sighting of the two Japanese minecraft at 0904 on 3 June, 470 miles southwest of Midway. 80-G-701843

Crew of the VP-23 PBY-5A that spotted the approaching Japanese fleet on 3 June. Rear (L-R): R.J. Derouin, Francis Mussen, ENS Hardeman (co-pilot), ENS Jewell M. "Jack" Reid (pilot), R.A. Swannow. Front row: J.F. Grammell, J. Groovers, P.A. Fitzpatrick.
80-G-19974

Further west patrolled ENS Jewell H. Reid, A-V(N). Thus far that morning, he had been enjoying a comparatively uneventful patrol—until he spotted the Japanese Transport Group. At 0925, he reported tersely: "Main Body." The news electrified Midway—the Japanese were on the way, just as predicted. "Jack" Reid maintained his search in the proximity of the Japanese, transmitting an amplifying report two minutes later, giving a bearing (262 degrees) and a distance (700 miles), the latter at the limit of the Midway-based patrols. Another PBY was directed to shape a course to the vicinity a short time later.

Reid, meanwhile, stayed closed to the Japanese, lingering, just out of reach. He reported six large ships in column formation at 1040. Twenty minutes later, Reid reported 11 ships steering directly east at 19 knots. He requested instructions; NAS Midway ordered him to return to base, a job well done. The other PBY, meanwhile, reached the vicinity and transmitted its contact report at 1130: two cargo vessels and two smaller ships, steering a roughly northeasterly course from the west southwest, 270 miles away.

Some distance away, in *Yorktown*, Frank Jack Fletcher and his staff mulled over the contact reports. At that time, TF 17 and TF 16 were steaming north by east, 320 miles from Midway. Fletcher estimated, correctly, that the ships spotted by the PBYs were not the sought-after carriers. He accordingly maintained his position north of Midway, keeping station at courses and speeds that would allow him to carry out aircraft operations to safeguard his own task forces; Spruance's TF 16 steamed 10 miles to the south. He then ordered *Yorktown* to launch a second scouting mission on 3 June,

and at 1300 10 SBDs took off to search again the same sector scouted that morning, but only to a distance of 175 miles (*vice* 200) out. Although the choice of sector was a wise one, the SBDs found nothing.

Meanwhile, on Midway, CAPT Simard, knowing from recent experience that a PBY would probably not survive a shadowing mission, ordered a special long-range B-17, equipped with extra gasoline tanks and with a naval observer on board to identify ships, to track the "main body" of the enemy fleet. Upon contacting the enemy, it was to broadcast positions to guide the attacking B-17s to the target. It took off at 1158. Shortly thereafter, Simard then ordered the first Army bombing mission, when he dispatched six B-17s (Flight 92) to attack the "main body" reported by ENS Reid. As MAJ Warner recorded in his liaison journal, Flight 92 cleared Midway at 1230, its return expected in about eight hours, with runway and searchlights to be switched on at 1930. Each B-17 was armed with a half bomb-load (four 600-pound bombs) and a bomb bay gasoline tank to enable them to get home.

At about 1623, the airmen spotted the Japanese ships, Walt Sweeney leading the formation around to attack from out of the sun. Forming into three flights—at 8,000, 10,000 and 12,000 feet—the B-17s deployed to the attack, dropping their "sticks" of bombs. LT James Moore, Sweeney's bombardier, who had never seen anti-aircraft fire before squinting into the Norden bomb sight in the nose of the "Flying Fortress," said in the interphone, "Say, that stuff sure looks pretty through here."

The attack surprised the Japanese. On board the ship carrying elements of the Kure Special Naval Landing Force battalion, an officer of that unit later wrote in

A Boeing B-17E "Flying Fortress" at Midway prior to the Battle. Her usual olive drab uppersurfaces appear to have been modified with sand paint—many B-17s on Midway at that time appear to have been camouflaged thus. Many of the -17's had recently arrived in the Hawaiian Islands from the mainland, and required the installation of extra gas tanks (to allow for longer range) and other special equipment.

his diary: "At last this is war." Witnessing the bomb splashes around some of the other ships in the column must have affected him, as he added: "I don't want to die before we reach our destination." In *Nankai Maru*, the first ship in the first division of ships bearing the occupation force, one Japanese sailor described in his diary how the air raid warning had sounded, followed by the sight of the B-17s far overhead. He saw several large bombs splash on both sides of *Argentina Maru*, the fifth ship in the first division. "The machine guns near the port side of our ship laid down a sweeping fire and our ship was not hit. . . . Our morale was very high." he wrote later, "It seemed like a maneuver." Six bombs fell "a short distance" from *Kiyozumi Maru*.

While some of the pilots claimed hits, they scored nothing more than a near miss with their ordnance, since hitting a moving ship from thousands of feet up was no mean feat. One of the targets, *Argentina Maru*, reported that bombs missed her by as much as 100 to 200 yards! As they cleared the area, though, the Army pilots seemed jubilant—"We headed for home in high spirits," Sweeney later recounted, "our only regret being that we had no more bombs." Ironically, the special B-17 sent out on the tactical scouting mission could not find

the "main body," only "two transports and two destroyers" at 1640, 700 miles from Midway.

As MAJ Warner had recorded in his journal, the runway lights were to be switched on at 1930 to enable the Army pilots to see their way into Midway. An hour elapsed before the first B-17s entered the landing pattern; the last—CAPT Willard Woodbury's—did not land until 2145.

In the meantime, before the Army planes had returned, four Navy pilots were briefed at about 2000, on the approach of the Occupation Force. LT William L. Richards, VP-44's XO, had been selected to lead four PBYs (three from VP-24 and one from VP-51) on a mission to find the Japanese, and carry out a torpedo attack. He would command the mission from LT(jg) Charles P. Hibberd's PBY, 24-P-12. At 2115, the quartet of "Catalinas," each carrying one Mk. XIII, Mod. 1 torpedo, took off from Eastern Island and, after rendezvousing, headed roughly west by south. Other than "Red" Richards, who had already been at Midway, the crews had flown their PBYs to Eastern Island only that afternoon; despite the 10-hour flight they had just made, not a man shrank from the mission that lay ahead.

As the PBYs droned through the clouds, the loose

Nankai Maru, one of the ships comprising the Occupation Force; she is seen here prewar, in the Panama Canal, 3 July 1937.
NH 47185

cruising formation became even looser—so much so in fact that ENS Allan Rothenberg's 51-P-5 drifted away around midnight and ENS Gaylord D. Propst's 24-P-11 about an hour later. Only LT(jg) Douglas C. Davis, A-V(N), in 24-P-7, remained with Richards.

Meanwhile, as the Army planes had been returning, Frank Jack Fletcher ordered a course change at 1940 that would take TF 17 to a launch point approximately 200 miles north of Midway at daybreak on 4 June. As it had done since the rendezvous on the morning of the 2d, TF 16 remained 10 miles to the south of TF 17. At midnight, *Yorktown* and her consorts were 271 miles from Midway. On board *Enterprise*, the VF-6 diarist wrote: "Contacts show the Japs [are] on their way in. Everyone getting ready for the main event . . . and everyone just a little noisier than usual. The torpedo pilots are damn sore because they get their big chance tomorrow and missed TBF's by a week after waiting three years. . . ."

That night, a junior officer in the battleship *Haruna* wondered what the people on Midway were doing at that moment, "not knowing tomorrow they are going to *Hell*."

CAPT Steele of ADM Nimitz' staff, however, entered somewhat more profound thoughts as the running summary account's last entry for 3 June: "The whole course of the war in the Pacific," he wrote, "may hinge on the developments of the next two or three days." He could not have known how right he was.

The pilots of the four PBYs flown in the night torpedo attack on 3/4 June 1942: (L-R) LT(jg) Douglas C. Davis, A-V(N) (VP-24); ENS Allan Rothenberg, A-V(N) (VP-51); LT William L. Richards (USNA Class of 1932) (VP-44); and ENS Gaylord D. Propst, A-V(N). 80-G-64819

CHAPTER SIX

. . . .

"Midway...
Had a Good
Fight on
its Hands..."

*T*he four lumbering "Catalinas" that had set out from Midway before the B-17s had returned, continued to hunt the enemy. At 0115 on 4 June, Richards' radar indicated "about ten ships" on the port beam, between 10 and 12 miles distant. For five minutes, he homed in on them until he spotted them in the moonlight, seven miles ahead. Although clouds obscured the ships heading the two columns, he could clearly see the silhouettes of the larger vessels.

Richards broke off to attack, throttling the PBY's engines back. Picking the last large ship in the first column—the oiler *Akebono Maru*—he made his torpedo run up the moon path; dropping down to 100 feet and closing within 800 of the "large transport or cargo ship," he fired his "fish" and then retired in a "sharp, right climbing turn" over her stern. Lookouts in the waist of 24-P-12 noted a "huge explosion and heavy smoke," as the torpedo barrelled into *Akebono Maru*'s bow, killing 11 men and wounding 13.

Davis started in immediately after Richards did, but, unsatisfied with his first approach, ascended to 2,000 feet. His second run cloaked by clouds, Davis glided in, engines throttled back, and fired his torpedo at the ship just ahead of the stricken *Akebono Maru, Kiyozumi Maru*. As 24-P-7 pulled away, Theodore E. Kimmel, AMM2c, fired his .50-caliber machine gun and briefly swept *Kiyozumi Maru*'s decks, wounding eight men of the Kure SNLF unit. Davis' torpedo, though, missed its target, as his crew reported seeing no evidence of a hit. Japanese antiaircraft fire, though, perforated 24-P-7's bow in several places, damaging the bomb sight, and holed the hull, wings, and tail; it also forced Davis to abandon his attempt to assess damage.

ENS Propst, meanwhile, had managed to find the Japanese on his own. Firing his torpedo at what was probably *Kiyozumi Maru*, he feinted to the right and then wrapped 24-P-11 into a tight left turn. The "Cata-

Bel Geddes diorama depicting the night torpedo attack by the four Midway-based PBY-5As on the Japanese occupation force, showing the torpedo striking *Akebono Maru*'s bow. 80-G-701846

The freighter *Kiyozumi Maru*, strafed by LT(jg) Doug Davis' PBY, is seen here in Limon Bay, during her 16/17 July 1937 transit of the Panama Canal. She was ultimately sunk at Truk by planes from TF 58, 17 February 1944. NH 42307

lina's" second pilot reported a flash indicating a hit, but Japanese records do not confirm it. Propst managed to escape the single Japanese plane that attempted to interfere with his retirement, by making "judicious use" of the scattered clouds.

ENS Rothenberg, having lost contact with the other planes about midnight, only encountered what he believed to be the "advanced screen" of the Japanese fleet. Ineffective antiaircraft fire twice came up at 51-P-5, and once an unidentified plane made several approaches, but stayed out of gun range each time. Unable to find the enemy ships when breaking out of the overcast, Rothenberg kept up the search for 30 minutes until, gasoline low, he turned the PBY around and headed back to Midway.

The morning of 4 June, meanwhile, found Fletcher's ships zig-zagging to the southwest at 13.5 knots, to allow them to be in a position 202 miles north-northeast of Midway when dawn broke at 0430. CINCPAC had warned of a Japanese approach from the northwest, an all out air attack on Midway about dawn, and that the enemy would continue to close to shorten the return flight of their planes—if that intelligence proved correct, Fletcher would be on the enemy's eastern flank, whence he could hit the Japanese before their planes could return from Midway to rearm and refuel. Although all indications were that the Japanese were right on schedule, if the enemy launched from a position north or northeast of Midway, Fletcher would find himself not on the enemy's flank, but between them and their target. As a precaution, he directed that *Yorktown* launch a search in the northern semicircle to a radius of 100 miles, knowing that the Japanese would have to be within 300 miles of Midway to launch planes.

Roused at 0130, the crews breakfasted in shifts between 0300 and 0400. In *Enterprise's* wardroom, LCDR C. Wade McClusky Jr., the CEAG, noted the absence of the usual quips, an air of hushed expectancy replac-

ing the more usual banter. Surprised to see LCDR Gene Lindsey out of his bunk, McClusky made a comment to that effect. "This is the real thing today," Lindsey replied, "the thing we have trained for, and I will take my squadron in."

Flight quarters had sounded on board all three carriers before dawn, although only *Yorktown* made preparations to launch aircraft immediately. On her flight deck sat 16 aircraft—the six F4F-4s of LT(jg) Richard G. Crommelin's second division of VF-3, which would provide the day's first CAP. Astern of them sat the 10 SBDs of "Scouting" Five that would search to the north.

TF 17 approached its 0430 launching position in fine weather—a light five-knot breeze from the southeast, the clouds cumulus and four-tenths overcast, the sea smooth, and visibility excellent. Only the wind posed a problem, as carriers must steam at high speed into the wind when conducting flight operations. The light southeasterly wind meant the Americans would have to steam away from the Japanese when they launched or recovered aircraft, thus increasing the distance that any strike planes would have to fly. At 0430, TF 17 altered course into the wind, and one minute later the first F4F wobbled into the air, the others following at short intervals. Then, "Scouting" Five's SBDs brought up the rear, fanning out into their assigned sectors.

Meanwhile, to the northeast, the *Kido Butai* was making the final preparations for launch. The four carriers carried a total of 227 operational planes: 73 Mitsubishi A6M2 Type 00 carrier fighters, 72 Aichi D3A1 Type 99 carrier bombers, 81 Nakajima B5N2 Type 97 carrier attack planes, and one Yokosuka D4Y1 Type 13 special reconnaissance plane. Spotted for launch on their decks was the day's first CAP of 11 "Zeroes" and a strike force of 108 planes—36 *kansen*, 36 *kanbaku*, and 36 *kanko*—to be led by LT Joichi Tomonaga, commander of the *Hiryu* Air Unit.

At 0300 on 4 June, VADM Nagumo ordered the 7th

Cruiser Division—RADM Takeo Kurita commanding—to shell Midway. Working up to top speed, the four 8-inch gunned heavy cruisers of that unit--*Mogami, Mikuma, Suzuya* and *Kumano* (flagship)—left their screening destroyers behind and sped off.

A little less than an hour and a half later, at 0428, with the *Kido Butai* 240 miles northwest of Midway, the first "Zero" of the CAP took off. By 0440, the entire striking force had gotten aloft; forming up quickly, it took departure at 0445. Mechanical difficulties compelled only one plane—a Type 97 from *Hiryu*—to return. Almost half of Nagumo's planes were then Midway-bound; since his intelligence estimates reported only 30 fighters to oppose his inbound strike, the admiral felt that the force he was hurling against the Americans would suffice.

Perhaps to ensure surprise, and not have his search planes spotted in advance of his strike group, Nagumo had specified that reconnaissance planes not be put aloft until after the strike group had departed. On board the heavy cruisers *Tone* and *Chikuma*, and the battleship *Haruna*, pilots and observers clambered into Aichi E13K type 00 and Nakajima E8N2 Type 95 reconnaissance floatplanes earmarked to conduct searches. *Kaga* and *Akagi* each launched one *kanko* for anti-submarine patrol in the vicinity of the task force. *Haruna's* Type 95, assigned the most northerly sector, was to fly out 150 miles, the six Type 00s were to scout the other sectors out to 300 miles. Launching the planes from the carriers, and from the battleship, went well; the only difficulties arose on board the cruisers, and delays ensued. A catapult malfunction delayed the launch of *Tone's* number four plane until 0500. Once the search planes were finally airborne, they fanned out toward their respective areas.

Having launched planes, the *Kido Butai* worked up to 24 knots to close Midway, while, on board the carriers, deck crews armed a second attack force with torpedoes and bombs fused for use against ships, in case the search planes spotted an American task force. Soon 36 *kanbaku* sat on the decks of *Hiryu* and *Soryu* (18 on each ship); 36 *kanko* (18 each on board *Kaga* and *Akagi*), and 25 *kansen*—seven in *Kaga* and six on each of the others. Planners earmarked many of the fighters, if needed, for CAP over the fleet.

Purposeful activity, meanwhile, had stirred NAS Midway long before dawn; at 0350, the first of the six F4F-3s of CAPT John F. Carey's division droned off into the darkness to fly the dawn CAP, to cover the take off of the B-17s and PBYs.

Pilots and aircrew of the Navy flying boats and Army bombers clambered into their respective aircraft, too, the former briefed for search, the latter for attack.

"Bombs are carried for expenditure on crippled ships only. Your mission," LCDR Brixner emphasized, "is to gather accurate information. The information is vital, it must be gotten in."

As they had done the previous days, the "Catalinas" began lumbering aloft at 0415: 11 VP-23 PBY-5s from the lagoon, and 11 VP-44 PBY-5As from Eastern Island. As it had for the previous week, VP-44 took the southern sectors and VP-23 the northern. A material casualty, however, compelled one PBY to return to Oahu—there was no room on Midway for lame ducks.

CAPT Simard was sending LTCOL Sweeney's 15 bomb-carrying B-17Es (and one B-17D to act as a pathfinder and photo ship) to the westward to attack the Japanese transport force they had bombed the previous day. Sweeney was told to monitor his radio closely for a possible change of targets, however; if the search disclosed the position of the Japanese carriers they were to attack them if they had the range to do so. The big bombers cleared Midway shortly after 0415, assembled over Kure Island, and shaped a course to resume the offensive against the enemy transports.

After the bombers departed, CAPT Kirk Armistead's six F2A-3s sat poised to reinforce Carey's division if necessary. By 0450, though, Midway stood down from the morning alert; while Armistead's planes stood down, Verne McCaul recalled Carey's patrol. Unfortunately, CAPT Francis P. McCarthy, USMC, and his wingman did not get the word, and they continued orbiting to the north. The rest were down by 0500. Soon after landing, 2ndLT Walter W. Swansberger's "Wildcat" became mired in the sand, temporarily reducing Carey's division to three. As soon as the Marines had landed, a B-17E took off on three engines to return to Hickam. Meanwhile, the rest of the island's 64 operational planes sat manned and ready, engines warm and radios energized.

For the men in the PBYs that had lumbered aloft at dawn for the search, all proceeded uneventfully. In the course of his flight, however, LT Howard P. Ady, of VP-23, spotted something below through the low cumulus clouds and scattered showers, and transmitted a report which soon galvanized the forces defending Midway into action—that he had spotted the "main body" of the Japanese fleet! He reported two carriers, three battleships, four heavy cruisers and six to eight destroyers. Upon receipt of Ady's report, Midway went on the alert. All air crews were instructed to man their planes and to stand by with their engines turning over.

LT(jg) William E. Chase, in another VP-23 PBY, encountered low cumulus clouds and scattered showers in the course of his patrol, too, when suddenly something caught his attention—what he estimated at over

50 planes, in formation, proceeding toward Midway. He immediately transmitted a warning in plain language at 0544: "Many planes heading Midway," 100 miles northwest by north of the atoll. Subsequently, Chase came upon a portion of the Japanese carrier force, and as he did before, used the rain squalls as cover. Japanese lookouts reported sighting a flying boat at about 0542 and again at 0551 (the latter by lookouts in the heavy cruiser *Chikuma*), but the PBY entered a "squall zone" at about 0553.

Upon receipt of Chase's report, COL Shannon ordered the antiaircraft gun groups to "Open fire on all planes not identified as friendly." Soon thereafter, CAPT Simard informed the colonel of the report of an enemy aircraft carrier sighted by his search planes 150 miles to the north-northwest. Radar reports multiplied: few planes at 93 miles; many planes at 89. At 0556, Shannon put his Marines on Condition One and the air raid alarm began to sound; Simard diverted the air-

borne B-17s toward the position of the Japanese carriers.

Meanwhile, the fleet submarine *Nautilus* (SS-168), LCDR William H. Brockman Jr., commanding, who had farsightedly instructed his radiomen to monitor the aircraft search frequency in advance of the time specified in OpPlan 29-42, intercepted Chase's "many planes heading Midway." "Alert to the requirements of the situation," Brockman determined quickly that the position given lay on the northern boundary of his patrol area, and set his course accordingly. Ironically, *Nautilus*, the slowest and least maneuverable boat in the submarine force, was the only one then closing on Nagumo's fleet.

At 0600, the reports of the location of Japanese carriers, provided by the seemingly ubiquitous PBYs, and reports of incoming aircraft, prompted Midway to clear the field of all operable aircraft. As the Japanese droned in disciplined formations toward them, VMF-221's operable fighters—21 F2A-3s and three F4F-3s—scrambled to intercept.

VMF-221 pilots, 14 July 1942. Front row (L-R): 2dLT William V. Brooks, USMCR; 2dLT John C. Musselman, Jr., USMCR; CAPT Philip R. White, USMC; CAPT William C. Humberd, USMC; CAPT Kirk Armistead, USMC; CAPT Herbert T. Merrill, USMC; CAPT Marion E. Carl, USMC; 2dLT Clayton M. Canfield, USMC. Rear row (L)R): 2dLT Darrell D. Irwin, USMCR; 2dLT Hyde Phillips, USMCR; 2dLT Roy A. Corry, Jr., USMC; 2dLT Charles M. Kunz, USMCR. 80-G-357094

Beneath the nose of a Douglas R4D-1 (BuNo 3143) from VMJ-252 stand surviving pilots of VMF-221, Ewa, 22 June 1942. (L-R, all ranks USMC unless otherwise noted) CAPT Marion E. Carl; CAPT Kirk Armistead; MAJ Raymond Scollin (who had been brought in to serve as an additional XO for MAG-22 prior to the battle, to specifically handle the fueling and arming arrangements for aircraft); CAPT Herbert T. Merrill; 2dLT Charles M. Kunz, USMCR; 2dLT Charles S. Hughes, USMCR; 2dLT Hyde Phillips, USMCR; CAPT Philip R. White; 2dLT Roy A. Corry, Jr., USMCR. Although Merrill survived the Battle of Midway, he would not survive the war; he was killed in a plane crash on Palmyra Island in March 1943. 80-G-357083

VMF-221

Plane No.	Pilot
First Division (F2A-3)	
MF-1	MAJ Floyd B. Parks, USMC*
MF-2	2dLT Eugene P. Madole, USMCR
MF-3	CAPT John R. Alvord, USMC*
MF-4	2dLT John M. Butler, USMCR
MF-5	2dLT David W. Pinkerton Jr., USMCR*
MF-6	2dLT Charles S. Hughes, USMCR
Second Division (F2A-3)	
MF-7	CAPT Daniel J. Hennessey, USMC*
MF-8	2dLT Ellwood Q. Lindsay, USMCR
MF-9	CAPT Herbert T. Merrill, USMC*
MF-10	2dLT Thomas W. Benson, USMCR
MF-11	CAPT Philip R. White, USMC*
MF-12	2dLT John D. Lucas, USMCR
Third Division (F2A-3)	
MF-13	CAPT Kirk Armistead, USMC*
MF-14	2dLT William B. Sandoval, USMCR
MF-15	CAPT William C. Humberd, USMC*
MF-16	2dLT William V. Brooks, USMCR
MF-17	2dLT Charles M. Kunz, USMCR*
MF-18	2dLT Martin E. Mahannah, USMCR
23	2dLT Walter W. Swansberger, USMCR**
Fourth Division (F2A-3)	
MF-19	CAPT Robert E. Curtin, USMC*
MF-20	2dLT Darrell D. Irwin, USMCR
Fifth Division (F4F-3)	
22	CAPT John F. Carey, USMC*
24	CAPT Marion E. Carl, USMC
25	2dLT Clayton M. Canfield, USMCR

*Section Leader
**Not assigned to this division, but "tagged on." He was flying an F4F-3 (BuNo 3989).

Parks' men grimly climbed. When he reached 5,000 feet, though, 2dLT Hughes felt his F2A-3's engine vibrating heavily and noticed it losing power. Reaching 16,000 feet, he saw that he was lagging behind. "The engine was [running] so rough," he concluded, "it would be suicide to try and fight the plane." He turned back.

2dLT Elmer P. Thompson, USMCR, who had relieved 2dLT Maurice A. Ward, USMCR, as squadron (VMSB-241) duty officer (Ward manned an SBD-2), shortly before the air raid alert had sounded, watched as all flyable planes vacated the airfield.

Quickly following the fighters came the six Grumman TBF-1s of VT-8. Once airborne, they joined up and stepped down in two three-plane sections. Fieberling led the first, with ENSs Earnest and Brannon on his wing; ENSs Gaynier and Lewis, and Woodside, AMM1c (NAP) brought up the rear. They climbed to 2,000 feet, and, at 160 knots, headed northwest. No sooner had they reached that altitude when two or three Japanese planes swept by, making one pass before breaking off the action—maybe preoccupied with protecting the Midway-bound strike group. Using the clouds for cover, Fieberling's flight evaded the fighters and climbed to 4,000 feet.

The four torpedo-armed Army B-26s followed the "Avengers." Soon thereafter, VMSB-241—16 Douglas SBD-2s and 12 Vought SB2U-3s—each plane laden with a 500-pound bomb, rose into the sky. Shortly after take-off, CAPT Bruce Prosser, in Norris' group, turned back when he noticed that the left side of his engine cowling had blown loose.

The two groups of Marine bombers rendezvoused 20 miles from the atoll and divided into two attack units, the SBD-2s under Henderson, and the SB2U-3s under Norris. On Sand Island, one VMSB-241 pilot, 2dLT Robert W. Vaupell, USMCR, his SBD-2 undergoing a spark plug change, could only watch the incoming Japanese. He and his radio-gunner, SGT Carl Hickman, grabbed the .30-caliber from the after cockpit of the "Dauntless" and set it up in a gun pit next to the plane. On Eastern Island, the same idea hit 2dLT Thompson, with no plane to man. He took the telephone from the VMSB-241 ready room and, along with PFC Thiesen, set it up in a machine gun pit in front of it, and there mounted a .30-caliber Browning and ammunition which he had removed from an inoperable SB2U parked nearby. CAPT Prosser, meanwhile, noticed the incoming Japanese strike as he taxied his "Vindicator" to a revetment; the free gun removed to be set up in an adjacent foxhole, VMSB-241 plane handlers pushed the SB2U into its enclosure and then headed for their stations.

John Ford, atop the powerhouse on Sand Island, noted the calm which appeared to settle over Midway after the planes had taken off. To him, Midway seemed "very quiet and serene." "There was nothing moving," he recalled later, "just a lazy sort of tropical island." CPL Eugene T. Card, radio-gunner in the SBD-2 flown by CAPT Dick Fleming, thought that Midway, as it slid further away from them as the "Dauntless" gained altitude, seemed "deserted."

As Henderson's and Norris' planes joined up at Point "Affirm," and Parks' were climbing to intercept, the inbound Japanese spotted the atoll about 0615. With the positions of the enemy carriers known, both Henderson and Norris soon acknowledged radioed instructions to attack an enemy carrier 180 miles northwest of Midway and set course accordingly.

As the Japanese were beginning their final approach, CAPT Francis P. McCarthy and 2dLT Roy A. Corry, USMCR, both flying F4F-3s (planes nos. 26 and 27, respectively), and who had been on patrol since 0400, unaware of the order to come in after the search planes had gotten aloft, learned of the incoming strike over their radios. McCarthy requested instructions. Told to land, refuel, and get airborne again, he and his wingman landed at about 0615. Soon thereafter, 2dLT Hughes taxied his "Buffalo" back to its revetment. At about 0625, thanks to quick work by the ground crews, who had only time enough to top off the tanks as best they could, McCarthy and Corry took off with enough fuel to enable them to get up to join their airborne shipmates.

The first, fourth, and fifth divisions (Parks', Curtin's, and Carey's), meanwhile, had been vectored out to intercept, while the second (Hennessy's) and third (Armistead's) had been told to orbit 10 miles out, "temporarily withheld in the event that another group of enemy would appear on a different bearing." At the outset, the enemy's disposition favored the Marines: *kanko* in the lead, with *kanbaku* behind and above them; the "Zeroes" trailed the entire formation. CAPT Carey was apparently the first on the air, radioing: "Tally ho! Large formation of bombers . . . accompanied by fighters . . ." a few moments before the Japanese spotted Midway.

The "Buffaloes" of Parks' and Curtin's divisions, and Carey's "Wildcats" hit the lead elements, and the first two *chutai* of six *kanko* from *Hiryu* suffered heavily in the opening moments of the battle: two slanted seaward in flames; a further three took heavy damage and trailed smoke. Among the latter was that in which LT Tomonaga, the strike commander (as well as the commander of *Hiryu's* first *chutai*), rode. Another plane forced out of formation was the Type 97 flown by *Hiryu's* second *chutai* leader, LT Rokuro Kikuchi. Like Tomonaga's plane, Kikuchi's caught fire; he eventually dropped out of formation and had to ditch on the way back to the Mobile Force. Another formation of Type 97s from *Soryu* suffered three planes hit, one of which failed to return to its carrier.

Marines at Battery "E" reported seeing two planes falling in flames soon after Parks' initial interception of the enemy. Nobody knew whose they were. Nor would anyone ever know how well Parks' division fared, from the American side, for no one in that group—Parks, Madole, Alvord, Butler, and Pinkerton—lived to tell the tale. CAPT Carey dove on the lead division and sighted-in on the leader; he claimed a shoot-down, but got a bullet through the windshield for his trouble. Making an above-side approach on the middle of the formation, Carey fired and thought he got the leader; at that moment, bullets tore into his Grumman. Shot through his right knee and left leg, the pilot continued his pass through the formation before throwing his plane into a dive, to head back to Midway.

In Carey's division, 2dLT Clayton Canfield picked out the number three man in the number three section and opened fire, flaming one *kanko* almost immediately. Marion Carl had tangled with the escorting "Zeroes" and had been forced to dive away, "heading straight down at full throttle" until the enemy gave up the chase. On the way back to Midway, Carl fought a short, sharp action with three "Zeroes"; he modestly claimed one downed and two damaged in the encounter before he found the skies empty of Japanese. Canfield joined up with Carey and covered his return to Eastern Island; Carey, unable to control his F4F-3 fully because of his wounded leg and the plane having a flat tire, ground-looped upon landing. Canfield's gear failed upon his return to Midway and he, too, made a forced landing.

Curtin and Irwin had followed Parks' five-plane division into battle; Irwin had seen Parks' division make an overhead pass on the enemy formation, followed by Curtin; after that time he never saw the other six planes again. Just as he was preparing to make a second run on the bombers, Irwin spotted a "Zero" on his tail; soon thereafter, the Japanese shot most of his left aileron away. Knowing that he could not maneuver his aircraft, he pushed the stick forward and threw his "Buffalo" into

1stLT (later MAJ) Floyd B. Parks, USMC, the CO of VMF-221 from 17 May to 4 June 1942. USMC

Bel Geddes' depiction of the lead elements of VMF-221, possessing an altitude advantage at the outset, intercepting the incoming Japanese planes, who were reported as approaching in tight "V" formations, on the morning of 4 June. 80-G-701850

Bel Geddes' version of VMF-221's "Wildcats" and "Buffaloes" tangling in mortal combat with the "Zeroes" escorting the Japanese attack group flying against Midway. 80-G-701851

Brewster F2A-3 (BuNo 01553), seen here after a landing accident at NAS Miami, 12 October 1942, while being used as a trainer, had been flown during the Battle of Midway by CAPT William C. Humberd. Maas

Grumman F4F-3 (BuNo 4006) flown on 4 June by CAPT John Carey, awaits removal from Sand Island after the battle. In the far background sit at least three F2A-3s and three SBD-2s. Note darker paint on the F4F's rudder, indicative of pre-battle repainting. 80-G-11636

a dive, coming out at 500 feet and heading for Eastern Island. He managed to land, keeping his head down in the cockpit.

Throughout the engagement, the Japanese showed "superb air discipline, staying in tight vee formations and keeping on their compass course . . ." The Marines had made their initial contact at about 14,000 feet, and after the first successful pass through the neat enemy formations, "Red" Parks' men found themselves dueling with an overwhelming number of "Zeroes." All of VMF-221's divisions broke into single-plane elements within a short time, and as the "Zeroes" gained the upper hand it became a melee in short order.

CAPT Philip R. White, in Hennessy's second division, took his first pass through the Type 99s, but became separated from his wingman, 2dLT Lucas, and

the rest of the division in so doing. After eluding one "Zero" he emerged from the clouds to claim one Type 99, and, later, damage a second before running out of ammunition. CAPT Herb Merrill made an overhead run on the bombers before being taken under fire himself, his right wing and instrument panel being hit first. After almost losing control of the F2A-3, Merrill dove again, and headed toward the reef, where "Zeroes" flamed his "Buffalo."

McCarthy (who, it will be remembered, had been decorated by ADM Nimitz on 2 May during the admiral's inspection of the atoll) and Corry had only reached 8,000 feet when eight "Zeroes" jumped them. Fighting singly, the two Marines did not fare well; Corry later reported he saw McCarthy shoot down one "Zero," and that he himself had shot one enemy plane off his section leader's tail before three "Zeroes" latched onto him. Spotting a *kanbaku* attempting to escape from the skies over Eastern Island, Corry fired a short burst into him before he then dove for the water in an attempt to get away from the "Zeroes." His fuel tanks leaking, Corry ultimately had to get back to Midway, staying low on the water.

2dLT Kunz suffered a harrowing experience: bullets passed just to each side of his head as he sat in the cockpit, creasing his scalp above each ear. As Ira Kimes later recalled: ". . . It was necessary for the group surgeon to give him several 'stiff shots' that night before he could be induced to sleep."

John Ford, meanwhile, had watched as the Japanese formations droned closer, reporting their inexorable progress to CAPT Simard over the phone. "Everybody was very calm," he observed; the attitude of everyone there amazed him. To his experienced eye, it seemed almost "lackadaisical . . . as though they had been living through this sort of thing all their lives."

The Type 99s from *Akagi* and *Kaga*, having suffered less at the hands of the fighters than the *kanko* from *Soryu* and *Hiryu*, neared their pushover point. Only moments before the latter planes had released their ordnance, 2dLT Hughes had gotten his "Buffalo" into the revetment. He watched the attack begin, perceived bombs being dropped, and then hugged the ground as they landed nearby. 2dLT J.C. Musselman Jr., USMCR, VMF-221's duty officer, had just reported to the CP on Eastern Island that McCarthy and Corry had just taken off when he noticed the bombers approaching Sand Island. He then headed for the nearest slit trench, just making it before the bombs began to fall.

As all operable aircraft had scrambled to clear the field, the nine 77-foot ELCO motor torpedo boats of MTBRON ONE then at Midway (two, *PT-29* and *PT-30*, were on patrol at Kure Island) had cast off from

Bel Geddes' representation of the Japanese dive-bombing Eastern Island on 4 June. 80-G-701852

the dock at Sand Island and stood out; they were under-way and moving out as the Japanese approached.[1] *PT-42* joined in with her .50-calibers as the Marine guns on shore opened up on the first wave. In addition, the boat detail from NAS Midway under BOSN C.R. Oliver Jr., had manned its posts, too: one 40-foot motor launch armed with a .30-caliber machine gun, two tugs armed with .30-caliber machine guns and Browning Automatic Rifles (BAR), and one tug armed with a .30-caliber machine gun and rifles.

"Red" Richards' PBYs were lumbering back from their night torpedo mission when they heard Midway broad-casting that an air raid was in progress. Wisely deciding to avoid contact with enemy planes, each pilot headed for Lisianski to wait out the attack.

Some of the outward-bound VMSB-241 pilots and radio-gunners, meanwhile, glancing behind them, saw heavy antiaircraft fire and columns of smoke beginning to rise from Midway as the Japanese strike unfolded. CPL Card, in CAPT Fleming's SBD-2, noticed that and told his pilot about it over the interphone. "Well, this is *it* all right," Fleming responded. "Midway," Card mused, "looked like it had a good fight on its hands."

John Ford, who only a few days before had thought that if there was to be a fight, it would not touch Mid-way, had focused his 16-mm. movie camera on the near-by hangar on Sand Island, figuring that that would be a major target. One bomb landed close to the power-house, however, and the world mushroomed up before the veteran director, a piece of shrapnel knocking him

momentarily senseless. The last thing he saw in his lens was "one big chunk coming for the camera." Awaken-ing to find his elbow and arm full of shrapnel, "knocked . . . goofy for a bit," Ford recovered and went doggedly on with his job. The Marines with whom he had been sharing the powerhouse roof bandaged him up them-selves, telling him: "Don't go near that Navy doctor, we will take care of you . . ."

Bombs soon demolished the powerhouse on Eastern Island; C.J. Stanfield Jr., Sea2c, on watch there, imme-diately left his station to seek help for the wounded. Unable to find any close at hand, he hefted C.L. Roper, MM2c, on his back, and braved the attack then still underway to carry his injured shipmate to an aid sta-tion where his wounds could be dressed.

From what the PT-boat sailors could see from the lagoon, at least 18 *kanbaku* dove from the northeast, pulling out of their runs in their vicinity. The sailors were determined to not let the enemy get away un-scathed: every time a Japanese plane came within range (the PT boats would hold their fire "until the range was closed for a sure chance for hits"), each boat opened up with her four .50-calibers—augmented in some cases by Thompson submachine guns and .30-caliber rifles. John Ford noted the PT boats' circling around out in the lagoon and the "awful blast" they were putting up. To him, it appeared as if the Japanese "couldn't figure out what the Hell they [the PT boats] were and . . . really gave the place a wide berth."

One "Zero" pilot, though, apparently had other ideas; he recovered from a steep vertical dive at about 25 feet over the lagoon and roared in, strafing one of the boats. *PT-25* took over 30 hits; fortunately, all damage (for-

1. Those same boats had been at Pearl Harbor on 7 December 1941, awaiting shipment to the Philippines, and had participated in the defense of the fleet that morning.

The 77-foot ELCO motor torpedo boat, *PT-25*, off Pearl Harbor, 5 February 1942, as seen from *Enterprise*. On 4 June, *PT-25* engaged a strafing "Zero." 80-G-7178

ward, around the cockpit and at the waterline) proved superficial. Three men, though, ENS J.L. Mote, USNR, L.D. Robinson, SC2c and H.A. Walker, RM1c, received superficial wounds from flying fragments. On board *PT-24*, Orville R. Mott, TM2c, changed the inboard barrel of the starboard .50-caliber machine gun, wresting off the old, hot, barrel, and burning his hands in so doing, while firing the outboard gun simultaneously. The gunners on board *PT-21* and *PT-22* caught one low-flying Japanese plane, flying westward, "tracers from both boats indicating perfect shooting," and the enemy aircraft crashed in the trees at Sand Island.

This heavy antiaircraft fire from both the Marines and the PT boats that had met the attackers proved heavy. One *Hiryu kanko* had gone down; two had been damaged. The barrage downed one *Kaga kanbaku* (FPO1c Watanabe, pilot; FPO3c Kimura, observer) as it was bombing the seaplane ramp on Sand Island—perhaps the same aircraft engaged by *PT-21* and *PT-22*.

The Marine fighter planes having been scattered, the "Zeroes" then raised "Merry Hell" strafing the installations on Eastern and Sand Islands. One "Zero," though, perhaps that flown by FPO1c Ito, from *Kaga*, hit by antiaircraft fire, crashed near the VMF-221 ready room. 2dLT Hughes saw two Brewsters attempting to fight the "Zeroes;" one "Buffalo" went down in flames; ground fire apparently saved the other. As Hughes later wrote: "Both [F2A-3s] looked like they were tied to a string while the Zeroes made passes at them." 2dLT Hyde Phillips saw one F2A-3 cross the northeast tip of Eastern Island to help out another.

A "Zero" shot down the would-be helper, though, and as Phillips watched, teamed up with another "Zero" in shooting at the helpless pilot in his parachute. From

his vantage point on Sand Island, LT Vaupell also noted two A6M2s strafing a Marine pilot after he had bailed out of his burning Brewster. John Ford saw it, too; unable to photograph it because of the distance, he watched through binoculars as a "Zero" even strafed the 'chute in the water; Ford thought that that "wasn't very chivalrous at the time." "I only prayed to God," Ford later recounted, "that I could have gotten a picture out of it."

Men in the PT boats in the lagoon also witnessed two "Zeroes" strafing a downed pilot.[2]

When the radar screen on Midway showed only retiring enemy planes, at about 0720, the call went out for the fighters to land by divisions, to refuel and rearm. When it became evident that those divisions had suffered heavily, the call went out for all fighters to land. A pitiful few responded: of the 25 planes that had engaged the enemy, only eight returned. Two of these were pronounced flyable again; 14 VMF-221 pilots were missing, four wounded.

Once the Japanese planes had cleared the area, MAJ Scollin surveyed the runways and put crews to work repairing them. The power plant had been demolished; gasoline lines from the main storage tanks had been broken near the powerhouse; bombs had hit in the vicinity of the sick bay and VMSB engineering tents; the Eastern Island CP had been demolished, as had the mess hall and post exchange. A detail of men gathered from the nearby slit trenches extinguished the fires at the mess hall; Hyde Phillips, whose plane had been out of commission that morning, found six boxes of blood plasma in the wreckage, and soon delivered it to the sick bay.[3]

One bomb had hit a VMF rearming pit, killing the four men there and setting off eight 100-pound bombs and 10,000 rounds of .50-caliber ammunition; the explosion scattered debris around the eastern end of runway number one. One bomb had cratered the center of number one, near its eastern end; one had hit on the shoulder of runway number three, near its junction with number two; and an instantaneous fused bomb had made a small crater 500 yards from the eastern end of runway one. Inspection parties also found the wreckage of a "Zero" scattered across the northern end of number one; a road scraper and a bulldozer soon had cleared the runway of debris. Losses, in terms of men, had been light: six Marines killed and approximately 20 suffering minor cuts and bruises. An Army Air Corps lieuten-

---

2. Although a search by *PT-26* failed to disclose anything soon thereafter, a later search (9 June) turned up the body of 22-year-old 2dLT Martin Mahannah, who had been with 221 only a week.

3. His plane was an F4F-3 (BuNo 1864) and it bore the number 28.

The wreckage of FP01c Watanabe's Aichi D3A1 Type 99 carrier attack plane ("Val") on Sand Island. Landing gear wheel hub and leg identifies this plane quite clearly as a *kanbaku*. Note photographer at far right. USN

The gutted interior of the seaplane hangar on Sand Island on 4 June, showing firefighters wrapping up their work. Note at least three Packard engines (spares for the 77-foot ELCO boats) in the left background. 80-G-17081

Burning oil tanks on Sand Island, with apparently unruffled "goonies" in the foreground. The smoke generated by this blaze helped to guide returning pilots back to Midway, much as the "Pillar of Cloud" guided the Children of Israel in the book of Exodus. 80-G-17056

Beyond the damaged laundry building (foreground), smoke boils into the sky from the burning oil tanks on Sand Island. 80-G-17057

ant and an enlisted man, taking shelter in a plane revetment, also died, as did MAJ Benson of the 6th Defense Battalion, when a bomb scored a direct hit on his Eastern Island CP.

On Sand Island, direct bomb hits tore out water lines, destroyed three oil storage tanks, demolished one corner of the laundry building and the squadron warehouse, totally destroyed the dispensary, Navy mess hall and galley, demolished the brig and contractors' superintendent's buildings, as well as the torpedo and bomb-sight building. Near-misses damaged the Navy machine shop, paint storage building, and garage. Bomb fragments damaged two PAA fuel storage tanks and four Navy diesel and fuel oil storage tanks; concussion slightly damaged the Navy BOQ and the Administration Building. Two Navy barracks buildings suffered badly damaged—but repairable—walls and windows. While most vehicles only received miscellaneous repairable damage, two pick-up trucks and a station wagon were demolished. With the exception of the power house, "an ideal target" owing to its size and location, most buildings constructed at Midway consisted of steel frames but with everything else—interior finish, walls, ceiling and flooring—made of wood. Roofs were of tar paper and wood. The prominent seaplane hangar on Sand Island stood badly damaged, completely burned with only 50 percent of the steel framing remaining in fair condition.

With the Japanese having cleared the area, *PT-20*, PT-22, and *PT-28* returned to the dock at Sand Island. Fire and rescue parties from these boats then went ashore to help with helping the wounded and fighting fires. ENS D.J. Callaghan and ENS Clark W. Faulkner,

USNR, bravely entered the burning seaplane hangar and salvaged rifles, ammunition, hand grenades and spare parts for Packard engines despite the prevailing "hazardous conditions and against the advice of others in the vicinity." The needs of the moment inspired others to almost reckless bravery: although warned that the whole area was "extremely dangerous," LT Clinton McKellar Jr., CO of MTBRON ONE, along with R.H. Lowell, MM2c, V.J. Miastowski, F3c, USNR, and J.B. Rodgers, S2c, cut their way through barbed wire and gingerly made their way through a minefield to organize firefighting parties near the large fuel oil dump.

PT-20 later proceeded out into the lagoon and took part in rescue operations. Herb Merrill had been thrown clear of his burning "Buffalo" as it had spiralled downward toward the sea. Taking to his parachute, the VMF-221 pilot landed in the water; slipping out of his 'chute harness, Merrill then struck out for the reef off Sand Island, eventually reaching it after two hours. Having suffered second degree burns, he clung, nearly blinded, to the reef until *PT-20* arrived at 0945. Seeing Merrill obviously suffering from shock and burns, Edward J. Stewart, SM3c, unhesitatingly dived in the water with a life ring at the end of a line and, braving the surf breaking on the jagged coral, then helped the injured Marine to safety.

Over the atoll hung a column of smoke, orange tongues of flame licking at its base, that expanded and boiled up into the sky. Through it all, however, the stars and stripes—raised in the midst of the attack—still flew from Midway. All hands prepared for whatever was to come, having no way of knowing whether the Japanese would be back . . . or not.

CHAPTER SEVEN

"No Bomber is a Match for a Bunch of Fighters..."

While Midway's defenders took stock of the damage and succored the wounded, the Japanese were encountering troubles of their own. At 0700, shortly after a message had been received on board *Akagi* from *Hiryu's* attack unit (0645) that it had completed its strike and was homeward bound, LT Tomonaga transmitted a message to the flagship of the Mobile Force, "There is need for a second attack wave." That, however, had come on the heels of *Kaga's* air officer's message (0640): "Sand Island bombed, and great results obtained." Tomonaga's report apparently carried more weight, for despite *Kaga's* optimistic tidings, the plane that had been held in reserve to deal with American ships, should they have been sighted, were to be rearmed with bombs. As long as Midway possessed the means with which it could operate planes, it threatened the Japanese. At 0715, Nagumo issued his orders: "Planes in second attack wave stand by to carry out attack today. Re-equip yourselves with bombs."

Shortly before 0700, meanwhile, as she plodded toward the Mobile Force, *Nautilus* spotted a formation of six planes—that she identified as "Flying Fortresses," but what may have been Fieberling's VT-8 detachment—heading toward the Japanese.

Soon thereafter, about the time VADM Nagumo was receiving word from LT Tomonaga that a second strike to neutralize Midway would be necessary, LT Fieberling spotted the enemy fleet, about 15 miles away, and deployed his little formation, the first planes from Midway to make their appearance against the Japanese. The six TBF-1s cut across the path of the four Army B-26s under CAPT James F. Collins Jr., which arrived almost simultaneously. From 8-T-1, Bert Earnest counted about 10 ships in the immediate vicinity ahead, "destroyers, cruisers, and at least one battleship forming a screen around two long carriers."

AVCDT Langdon K. Fieberling, USNR, circa 1937. One of the original officers assigned to fit out the then-new VT-8 in the summer of 1941, he led VT-8's Midway detachment in its attack on the *Kido Butai* on 4 June. USN

ENS Oswald J. Gaynier, A-V(N), circa 1941. The 27-year-old "Os" Gaynier was one of the pilots of the VT-8 detachment operating from Midway. Lucabaugh

ENS Albert K. "Bert" Earnest's Grumman TBF-1 (BuNo 00380), after landing on Midway on 4 June 1942, the sole survivor of six that had set out that morning to attack the Japanese carrier force. Note the full side code 8-T-1. Earnest, via Lawson

VT-8 Detachment (Grumman TBF-1)

First Section

8-T-16 (BuNo 00399)   LT Langdon K. Fieberling
ENS Jack Wilke, A-V(N)*
Arthur R. Osborn, RM2c

8-T-19 (BuNo 00398)   ENS Charles E. Brannon, A-V(N)
William C. Lawe, AM3c
Charles E. Fair, AOM3c

8-T-1 (BuNo 00380)   ENS Albert K. Earnest, A-V(N)
Harry H. Ferrier, RM3c
Jay D. Manning, Sea1c

Second Section

8-T-12 (BuNo 00391)   ENS Victor A. Lewis, A-V(N)
Nelson L. Carr, AM3c, USNR
John W. Mehltretter, EM3c

8-T-4 (BuNo 00383)   ENS Oswald J. Gaynier, A-V(N)
ENS Joseph M. Hissem, A-V(N)*
Howard W. Pitt, Sea1c

8-T-5 (BuNo 00384)   Darrel "D" Woodside, AMM1c(NAP)
Arnold T. Meuers, Ptr2c
Lyonal J. Orgeron, AOM3c**

*Indicates on temporary duty with VT-8, from VP-24.
**Indicates on temporary duty with VT-8, from VP-44. He replaced William L. Coffey Jr., AMM1c, who had flown in Woodside's crew from Ford Island to Midway.

The VT-8 detachment had no sooner spotted the enemy when they found themselves bedevilled by "Zeroes" (about 27 were airborne at the time). The fighters nipping at them all the while, the TBFs dove in formation through the clouds, to within 150 feet of the Pacific. Though outnumbered, Fieberling's men pressed home their attack in the teeth of heavy antiaircraft and fighter opposition until only one of their number remained.

The second pass by the "Zeroes" killed Earnest's gunner, Manning, as cannon and machine gun shells smashed the turret. Harry Ferrier, down in the tunnel position of the "Avenger," looked up and forward when he heard Manning's machine gun quit abruptly, and saw the dead and bleeding gunner. Much like the adolescent hero in Stephen Crane's *The Red Badge of Courage*, the frightened, 18-year old Ferrier matured in an instant.

Shells then demolished part of 8-T-1's hydraulic system; the tail wheel dropped down in the slipstream and blocked Ferrier's field of fire. Soon thereafter, a shell creased his scalp and knocked the young radio-gunner unconscious, and he slumped, dazed and bleeding, against the side of the fuselage. Earnest felt the sting of shrapnel in his right cheek as a shell exploded outside of the cockpit, to starboard. Still several miles from the Japanese ships, the fighters shot away his elevator wires, and Bert Earnest felt 8-T-1 buck toward the ocean; thinking that he had lost control of the plane, he jettisoned his torpedo at what he took to be a light cruiser. He then regained control using the elevator tab, and kept his battered bomber in the air.

Free of the torpedo, the plane rose slightly; using a trim tab to get a few needed feet of altitude, Earnest kept BuNo 00380 airborne. For 10 minutes, attacking "Zeroes" toyed with the lone TBF before they left it alone; as Earnest later remembered that moment: "Although they made runs on me . . . no vital parts of the plane were hit and it continued to perform very well." Only then allowing himself the luxury of looking back, Earnest saw "no signs of any ships having been hit." Having seen none of the other five planes since about the time his elevator wires had been shot away, he found himself alone. Necessity prompted him to take stock of his situation: his TBF-1 had sustained some 70-odd bullet and cannon shell hits; he had lost control of his elevators (he had to fly by the trim tabs alone); his bomb bay doors hung open; his compass was inoperative; one main gear could not be extended. His gunner was dead, both he and his radioman had been wounded.

CAPT Collins and his pilots, meanwhile, had spotted the Japanese ships about five minutes after Fieberling had done so, and turned first to the left, then to the right to evade the antiaircraft fire from the *Kido Butai* below. Noting momentarily the Navy planes approaching from the right and crossing their path, at about 0710 (when Japanese records indicate the torpedo planes divided into "two groups") Collins' troops ran into heavy antiaircraft fire shortly before six A6M2s from the CAP barrelled into them, head-on, at 700 feet.

AVCDT Joseph Hissem, circa 1941. As an ensign, he was one of two VP-24 pilots who volunteered to serve as navigators for the land-based VT-8 detachment during the Battle of Midway. Both Hissem and ENS Jack W. Wilke, the other volunteer, failed to return. USN

ENS "Bert" Earnest and his radioman, Harry Ferrier, at Guadalcanal, 1942, were the only survivors of the Midway-based VT-8 detachment. USN

Another view of BuNo 00380, showing the large hole in the starboard elevator, taken 7 June 1942. Earnest earned one Navy Cross for participating in the attack on the Japanese fleet, and another for bringing the shot-up airplane home so that it could be evaluated. USMC

Glad to be alive: CPL Frank L. Melo, Jr., of Astoria, Long Island, N.Y. He was awarded a DFC for his service as radio operator and gunner in the B-26 flown by 1stLT James P. Muri. 22710 A.C.

B-26 Unit

69th Bombardment Squadron (Medium)
38th Bombardment Group

B-26B   CAPT William F. Collins Jr.
           2dLT Colin O. Villines
           2dLT Thomas N. Weems Jr.
           SGT Jack D. Dunn
           TSGT Raymond S. White

B-26B   1stLT William S. Watson
           2dLT L.H. Whittington
           2dLT J.P. Schuman
           SSGT Richard C. Decker
           CPL Albert E. Owen
           CPL Bernard C. Sietz

18th Reconnaissance Squadron (Medium)
22d Bombardment Group

B-26   1stLT James P. Muri
(42-1391) 2dLT P.L. Moore
           2dLT William W. Moore
           2dLT Russell H. Johnson
           TSGT John J. Gogoj
           CPL Frank L. Melo Jr.
           PFC Earl D. Ashley

B-26   1stLT Herbert C. Mayes
(42-1424) 2dLT Gerald J. Barnicle
           2dLT Garnett M. McCallister
           SSGT Salvatore Battaglia
           PVT Benjamin F. Huffstickler
           PVT Roy W. Walters

Lamenting bitterly not having more and heavier-caliber nose guns to challenge the attackers, the pilots of the B-26s took their planes down to 200 feet. The "Zeroes" apparently splashed the number two and three ships of the formation (1stLT William S. Watson's and 1stLT Herbert C. Mayes') in rapid succession, or at the very least broke up what had hitherto been a formation. As an officer in *Haruna* later recounted: "a large-model enemy attack plane was shot down and disappeared spectacularly beneath the water"— perhaps one of the B-26s.

Collins then made his attack from about 20 degrees off the bow of his target—the flagship *Akagi*, which was turning into the group of approaching torpedo planes to starboard. On the inside of the carrier's turning circle, Collins reasoned that "he [*Akagi*] would have a slim chance to miss our torpedo if it made a true run . . ." But miss they did. Eight hundred yards from *Akagi*, Collins fired his Mk. XIII from an altitude of about 250 feet; 2dLT William W. Moore, 1stLT James P. Muri's navigator, saw the torpedo cleanly enter the water and churn towards the target.

Muri pressed in even closer, holding off firing his "fish" until between 450 and 500 yards away from his target, when he released at an altitude of 150 feet. He turned "into and over the carrier" after his drop, "thus missing most of his antiaircraft fire." The retribution wrought on the enemy was small: *Akagi* lost two men killed and suffered three wounded by strafing during the attacks of the torpedo planes. In return, no hits had been scored.

Both surviving "Marauders," like the sole TBF-1, had suffered heavily. Several hundred rounds had holed Muri's ship, with at least 25 in each main fuel tank (the leak-proofing, though, proved excellent); cannon shells and bullets had smashed the power turret; all propeller blades had been damaged and the left tire shot off. All three of his gunners, Gogoj, Melo, and Ashley, had been badly wounded, and his co-pilot, Pete Moore, had had to man the tail gun at one point! Collins' plane had its hydraulic system shot out and "numerous holes" in the ship. Faulty guns plagued both B-26s; in Collins' plane the turret guns "hung-up repeatedly," and one tail gun "would not fire after the first burst." Both pilots complained of the lack of fixed, forward-firing guns, and training for gunners; as Collins later observed in frustration: "...No bomber is a match for a bunch of fighters and particularly so when the few guns it has won't shoot and the gunners have not had sufficient training to shoot them."

Several miles away, meanwhile, *Nautilus*, at periscope depth, neared the *Kido Butai*; Brockman saw smoke and antiaircraft bursts in the sky ahead at about 0710, the time Fieberling and Collins were commencing their attacks. *Nautilus* then went to general quarters and crept toward her quarry. Because of the fact that she was running submerged, she failed to receive Commander TF 7's report, sent at 0715, that reflected the PBY sighting of the Japanese striking force—an academic message in that she had been the only submarine to have picked up Chase's initial contact report giving the bearing at which the Japanese could be found.

Two other submarines, *Gudgeon* (SS-212) and *Grouper* (SS-214), intercepted RADM English's report, and, like *Nautilus*, altered course accordingly. *Grouper*,

a comparatively new "boat," commissioned on 19 February 1942 and recalled from her maiden war patrol, went to general quarters at 0726, and, running on the surface, sped toward the reported bearing. Spotting what looked like planes taking off from a carrier five minutes later, LCDR Claren E. "Duke" Duke took *Grouper* down to stalk the *Kido Butai* submerged.

At about the same time, LT(jg) Robert S. Whitman (a husky New Yorker, from Binghamton, known to his classmates at the USNA as "Whit" or "Scottie"), flying 44-P-12 (BuNo 04975), ran across the Occupation Force. He reported antiaircraft fire, and that he was being attacked by enemy planes. Some 340 miles west of Midway, Whitman and his crew fought a gallant battle against Mitsubishi F1M2 Type 00 floatplanes ("Petes") from the seaplane carrier *Chitose*. In the fight, enemy bullets killed Whitman, ENS Walter H. Mosley, A-V(N), Clarence J. Norby Jr., AMM3c, William H. O'Farrell, RM3c, and James W. Adams, ACRM, mortally wounded ENS Jack H. Camp, A-V(N), and set the

This view shows a B-26 fitted with a torpedo at Adak, Alaska, 5 November 1942. During the Aleutian phase of the Battle of Midway, torpedo-carrying B-26s attacked the carriers *Ryujo* or *Junyo* and the heavy cruisers *Takao* or *Maya*. Like the Midway-based "Marauders," though, these attacks were likewise unsuccessful. 80-G-33813

Martin B-26 "Marauder" and her crew. 1st LT James Muri (2d from left, in front) brought his B-26 back to Midway with over 500 holes in the airframe. 22850 A.C.

Midshipman Robert Scott Whitman, circa 1939. Killed in action with floatplanes from *Chitose* on 4 June, when his PBY was shot down, he would be the only patrol plane commander to die in action at Midway. 1939 *Lucky Bag*

lumbering "Catalina" ablaze.[1]

As fire engulfed the PBY, Philip L. Fulghum, AOM2c, continued to man his .50-caliber machine gun, and fired at the Mitsubishis, sending one away trailing smoke. On his own initiative, with a crash imminent, Fulghum then released the plane's two 500-pound bombs. After the battered flying boat had crashed into the ocean, Virgil L. Marsh, AMM1c, despite the roaring flames, freed a rubber life raft from the plane; John C. Weeks, AMM2c, although seriously wounded, set to work repairing the holed raft; Fulghum assisted the wounded men, who included ENS Camp and ENS Lee C. McCleary, A-V(N), into the rubber boat.

Elsewhere in the skies that morning, Henderson's and Norris' men had, meanwhile, had an uneventful flight. At one point, Gene Card, Dick Fleming's radio-gunner, had looked over at 2dLT Albert Tweedy's plane and given Raymond, his back seat man, the 4.0 sign. Raymond grinned and waved back. Time rolled by until around 0700, when Fleming, who had often told his radioman that he "might have to take over while he worked on his chart board" and had occasionally let Card fly while on patrol, let his radio-gunner put the stick in and hold the course. "Imagine me flying point,"

1. ENS Mosley had had an eventful wartime career up until his death. He had been at Pearl Harbor when it was bombed on 7 December 1941 and survived being shot down by Japanese planes off Darwin, Australia, on 19 February 1942. The pilot of the latter plane was a future CNO, then-LT Thomas H. Moorer, USN.

he mused, "out Jap hunting."

While the Marines were still "Jap hunting," LTCOL Sweeney's B-17s were droning along at 20,000 feet through the towering cloud formations that stretched from 1,000 to 6,000 feet, with high broken clouds further aloft at about 18,000. Thinking it impractical to bring a formation of 15 planes in to attack at 1,000 feet, and that the cloud conditions precluded identifying targets clearly, Sweeney kept his men at 20,000. At about 0732, the B-17 formation found Japanese ships, and had remained undetected. Still, however, they identified no carriers. They continued to hunt.

As the Americans were approaching, their presence unknown to the Japanese at that point, VADM Nagumo was digesting unsettling news that compelled him to postpone his planned second strike on Midway. At 0728, *Tone's* no. 4 plane had spotted a formation of 10 surface ships, 240 miles north by east of Midway. Maddeningly for Nagumo, the report contained no details as to ship types, and proved to be inaccurate in that it placed the American force 31 miles further away from the *Kido Butai* than it actually was.

At 0739, shortly after his carriers had begun recovery of the morning's strike, Nagumo ordered a course change to allow him to meet the unexpected American challenge, and at 0745, he issued new orders: "Prepare to carry out attacks on enemy fleet units. Leave torpedoes on the planes which have not yet been changed to bombs . . ." Two minutes later, he directed *Tone's* plane to "Ascertain types [of ships] and maintain contact . . ." Nagumo, like Fletcher, may have been leery of launching a full strike against a foe whose composition had not been established for certain—as had been done in the Coral Sea, when an all-out strike had sought out *Neosho* (AO-23) and *Sims* (DD-409).

Shortly after Nagumo had ordered that course change, *Grouper* found herself the object of attention from one of the *Kido Butai's* inner air patrol aircraft, as a plane strafed her periscope and forced her down. Over the next few hours, destroyers would depth-charge the untried fleet boat, and keep her submerged and ineffective.

For the pilots and radio-gunners of VMSB-241, meanwhile, almost another hour went by after CAPT Fleming had let his rear-seat man first take the "stick," when suddenly, Card noticed 1stLT Daniel Iverson's SBD-2 closing up fast, with Iverson gesturing down to port. Card craned his neck but did not see anything; then Fleming broke in over the interphone: "We've made contact. There's a ship at 10 o'clock. Do you see it?" As the minutes passed, more ships—including two carriers—appeared beneath the breaks in the clouds.

VMSB-241

Plane
No.   Pilot/Radio-gunner

First Division (SBD-2)

Command Section
1 MAJ Lofton R. Henderson/PFC Lee W. Reininger
2 CAPT Richard E. Fleming, USMCR/CPL Eugene T. Card
3 TSGT(NAP) Clyde H. Stamps/PFC Horace B. Thomas

First Section
4 CAPT Elmer G. Glidden Jr./CPL Meade T. Johnson
5 2dLT Thomas J. Gratzek, USMCR/SGT Charles W. Recke

Second Section
6 1stLT Daniel Iverson Jr., USMCR/PFC Wallace J. Reid
7 2dLT Robert J."R" Bear,USMCR/PFC Truell L. Sidebottom

Third Section
8 CAPT Armond H. DeLalio, USMCR/CPL John A. Moore
9 2dLT Maurice A. Ward, USMCR/PFC Harry M. Radford

Fourth Section
10 2dLT Albert W. Tweedy, USMCR/SGT Elza L. Raymond
11 2dLT Bruno P. Hagedorn, USMCR/PFC Joseph T. Piraneo

Second Division (SBD-2)

First Section
16 2dLT Richard L. Blain, USMCR/PFC Gordon R. McFeely, USMCR
17 2dLT Bruce Ek, USMCR/PFC Raymond R. Brown
13 2dLT Jesse D. Rollow Jr., USMCR/PFC Reed T. Ramsey

Second Section
19 2dLT Thomas F. Moore Jr., USMCR/PVT Charles W. Huber
15 2dLT Harold G. Schlendering, USMCR/PFC Edward O. Smith

MAJ Lofton R. Henderson, USMC, CO of VMSB-241 from 17 April to 4 June 1942, in a view taken around the time of his promotion to major on 2 July 1941. "Henderson Fields" at Guadalcanal and Midway were named in his honor, as was the destroyer *Henderson* (DD-785).
USMC photo 412669

Henderson and his group, flying at 9,500 feet, sighted the Mobile Force at 0755, the squadron commander informing Fleming, in the formation's command element, of two enemy flattops on the port bow. Henderson, who had been flying off to one side of the group, shepherding his young charges along, then slid back into the lead of the formation to take it in. As he did so, Card heard his pilot shout: "Here they come!"

As Henderson and his men began to let down to attack *Hiryu*, the carrier's CAP slashed tenaciously at them. 1stLT Iverson, whose radio was out of commission and who had just joined up in the squadron commander's box from CAPT Elmer Glidden's, saw "Zeroes" attacking Henderson's SBD-2. The major gamely kept the squadron intact until his "Dauntless" slanted toward the water, trailing smoke.

With Henderson having been shot down, Fleming, who had expressed a "keen desire to finish one Japanese carrier" a few days before, assumed the lead of the division, and pressed home his attack through a storm of antiaircraft fire and a swarm of "Zeroes," releasing his bomb at *Hiryu* and pulling out at just 400 feet.

2dLT Albert W. Tweedy maintained his position on

Henderson's wing until the end, and "Zeroes" shot him down, too. CAPT Armond DeLalio, leading the third box of the first divison, saw "Zeroes" attack the SBD-2 flown by 2dLT Thomas Gratzek, and that "Dauntless," its fuselage breaking into flames behind the engine, left the formation. Two other SBD-2s of the first division went down to the guns of the nimble enemy fighters— Ward's and Hagedorn's—and one (Ek's) of the second.

Gene Card, who had been wounded, tried to keep the "Zeroes" at bay while his pilot masterfully took the SBD-2 close to the water and kept jinking to keep the fighters off balance for a 20-mile chase. With his "instruments . . . a mess and the compass . . . gone," Fleming told Card: "We may have to sniff our way home."

Dan Iverson, in a dive with two "Zeroes" astern and firing, yanked his bomb release at 300 feet before he pulled out. Two additional fighters joined up on his two tormentors and they took turns trying to knock him down as he cleared the area and headed for the clouds at full throttle. "I could not estimate my speed," he recalled later, "as my airspeed indicator was out of commission." On top of that, a bullet had severed his throat microphone chord. Bob Bear, Dan Iverson's wingman and the last man to take off from Eastern Island, made a broadside dive on *Hiryu*, cutting loose with his fixed guns as he released his bomb. His strafing may have accounted for the four men killed and several wound-

VMSB-241 pilots, sometime between 17 April (when MAJ Henderson took command) and 28 May 1942 (when Smith and Frazer were detached). Those present (L-R, all USMCR(V) unless otherwise noted): front row, seated: 2dLT Albert W. Tweedy, 1stLT Bruce Prosser (the only one in the group who appears to be wearing non-regulation *sandals*, MAJ Lofton R. Henderson, USMC (CO); CAPT Leo R. Smith, USMC (XO); 1stLT Elmer G. Glidden, Jr. Middle row (kneeling): 2dLT Thomas J. Gratzek, 2dLT Robert W. Vaupell, 1stLT Daniel Iverson, Jr., 2dLT Jesse D. Rollow, Jr., 2dLT Harold G. Schlendering, TECHSGT (NAP) Clyde H. Stamps, USMC. Rear row (standing): 2dLT Maurice A. Ward, 1stLT Richard L. Blain, 2dLT Sumner H. Whitten, 2dLT Thomas F. Moore, Jr., 1stLT Armond M. DeLalio, 2dLT Bruce Ek, 1stLT Leon M. Williamson, 1stLT Richard E. Fleming, 2dLT Robert J. Bear, MARGUN (NAP) Howard C. Frazer, USMC, 2dLT Bruno P. Hagedorn. 80-G-40283

ed suffered by *Hiryu* at that point in the battle.

As 2dLT Thomas F. Moore Jr., had circled the target, he became aware of "Zeroes" besetting him. His gunner, PVT Charles W. Huber, soon informed the pilot, however, that his gun had jammed and that he was unable to clear it. Moore responded by telling him to keep pointing his weapon at the fighters "even though he couldn't fire." Finding himself attracted to the "huge rising sun insignia" on *Hiryu's* light yellow flight deck, Moore established an aiming point well aft, and pushed over into a steep dive. Releasing his bomb at 400 feet, he found himself still sorely beset by the "Zeroes," whose pilots, apparently having seen that all they had to contend with was a wounded gunner with an inoperable machine gun, nipped closer with their firing passes. Pulling out of his dive between 25 and 50 feet off the water, Moore looked around to see where his bomb had hit, but, noting the presence of at least three enemy fighters on his tail, quickly abandoned his curiosity! Eventually succeeding in evading them, Moore set course for home.

The battered remnant of Henderson's boxes cleared *Hiryu's* vicinity, apparently having scored only one near miss. Two other bombs splashed 50 meters from the ship; one 80 and another 150. "Zeroes" had accounted for six planes shot down. Radio-gunners in the SBDs, however, managed to extract some retribution, downing a section leader from *Hiryu*. The "Zeroes" hounded the surviving SBDs for several minutes before the Marines managed to escape into the clouds with their riddled aircraft.

Soon after the last of the Marine SBDs had cleared the area, VADM Nagumo received more word from *Tone's* diligent airmen at 0820: "The enemy is accompanied by what appears to be a carrier." That an American carrier was definitely in the vicinity was unexpected. Nagumo's order to re-arm to go after surface ships, however, rendered it impossible to launch a strike swiftly. It would simply have to wait.

Nautilus, in the meantime, had seen masts over the horizon at 0755, and, like *Grouper*, had gotten strafed for the trouble. Going down to 100 feet, she picked up echo-ranging sounds for the first time—evidence that she had been detected. Again at periscope depth five minutes later, Brockman sighted what looked to him like a battleship and three "cruisers," and decided to go for the former. Again sighted by prowling aircraft, and bombed for the first time, *Nautilus* continued to press on, continuing to hear echo-ranging sounds from at least two enemy ships. For about the next quarter of an hour, Japanese destroyers kept *Nautilus* lying low. She came to periscope depth at 0824.

"The picture presented on raising the periscope was one never experienced in peacetime practice," Brockman noted later, "Ships were on all sides moving across the field at high speed and circling away to avoid the submarine's position." During the depth charging, the shock of the explosions had sheared a torpedo retaining pin on one of *Nautilus'* deck tubes, and the "fish" was running "hot," leaving a trail of bubbles. Brockman attempted a torpedo attack on the "battleship" in his periscope view but missed; one torpedo had not fired. *Nautilus'* presence caused a considerable "stir," and both the light cruiser *Nagara* and the destroyer *Arashi* attacked with depth charges.

Even as *Nautilus* was causing such consternation, and as operations proceeded apace to re-arm a portion of a strike with torpedoes instead of bombs to contend with an American task force off lurking over the horizon, a new group of foes appeared to torment Nagumo's men: the rest of VMSB-241, whose SB2U-3s, which followed the SBDs, would likewise run a gauntlet. Norris' men had spotted the enemy fleet about 0815 and the leader commenced a shallow dive through the overcast from 13,500 feet. Norris, spotting the battleship *Haruna*, peeled off immediately to the right in a steep dive, followed by 2dLTs Kenneth Campion and George Lumpkin. As he did so, Norris forehandedly radioed his pilots the course home.

LCDR William H. Brockman, Jr., CO of *Nautilus* (SS-168), seen here on 26 August 1942, would earn a Navy Cross for the "skill, determination, courage and fortitude" he displayed at Midway. He went on to receive two further Navy Crosses and the Silver Star, as well as four letters of commendation for his World War II service. 80-G-13035

Lumpkin, following the leader, found the antiaircraft fire heavy, and the air rough, making it "practically impossible to hold the ship in a true dive." On top of that, he discovered much to his dismay that the bomb-release mechanism would not work. Pulling out of his dive slightly to the south of the battleship, Lumpkin heard his radio-gunner, PFC George A. Toms, reporting the proximity of "Zeroes" and firing his .30-caliber machine gun to keep them at bay.

Five miles from the enemy ships, Norris' second box, led by 2dLT Allan H. Ringblom, a former Miami traffic policeman and one of the "greenest group [of second lieutenants] ever assembled for combat," encoun-

Nautilus (SS-168), off Mare Island, 12 April 1942. The men handling torpedoes on her deck give a good indication of this "boat's" size; her two 6-inch guns are prominent in this view taken upon conclusion of the ship's first wartime overhaul. 19-N-29179

CAPT (later MAJ) Benjamin W. Norris, USMC, who became XO of VMSB-241 on 28 May 1942, CO on 4 June upon the death of MAJ Henderson, and who was lost on the night of 4 June. USMC photo 14274

VMSB-241 SB2U-3 Unit

GROUP ONE
1 MAJ Benjamin W. Norris/
   PFC Arthur B. Whittington, USMCR
2 2dLT George T. Lumpkin, USMCR/
   PFC George A. Toms
3 2dLT Kenneth O. Campion, USMCR/
   PVT Anthony J. Maday
4 2dLT George E. Koutelas, USMCR/
   PFC Warren H. VanKirk, USMCR
10 2dLT Orvin H. Ramlo, USMCR/
   PVT Teman Wilhite

GROUP TWO
9 CAPT Leon M. Williamson, USMCR/
   PFC Duane L. Rhodes
6 2dLT James H. Marmande, USMCR/
   PFC Edby M. Colvin
7 2dLT Jack Cosley, USMCR/
   PFC Charles E. Cayer
8 2dLT Allan H. Ringblom, USMCR/
   PVT Eugene L. Webb
11 2dLT Sumner H. Whitten, USMCR/
   SGT Frank E. Zelnis
12 2dLT Daniel L. Cummings, USMCR/
   PVT Henry I. Starks

tered its first A6M2s. Having had a relatively "quiet and uneventful trip to meet the enemy," Ringblom quickly realized his predicament as the ash-gray fighters barrelled through the formation.

"Tail-end Charlie" was 2dLT Daniel L. Cummings, USMCR, who had only transferred into the squadron from VMF-221 on 1 June, and whose radio-gunner, 18-year-old PVT Henry I. Starks, had never fired aerial gunnery. Unable to "be an effective shot much less protect himself," Starks died in a "Zero's" first pass. The SB2U gunners believed that they had achieved some retribution, though, as 2dLT Whitten's radio-gunner, SGT Frank E. Zelnis, claimed a "Zero." Whitten later recounted that he saw an inverted "Zero" slanting seaward. Norris' men, however, had failed to score any hits on *Haruna*.

Getting home proved an ordeal for the men who survived. Bert Earnest nursed the crippled TBF-1 back home, ultimately using the pillar of cloud from the burning oil tanks on Sand Island as a point of reference. CAPT Collins neared Eastern Island and discovered that he could not extend his nose gear; at 0915, airfield controllers ordered both Collins and Earnest to bail out, along with their surviving crews. However, as NAS Midway's war diary noted: "They [Collins and Earnest] came in and landed anyhow."

Earnest's starboard landing gear buckled and the shot-up "Avenger" slewed off to one side. LT Muri brought in his B-26 with his left main tire shot away and, as MAJ Warner observed, "did a beautiful job of [landing] it off the left side of the runway clearing the mat." CAPT Collins, his nose gear out, simply let his B-26 come in on its nose, swerving to the right and off the runway so that he would not obstruct it. MAJ Warner marvelled at the skillful manner in which each pilot brought his damaged ship in. None of the pilots could tell if their attack had resulted in any damage: Earnest reported making a run on an enemy carrier but did not observe the result; the B-26s likewise reported unknown results.

The Marines had trouble getting back, too. 2dLT Harold G. Schlendering, his elevator controls shot away and his radio-gunner, PFC Edward O. Smith, dead, coaxed his SBD to within eight miles of the reef at Midway before his engine failed. Bailing out, he was picked up by *PT-20*. Tom Moore, with his gunner, PVT Huber, wounded, could not find Midway; an inoperative radio (he could neither send nor receive) did not help. Finally, Huber called Moore's attention to a smudge of smoke off on the horizon—Sand Island's burning oil tanks.

CAPT (then-2dLT) George T. Lumpkin (2d from left) and Dan Cummings (R), seen here at Guadalcanal later in 1942. Elmer P. Thompson is at far left.
Cummings

Moore later wrote, gratefully, of Huber, "due to his keen observation in sighting the smoke when the pilot was lost, he is directly responsible for himself, the pilot, and the SBD returning to Midway . . ."

CAPT Richard L. Blain, tried to reach Midway, too, but without success. Forced to ditch in the open sea, the two Marines broke out the rubber boat and their emergency rations. Blain and his radio-gunner, CPL Gordon McFeely (who had been a truckdriver in MAG-22's headquarters and service squadron until late April), then settled down to await the rescue they hoped would be soon in coming.[2]

The men from MAJ Norris' group had adventures of their own on the return flight. Clearing the Japanese formation on a southwesterly course, 2dLT Lumpkin found himself joined by Ken Campion, and started to turn back toward Midway when he noticed a Type 95 reconnaissance floatplane, from one of the battleships, coming up on the starboard side. Both Lumpkin and Campion turned their "Wind Indicators" toward the enemy aircraft and fired bursts into him as he turned and retired toward the enemy fleet. Campion rashly followed. At that moment, PFC Toms informed his pilot of the proximity of more "Zeroes," and Lumpkin quickly pulled up into the overcast and stayed there, flying on instruments for the next five minutes. Campion was never seen again—he probably fell victim to the same enemy fighters that Toms had seen.

2dLT Orvin H. Ramlo, originally assigned to VMF-221 but who had volunteered to fly in VMSB-241, had carried out his attack on *Haruna* in the face of heavy

fighter opposition. The "Zeroes" wounded PVT Teman Wilhite, his radio-gunner, but the game Marine kept them at a distance, holding off three Japanese fighters that tried for 30 minutes to knock down Ramlo's holed SB2U-3. Once free of the fighters, Ramlo had company for most of the flight back to Midway: 2dLT James H. Marmande, but 10 miles short of the atoll Marmande's plane simply "disappeared." No trace of it, nor of its crew, was ever found.

2dLT Ringblom flew the course prescribed by MAJ Norris, but failed "to compensate for wind, variation, and compass" and found Kure—not Midway. His radio failed soon thereafter, and he flew on, beginning to doubt Norris' directions. Turning 180 degrees, he happened across Midway soon thereafter but about 10 miles from the reef his "Vindicator" ran out of gas. Gliding to a water-landing in front of a PT-boat near Sand Island, Ringblom and his radio-gunner, PVT Eugene L. Webb, soon found themselves the guests of *PT-26*, the pick-up being made so quickly after the SB2U-3 hit the water that the pilot had not even inflated his life jacket!

Dick Fleming had meanwhile joined up with CAPT Glidden; Lumpkin joined Dan Iverson. Making a fine three-point landing and holding the plane straight on the strip in spite of a flat left tire, Fleming turned his SBD-2 off the runway and applied the brakes. As Marines rushed up, Fleming climbed out and announced: "Boys, there is one ride I am glad is over," before he shook hands with Gene Card. Their SBD-2 had been holed 179 times. Dan Iverson's SBD-2 had taken 219 hits; his hydraulic system shot away, Iverson managed a landing on one wheel.

Cummings, meanwhile, who had attacked a destroyer with his bomb, made it through the slashing attacks

2. They remained adrift until the morning of 6 June, when a VP-23 PBY landed and picked them up. It was a small world, indeed for the patrol plane commander turned out to be LT Samuel I. Ogden A-V(N), USNR, who had been a classmate of Blain's at Pensacola!

2dLT Iverson stands on the wing root of his SBD-2, while another Marine examines the tail surfaces. USMC Photo

Two views of 2dLT Daniel Iverson's Douglas SBD-2 (BuNo 2106). Note painted-out mission letter ahead of the plane number, 6 (probably a "B," since the plane had been operated by VB-2, in *Lexington*, 12 December 1941-15 April 1942); and recently overpainted rudder stripes. On the original print, the recently repainted centers of the insignias (where the red areas had been painted over with white) are plainly visible. USMC

of the "Zeroes," with his "old, obsolete SB2U-3 . . . almost shot out from under me . . ." Using full right rudder and right aileron, with his elevator controls frozen and his instruments shot away, he eventually made it to within five miles of Midway when his gasoline gave out and he had to "ditch." Only having enough time to confirm his worst fears that Starks was dead, Cummings swam away from the rapidly sinking "Vindicator" to be picked up by *PT-20*. Once on board, Cummings found himself in the company of his squadronmate, 2dLT Schlendering, and Herb Merrill.

Even as the scattered elements of the Navy and Marine aircraft that had set out from Midway were making their sometimes tortuous way home, often every

man for himself or in battered pairs, and *Nautilus* was dodging the enemy's anti-submarine efforts, the B-17s were continuing the search for the elusive carriers. Finally, CAPT Paul Payne spotted the flattops emerging from beneath the cloud cover, and Sweeney deployed his group to attack, by flights, at 0810. He divided his ships into three groups, each taking a carrier.

Sweeney's first two flights (including his own, consisting of himself, CAPT Gregory and LT Woodbury) dropped 44 500-pound demolition bombs on one flattop. The second element—CAPT Tokarz, CAPT Sullivan and CAPT Payne—claimed one hit on her stern. The third flight—CAPT Cecil Faulkner, LT Steedman, and LT Andrews—claimed one hit on a second carrier's port bow, "one waterline hit amidship," one possible hit and five near misses. The fifth element—LT Wuertele and LT Grundeman—attacked the carrier attacked by the third element and came away claiming one direct hit, one "possible" hit, and two near misses. A third carrier came under attack by the fourth element—LTCOL Brooke Allen, LT Williams and LT Eberenz—that claimed one hit and two near-misses. The airmen assessed the antiaircraft fire, which began almost as soon as the B-17s bomb bay doors opened, as "heavy and at the proper altitude," but it generally burst behind the B-17s. Sweeney assessed the fighter attacks, coming from below and from the forward quarter, as "pretty, but not effective." "Their heart was not in their work," he later wrote, "and in no case was an attack pressed home." The Army bombers suffered only slight damage; only one man, the tail gunner in CAPT Faulkner's B-17E, suffering a cut finger. In return, the Army gunners claimed two "Zeroes" downed, and the pilots were jubilant, confident that they had dealt the *Kido Butai* a heavy blow. As Walt Sweeney later wrote, "We didn't have time to wait and see them sink, but we left knowing they were badly crippled." Had they waited, they would have seen that, in fact, none of their bombs had even scratched paint, having landed astern of *Kaga* and 500 meters wide of *Akagi*. They had, however, again seriously disrupted Nagumo's routine.

The B-17s returned to Midway after 0930, and landed on the shrapnel-littered runways, four of the B-17s blowing tires. Owing to the damage to the gasoline pumping system, reservicing the B-17s took time, as all of the fueling had to be done by hand, from 55-gallon drums. Sweeney ordered each plane commander to get aloft again as soon as possible, particularly since VMF-221 had few fighters with which to protect the airfield a second time.

Trailed by a destroyer, *Akagi* turns to starboard, in this view taken from one of the 14 B-17s, flying at 20,000 feet on the morning of 4 June 1942, that attacked the *Kido Butai* at that time. Despite claims of their setting three carriers afire during this attack, the B-17s scored no hits. 57576 A.C.

Bill Brockman soon discovered that his old friend, the "*Jintsu*-class cruiser"—which was, in fact, the destroyer *Arashi*—lingered in the area as the rest of the *Kido Butai* sped away, Nagumo radioing Yamamoto of his sighting of an American task force formed around one carrier, and of his intentions: "We are heading for it." *Arashi* was to drive off the troublesome sub or sink her. The submarine endured her second depth charge attack, diving down to 150 feet, and stayed at that depth for 20 minutes, after which time Brockman brought *Nautilus* up again to have a look around. Spying a car-

rier at 0900, *Nautilus* again closed, only to have a destroyer pick up her scent. After firing a torpedo at his tormentor, Brockman took his "boat" down again, this time going down to 200 feet at 0918 after six depth charges exploded close by.

Ultimately, apparently satisfied that her attacks had driven off or sunk the persistent submarine, *Arashi*—a bone-in-teeth and a vivid white wake stretching astern—set course to rejoin the *Kido Butai* at a good clip. While thinking she had hindered one intruder, she would inadvertently help one far more deadly.

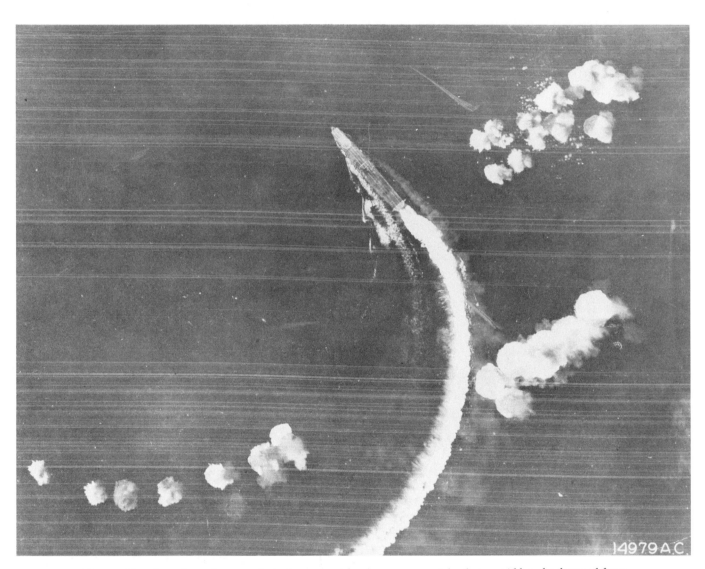

Hiryu, with at least three planes on deck abreast her island, maneuvers violently to avoid bombs dropped from B-17s on 4 June. 14979 A.C.

CHAPTER EIGHT
. . . .

"Well, Murray, This is it..."

Ady's terse "Enemy carriers," *sans* amplification, at 0534 had abruptly ended the suspenseful wait in TF 16 and TF 17 for word on the enemy's whereabouts. Ten minutes elapsed, though, before LT(jg) Chase's "Many planes heading Midway . . ." came through. This, although it confirmed CINCPAC's intelligence reports and told of the enemy's presence, did not give his position.

At 0600, as planes from Midway were scrambling to get airborne in the path of Tomonaga's incoming strike, Fletcher had ordered Spruance to steam to the northwest. TF 17, with a search aloft, would continue northeast toward her "point option" and recover her planes. At 0603, as TF 16 was settling on its new course, Fletcher and Spruance received Ady's unauthenticated report pinpointing two carriers and battleships 175 miles to the southwest.

Ady, however, had mentioned only two carriers—the smokescreen laid by the light cruiser *Nagara* and the battleship *Kirishima* had apparently worked well in misleading the Americans—not the four or five flat-tops operating in one group as projected in Op-Plan 29-42. A skeptical Frank Jack Fletcher thus wanted more hard evidence before he committed his planes. In the Coral Sea, a search had yielded a report of two carriers on 7 May; two air groups had been sent out only to discover that the two "carriers" had, in fact, been "cruisers." Fortunately, a searching B-17 had found one carrier (*Shoho*) so that the strike was rerouted and that target sunk.

Launching a strike against the two reported carriers then approaching Midway meant that the enemy lay at the range limit of the TBD and F4F; Fletcher's planes would have little fuel reserve to allow for combat maneuvering nearer the target. It would also allow for virtually no errors in navigation. By the same token, the admiral also recognized that his own search was homeward bound. Having no further contacts from either his or the Midway-based planes, these carriers reported by the PBY seemed to be the only ones around.

RADM Frank Jack Fletcher, USNA Class of 1906—a "strenuous son of the Middle West" broke his flag in *Yorktown* (CV-5) on New Year's Day 1942, and commanded TF 17 in modest and workmanlike fashion during its operations in the Pacific theater in the early part of the war. Fletcher has been more fairly appraised in the more recent historiography of the Pacific War. USN

RADM Raymond A. Spruance (seen here as a VADM), USNA Class of 1907, a man physically and morally courageous; a quiet man gifted with a transcendent fighting spirit. "Power of decision and coolness in action," wrote Samuel Eliot Morison, "were perhaps [his] leading characteristics." USN

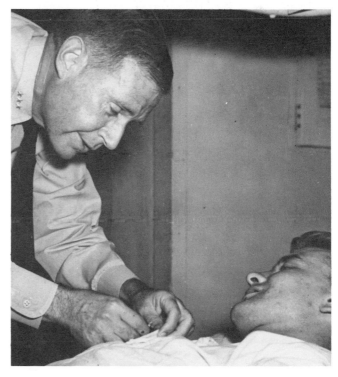

Weighing his options, Fletcher ordered Spruance to "Proceed southwesterly and attack enemy carriers as soon as definitely located," and informed him: "I will follow as soon as planes recovered."

At 0614, with Nagumo's planes enroute to Midway, the initiative lay with Spruance, who wanted to launch his strike as soon as possible. His only reservations concerned the range of his fighters and torpedo planes. Allowing a reserve for combat maneuvering, his staff placed this at 175 miles. Assuming that the enemy maintained his present course, thus shortening the distance their strike would have to fly to return to their ships, at 0700, they would be 155 miles to the west southwest of TF 16. Spruance decided on an 0700 launch.

Meanwhile, TF 17 proceeded toward "point option." Shortly before 0630, the 10 SBDs of *Yorktown*'s dawn search orbitted overhead, reporting no contacts. The carrier quickly launched her second CAP of the morning, VF-3's fourth division, under LT(jg) Art Brassfield. The flight deck thus cleared, *Yorktown* recovered the 10 SBDs from the dawn search and LT(jg) Crommelin's CAP. Flight operations then completed, Fletcher turned TF 17 to the southwest, and increased speed to 25 knots to follow TF 16. Still concerned about the number of Japanese carriers in the area, he laid no plans to launch TF 17's strike, hoping that further contact reports would clarify the situation. Until then, much to the chagrin of the men perspiring in their flight gear in the ready rooms, *Yorktown*'s squadrons were to be held in reserve.

On board *Enterprise* and *Hornet*, which had had two false-starts that morning already, the receipt of the 0603 contact report again triggered activity in the air department. Spruance's air staff, though, did not immediately signal *Hornet* of the intended launch time. At 0615 *Hornet*'s air plot got the ready room teletypes clattering with the Japanese position, course, and speed. Thereafter, the bullhorn summoned the 10 VF-8 pilots who would fly the day's first CAP to man their planes, followed shortly by the pilots of the strike escort. Finally, the horn summoned all strike group pilots except the CHAG and the four squadron COs.

When *Enterprise* showed no indication that she was going to launch, however, *Hornet*'s men filed back to their respective ready rooms. At 0653, though, Browning belatedly signalled Mitscher of Spruance's intention to launch at 0700: the strike groups would use a "deferred departure"—each group's squadrons forming up over their carrier and departing en masse, and to use search and attack procedure en route, due to the lack of continued sighting reports.

No provision was made for the two air groups to operate together. Pre-war doctrine dictated the formation of separate air groups into a single massed strike under the senior group commander, but this was not implemented. As events were to show, this proved to be very fortunate, as McClusky, while some felt that he was unfamiliar with dive bombers (he had recently been skipper of VF-6), possessed more combat experience than did the CHAG, CDR Stanhope C. Ring.

Neither carrier in TF 16 had provided a specific "point option" course. To the *Hornet* pilots, in their first action, this oversight does not seem to have been given much notice. The men in her squadron, drilled in peacetime doctrine, were simply expected to follow the leader. This was not true for the *Enterprise* squadrons, whose commanders had been told that TF 16 would close the enemy behind the attack group, shortening their return distance, and they briefed their pilots accordingly.

LCDR Lindsey appeared to give the final briefing to the VT-6 pilots; his being there startled those who had not seen him since his accident on 28 May. It is unclear how much LT Arthur V. Ely, VT-6's XO, had told Lindsey of the discussions held the day before with the other squadron commanders. But apparently Lindsey misunderstood how the escort was going to be deployed, since he had told the squadron to expect "close" fighter support. Since "Doc" Ely expected support to be on hand, he apparently felt it unnecessary to correct his skipper.

A surprise also awaited LCDR Wade McClusky, CEAG, before launch. He was in his office gathering up his flight gear when the regular CEAG radio-gunner, John Murray O'Brien, ACRM, from VF-6, stumbled in with a tale of woe: he had fallen down and broken his glasses; without them he could barely see. McClusky sent word to Bombing SIX to provide him a new radioman, and a few minutes later Walter G. Chochalousek, ARM1c, showed up. Although new to the ship, Chochalousek had seen action with *Lexington*'s VT-2 in the raid on Salamaua in March. After Browning's signal, *Hornet*'s pilots again manned their planes. Mitscher then summoned the CHAG and the four squadron commanders to a hasty meeting with CDR Apollo Soucek, the air officer, to discuss the course the strike group should take to find the Japanese. Considerable disagreement ensued. Ring finally asked each of the pilots present, as well as himself, to solve the navigational problem using the available data. Although a comparison of plots yielded as many options as the number of people who had figured them out, Ring chose his own course, 265(T). LCDR John C. Waldron, VT-8's skipper, disagreed, but Ring's decision stood.

About 0650, the two carriers separated, each becoming the center of her own task group—*Enterprise* with the heavy cruisers *Northampton* (CA-26), *Pensacola*

While one "Wildcat" climbs (L), *Enterprise* launches another from her deck on the morning of 4 June 1942; *Northampton* (CA-26) steams in the background, in this view taken from *Pensacola* (CA-24)—the first photo taken by her photographer that day. Planes spotted aft are F4F-4s and SBDs; no TBDs have been brought to the flight deck at that time. 80-G-32224

Eleven of the 14 VT-6 "Devastators" to be used in the morning attack on 4 June are spotted aft on *Enterprise*'s flight deck. At left is plane no. 2, the TBD-1 (BuNo 1512) flown that morning by ENS Severin L. Rombach, A-V(N); W.F. Glenn, ARM2c, radiogunner. In left background steams one of the carrier's plane guards; at right is *Pensacola* (CA-24). 80-G-41686

While planes from her air group orbit the task force (center background), the SBDs that had not been launched are cleared from the flight deck. 80-G-32225

(CA-24) and *Vincennes* (CA-44), and the destroyers *Balch* (DD-363), *Benham* (DD-397), *Aylwin* (DD-355), *Monaghan* (DD-354) and *Phelps* (DD-360); *Hornet* with *Minneapolis* (CA-36) and *New Orleans* (CA-32), light cruiser *Atlanta* (CL-51) and destroyers *Maury* (DD-400), *Ellet* (DD-398), *Worden* (DD-352) and *Conyngham* (DD-371). At 0656, each group swung into the wind, toward the southeast, gradually working up to 28 knots.

Promptly at 0700—at about the time, as we have seen, VADM Nagumo was getting word that a second strike on Midway would be necessary and Langdon Fieberling was spotting the Japanese force—each carrier commenced getting her planes off. Spotted first on each ship were the F4Fs forming the first CAP of the day.

About every 20 seconds, a plane roared purposefully down the deck and over the ramp. Fighting EIGHT contributed eight F4Fs in two four-plane divisions, led by LTs Edward J. O'Neill and Warren W. Ford, to fly "hi cap." These immediately set out on the laborious climb to 18,000 feet. Fighting SIX also launched eight F4Fs for CAP, in four-plane divisions led by LT Roger W. Mehle and LT(jg) Frank B. Quady, to fly "lo cap." Immediately after *Hornet*'s CAP came LCDR Samuel G. "Pat" Mitchell's 10-plane strike escort. Only one of the F4Fs had any difficulty: ENS John McInerny, A-V(N), had trouble starting his engine, but just as his plane was about to be struck below he managed to coax the engine to life and roared aloft. They also started the long climb to altitude, making gentle turns over *Hornet*, waiting for the dive bombers they would escort to form up.

Spotted next were *Hornet*'s 34 SBD-3's: the first 15 from LCDR Walter F. Rodee's VS-8; the next two, CHAG (CDR Ring) and his wingman, ENS Clayton E. Fisher of VB-8—each armed with a 500-pound bomb. Finally, came VB-8's 17 planes, each armed with a 1,000-pounder. Ring instructed Rodee and LCDR R.R. Johnson to use "group parade formation," a giant vee of vees with the CHAG section at the apex and the two squadrons abreast, VS-8 to starboard and VB-8 to port, instead of division step-down formation. The escort took station above and behind their charges, LCDR Mitchell's division with VB-8, LT Stanley E. Ruehlow's section with the CHAG, and LT Richard Gray's division with VS-8. By 0730 the last SBD was up. While forming, the group started the long climb to 19,000 feet, the fighters continuing about 2,000 feet higher.

Even as the last SBD was launched, the plane handlers of the *Hornet* air department started bringing up VT-8's remaining nine TBDs. As the pilots were preparing to take off, LCDR Waldron took ENS George H. Gay, A-V(N), the squadron navigation officer, aside, told him to disregard the data previously given, and confided to

the young pilot that he was convinced that Ring was taking the wrong course. He then told Gay to follow him, adding: "Just track me so if anything happens to me, the boys can count on you to bring them back." Twelve minutes after they had been spotted, the 15 TBD-1s of VT-8 began taking off.

At 0746, Ring signaled for his group to take its departure, just as the last of Waldron's TBDs were taking off. Making a "running rendezvous," VT-8 climbed to 1,500 feet and departed around 0750, joining the rear of *Hornet*'s formation. The TBDs had cleared *Hornet* just in time, for at 0754 ENS Stephen W. Groves, A-V(N), of the CAP made a "deferred forced landing." *Hornet* immediately scrambled another VF-8 F4F to restore the CAP to eight.

On board *Enterprise*, her men, too, had anxiously awaited the word to take off. The wait proved especially difficult on the radio-gunners who, standing by their individual aircraft and not being in the squadron ready rooms, found themselves ignorant of the little information available. The two false alarms left most wondering if anybody knew what was going on. James F. Murray, ACRM, of VB-6, soon saw that the third call to man planes would be unlike the first two. As his pilot, LT Richard H. Best, the squadron CO, clambered on board the SBD, he said simply: "Well Murray, this is it."

As the CAP fighters roared down the deck, the pilots of the 37 SBDs spotted for launch started their engine and cockpit checks. At 0706, the first of Scouting SIX's 16 SBD-3s lumbered aloft; only one, LT Frank A. Patriarca's, would have to be left behind: unable to get full power from the engine of S-13, the leader of the sixth section was waved up to the number one elevator and struck below. The rest managed to get off without incident. Next off was LCDR McClusky and his two VS-6 wingmen. Due to the limited deck run available, the first six of those SBDs carried only a single 500-pound bomb. The last 12 each carried two 100-pound bombs in addition to the 500-pounder.

Bombing SIX brought up the rear. Although 18 SBDs had been spotted, mechanical casualties compelled deck hands to strike B-4, B-17, and B-10 before take off. By 0725 the other 15 SBDs had made it aloft, each armed with a 1,000-pounder. In a deferred departure, they orbited *Enterprise* as they formed up and started the long climb to 20,000 feet, waiting for their escort and the torpedo planes.

On board *Enterprise*, after the last SBDs had left the ship, plane handlers commenced spotting the 10 F4Fs and 14 TBDs that would accompany them—ideally a procedure that would have started while the last of the dive bombers were taking off. In the light wind conditions prevalent that day, though, Best's SBDs—each car-

Scouting SIX forms up over TF 16 in this view taken from *Pensacola*. Single plane is probably S-14, flown by ENS John C. Lough, whose section leader, LT Frank Patriarca, is deck-bound with an engine that won't start, and is thus unattached at that moment. He is closing in on LT Charles R. Ware's division, which is in turn trying to close up on the first two. USN

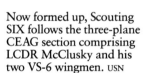

Now formed up, Scouting SIX follows the three-plane CEAG section comprising LCDR McClusky and his two VS-6 wingmen. USN

rying a full load of fuel and a 1,000-pound bomb—needed the entire flight deck to get aloft. Consequently, the re-spot of the deck could not start until the last SBD had cleared it. It took 20 minutes to re-spot—repairs to a balky TBD (that was eventually fixed) consumed some of that time—and to McClusky, orbiting overhead, "action on the flight deck seemed to come to a standstill."

In the flag shelter, Spruance grew restive over the time being lost as the SBDs circled, burning fuel, while the contact grew colder and the chance of enemy detection of his force grew greater. Finally, at 0745 he felt he could wait no longer; even as the first F4F was being launched,

he signalled McClusky to "Proceed on mission assigned." McClusky carefully considered the problem on his plotting board, using his estimate of the Japanese course and speed. His solution placed his point of interception as bearing roughly southwest.

While *Enterprise* and *Hornet* were getting their planes aloft, TF 17 steamed to the southwest at 25 knots, and Frank Jack Fletcher faced the critical decision of when to commit *Yorktown's* aircraft. The experience at Coral Sea probably fresh in his mind, he knew that it would be folly to commit all of his planes to strike two carriers while two or three more lurked unreported elsewhere. He decided to wait until further searches

LT(jg) Frank Fisler, of VP-51, flying a VP-23 PBY-5B (BuNo 2389), flies near TF 17 at around 0730 on 4 June 1942. On *Yorktown*'s flight deck, from forward, are the day's first CAP, the VB-3 and V"S"-5 search flights, and, aft, the TBD-1s from VT-3, which are spotted to take off first in the strike. 80-G-21628

An SBD makes a pass over *Yorktown*, perhaps to drop a message to avoid breaking radio silence. Aft on the carrier's flight deck sit the TBDs of Torpedo THREE. 80-G-23842

A TBD-1, torpedo underneath, en route to the Japanese fleet. Varying theories as to the identity of this plane have come up over the years, but the most convincing is that it is from VT-3, since other photographs in sequence were taken from the heavy cruiser *Portland*. 80-G-21668

could ascertain the whereabouts of the others.

Fletcher was not the only one worried about the location of enemy carriers. So, too, was Nagumo. The report of the American carrier sent in by *Tone's* no. 4 plane worried him. Thus, at 0830, *Soryu* launched a new airplane on its maiden mission of war—the ship's only operable Yokosuka Experimental Type 13 carrier bomber (later code-named "Judy"). At the controls was PO1 Masatada Iida; SPO Isamu Kondo was in the rear seat. Iida set course to fly to the point indicated by *Tone's* no. 4 plane.

Meanwhile, reporting of a snooper shortly after 0800 changed the complexion of things on *Yorktown's* flag bridge, and Fletcher, after conferring with CAPT Buckmaster, *Yorktown's* air officer, CDR Murr Arnold, and the CYAG, CDR Oscar Pederson, decided at 0838 to launch a limited strike—17 SBDs of VB-3, 12 TBDs of VT-3, and six F4Fs of VF-3—to attack the same carriers against which Spruance had sent his planes. He would hold the 17 SBDs of V"S"-5 in reserve for use in a search or for a second attack.

That did not please LT Wallace C. Short of "Scouting" FIVE, whose squadron had recently fought in the Coral Sea, knocking *Shokaku* out of action, and wanted another crack at a Japanese carrier. Fletcher, however, remained firm; V"S"-5 would stay on board.

The arrangement likewise did not please "Jimmy" Thach, who was to lead the escort. Knowing how his fighters would be seriously outnumbered, he had planned on using his new "beam defense" tactic—which required four-plane divisions—to give his men a fighting chance against the "Zeroes." The "Thach Weave" would not work with six planes instead of eight, and despite Thach's representations to that effect, Murr Arnold explained that CAPT Buckmaster wanted three six-plane divisions for CAP. Thach would have to settle for a six-plane escort.

With the strike composition decided, Arnold and Pederson carefully considered the contact reports, now two hours old, and their best estimates of what the enemy would do. The reported enemy course was into the wind, toward Midway. They figured the Japanese would maintain it, at least until they recovered their planes, and allowed for a maximum rate of advance along this base course. That placed the estimated point of contact to the southwest of TF 17's 0900 position.

They reasoned that if the strike group arrived at that point and found no enemy ships, it would turn to the northwest and fly a reciprocal of the projected Japanese course. If the Japanese deviated from it, a good chance existed for their men to find the enemy.

In March, during the strike on Salamaua and Lae, *Yorktown* had launched her torpedo planes first, followed by the dive/scout bombers and the fighters. The faster aircraft overtook the slower ones and thus dispensed with the time- and fuel-consuming joinup over the task force. This "running rendezvous" minimized the TBD-1's and F4F-4's range limitations, allowed a fuel reserve for combat maneuvering, and promised the best way to achieve a coordinated attack.

In contrast to the comparatively rocky departure of planes from *Enterprise* and *Hornet*, *Yorktown's* launch went smoothly. LCDR C.C. Ray, *Yorktown's* communications officer, remembering a sighting report fiasco in the Coral Sea less than a month before, had had his yeomen round up all of the code books and put them in a safe. If the scouts had anything to report, Ray enjoined the squadrons, do so in *plain language*!

Yorktown turned into the wind and commenced launch, steaming to the southeastward and drawing away from TF 16. "Lem" Massey's TBDs led, departing at 0840 and climbed slowly to 1,500 feet, heading to the southwest. Next came LCDR Max Leslie's 17 SBDs, each armed with a 1,000-pound bomb. They formed up and started climbing, slowly circling TF 17 until 0902 when they took their departure. At 0905 Thach's six F4Fs took off, formed up, and followed Leslie.

With the strike group off, *Yorktown* shuffled her CAP. At 0920, LT William N. Leonard, a VF-42 veteran and the man who had relieved Don Lovelace as VF-3's XO, took aloft the six F4Fs of his division; soon thereafter, *Yorktown* recovered LT Brassfield's division to rest and refuel. The carrier, meanwhile, re-spotted her flight deck with Wally Short's 17 SBDs, each armed with a 1,000-pound bomb, and the six F4F-4s of LT(jg) Dick Crommelin's division.

As the last of the strike planes disappeared from view, little remained for Fletcher and Spruance, and the men on board the ships of TF 16 and TF 17, to do but wait. In the air, 151 aircraft, manned by 278 officers and enlisted men—their friends and shipmates—droned toward the Japanese.

LT William N. Leonard takes off in his Grumman F4F-4 (BuNo 5244), plane no. 13, for CAP duty on the morning of 4 June 1942, as photographed by William G. Roy, PhoM2c. Note .50-caliber Browning machine gun protected by a mattress slung on the lifeline—one of the many jury-rigged mounts on board at that time. 80-G-312016

CHAPTER NINE

"Skipper, There's A Zero on My Tail..."

Within at least one portion of that winged host of Americans on its way to do battle with the enemy, however, all was not well. John Waldron, convinced that the CHAG was leading them the wrong way, broke radio silence and contacted him at about 0820. The two strongly disagreed over the course to follow, and Waldron eventually told Ring, in effect, that he would lead his squadron to the enemy even if he had to do so alone. At 0825, Waldron headed to the southwest. Some 20,000 feet above, unbeknownst to the men of Torpedo EIGHT, Jim Gray and VF-6 were conforming to VT-8's movements. Gray assumed that they knew where they were going, and would summon him if they needed help.

Torpedo EIGHT, in right echelon formation, flew in two divisions—the first, under Waldron, consisting of eight TBDs in four two-plane sections, and the sec-ond, under the XO, 31-year-old LT James C. Owens, Jr., of two two-plane sections and one of three. For about 30 minutes, the squadron droned over the Pacific, shepherded by Gray's VF-6 division, until Waldron noted a "fighter" tailing them—*Tone*'s no. 4 plane, homeward bound from its mission in the vicinity of the American task forces, which, although miscounting, warned VADM Nagumo's flagship at 0855: "... Ten attack planes heading toward you ..."

As VT-8's first division shifted into a scouting line so that it could scan more ocean, Jim Gray lost sight of the TBDs as they passed beneath a cloud layer. The VF-6 leader felt that that boded well for the torpedo planes—it would give them cover. At 0910, LT(jg) John C. Kelley, leading Gray's second division, called the skipper's attention to something at "one o'clock down." Initially, Gray thought Kelley meant aircraft, but beyond the cloud bank he soon discerned the tell-tail white wakes of the Japanese fleet.

Torpedo EIGHT, meanwhile, unfamiliar with flying a scouting line, began to straggle: ENS "Tex" Gay, the "tail-end Charlie" in the second division, could hardly see the TBDs at the end of the line. Waldron, seeing his struggling charges, gave the order to re-form and close up. No sooner had his first division re-formed, he spotted smoke on the horizon ahead.

In Waldron's path steamed the Japanese carriers, on board which the passage of time had diminished the tension prompted by the American attacks earlier that morning. They had just completed the recovery of the planes from the strike on Midway and had reorganized the CAP; 21 "Zeroes" orbitted overhead, three of which

Pilots of Torpedo EIGHT, on board *Hornet* around mid-May 1942. Standing (L-R): LT James C. Owens, Jr., ENS E.L. Fayle, A-V(N), LCDR John C. Waldron, LT Raymond A. Moore, ENSs [all A-V(N)] Ulvert M. Moore, William R. Evans, Jr., Grant W. Teats, LT(jg) George M. Campbell. Kneeling (L-R): ENSs [all A-V(N)] Harold J. Ellison, Henry R. Kenyon, Jr., John P. Gray, George H. Gay, Jr., LT(jg) Jeff D. Woodson, ENS William W. Creamer, A-V(N), and AP1c Robert B. Miles (NAP). Horan

were waiting to land; six sat on *Kaga*'s flight deck.

Having recovered the morning strike, Nagumo began focusing his attention on the reported American carrier to the east. An hour would be necessary to organize a proper strike, but the admiral planned to launch planes at 1030 to deal with the enemy carrier. At 0917, Nagumo ordered a course change to the northeast, to close the enemy. As his ships turned, though, *Chikuma* and *Tone* almost simultaneously spied a group of American torpedo planes 35 kilometers to the northeast. At 0920, *Kaga* scrambled her six standby "Zeroes."

After he had unsuccessfully attempted to inform Ring that he was attacking, Waldron selected the carrier to his left as his target, and ordered Owens to swing the second division out to starboard to make a split attack. Before the men of Torpedo EIGHT knew what hit them, though, the "Zeroes" were upon them. One A6M2 shot down the left-hand TBD in Waldron's division almost immediately. Seeing the "Zeroes" swarming around the XO's division, still relatively close at hand, Waldron recalled Owens, who quickly formed his planes on the CO's in a tight right echelon of divisions.

Meanwhile, Waldron led VT-8 down to make a low approach to keep off the fighters. The "Zeroes," however, slashed savagely at the lumbering TBDs from abeam and astern. "Tex" Gay, flying in the rear of the formation, noted "some [TBDs] were on fire and some did a half-roll, and crashed on their backs, completely out of control." At least one exploded in mid-air.

Early in the attack, Waldron decided to attack the carrier in the center, *Soryu*. Two more TBDs splashed before one A6M2's bullets hit the CO's left wing tank, and his TBD burst into flames. Gay saw Waldron start to climb out onto the starboard wing to escape the fire consuming the cockpit, just before T-16 hit the water and disappeared. The rest staggered doggedly on, the "Zeroes" decimating them. Gunfire fatally wounded Gay's radio-gunner, Robert K. Huntington, ARM3c, and then hit Gay in the left arm. Extracting the 7.7-mm. round, for want of a better place, he put it in his mouth.

As VT-8's remnant approached *Soryu* from ahead on her starboard bow, she began turning to starboard, presenting her port side to the three TBDs—Gay's and two others; one ahead, the other ahead and to port. Gay swerved to port to avoid another pass by a "Zero," and pulled up to take a shot as it zoomed past. When he turned back to starboard, he could see one of the TBDs slanting down, out of control; the other had disappeared. The fighters had whittled VT-8 down to its last plane.

When he estimated he was within 1,000 yards of his target, Gay pulled up to 100 feet and slowed to 80 knots to drop his torpedo. After the electrical release failed, he switched the stick to his injured left hand, reached across his body with his right and pulled the manual release to fire his "fish"—virtually on top of *Soryu*. Not wanting to overfly her and expose himself to her starboard antiaircraft batteries, he turned to head out over her stern, noting the flight deck full of planes being rearmed and refueled. Then he was past her, low to the water, heading for a hole in the screen. The Japanese, however, placed a formidable obstacle in his way.

At 0932, compelled to do so by VT-8's assault, *Akagi* had scrambled five A6M2s to increase the CAP, and these cornered VT-8's last airborne aircraft. One burst destroyed most of his controls and the TBD headed for the water. Gay, having marginal elevator control, managed to keep the nose up as the right wing hit the water, and although the big Douglas cartwheeled into the ocean, Gay survived the ditching and clambered from his cockpit with his life raft in the center of the Japanese fleet. He decided to hide beneath it, making himself as inconspicuous as possible.

After the destruction of Waldron's squadron, VADM Nagumo, ignorant of the new onslaught winging its way toward him, confidently radioed Yamamoto: "Carried out air attack of Midway at 0630. Many enemy shore based planes attacked us subsequent to 0715. We have suffered no damages. At 0728 enemy composed of one carrier, seven cruisers and five destroyers sighted . . . on course southwest, speed 20 knots. After destroying this, we plan to resume our Midway attack . . ."

At about that time, as Waldron's men were going after *Soryu*, Jim Gray, circling, stayed about 15 miles ahead of the Japanese, wondering where everyone else was. He tried in vain to contact McClusky. Given the situation, he felt he could do little except wait, and hope he could assist McClusky when he finally did arrive.

The squadron Gray was to cover, Torpedo SIX, had, meanwhile, formed up in two divisions, each with seven TBDs, the first flying left echelon and second in right echelon off the first. Other than the understandable apprehension over the failure of the expected fighter escort to arrive, things had gone smoothly. Lindsey's first inkling of the proximity of the Japanese came shortly after 0930 when he spotted smoke over his starboard wing. Turning the squadron to the northeast to investigate, he soon saw the wakes of many ships, bearing northwest by north, before him. Nagumo's course change at 0917 would have put some distance between the Japanese and Gene Lindsey if Waldron's men had not compelled the *Kido Butai* to take evasive action to avoid their brave charge, slowed the enemy's rate of advance, and provoked the screening ships to lay smoke—a tactic that instead of cloaking the carrier's movements called attention to them.

To Lindsey, the Japanese fleet, with three carriers at its heart, appeared to be in a loose, scrambled formation. The VT-6 skipper attempted to contact McClusky but, receiving no response and having no fuel to spare, realized that his squadron was on its own. Picking the closest carrier, *Kaga*, as his target, he turned the squadron to port and altered course to due north, placing her in his one o'clock position as he approached from the south. About 20 miles out, Lindsey split his formation, telling "Doc" Ely to take the second division in while he would continue northward to gain *Kaga*'s opposite side.

At 0938, lookouts in the Japanese ships sighted that new group of torpedo planes deploying for the attack. At that moment, some 30 A6M2s orbited the formation, five of which were about to land. Most of the others ranged out to the southeast at low altitude, some of those possessed very little ammunition after the recent slaughter of Waldron's TBDs. At 0940, *Tone* fired a salvo, the bursts directing the "Zeroes" toward Lindsey. Five minutes later, after turning into the wind, *Akagi*

and *Soryu* launched six A6M2s to reinforce the CAP.

Shortly after VT-6 split, *Kaga* turned to the north, drawing Ely astern and forcing Lindsey to struggle to gain the carrier's port bow. Ill-suited for a lengthy stern chase, as a TBD could only make 100 knots with the drag-producing torpedo slung beneath it, VT-6 closed *Kaga* at an agonizingly slow pace. The first "Zeroes" hit Ely's division just as he reached the outer screen. Trading altitude for speed and beset by growing numbers of enemy fighters, Ely led his men down to the wavetops.

Meanwhile, as VT-6's attack developed, Jim Gray, orbiting at 22,000 feet on the far side of the Japanese fleet, had no inkling of Lindsey's proximity. Further, the fuel gauges in his "Wildcats" were soon showing only a third of a tank remaining in each plane. At 0952, Gray radioed *Enterprise*: "This is Gray. We are over six destroyers, two battleships, two carriers"—the first contact report Spruance had received.

By 1000, Gray realized that he could wait no longer, for even if McClusky were to show up, his fighters no longer had the fuel to engage the enemy. He considered

Pilots of Torpedo SIX, on board *Enterprise*, 20 May 1942. Front row (L-R): LT(jg) Samuel L. Prickett; Harry A. Mueller, CAP; Albert W. Winchell, AP1c (NAP); ENS Jamie S. Morris, A-V(N); LT(jg) Lloyd Thomas, A-V(N); ENS Flournoy G. Hodges, A-V(N); LT(jg) John T. Eversole; Stephen B. Smith, CAP; Robert Laub. Second row (L-R) LT(jg) Randolph M. Holder, A-V(N); ENS John W. Brock; ENS Edward Heck, Jr., A-V(N); LT Paul J. Riley; LCDR Eugene E. Lindsey (CO); LT Arthur V. Ely (XO); LT(jg) Severin L. Rombach, A-V(N); ENS Irvin H. McPherson, A-V(N); Thomas E. Scheaffer, CAP. USN

strafing the enemy ships, but demurred, thinking that he could cause little damage. The problem of how to get home then remained. Having followed the torpedo planes all the way and trusted in their navigation, Gray had no idea where "home" was. He counted on using *Enterprise*'s YE homing signal—a line of sight device—to get back to the ship, and at 22,000 feet he enjoyed a better chance of picking it up at that altitude than far below.

With his group representing more than a third of *Enterprise*'s fighter strength, Gray felt it behooved him to get them back to defend the ship. Before turning for home, though, hoping to aid McClusky, Gray again transmitted a report: "This is Gray. We are returning to the ship due to lack of gas. We have been flying over the enemy fleet. They have no combat air patrol. There are six destroyers, two battleships, and two carriers. Course about north."

Even as Gray was transmitting, however, his presence drew a reaction from the Japanese. At 1000, *Soryu* launched three "Zeroes" to attack a "horizontal bombing unit." Before the trio could reach him, though, Gray had turned east toward TF 16.

Some 20 miles to the west, however, the squadron Jim Gray was supposed to protect—VT-6—was locked in a desperate struggle with the Japanese. The enemy pilots operated with cool, efficient teamwork, making high side approaches from both quarters, "scissoring" a TBD in a cone of fire. Whichever attacker drew defensive fire would break off early while the other would bore in. The "Zeroes" would range in with their 7.7-mm. machine guns and then, once they saw their bullets striking home, would cut in with the 20-mm. guns. Several times, Ely tried to contact Gray, to no avail, until a "Zero" splashed him, the first VT-6 plane to go down. ENS John W. Brock spotted a "Zero" pulling up directly ahead as it recovered from a run from astern. He impulsively pulled up to give the A6M2 a burst from his fixed machine gun, but in so doing pulled out of formation long enough to allow another "Zero" to splash him. Douglas M. Cossitt, ARM3c, radio-gunner in MACH A. Walt Winchell's T-8, saw another TBD take a direct hit on its torpedo and disappear in a blinding flash.

Eventually, only Winchell's and CHMACH Stephen Smith's TBDs remained out of Ely's second division, each seeking the dropping point. As many as five "Zeroes" shot up Winchell's TBD, holing the fuel tanks. Even after the pilot had fired his torpedo, the enemy pilots persisted in attacking T-8. Ultimately, after what seemed to Cossitt an eternity, the Mitsubishi pilots gave up and left them alone. Not finding any friendly planes to join, Winchell set course back to TF 16.

Emblazoned with a "black cat" insignia, Smith's T-11, meanwhile, seemed to bear a charmed life. One burst holed the right wing tank, another shattered his instrument panel, destroying the compass; a third rendered both free guns inoperative. His guns out of action, Wilfred N. McCoy, Sea1c, a tall, young man on his first combat mission, huddled in the rear cockpit, trying to make himself as small as possible, while Smith sought a good dropping point. With *Kaga* swinging around to show her stern to Lindsey's first division, the big carrier began steaming across Smith's path. Picking an aiming point on the ship's starboard side, Smith fired his torpedo. As McCoy reported a true run, the pilot turned across *Kaga*'s bow, heading out to the north. Fortunately, after T-11's torpedo had splashed into the water and begun churning toward the target, the "Zeroes" bothered Smith no more. Once clear of the Japanese formation, and seeing no other friendly planes in the vicinity, he, too, set course for home.

Lindsey's first division, meanwhile, found the going difficult, too. *Kaga*'s turn to the north had left VT-6 well clear of the Japanese screen on her port quarter. While headed northward, Lindsey could see that Ely was well within the Japanese screen, and from the radio transmissions, could hear of his second division's plight. Finally drawing even with *Kaga*, Lindsey turned northeast to commence his attack. Like Ely's men, though, they had just about reached the outer screen when "Zeroes" set upon them. Increasing numbers of the ash-gray fighters, some fresh from the massacre of VT-6's second division, arrived on the scene. Several times, Lindsey sought help from Gray, but to no avail.

Many of the "Zeroes," out of 20-mm. ammunition, though, found it harder to land the killing blow. While the TBDs fought back—William C. Humphrey, ARM1c, radio-gunner in LT(jg) Laub's T-4, flamed one *Akagi* "Zero" that came too close—the odds proved too great. One by one, four TBDs of VT-6's first division cartwheeled into the ocean: only three survived the onslaught—LT(jg) Laub's, ENS Irvin H. McPherson's, and ENS Edward Heck, Jr.'s—and retired unpursued. By 1015, they had all passed beyond the Japanese screen.

Between 0915 and 0940 VT-8 and VT-6 had found the Japanese carriers, each discovering an apparently undamaged enemy. In both air groups, though, the SBDs had left the task force before the TBDs, proceeding at a cruising speed some 20 knots faster, yet the torpedo planes had arrived first. Only VT-6 had observed any signs that the Japanese had been attacked, but only by other torpedo planes. The question of the whereabouts of the dive bombers went unanswered as one TBD after another had slammed into the sea.

Unbeknownst to the brave men in the TBDs, the

route of the SBDs to the scene of battle had been fraught with misfortune. *Hornet*'s group had been the first away from TF 16, heading west on a course of 265 from Midway. Visibility in the area was about 30 miles at 5,000 feet, somewhat less at the higher altitude of the dive bombers. By 0900, however, as the group neared the expected interception point, below stretched only an empty ocean.

At that juncture, VF-8's fuel situation, however, demanded immediate attention. Two of "Pat" Mitchell's pilots had already assessed their dwindling gasoline state—ENSs John McInerny and John Magda, A-V(N)—and had broken for home. The former noted smoke to the southeast, and while thinking that that might betoken the presence of the Japanese, did not have the fuel to investigate.

Mitchell, although perturbed by the insubordinate actions of two junior pilots, soon concurred that VF-8 was in a fix. No enemy lay in sight, but even if one were to appear, the F4Fs had no fuel left for combat maneuvering. The only course open was to try and get home, so, about 0910 Mitchell commenced a shallow turn to starboard, collected his seven remaining F4Fs and followed McInerny and Magda—although because of the opposite direction of the turn (the two ensigns had turned to port) they ended up several miles north of them. Since he could not pick up *Hornet*'s "hayrake" on his ZB gear, Mitchell polled his pilots by Morse hand signals to see who was. Discovering that LT Stanley E. Ruehlow was receiving it, he motioned him to take the lead.

After the abrupt departure of his escort, meanwhile, Ring continued to head west. By 0915 he and his men had reached the intercept point but still could see no enemy ships. Five minutes later, at about 0920, he heard John Waldron announce over the radio that he was attacking. Over the ensuing minutes, other transmissions reflected VT-8's bloody demise.

The CHAG, while leading his men doggedly westward, adopted no search pattern to find the enemy who lay, from Waldron's desperate radio messages, to the southeast. Frustrated, "Ruff" Johnson, given the last known position of the Japanese, turned VB-8 that direction and deployed it in a scouting line. Johnson's plan was sound and his navigation excellent, but Nagumo's turn to the northeast at 0917 had moved the *Kido Butai* 30 miles to the east and resulted in his men passing just west of the Japanese. By 1030 it was clear to VB-8—its numbers reduced by one as ENS Troy Guillory's SBD had shed its reduction gear and compelled him to "ditch"—that they had missed their quarry. Johnson and his men kept searching until shortly before they reached Kure at 1015; still not having found the enemy, they

commenced their return. One section picked up *Hornet*'s YE and shaped a course home; the rest picked up *Enterprise*'s changed YE signal. Unable to find their own ship they set course for Midway instead.

After Johnson's departure, meanwhile, Ring sent his wingman, ENS Fisher, over to VS-8 to tell their squadron CO, LCDR Walter Rodee, to follow him. Rodee did so until 0945 when it became clear he did not have the fuel to keep up a westward course. He turned VS-8 to port and took up an easterly course to return to *Hornet*. CHAG, alone, continued west for several minutes before his dwindling fuel supply forced him to turn for home, too.

Unknowingly, on the outward leg, *Hornet*'s air group had passed about 60 miles north of the Japanese carrier force as it pounded southeast toward Midway. Nagumo's 0917 turn had brought the *Kido Butai* back to the north, and between 1015 and 1030, VS-8 passed some 25 miles north of the Japanese, who remained hidden behind the high altitude overcast. Around 1030, several of the pilots in the rear of the squadron noticed smoke to the south, but believed it came from Midway, which they knew had been under attack that morning!

For Wade McClusky, the mission had not gone smoothly either—the delay in launching the TBDs and F4Fs, and the unexpected signal sending the SBDs on alone. Not only did that leave the dive bombers bereft of any fighter escort, but foiled any chance of a coordinated strike. Setting out on a southwesterly course, the 33 SBDs continued to climb to 19,000 feet. McClusky estimated that his group should sight the Japanese around 0920 after an outbound leg of about 150 miles.

RADM Spruance considered LCDR C. Wade McClusky (seen here 29 January 1942 as CO of VF-6) as "the outstanding hero of the Midway battle." McClusky's decision to press on and seek out the enemy, the admiral declared, "decided the fate of our carrier task force and our forces at Midway . . ." 80-G-464482 (cropped)

The lengthy climb proved difficult for several of the group's aircraft. Unable to coax full power from his engine, LT(jg) Edward L. Anderson had to level his section off 2,000 feet below the rest of VB-6's third division. ENS Eldor Rodenburg, of VS-6, turned back with engine trouble, some 90 miles from home, reaching *Enterprise* at 0930.

When McClusky and the *Enterprise* air group reached the estimated interception point at 0920, meanwhile empty ocean lay beneath them. McClusky checked, and found his navigation sound. During the flight to that point, McClusky had, using binoculars, scanned the horizon from right to left, and had seen no trace of the enemy, whom he had given a rate of advance of 25 knots—the maximum he expected a carrier group to make. Sure that the Japanese could not be to his left, he had kept looking off to his right, feeling that the enemy had changed course to the east or west, or, more likely, had reversed course.

Normally, a situation such as that would have dictated an expanding box search, but McClusky did not feel that his men had the fuel for it. Modifying the procedure, McClusky decided to continue to the southwest, to allow for any westward change of course, head out for 35 miles, then turn to the northwest and fly the reverse of the last known Japanese course. If necessary, he would then turn due east, intending to hold that course until 1000.

Heading northwest, near the end of the leg, at 0955, McClusky spied the wake of what he believed was a cruiser making knots to the northeast. Concluding she was a liaison vessel between the occupation force, known to be to the south, and the striking force, he decided to follow her. The ship pointing like an unerring arrow toward the *Kido Butai* was the destroyer *Arashi* which, having depth charged *Nautilus* for the last time at 0933 and perhaps assuming that she had finally driven off the persistent submersible, was speeding to rejoin Nagumo.

Getting to that point, however, had not been easy. While the fuel gauges of *Enterprise*'s SBDs had long passed the half-way mark, several SBDs in VB-6 were also running out of oxygen. Seeking to save weight so that his SBDs could carry a full load of gas, Best had ordered only two oxygen bottles carried, instead of six. After the turn to the northeast his number two wingman, LT(jg) Edwin J. Kroeger, signalled Best's radio-gunner, Jim Murray, that his gunner was having oxygen problems and he was going to have to drop to a lower altitude. Best, whose aircraft were carrying the 1000-pound bombs, knew he had "lost" several aircraft before leaving, and, not wanting to lose any others, signalled "Bud" Kroeger to hold formation. He brought the whole squadron down to 15,000 feet, and then removed his own oxygen mask to show the other pilots that one did not need oxygen at that altitude—and so he could experience everything they did in case any problems did occur. Best's decision proved to be wise, for at least three other aircraft had oxygen problems and the drop in altitude allowed all four to maintain formation. That drop, however, could not help ENS Tony Schneider, who, although he had had engine trouble from the outset, had unfalteringly continued to hold formation.

As McClusky overtook *Arashi*, his eyes "were practically glued to his binoculars," until, at 1000, about 35 miles ahead, he sighted the wakes of many ships at high speed—an outer screen of destroyers, an inner screen of cruisers and battleships, and, in the center, four carriers. At 1002 McClusky radioed Spruance: "This is McClusky. Have sighted the enemy." In *Enterprise*'s flag shelter, CDR Miles Browning lunged for the microphone and urged McClusky to attack. McClusky had every intention of doing so, but it would take another 15 minutes for him to get in position.

Enterprise's SBDs had been in the air for more than three hours when the ships came into view, and many of McClusky's pilots thought they had returned home. Tony Schneider felt relieved, for after sighting the ships his engine began sputtering from fuel exhaustion, and he started the long glide toward them and a water landing—until he saw a battleship, a type of warship neither TF 16 nor 17 contained. He made a U-turn immediately, intending to land as far from those ships as possible. For the others, the sight of bright yellow flight decks, highlighted by a big red "meatball" forward, dispelled any doubts as to the nationality of the fleet that lay before them!

In the meantime, the Japanese found themselves confronted by a new foe. *Yorktown*'s air group had encountered no such obstacles as those that had vexed *Enterprise*'s and *Hornet*'s, heading out, as planned, southwest by west in three separate elements. The TBDs and F4Fs, at low level, navigated by the whitecaps, and used the convenient clouds to screen their passage. During the long climb to 16,000 feet, Leslie's SBDs had slowed to about 110 knots. In the 45 minutes since TF 16 had launched its strike groups, visibility had improved significantly, enabling "Jimmy" Thach to find and follow the SBDs.

Safely clear of TF 17, about five minutes after departure, Leslie and his men began arming their bombs. "Faulty electrical release connections," though, allowed not only Leslie but three of his pilots, ENSs Isaman, Lane, and Merrill, to accidentally jettison their ordnance into the sea below. Jittery enough anyway, Thach's pilots had their peace of mind tested when one, then another, and two more, geysers of spray shot up from the water below. Leslie—then left with only 13 effective planes—immediately broke radio silence and ordered his pilots to forsake the electrical release and arm their bombs manually.

At 0945, Leslie and Thach caught up with VT-3 as it flew in right echelon formation, at 1,500 feet, with Massey's first division in the lead, LT Patrick H. Hart's second division stepped down behind, with the individual wingmen stepped up on their leaders. Thach motioned MACH Tom Cheek to place his section close astern of the TBDs and about 1,000 feet above as the close escort, and placed his own division 3,000 feet above Cheek. Far above the TBDs, the F4Fs and SBDs, in view of their higher cruising speed, made lazy S-turns to enable them to keep station with the slower torpedo planes.

At 1003, as the *Yorktown* group approached the end of their outbound leg, Lloyd F. Childers, ARM3c, radio-gunner in MACH Harry L. Corl's T-3, spotted three columns of smoke to starboard. He pointed out the smoke to Corl, who then rocked his wings to attract Massey's attention. Massey altered course toward the smoke. Far above, Leslie noted VT-3's movements and, turning to follow, radioed Massey asking, in code, if he had sighted the enemy. Although he received no response, at 1205, his radio-gunner, William E. Gallagher, ARM1c, pointed out the answer to his query: the Japanese lay 25 miles ahead.

Massey led VT-3 in a gradual climb up to 2,600 feet, intending to use a high level approach and trade altitude for speed during a fast glide to the dropping point. While this rendered the TBDs more vulnerable to fighter attack, Massey knew he had Thach and his men to give them support. Torpedo THREE was about 16 miles from the nearest carrier when, at 1010, *Chikuma* signaled *Akagi* that she had spotted 20 American torpedo planes, and fired a salvo from her main battery to direct the CAP toward the new attackers.

When *Chikuma* spotted VT-3, the Japanese were still fending off VT-6's desperate assault on *Kaga*. At 1000, under intense pressure, that carrier had launched six A6M2s to help drive off the stubborn torpedo planes. At the same time, *Soryu* had launched three fighters to intercept Fighting SIX. Several minutes later *Akagi* recovered three "Zeroes" which were low on ammunition, leaving 37 Mitsubishis aloft. Of these, 14 (two from *Akagi* and 12 from *Kaga*) flew on station close to the carriers, 10 (seven from *Akagi* and three from *Soryu*) were pursuing the remnants of VT-6, and the other 13 (three from *Kaga*, seven from *Hiryu*, and three from *Soryu*) were ranging to the southeast. Additionally, *Hiryu* and *Soryu* prepared to launch three A6M2s apiece—these were aloft by 1015.

Directed by *Chikuma*'s bursting shells, the "Zeroes"—including those hounding VT-6's retreating TBDs—began coverging on the *Yorktown*ers. The early arrivals set up Thach's division, which descended, gained maneuvering speed, and attempted to help VT-3. In the

Torpedo THREE's pilots at Kaneohe, 29 May 1942. Kneeling (L-R): ENS David J. Roche, A-V(N); MACH John R. Baker, NAP; LT(jg) Donald E. Weissenborn, A-V(N); to right of map (R-L): LT(jg) Richard W. Suesens; ENS Oswald A. Powers, A-V(N); LT(jg) Fred C. Herriman, A-V(N). Standing (L-R): Wilhelm G. (Bill) Esders, CAP; ENS Carl A. Osberg, A-V(N) ENS Wesley F. Osmus, A-V(N); MACH Harry L. Corl; LT(jg) John N. Myers, A-V(N); RE Werner I. Weis (NAP) in front of ENS Leonard L. Smith, A-V(N); CHMACH John W. Haas, LCDR Lance E. Massey (CO) (pointing at map), ENS Gerald R. Stablein, A-V(N); LT Patrick H. Hart (hatless), ENS John M. Armitage, A-V(N); ENS Otho H. Schneider, A-V(N).
Esders

early stages of that descent, an A6M2 got below and behind the F4Fs and shot down the trailing "Wildcat," piloted by ENS Edgar R. Bassett, A-V(N).

Thach descended to 3,000 feet before it became clear that he and his men might all suffer Bassett's fate if they did not start maneuvering defensively against upwards of 15 "Zeroes" that were carrying out a series of fierce, relentless attacks designed to break up VF-3's formation. He knew their only chance for survival lay in his division's holding on and countering each onslaught.

Initially, the Americans flew in a line astern with Thach leading. As each "Zero" made its run he would turn away from the attack, leaving the Japanese pilot with a difficult full deflection shot. Though effective, it left little opportunity for counterattack and compelled Thach to modify his defense. As before, when the attacking "Zero" neared firing position, VF-3's skipper would turn away and then quickly reverse course. Using this procedure, he got in some long-range shots as the Mitsubishis climbed away. During one attack, the Japanese pilot slowed as he pulled out. Thach, at close range, opened fire, and the A6M2 abruptly stalled and slanted seaward.

LCDR John S. Thach, seen here as CO of VF-3, 5 May 1942, in the cockpit of his "Wildcat." His role in the development of aerial combat tactics (the "Thach Weave") helped the U.S. Navy to fight the superb Mitsubishi "Zeroes" they faced in the Pacific War. 80-G-64822

During the action, while Thach used his beam defense tactic and partially turned the tables on his attackers, that did not entirely relieve the pressure. More and more often, though, the Japanese passed up following their target through the turn rather than face a head-on pass with another F4F, and both Thach and his wingman, ENS R.A.M. Dibb, A-V(N), shot down A6M2s that pressed their attacks too close.

Though Thach's tactics had enabled VF-3 to make the best of a bad situation, the Japanese fighters kept him from fulfilling his primary mission of protecting Massey's TBDs.

Although the first "Zeroes" to arrive jumped Thach's F4Fs, only a short time elapsed before the "Zeroes" were taking on the TBDs. Lloyd Childers, facing aft in T-3, on Massey's right wing, suddenly heard his pilot, Corl, yell in his high-pitched voice, "Up ahead! Up ahead!" The reason for Corl's agitation soon became apparent as Childers saw a "Zero," head-on, apparently intent on passing between T-1 and T-3. The radio-gunner quickly drew a bead on the Mitsubishi with his single .30-caliber machine gun, to snap off a few rounds as the A6M2 flew by, but when he squeezed the trigger nothing happened—he had forgotten to click off the safety.

Astern of VT-3, Tom Cheek saw the same "Zero" flash through Massey's formation and shot him down. He then saw two "Zeroes" on the left of the formation start a run on VT-3's lead section, but, unable to get to them, scared them off by firing ahead of them. The startled Japanese snapped into a steep climb to avoid him. Breaking right, Cheek next chased off an enemy fighter making a beam attack on Massey's trailing section. When he turned back, he saw the TBDs, losing altitude and pulling away from him.

About 14 miles from the nearest enemy carrier, the first "Zeroes" had attacked VT-3. Initially, the squadron held its altitude, only loosening formation to allow the individual aircraft to jink up and down to avoid the Japanese fire. About 10 miles out, however, under mounting pressure from the growing number of "Zeroes," Massey nosed over, gaining speed for the approach to his target. As VT-3 started to lose altitude, it passed underneath a large cloud formation, and disappeared from the view of both Thach and Leslie.

Meanwhile, Cheek, now behind VT-3, saw two A6M2s to the right of VT-3 and headed toward them. As he approached, a "Zero" cut in front of him; he had just about caught up with it when VT-3's radio-gunners sent it spiralling into the ocean in flames. Pulling up, Cheek suddenly found a Mitsubishi on his tail; fortunately, his wingman, ENS Daniel C. Sheedy, A-V(N), had stuck with his section leader through all of his maneuvers, and chased the A6M2 off.

Cheek then noticed that VT-3 had almost disappeared from view below the clouds, but that their formation was still intact except for the last TBD which was afire and falling, a parachute descending in its wake. Hoping to catch VT-3 on the far side, Cheek headed into the clouds, with Sheedy behind him.

Torpedo THREE, well into its descent, lost the tail-end plane to attacking A6M2s. For ENS Wesley F. Osmus, A-V(N), and his radio-gunner, Benjamin R. Dodson, Jr., ARM3c, the end came with fiery swiftness as the TBD's fuel tanks exploded in flames that quickly spread to the cockpit. Still at 1,500 feet, Osmus, his face and hands burnt, had no choice but to bail out. Dodson, either already dead or wounded and unable to extricate himself from the falling aircraft, did (or could) not.

As he followed Cheek, Sheedy found himself the prey of another "Zero" that shot up his cockpit. Wounded in the right shoulder and ankle, most of his instruments gone, and his right landing gear damaged, he ducked his battered F4F into a cloud, hoping to stick with his section leader.

Cheek, meanwhile, emerged from the cottony whiteness into a veritable swarm of ash-gray fighters; he dueled with one in a head-on pass, rolled left, damaged a second with a beam attack, and plunged into the safety of a second cloud. Doubling back to foil any pursuers, he popped out the bottom and found himself alone over the heart of the Japanese fleet. Knowing that his part in this fight was over, and low on the water, dodging antiaircraft bursts, he headed for home.

Emerging from that first cloud, Sheedy, too, found himself alone with a quartet of "Zeroes" chasing him. Wounded, in a shot-up airplane, little remained for Sheedy to do but run. Heading for the water to gain speed, he found an A6M2 ahead. At wave-top height, head-on, the two exchanged fire then, at the last instant, both turned to avoid colliding. As they did so, the "Zero" dipped a wingtip into the ocean and disintegrated upon impact. Alone, but well clear of the Japanese, Sheedy, too, pointed his F4F home.

Shorn of its escort, VT-3 then faced its tormentors alone. Recognizing immediately that *Hiryu* and *Soryu*, the most easterly of Nagumo's carriers, would be the objects of the new American attack, the captains of those two ships had ordered them turned into the wind between 1013 and 1015, and launched three fighters apiece to reinforce the CAP. *Soryu*, the closest to VT-3, then swung to the northwest, showing her stern to it, while *Hiryu* turned back to the northeast.

Thanks mainly to VF3's efforts, Massey's squadron had emerged from the initial interception—with the exception of Osmus—unscathed. While VT-3 had outdistanced many of the A6M2s tangling with its escort, all too soon the prevailing doctrine of torpedo attack compelled the TBDs to level out at 150 feet and drop their airspeed to 110 knots. Almost immediately, two "Zeroes," concentrating on the lead section, hit them.

Maneuvering to avoid the American attack, both *Akagi* and *Soryu* had swung to the northwest leaving

Massey with a long stern chase into the heart of the Japanese formation. Realizing that little chance existed of achieving a good dropping position on his original target, Massey turned to the northeast, trying for the most northerly carrier, *Hiryu*. With a long approach at low speed, "Lem" Massey and his men faced mortal combat with a mounting number of enemy fighters.

Massey had barely started the long run to the north when six to eight A6M2s caught up to the TBDs. The "Zeroes" attacked from all points of the compass in the beginning of what Lloyd Childers called "a melee with about 30 Zeroes going crazy in the most undisciplined, uncoordinated attack that could be imagined . . ." After one of the passes Corl's elevator controls were hit and T-3 started for the water. Believing they were going in, Corl jettisoned his torpedo and, as if talking to himself said, "I think we're going to have to ditch." Minus the torpedo, Corl discovered he could keep the nose up with the tab control, and he rejoined the lead section.

Running parallel with the target, about a mile from the dropping point, the "Zeroes" splashed "Lem" Massey. Hit in the fuel tanks, T-1 erupted in flames. Massey's number two man, Wilhelm G. Esders, CAP, saw the skipper stand up in the cockpit, struggling to avoid the heat. His gunner, Leo E. Perry, ACRM, was still firing at their attacker when the TBD smashed into the sea.

Now leading the squadron, Esders turned into his final run. Even as he did so, another TBD, in flames, hit the water. As the rest of the squadron followed Esders, Corl, having jettisoned his torpedo, broke to the east to get clear. Approaching the dropping point, the five remaining TBDs each fired their "fish" between 600 and 800 out. As Esders fired his, he heard his radio-gunner, Robert B. Brazier, ARM2c, call out over the interphone that he had been hit and could no longer man the guns. After the drop, Esders banked T-2 sharply to the right and headed east, clearing *Hiryu* by several hundred yards. The other four TBDs crossed the carrier's bow, one crashing into the sea, the "Zeroes" still making runs on them. Soon the others, too, were gone.

Like the stirring response attributed to John Paul Jones, Harry Corl and Bill Esders had just begun to fight—getting clear of the Japanese fleet lay ahead of them. About three miles from the carrier, two A6M2s immediately started making runs on T-3. For 10 minutes, Corl and Childers endured repeated, alternating high-side attacks. Initially they came from the rear, but Childers accurate fire soon discouraged them and they switched to runs from abeam or from the forward quarter. Although Corl jinked and skidded to throw off the enemy's aim, the Japanese scored numerous hits on T-3. On one of the beam attacks, two 7.7-mm.

bullets hit Childers in the left leg. Minutes later, while trying to shoot at an attacker coming from up forward, he was hit by another 7.7-mm. round above the right ankle, breaking bones in his leg. In agony from his last wound, Childers continued to man his gun until it jammed. Watching the A6M2s attack again, one from the left and the other from the right, he struggled to clear the gun, but without success. As the two came in yet again, he pulled out his .45-caliber pistol and, in desperation, fired a half a clip at each one. Having exhausted his ammunition, Childers observed what he took to be a miracle: the "Zeroes" left!

Bill Esders encountered a similar situation. As he turned east after dropping his torpedo, two "Zeroes," joined soon thereafter by another pair, jumped T-2 almost immediately. With Brazier seriously wounded and unable to defend the plane from the rear, Esders knew that the responsibility of keeping the plane in the air lay with him. A month earlier, "Jimmy" Thach had lectured the VT-3 pilots on how best to survive being caught alone by enemy fighters. Now, following Thach's advice, Esders descended to only 20 feet over the water and slowed T-2 to 85 knots. Watching each "Zero" start its run, he would wait for the enemy to open fire and try to "walk" his bullets across the water into the TBD. Just as they were about to hit, he would turn into the attacker, spoiling the Japanese pilot's aim. Having gained speed in its dive, the "Zero" was forced to over-shoot or risk stalling into the water. The four Mitsubishis pursued Esders for more than 15 miles until, one by one, they broke away. Finally, only one adversary remained. Slowing down as much as he dared, the Japanese flew along on Esders' port side, and in a gesture of chivalry amidst a conflict very much devoid of it, raised his right hand and waved. Having acknowledged the unknown American's skill, the "Zero" snapped into a climb and headed back whence he had come.

An excerpt from LCDR "Jimmy" Thach's action report concerning VF-3's escorting Torpedo THREE's TBDs at Midway. "Six (6) F4F-4 airplanes," he declared, "cannot prevent 20 or 30 Japanese VF [fighters] from shooting our slow torpedo planes. It is indeed surprising," he marveled, "that any of our pilots returned alive."

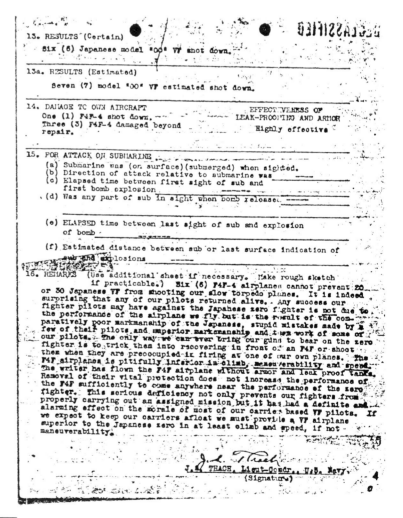

Editor's Note: See Appendix (Ewing and Tillman) for further comments on Ring, Esders, Gay, Waldron and others as well as treatment of the new F4F wildcat's problems at Midway.

-100-

CHAPTER TEN

. . . .

"...Like a Haystack in Flames"

Although he had emerged from the American onslaught unscathed, Nagumo found his orderly formation in disarray; *Soryu* had been pulling ahead of *Akagi* and *Kaga*—although her recent excursion to the west to avoid VT-3 had brought her back toward *Akagi*—while *Hiryu*, pounding north at 30 knots to get away from the same squadron, ended up on the horizon, barely visible from the flagship. The carriers stretched in a ragged line from *Kaga* to the south to *Hiryu* in the northeast.

Nagumo had had to recover his Midway strike planes, some of which had been damaged and all low on fuel. Those had had to be struck below and planes earmarked for the second strike brought to the flight deck; since he had ordered the shift in ordnance, weapons that would normally have been stowed below were shunted off to the side on the hangar decks—a violation of safety regulations that had been overlooked in view of the need for haste. Nagumo might have delayed landing the first attack group, but to do so would have meant that some planes would have been lost; knowing he had very few spares, he apparently minimized what danger one carrier could pose to his four.

Since completing recovery operations at 0938, the Japanese had been working frantically to get a strike group ready to seek out the American carrier. By 1020 the work was almost done: on *Akagi*'s flight deck sat six *kansen* and 18 *kanko*; in both *Hiryu* and *Soryu*, the crews were in the process of bringing six *kansen* and 18 *kanbaku* up to the flight decks. Of *Kaga*'s group, her 27 *kanko* were ready, but the gallant attack of the TBDs had compelled her to divert her escort fighters to reinforce the CAP.

Arashi, the ship whose wake had attracted Wade McCluskey's attention, was returning to the *Kido Butai* when she spotted a man in the water. She hove to and lowered a boat, whose crew soon picked up an Amer-

ican pilot: ENS Osmus, whose TBD had been shot down during the Torpedo THREE's approach to the Japanese fleet. The initial interrogation yielded information on who their captive was, and where he was from. His wounds were treated and he was fed. Soon, however, *Arashi* would be near the *Kido Butai*, where events there would ultimately bode ill for the stocky young man who hailed from Chicago.

The massacre of the squadron in which Osmus had flown, VT-3, and the desperate battle of Thach's escorts, however, had not been in vain, because their travail had left the skies open to McClusky's 32 SBDs, rapidly approaching from the southwest. The CEAG, who had just radioed his contact report to Spruance, could see four carriers, but didn't think that his planes could sink or disable more than two. Deciding to attack the two closest carriers (*Kaga* and *Akagi*), he instructed Gallaher to attack the left-hand CV with VS-6 and Best to attack the right-hand CV with VB-6. He attached his three planes to Gallaher's, and added: "Earl, follow me down."

Dick Best knew which target was his. An expert dive bomber pilot (unlike McClusky, who had, up until recently, flown fighters), well-versed in bomber doctrine, he knew that VB-6 should take the closer ("left-hand") carrier while VS-6 took the one further away (the "right-hand" carrier), so the targets would come under attack at the same time and split the antiaircraft fire. He radioed McClusky: "Group commander from six baker one. Am attacking according to doctrine." Best and McClusky, however, were apparently sending their respective messages simultaneously, for neither received the other's intentions. Unknowingly, both VB-6 and VS-6 were beginning a shallow ascent toward the same target.

During the high-speed run to the pushover point, Best and Gallaher deployed their squadrons, first division in the center, second to port, and third to starboard, to split the antiaircraft fire. No matter which way the target turned, someone would end up diving down the length of the target.

One remarkable fact struck each *Enterprise* pilot at that juncture: the lack of Japanese fighters. In the prevailing excellent visibility over the heart of the enemy fleet, none had molested VB-6 and VS-6. They had heard some radio chatter from VT-6 earlier and it looked like there was a torpedo attack in progress at that point, but no fighters had come their direction.

Dick Best, VB-6 up-sun of the target, had just started to push the stick forward when several blue blurs streaked by ahead of him. Hauling back, Best realized that McClusky was diving on *his* target. Closing his dive flaps and flicking his elevators up and down, he gave the "close up" signal.

CEAG Section (USS *Enterprise* CV-6)

GC LCDR C.W. McClusky Jr./Chochalousek, W.G., ARM1c
S-8 ENS W.R. Pittman, A-V(N)/Adkins, F.D., AMM2c
S-11 ENS R.A. Jaccard, A-V(N)/Pixley, P.W., RM3c

Scouting Squadron SIX

First Division

S-1 LT W.E. Gallaher/Merritt, T.E., ACRM(AA)
S-2 ENS R.W. Stone, A-V(N)/Bergin, W.H., RM1c
S-3 ENS J.Q. Roberts, A-V(N)/Swindell, T.R., AOM1c
S-7 LT(jg) N.J. Kleiss/Snowden, J.W., RM3c
S-18 ENS C.E. Dexter, A-V(N)/Hoff, D.L., RM3c

Second Division

S-10 LT C.E. Dickinson Jr./DeLuca, J.R., ARM1c
S-15 ENS J.R. McCarthy, A-V(N)/Howell, J.E., RM2c
S-12 ENS C.D. Peiffer, A-V(N)/Jeck, F.C., RM3c
S-16 LT(jg) J.N. West/Stitzelberger, A.R., RM2c
S-17 ENS V.L. Micheel, A-V(N)/Dance, J.D., RM3c
S-14 ENS J.C. Lough, A-V(N)/Hansen, L.D., RM2c

Third Division

S-4 LT C.R. Ware/Stambaugh, W.H., ARM1c
S-5 ENS F.W. O'Flaherty, A-V(N)/Gaido, B.F., AMM1c
S-6 ENS J.A. Shelton, A-V(N)/Craig, D.W., RM3c

Bombing Squadron SIX

First Division

B-1 LT R.H. Best/J.F. Murray, ACRM(PA)
B-2 LT(jg) E.J. Kroeger/Halterman, G.W., RM3c
B-3 ENS F.T. Weber, A-V(N)/Hilbert, E.L., AOM3c
B-5 LT(jg) W.E. Roberts, A-V(N)/Steinman, W.B., AMM1c
B-6 ENS D.W. Halsey, A-V(N)/Jenkins, J.W., RM3c

Second Division

B-7 LT J.R. Penland/Heard, J.F., ARM2c
B-8 ENS T.F. Schneider, A-V(N)/Holden, G.L., ARM2c
B-9 ENS E.A. Greene, A-V(N)/Muntean, S.A., RM3c
B-11 ENS T.A. Ramsey, A-V(N)/Duncan, S.L. ARM2c
B-12 ENS L.A. Hopkins, A-V(N)/Anderson, E.R., RM3c

Third Division

B-13 LT(jg) J.J. VanBuren/Nelson, H.W. Jr., ARM1c
B-14 ENS N.F. Vandivier, A-V(N)/Keaney, L.E.J., Sea1c
B-15 ENS G.H. Goldsmith, A-V(N)/Patterson, J.M. Jr., ARM3c
B-16 LT(jg) E.L. Anderson/Mason, S.J. Jr., ARM2c
B-18 ENS B.S. Varian Jr., A-V(N)/Young, C.R., ARM3c

At 1022, McClusky abruptly pushed over into this dive—a sudden move that surprised his number two man, ENS William R. Pittman, who had expected to dive last so that he and ENS Richard A. Jaccard—whose SBDs had been fitted with cameras—could photograph the results of the attack. Seeing Pittman pause, Jaccard followed the CEAG, and, in combat for the first time, accidentally lowered his wheels instead of opening his dive flaps! Pittman brought up the rear.

Gallaher, following McClusky, led VS-6's 14 SBDs practically through VB-6's formation. In the confusion, although most of Best's pilots missed his signal to reform, LT Joe Penland, leader of the second division, did not. Penland saw Best abort his dive, but unsure that Best meant for everyone to follow him, delayed his dive momentarily. Then, noticing a lot of misses on the carrier below, he decided to attack her. Bombing SIX's second and third divisions, as well as Best's second section—11 SBDs in all—were soon following McClusky in his dive.

Descending toward *Kaga* at five-second intervals, the 28 SBDs were well into their dives before the Japanese spotted them, opened up with their antiaircraft guns, and began taking evasive action which caused the first three bombs to miss her.

The fourth bomb, however, hit squarely. Earl Gallaher's plunged into the flight deck aft, amidst *Kaga*'s fully fueled and armed *kanko*. As he pulled out, Gallaher violated his own rule by looking back to see the results of his attack. As he saw the explosions blossom up from *Kaga*'s deck, he said to himself, "*Arizona*, I remember you"—he had been one of the *Enterprise* air group pilots flying into Pearl Harbor on 7 December 1941, and had seen what Japanese bombs had done to the first ship he had served in upon graduation from the Naval Academy.

After Gallaher, ENS Reid W. Stone missed to port. Then came ENS John Q. Roberts, who had begged Gallaher to allow him to fly the mission, declaring: "I'll see that my bomb hits even if I have to take it aboard." His SBD evidently damaged by flak, Roberts released his bomb but never pulled out. Following behind him, LT(jg) "Dusty" Kleiss saw Roberts' S-3 hit the water several hundred yards to starboard of *Kaga*. Roberts and his radio-gunner, Thurman R. Swindell, AOM1c, died instantly.

Seeing Gallaher's bomb turn the after end of the target into a sea of flames, "Dusty" Kleiss shifted his aim to the big red "meatball" forward. He released his 500-pounder at 1,500 feet; his two 100-pound incendiaries at 1,000. Looking over his shoulder as he pulled out, he saw the blast as his bomb hit abreast the forward elevator. Shortly after his radio-gunner, Snowden, had scared off a "Zero" that attempted to shoot them down, Kleiss noticed a second carrier in trouble; an awesome sight, it looked "like a haystack in flames." ENS James C. Dexter's bomb hit a refueling cart parked in front of *Kaga*'s island and the resulting explosion bathed the bridge in flaming gasoline; among those severely burned was the carrier's captain.

The second division leader, LT Clarence E. Dickinson Jr., dove on *Kaga*'s port side from abaft the beam and put his bomb amidships. One-by-one the rest followed, and while it is unclear how many more bombs may have hit *Kaga*, VS-6 claimed three more and VB-6

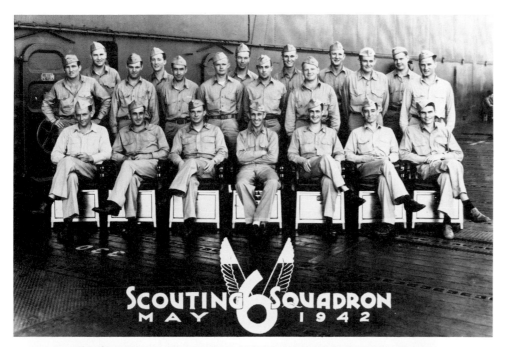

Pilots of Scouting SIX, on board *Enterprise*, 12 May 1942. Seated (L-R): LT(jg) J. Norman West; LT Frank A. Patriarca, LT Charles R. Ware, LT Wilmer E. Gallaher (CO), LT Clarence E. Dickinson, Jr., LT(jg) Norman J. "Dusty" Kleiss, ENS John R. McCarthy, A-V(N).Second row (standing) (L-R): ENSs [all A-V(N)] John Q. Roberts, Carl D. Peiffer, James A. Shelton, William R. Pittman, John C. Lough, Vernon L. Micheel, Eldor E. Rodenburg, Thomas F. Durkin, Jr., Richard A. Jaccard, Frank W. O'Flaherty, Clarence E. Vammen, Jr., James C. Dexter, Reid W. Stone, William P. West. 80-G-71989

Pilots of Bombing SIX, on board *Enterprise*, 3 June 1942. Seated (L-R): LT(jg) Edward L. Anderson, LT Harvey P. Lanham, LT Lloyd A. Smith (XO), LT Richard H. Best (CO), LT Joe R. Penland, LT Horace R. Moorehead, Jr., A-V(S); LT(jg) John J. Van Buren. Standing (L-R) [all A-V(N)]: ENS Eugene A. Greene, ENS George H. Goldsmith, ENS Stephen C. Hogan, Jr., ENS Norman F. Vandivier, ENS Don L. Ely, LT(jg) Wilbur E. Roberts, ENS Lewis A. Hopkins, LT(jg) Edwin J. Kroeger, ENS Delbert W. Halsey, ENS Frederick T. Weber, ENS Thomas W. Ramsey, ENS Tony F. Schneider, ENS Bertram S. Varian, Jr., ENS Arthur L. Rausch, ENS Harry W. Liffner. Goldsmith via Horan

Bel Geddes reconstruction of the attack by Bombing SIX and Scouting SIX on *Akagi* and *Kaga* on 4 June. 80-G-701869

at least two. The Japanese gave up counting after Dickinson's hit, for *Kaga*, her air group trapped on deck, was clearly doomed. Violent secondary explosions, triggered by aviation fuel and torpedo warheads, ripped the ship's vitals. Among those who died a fiery death in *Kaga*'s travail were four senior officers from her air unit: LCDR Tadashi Kusumi, her air unit commander; LT Shoichi Ogawa, her carrier bomber squadron CO, and two *buntaicho* (division officers), LT Minoru Fukuda and LT Ryotaka Mikami.

After having gathered what he could of his squadron, Dick Best turned to starboard and sped northeast for the next carrier. Approaching his new target as she headed into the wind to launch planes, Best, again upsun, saw neither antiaircraft fire nor "Zeroes." Then, after checking the spacing of his remaining planes, he barked over the radio: "Don't let this carrier escape."

At 1026, as *Akagi* began to pass under the leading edge of B-1's wing, Best started the routine: pull back the throttle, split the dive flaps, put the propeller into full pitch, switch the mixture to full rich, put the carburetor heat on, push the stick forward to start the dive, kick the nose aside so he could see the target, then ease her over to vertical and use the aileron for any course corrections, and adjust the tab as the speed increases. In every practice dive, he had done it exactly this way. Murray sang out every loss of 1,000 feet. At 3,500 feet Best pulled back on the stick, easing B-1 back to a 70 degree dive, and started to look for his aiming point in the three-power telescopic sight. Centering the crosshairs on a point abreast the bridge, in the middle of the flight deck, Best pulled the release at 1,500 feet and felt the welcome surge as the bomb fell free.

Behind Best, at 150-foot intervals, came his wingmen, LT(jg) "Bud" Kroeger and ENS Fred T. Weber. Following Best all the way, they, too, dropped at 1,500 feet and pulled out. Best's bomb penetrated *Akagi*'s amidships elevator and exploded on the hangar deck, detonating torpedoes and bombs carelessly stowed there. Kroeger's penetrated the port edge of the flight deck and exploded in the sea alongside. Weber's landed well aft amidst *Akagi*'s spotted *kanko*, wrecked water mains, and jammed the ship's rudder. Soon, *Akagi*, like *Kaga*, was afire throughout her length.

While McClusky's dive bombers had been coming up from the southwest, several miles to the east came VB-3. Shortly after sighting the Japanese, Leslie had overheard radio chatter concerning fighters attacking VT-3, and soon afterward, that squadron had disappeared from view below the scattered clouds. At 1015, having received no message from Massey that he had started his attack, Leslie turned to the north, delaying so that he could coordinate with the torpedo planes.

LCDR Tadashi Kusumi, *Kaga*'s air unit commander, who had led *Hiryu*'s *kanko* in the first attack wave at Pearl Harbor, perished in *Kaga*'s blazing demise. Prange

LT Shoichi Ogawa, who had led *Kaga*'s *kanbaku* in the second attack wave at Pearl Harbor, also did not escape the destruction visited upon *Kaga* by *Enterprise*'s SBDs. Prange

At 1020, Leslie radioed Massey, asking if he was ready to commence his attack, to which VT-3's skipper had responded in the affirmative. Moments later, though, Massey's voice came over the radio again, frantically calling for fighter support.

Deciding to go after the easternmost of the three carriers—*Soryu*—Leslie signalled VB-3 to deploy, and began descending to 14,500 feet. At 1023, the enemy carrier began a turn to starboard and soon settled on a course into the wind; Leslie's radioman reported that it looked as if she was starting to launch planes. At 1025, Leslie patted his head, the signal for the squadron to follow, pushed forward on the stick, and entered his dive. At 10,000 feet, he opened fire with his fixed .50-caliber guns, aiming at the carrier's bridge; he continued strafing until they jammed at 4,000 feet.

"Diving from the north," all of Leslie's pilots "had a steady dive along the fore and aft line of the target." LT(jg) Paul A. Holmberg, then in the lead, pulled both the manual and electrical releases for his bomb, which plummeted down to explode "directly in the midst" of the 18 *kanbaku* spotted forward; one Type 99 cartwheeled over the side in the force of the explosion. As Holmberg pulled out at 200 feet, his excited radio-gunner yelled: "It's a HIT!"

LT Harold S. Bottomley steadied his telescopic sight on his aiming point and pressed the electrical bomb release at 2,500 feet, before he reached down and pulled the manual release just to make sure he got rid of his bomb. Flattening out at 500 feet, he slammed his throttle wide and switched off the carburetor heat, adjusted the trim for the loss of the weight of the bomb, and headed for open water. As B-10 raced for a hole in the screen, Bottomley heard his radioman, Daniel F. Johnson, AMM2c, shout: "We got her!" Unable to resist the temptation, Bottomley glanced aft "to see the target completely enveloped in flames as bombs explode[d] in the pack of massed aircraft."

ENS Charles S. Lane, one of those who had lost his bomb, machine-gunned *Soryu* all the way down in his dive. LT DeWitt W. Shumway, VB-3's XO and the third division leader, saw at least "five direct hits and three very near misses" on *Soryu* that transformed her into a mass of flames, smoke, and confusion.

Japanese reports confirm three direct hits: one amidships, one forward of the forward elevator, and one near the after elevator, amongst the spotted aircraft. Explosions destroyed fire mains, and touched off fires that soon enveloped the ship, detonating bomb and torpedo magazines, machine gun ammunition and gasoline. By 1040, her engines had stopped; unmaneuverable, the doomed ship was ordered abandoned at 1045. Her captain, CAPT Ryusaku Yanagimoto, ordered his men to seek their own safety, and would allow no man to approach him. The flames soon enveloped him, too, as he shouted "banzais" to the end.

Correctly believing the carrier doomed, LT Osborne B. Wiseman and ENS John C. Butler, A-V(N), attacked a nearby battleship, claiming a hit on her stern and a near-miss. ENSs Robert M. Elder, Randy Cooner, and Milford A. Merrill (the last *sans* bomb), dove on what they took to be a light cruiser—actually the destroyer *Isokaze*—and claimed a hit on her fantail and a near-miss.

LT(jg) Paul A. Holmberg, USNA Class of 1939, who won a Navy Cross at Midway; he scored the first hit on *Soryu*.
Holmberg

Bombing Squadron THREE

FIRST DIVISION
B-1 LDCR M. F. Leslie/Gallagher, W. E., ARM1c
B-2 LT(jg) P. A. Holmberg/LaPlant, G. A., AMM2c
B-3 ENS P. W. Schlegel, A-V(N)/Shropshire, J. A., ARM2c
B-4 ENS R. K. Campbell, A-V(N)/Craig, H. H., AMM1c
B-5 ENS A. W. Hanson, A-V(N)/Godfrey, J. J., ARM3c
B-6 ENS R. H. Benson, A-V(N)/Bergeron, F. P., ARM3c

SECOND DIVISION
B-7 LT(jg) G. A. Sherwood/Bennett, H. D., ARM2c
B-8 ENS R. M. Isaman, A-V(N)/Weaver, S. K., ARM3c
B-9 ENS P. W. Cobb, A-V(N)/Zimmershead, C. E., AMM2c
B-10 LT H. S. Bottomley, Jr./Johnson, D. F., ARM2c
B-11 ENS C. S. Lane, A-V(N)/Henning, J. L., ARM2c
B-12 ENS J. C. Butler, A-V(N)/Berg, D. D., ARM3c

THIRD DIVISION
B-13 LT D. W. Shumway/Coons, R. E., ARM1c
B-14 ENS R. M. Elder, A-V(N)/Till, L. H., RM3c
B-15 ENS B. R. Cooner, A-V(N)/Bassett, C. R., ADM2c
B-16 LT(jg) O. B. Wiseman/Dawn, G. U., ARM3c
B-17 ENS M. A. Merrill, A-V(N)/Bergeron, D. J., RM3c

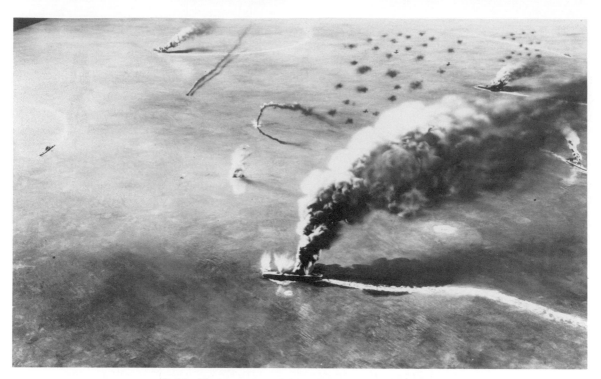

Bel Geddes' depiction of the attack on *Hiryu*. 80-G-701885

Pilots of Bombing THREE relax on board *Enterprise* (CV-6), April 1942, on temporary duty in that ship, as they spelled Scouting SIX, which had suffered heavy losses in the early raids. Front (L-R): ENS John Q. Roberts, A-V(N)*; LT Ralph W. Arndt; LT DeWitt W. Shumway (XO), LCDR Maxwell F. Leslie (CO); LT Harold S. Bottomley Jr.; ENS John C. Lough, A-V(N)*. Rear (L-R): LT(jg) Gordon A. Sherwood; ENS Roy M. Isaman, A-V(N); ENS John C. Butler, A-V(N); ENS John Bridgers, A-V(N); ENS Robert M. Elder, A-V(N); ENS Carl D. Peiffer, A-V(N)*; ENS Charles S. Lane, A-V(N); ENS Bunyan R. Cooner, A-V(N); ENS Robert K. Campbell, A-V(N); ENS Paul W. Schlegel, A-V(N), USNR; ENS Frank W. O'Flaherty, A-V(N)*. (*Indicates on temporary duty from VS-6. Ironically, all four would be lost at the Battle of Midway, in VS-6, on 4 June). NH 95555

The arrival of the SBDs had caught the Japanese in the midst of frantically recalling the fighters chasing VT-3 and engaging Thach's F4Fs. Unfortunately for the enemy, nightmarish radio conditions—some 40 pilots in the air all using the same frequency—hindered his ability to vector planes to the new attackers. Many of the "Zero" pilots' first indication of trouble was the smoke from the burning carriers that instantly alerted them to the latest threat. Soon, most of the "Zeroes" not actually engaging VT-3 were charging in from the south and east to take on the SBDs.

Attacking from the northwest, VB-3's pilots pulled out to the south of Soryu and immediately started their retirement. Briefed to head toward Midway, Leslie headed southeast after pullout. Slipping by the "Zeroes" engaging Thach and Cheek, he arrived at the squadron rendezvous and began circling. Joined soon thereafter by ENS Aldon W. Hanson, Leslie started for home after a Japanese destroyer started shooting in their direction.

The rest of VB-3 had encountered surprisingly heavy antiaircraft fire during pullout that, while it caused little damage, forced most of the pilots to the east to avoid it. With Leslie missing, LT Shumway gathered 10 of the squadron's SBDs, that, in retiring north of Thach's fight and well south of the "Zeroes" splashing Massey's TBDs, had clear sailing. Only ENS Roy M. Isaman in B-8 encountered any aerial opposition—a Type 95 floatplane on anti-submarine patrol—that he outran.

"Lefty" Holmberg had noted that his plane had been hit in the dive, and noticed fluid spilling into his cockpit after pullout. Waiting for his engine to seize, he was surprised when it kept purring smoothly. Having an aviation machinist's mate as a radio-gunner, Holmberg asked him was could be wrong. LaPlant responded that since the oil pressure was steady, it had to be the hydraulic fluid. They could get home after all.

Pulling out west of Akagi, Dick Best dodged his way through the Japanese screen and re-formed his section, then turned to the east to start his retirement. Soon thereafter, a "Zero" attempted to get on Best's tail, but Jim Murray drove off the A6M2 with a burst from his twin .30-calibers. Continuing his climb to 3,000 feet, Best turned southeast, following his instructions to retire toward Midway until clear of the enemy.

During the turn, ENS Weber began to straggle and was soon some 600 yards behind the other two SBDs when one of the Type 95 floatplanes on anti-submarine patrol jumped him. Too far back for the gunners in the other SBDs to support him, Weber benefited from the fact that his opponent was not a "Zero." He was able to avoid the two passes the Japanese pilot made and scuttle back into formation. He was able to clear the enemy without further incident. When he returned to the ship later, he swore to Best that he would never straggle again!

McClusky and VS-6 enjoyed no such good fortune. Enterprise's pilots had been briefed to retire to the southeast, toward Midway, until they were well clear of the enemy before turning for home. Recovering from their dives west of Kaga, the SBDs headed through the inner screen, then turned to port to head southeast. Unfortunately, this led the retiring SBDs into the midst of the "Zeroes" swarming to the defense of their carriers.

Retiring at wave top height and full throttle, McClusky managed to break through the screen without any damage, only to discover that not only had he lost both of his wingmen, but that three carriers—not two—lay burning.

Assuming that Hornet's pilots had hit the third one, he had just determined his return course when a stream of tracers laced the water in front of him. McClusky's glancing astern, as Chochalousek returned the fire, yielded the sight of two "Zeroes." A former fighter pilot, the CEAG knew how to handle himself—staying 20 feet off the water, he watched each "Zero" commit himself before he then wrapped the SBD into a steep turn into the attacker, presenting the latter with a difficult full deflection shot and giving Chochalousek a clear field of fire. For five minutes the A6M2s pursued, until one of them caught GC with a burst that holed the left side of the cockpit.

McClusky, feeling as if his "left shoulder was hit with a sledge hammer," and sure it was the end, after several seconds of silence yelled to Chochalousek and asked if he was OK. Receiving no answer he painfully turned to look and discovered that his unscathed gunner had shot down the "Zero" that had hit them and forced the other to give up the chase. They were fortunate. Their SBD had been hit 55 times.

Floyd D. Adkins, AMM2c, ENS Pittman's radio-gunner, experienced an adventure during the dive on Kaga. As the SBD plunged down, Adkins' twin .30-calibers broke loose from the ring; grabbing the guns, he pulled them into his lap. As S-8 pulled out, though, the G-forces jammed the gun barrels into the housing that held them when they were not in use. After freeing them, Adkins unbuckled his seat belt, stood up, and tried to work the Brownings back onto the gun ring against the slipstream. Still toiling at that task, Adkins glanced up; seeing a "Zero" starting a run, he immediately informed Pittman that they had a fighter on their tail and advised taking evasive action because the free guns might be ineffective. Knowing the Japanese pilot would break to the right, Adkins pushed his guns onto the right edge of the rear cockpit and as the "Zero" zoomed past, poured in a telling burst that sent it slanting toward the water.

Pittman and Adkins, however, were not out of the proverbial woods yet, since S-8 had been hit several times, including a 20-mm. hit that blew a hole the size of a soccer ball in the almost-empty starboard inboard fuel tank. More importantly, however, Pittman had little idea where *Enterprise* was. He headed east, hoping he would run into some friendly planes on the way, and soon spotted two SBDs up ahead. Drawing nearer he recognized S-1, the CO's aircraft, along with ENS Stone's S-2. He slipped into position on Gallaher's wing. Their number soon grew as, first ENS Jaccard, and then, much later, ENS Campbell, joined up. Together they set course to the northeast.

Pulling out of his dive, "Dick" Dickinson, leading VS-6's second division, saw three "Zeroes" charging in from his starboard side several hundred feet below him. Realizing his predicament if they headed for him, he frantically pulled the lever to close his dive flaps to increase his speed. The first two "Zeroes" headed by, chasing some first division SBDs, but the third pulled into a zoom climb and turned to get on S-10's tail. As the "Zero" flashed in, Joseph F. DeLuca, ARM1c, Dickinson's gunner, fired and turned the Japanese away.

Free of the "Zero," Dickinson noticed a destroyer off to his right, firing at them. The ship had his range but, strangely, her shells were bursting well in front of the SBD, due to the fact that, instead of 220 knots, he was barely doing 95. Apparently, moisture in the dive flap hinges had frozen during the long dive from high altitude and locked his flaps fully open. A veritable comedy of errors ensued as Dickinson jammed on full throttle and pulled every lever in the cockpit trying to get them loose. By the time Dickinson had regained his airspeed the rest of the squadron had passed him.

Suddenly, spying a "Zero" stalking another SBD, Dickinson banked in behind the Japanese and opened fire, forcing him to abandon his attack. After scaring off the A6M2, though, Dickinson found himself alone. Low on fuel, too, he could not afford to open up on the throttle to catch up with several SBDs he could see well ahead of him. All he could do was throttle back and hope he had enough gas to reach TF 16.

Pulling out of his dive at 500 feet, behind Dickinson, ENS John R. "Charlie" McCarthy saw the "Zeroes" he had expected before push-over. As Dickinson's number two man, he initially considered rejoining his division leader, but the latter had lost so much airspeed he found it virtually impossible to stay with him. His radio-gunner, however, Earl E. Howell, ARM2c, called out that there was a "Zero" climbing onto their tail, prompting McCarthy to give up on Dickinson and head for the water. When the Japanese was committed to his

firing pass, Howell called out for McCarthy to break left, and then cut loose with his free guns. McCarthy heard a few bursts from Howell's guns, then the radio-gunner's voice over the intercom: "I think I got him!" Sure enough, as he broke back to the right to continue away from the Japanese carrier, McCarthy saw the "Zero" on fire and turning upwind to make a water landing.

Alone, McCarthy started looking for other SBDs in the area that he could join, and soon spotted some attempting to form up under heavy "Zero" attack, and hastened to join them. By the time he arrived, the first section was already closed up, and he recognized LT Charles R. Ware—Scouting SIX's flight officer and an experienced pilot, well-versed in section defensive tactics—in the lead.

On temporary duty with VS-6, Ware had served in *Yorktown*'s VS-5 under LCDR William O. Burch, who had taught his pilots fighter tactics to enable them to survive in aerial combat. Some of Burch's students had done well at Coral Sea, and Ware put *his* instruction to good use at Midway. Nominally the third division leader, he had lost his second section when Patriarca had been unable to take off and Lough had been shifted to the second division. Pulling out of the dive in a veritable sky full of "Zeroes," Ware's first action had been to rally his section, as well as any other SBDs, in the area; he soon drew four SBDs to him. By the time McCarthy arrived, Ware had formed the first section with ENSs James A. Shelton and Carl D. Peiffer on his wing. Since McCarthy was the next senior in both rank and experience, the other two SBDs, flown by ENSs Frank W. O'Flaherty and John C. Lough, formed the trailing section on him. Like McCarthy, both Peiffer and Lough were part of the second division, but with Dickinson *hors de combat* they had rallied to Ware, trusting the veteran to lead them to safety.

With "Zeroes" swarming above the formation in ever increasing numbers, Ware led his planes down to the deck, and slowed to conserve fuel. Following the same pattern they had used while fighting Thach's F4Fs, the Japanese initiated a series of individual high speed firing passes. When a Japanese pilot committed himself to the attack, Ware responded by turning into him while McCarthy slid his section to the outside of the turn, opening a clear field of fire for the six rear gunners. By staying close to the water, Ware denied the Japanese pilots the opportunity to press their attacks close and recover under the SBDs' unprotected bellies. Faced with the concentrated fire of 12 .30-calibers, a "Zero" pilot inevitably broke off his attack.

Although the division had suffered little damage, ammunition and, most importantly, gasoline, became critical. Using Morse hand signals, Ware's division compared their fuel counts, and the watchwords became "conserve fuel, conserve ammo." After the long search to find the enemy and the long air battle, all pilots were low on fuel.

Even in the face of the fighter attacks, Ware had managed to maintain a base course to the southeast. After a 12-15 minute running fight with the "Zeroes," his makeshift division had managed to cover eight miles and clear the Japanese screen, beyond which the attacks finally subsided. Ware followed his instructions and headed toward Midway only after he was well clear of the *Kido Butai*. Much time elapsed as the division circled the enemy fleet, during which time they climbed to 1,200 feet. Free of the weight of bombs, and having burned up much fuel, Ware's SBDs were almost as nimble as fighters. Free of the "Zeroes," it was then a matter of trying to relax and get as close to home as they could.

Hard on the heels of the scouts had been the 11 SBDs of Bombing SIX that had bombed *Kaga*, led by LT Joe R. Penland of VB-6's second division. As he pulled out of his dive at 500 feet, his radio-gunner, Harold F. Heard, ARM2c, called his attention to the fact that the dive flaps were still open. Also frozen by a moisture buildup, several seconds—enough time for B-7 to lose all speed gained in the dive—elapsed before Penland could get them closed. A "Zero" attacked the SBD as the pilot was still struggling with the locked flaps. Fearing a low-level running battle, Penland pushed the throttle forward and climbed. Soon, three "Zeroes" were taking turns attacking the SBD, as the pilot put his aircraft into every twist and turn he knew how to make. Although Heard put up a stout defense with his free guns, the Japanese managed to get close enough to perforate B-7's wings with enough 20-mm. holes to begin draining the fuel tanks. His controls undamaged, though, Penland eventually reached the safety of a cloud formation.

When he emerged from the far side of the whiteness, the "Zeroes" were gone. Penland did spot another SBD heading their way, however, and throttled back to allow it to join up. Soon the third division leader, LT(jg) John J. Van Buren, in B-13, slid up alongside. With B-7's life blood flowing out of the punctured fuel tanks, it was obvious to both pilots that Penland was going to be in the air for only a few more minutes. Van Buren signaled Penland he'd stick with him. About five minutes later, B-7's tanks ran dry and Penland started toward the water. Losing altitude steadily, he turned into the wind on his final approach. Although busy with the preparations for ditching, Penland noticed Van Buren turn to follow him. Quickly gaining on his slower companion, Van Buren flashed past Penland when he was about 100 feet off the water, gave him a good luck wave, and turned for home. Moments later Penland executed a perfect, power off, forced landing. The plane stayed afloat long enough to allow he and his radio-gunner to save all their emergency equipment and rations before they started paddling toward Midway.

Behind Penland, the men of the second division emerged from their dives between 200 and 300 feet, in a maelstrom of antiaircraft fire and fighters. Their leader being effectively *hors de combat* little opportunity existed to join up for mutual defense; circumstances forced each to retire individually. A "Zero" jumped ENS Lewis A. Hopkins, in B-12, immediately after pullout. Heading down to water level, Hopkins countered the "Zero" by turning into each attack, opening up the field of fire for his gunner, Edward R. Anderson, RM3c. Although the A6M2 made several passes on the lone SBD, B-12 suffered only superficial damage before the Japanese pilot gave up the chase.

Once clear of the Japanese fleet, Hopkins set to work with his plotting board trying to figure out where he was. About that time, ENS Eugene A. Greene and Samuel A. Muntean, RM3c, in B-9, joined them. Using Morse hand signals the two pilots agreed on the best course towards home, throttled back to a speed that allowed for maximum range.

The last SBDs of VB-6 in the dive were those of LT(jg) Van Buren's third division and LT(jg) Roberts' section of the first division. By that point, numerous "Zeroes" filled the sky south of *Kaga*, and from the moment they started their withdrawal the Americans found themselves under attack. Initially, the "Zeroes" did not press home their assaults, as most of them, low on ammunition, faced too many widely separated targets. As the battle shifted southeastward, though, the number of Japanese fighters increased and the Americans found themselves in a wild melee.

Roberts and his wingman, ENS Delbert W. Halsey, were able to rendezvous almost immediately after pullout. Seeing a couple of third division SBDs off to starboard, each under attack by two "Zeroes," they turned to join the closest. As they drew nearer, though, A6M2s set upon Roberts and Halsey as well. The Japanese followed their pattern of individual hit and run passes, mostly targeting Halsey's trailing SBD, and after the first passes Roberts could see B-6 trailing fuel.

The SBD ahead was ENS Norman F. Vandivier's. Doing a marvelous job dealing with his attackers, he kept within 50 feet of the water, and held his base course as each "Zero" started a pass. Then, once the enemy pilot was committed to his run, Vandivier turned B-14 into the attacker, setting up his gunner, Lee E. J. Keaney,

Sea1c, and leaving the Japanese pilot a difficult full deflection shot. When the three planes finally joined, Vandivier took the lead. Spotting another SBD coming up from their starboard he turned to enable it to join up.

The approaching "Dauntless" was ENS George H. Goldsmith's B-15. As he had pulled out of his dive at 300 feet, two "Zeroes" immediately pursued. When the Japanese finally caught up they roared in from astern, the first "Zero" pressing home its attack to within 100 feet, flashing underneath B-15, and recovering off to the right, having scored numerous hits in B-15's after cockpit and tail, destroying the radio and ZB equipment, and in the right wing, holing the inboard fuel tank. Goldsmith switched the gas selector to that tank to use as much of the fuel as he could. During that critical moment both of the free guns jammed, leaving his radio-gunner, James W. Patterson Jr., ARM3c, defenseless.

As the second "Zero" commenced its first run, Goldsmith descended to 20 feet, watching the Japanese open fire with his machine guns, trying to "walk" the bullets across the water and into the SBD before cutting in with his 20-mm. guns. As the splashes drew closer, Goldsmith "jinked" toward them and saw the cannon shells lace the water where he had just been. The "Zeroes" made a total of four runs, the last occurring just as he rendezvoused with Vandivier and took station on his right.

Shortly after Goldsmith joined, the Americans could see two more SBDs heading toward them—the third division's second section, led by LT(jg) Edward L. Anderson. After pullout, "Andy" Anderson had found himself over the heart of the *Kido Butai*, with a battleship off to starboard. Seeing numerous "Zeroes" milling about, he took his SBD close to the water, holding between 150 and 200 feet, but none made more than a tentative pass at him and he was able to join his wingman, ENS Bertram S. Varian. Seeing the three SBDs forming up ahead, he decided to close for defensive purposes. The pair had almost reached Vandivier when three "Zeroes" hit them in rapid succession. One particular Japanese pilot proved very aggressive. Flashing past B-16 after one run, he pulled his "Zero" into a full loop less than 500 feet off the water and raced back for a second. The three Mitsubishis made several passes each and shot-up both SBDs, hitting B-16 repeatedly, especially in the after portion of the fuselage and tail, shredding all the fabric on the after control surfaces and practically shooting the rear cockpit to pieces, damaging the radio, destroying the interphone, and peppering Anderson's radio-gunner, Stuart J. Mason Jr., ARM2c, about the head with fragments and shrapnel. Mason's wounds bled profusely, filling his goggles with blood, severely hampering his gunnery. Fortunately, though, the fuel tanks had not been hit. Varian, however, did not fare so well, as B-18 took several hits in the wings which holed his fuel tanks.

Finally, after this last series of attacks, the "Zeroes" broke away. Throughout the engagement the Americans had made steady progress away from the *Kido Butai*, and emerged some 20 miles to the east of it. Shortly before the "Zeroes" left, however, the tanks in B-6 ran dry and ENS Halsey reported over the radio that he was going to have to make a forced landing. Anderson, with a wounded gunner, and a wingman losing fuel, continued to the northeast, but the others circled once and watched as Halsey turned into the wind and made a flawless power-off landing. He and Jenkins were last seen getting into their raft.

As Vandivier, Roberts, and Goldsmith resumed their retirement toward home they saw another "Dauntless" approaching—the third division leader, Van Buren, on his way home after leaving Penland. When Van Buren joined up, he assumed the lead; Vandivier formed on him and Goldsmith took station on Roberts. With the enemy gone, the four commenced a shallow climb toward home.

Bill Brockman had waited, meanwhile, for a decent interval to pass before he took *Nautilus* back up to periscope depth. Finding empty ocean, he resumed stalking the *Kido Butai*. At 1029, "large clouds of smoke" on the horizon betrayed the force's presence, and after intercepting a message that gave the location of a "damaged carrier," Brockman set a course in that direction. A little over an hour later, at 1145, *Nautilus'* skipper could see that a carrier—*Kaga*—lay at the base of one of those columns, apparently stopped and burning. At about the same time, "Duke" Duke, in *Grouper*, saw the smoke from what appeared to be two more burning carriers—probably *Akagi* and *Soryu*—10 to 12 miles away, and began his submerged approach. Moments later, a Japanese plane bombed *Grouper*, forcing her down to 140 feet as he maintained his approach course on the enemy ships.

As the planes from TF 16 and TF 17 cleared the area, the Japanese took stock of their situation. On board *Akagi*, raging fires, after consuming the ship's entire hangar area, swept forward, and threatened the bridge. Damage to the pumping system had severely hindered fire-fighting efforts and compelled Nagumo to transfer his flag to *Nagara* at 1046. At 1050, RADM Hiroaki Abe, commander, 8th Cruiser Division, radioed ADM Yamamoto, informing him of the fires he could see raging on board *Kaga*, *Soryu* and *Akagi*, of the intent to have *Hiryu* locate the American carriers, and of the retirement to the north to assemble forces. On board

Arashi, the Japanese subjected ENS Osmus to more intensive interrogation as the sight of three burning carriers lay before them, fueling their desire to find out more of what he knew. *Arashi* was soon involved in assisting the crippled *Akagi*.

The three rising smoke columns had not only attracted *Nautilus* and *Grouper*, but also alerted RADM Tamon Yamaguchi to the disaster that had befallen the *Kido Butai*. On board his flagship, *Hiryu*, only 34 operational aircraft remained: six *kansen* and 18 *kanbaku* on her flight deck, one *kansen* and nine *kanko* on the hangar deck. Aloft, 31 *kansen*, from all four carriers, remained airborne.

RADM Abe ordered Yamaguchi to attack, but the admiral needed little urging. He and his flag captain, *Hiryu*'s CO, CAPT Tomeo Kaku—the only naval aviator among the four carrier captains of the *Kido Butai*—planned to launch a strike immediately, regardless of the fact that the attack group would be comprised of only fighters and bombers, and no torpedo planes—when the *kanko* were ready, they would follow. At 1045, *Hiryu* commenced launching her first counterattack—18 *kanbaku* under LT Michio Kobayashi, escorted by six *kansen* under LT Yasuhiro Shigematsu. Twelve of Kobayashi's Type 99s carried one 250-kg. bomb suitable for use against ships, but six carried 242-kg. bombs—there had not been time to shift to more proper ordnance after the cancellation of the second attack on Midway. At 1054, Yamaguchi signalled: "All our planes are taking off now for the purpose of destroying [the] enemy carriers." He added that nine *kanko* and three *kansen*

would follow in an hour's time. He planned to proceed toward the enemy and give battle. In the meantime, one destroyer, was dispatched to each of the stricken carriers, and Yamaguchi requested Abe to maintain contact with the American flattops by the use of cruiser-based float reconnaissance planes.

One reconnaissance plane was doing just that: *Soryu*'s Type 13 bomber flown by Iida, who had flown to the point indicated by *Tone*'s no. 4 plane but found only an empty ocean. He turned to make the return flight, but came upon an American aircraft, which he took to be returning to its parent carrier. The sight of American ships confirmed the correctness of his decision, and at about 1110 SPO Kondo radioed a message that confirmed the presence of three task groups, each with an aircraft carrier contained within it. Unfortunately for the Japanese but fortunately for the Americans, the message was never received.

Nevertheless, at 1230, Nagumo notified Yamamoto of the crippling of three of his carriers, and that he had transferred his flag to *Nagara*. "After attacking the enemy," he radioed, "I plan to lead my forces to the north." In the meantime, ahead of the outward bound Japanese force, *Chikuma*'s no. 5 plane, one of those that had relieved *Tone*'s no. 4 plane, had lingered in the vicinity of the American task forces, transmitting important weather information: at 1132, it signalled Kobayashi: "I will lead you to the target by radio." *Tone*, meanwhile, recovered her no. 4 plane, which had rendered such fine service: only 50 liters of gasoline remained in her tanks!

Like RADM Fletcher, VADM Nagumo had to vacate his carrier flagship for the relative sanctuary of a cruiser. In the latter's case, the light cruiser *Nagara* (seen here at Shanghai, China, in 1936) became flagship after mortal damage on board *Akagi* forced the Japanese admiral to transfer his flag. NH 50960

Yorktown turns into the wind to launch a 12-plane CAP early on the afternoon of 4 June. Shortly afterward, she recovered the two VB-6 SBDs flown by LT(jg) W.E. Roberts and ENS G.H. Goldsmith both of whom had insufficient fuel to reach *Enterprise*. 80-G-21626

CHAPTER ELEVEN
....

"Incontestable Mastery of the Air"

*A*s the last of Spruance's strike had departed the vicinity of TF 16 shortly after 0800, his force had steamed roughly southwest by west, to close the enemy and shorten the return distance for his planes. Soon thereafter, at 0815, *Enterprise*'s radar picked up a bogey roughly 30 miles south by east—*Tone*'s no. 4 search plane. For the next hour, the Japanese skillfully eluded the CAP.

At 0930, TF 16 had adopted a course that would take them roughly southeast by east, into the wind, to rotate the CAP; to do so, however, the ships had to work up to 27 knots because of the prevailing light winds. The recovery took 20 minutes, and at the end of that period of high-speed steaming, TF 16 found itself some 35 miles east of where the returning strike pilots had been briefed to find it.

Some of those returning, however, would never reach TF 16. "Pat" Mitchell's 10 F4Fs attempted to home in on *Hornet*; shortly after 1000, his main group, led by Stan Ruehlow, sighted ship wakes to port, but, tragically, failed to recognize what proved to be TF 16. ENS George R. Hill, A-V(N), ran out of fuel first, followed by ENSs McInerney and Magda (who ditched together) and then the rest: LT(jg) Minuard F. Jennings and ENS Humphrey L. Tallman, A-V(N), together; ENS C. Markland Kelly Jr., A-V(N) (Tallman's flight school classmate); ENS Johnny A. Talbot, A-V(N), and finally LT(jg) Richard Gray, Ruehlow and Mitchell. By 1045, all of *Hornet*'s F4Fs assigned to the strike group had splashed down in the Pacific.

"Red" Richards' four PBYs, meanwhile, had been keeping clear of Midway since the report had been broadcast at 0641 that the atoll was under attack by the Japanese. Richards, Davis, Propst and Rothenberg had each set a course for Lisianski, only to encounter a storm front of moderate intensity centering over that island and forcing them to try for Laysan instead. LT(jg)

Davis reached that destination first, at 1000; Richards arrived next, at 1045, and Rothenberg at 1105. Davis and Rothenberg each had only 10-20 gallons of fuel remaining; Richards, 50. The fourth PBY, flown by ENS Propst, ran out of gasoline near Lisianski around 1045, and had to land in the open sea. *YP-290* lay at Laysan to welcome the three PBYs, and commenced refueling them soon after their arrival. Using five-gallon tins, the operation had to be conducted by hand, and consumed much time.

In the interim, as the morning passed on board *Enterprise* and *Hornet*, apprehension reigned over the lack of news from the strike group until, between 1025 and 1030, the carriers picked up radio messages which those on board *Enterprise* could identify as McClusky's pilots. By that point, though, no one knew exactly what they had been attacking, adding further to the mystery. At 1040, TF 16 again turned into the wind, to enable *Hornet* to recover the four remaining F4Fs from the first CAP. Moments later, *Enterprise* recognized her returning F4Fs and after clearing the deck by launching her third CAP, recovered Jim Gray and his men, who, in returning at high altitude, had been able to follow the YE signal back to the ship. Spruance debriefed Gray immediately, but the pilot could relate little of what had happened, since his fuel state had compelled him to retire. The 15 minutes it had taken to recover him and his men, though, took TF 16 further east.

At 1100, *Hornet*'s radar picked up a large flight of planes—soon recognized as SBDs—approaching from the bearing roughly south by west, 59 miles distant. TF 16 again turned into the wind, clearing her deck by launching two CAP divisions. CHAG landed first, followed by Walt Rodee's 16 SBDs and Clayton Fisher of VB-8; at the same time, *Enterprise* recovered two CAP divisions.

The intact bomb loads beneath *Hornet*'s SBDs betrayed the fact that the mission had not gone as planned. Neither VB-8 (with the exception of Fisher), VT-8 nor VF-8 had returned; Ring let Rodee report what little information he possessed on what had gone wrong. Less than an hour later, at 1145, LT Alfred B. Tucker and his two wingmen arrived over TF 16 and soon landed; they, too, could add nothing to what had happened to the rest of *Hornet*'s air group. NAS Midway soon dispelled the mystery of what had become of the rest of VB-8, however, when it radioed that 11 SBDs had reached safety there.

Learning the course to Midway from a returning PBY, "Ruff" Johnson had decided to land there, refuel, and return thence to the ship. ENS Thomas J. Wood, A-V(N), however, ran out of gas short of Midway and had to ditch, both pilot and radio-gunner emerging safely from their plane. Lacking the proper identification, Johnson had ordered his men to jettison their bombs off the reef to show their friendly character. Midway's defenders, however, hearing the air raid alarm at 1115, expecting the Japanese to return, proved that they weren't to be trifled with, and antiaircraft fire holed three SBDs before the Marines recognized them.

One of the Bombing EIGHT SBDs would not reach the airstrip to touch down. ENS Forrester C. Auman, A-V(N), ran out of gas over the lagoon and had to ditch there; at 1141 *PT-28* proceeded to the spot and rescued Auman and his radio-gunner. The "Dauntless" then sank on its back in 20 feet of water. Later, after first turning the plane over with a towline to afford access to it, divers from *PT-22* salvaged the machine guns, equipment, confidential and personal gear from the SBD.

By that point in the day, only seven of the B-17s had been reserviced and were ready for flight. At 1253, LTCOL Sweeney reported that unless otherwise directed, he would send seven of the B-17s back to Oahu, since he possessed almost twice as many planes as protective revetments for them, and some of the planes were experiencing engine difficulties. CAPT Simard failed to respond to the message, owing to the turmoil in the communications system, so Sweeney proceeded ahead. The seven B-17s cleared Midway, headed for Hickam Field, thus leaving eight B-17s, four of which were effective. While the alarm occasioned by the approach of Johnson's VB-8 planes was false, it nevertheless helped to alleviate some of the overcrowding on Eastern Island.

As MAJ Warner later wrote, the time coinciding with the arrival of *Hornet*'s planes was the "most critical . . . of the whole engagement." Their arrival caused "considerable confusion" as the one flyable F4F-3, flown by CAPT Carl, got airborne, as did four B-17s. "If the enemy had returned at that time," Warner later explained, "our losses on the ground would have been disastrous." Only eight bunkers existed for B-17s and four for B-26s, so seven "Fortresses" had to be dispersed along the runways, "a base that near the scene of action is so vulnerable that the planes have to be flown away to be saved." A few "Zeroes" with incendiary ammunition, he went on, "could have destroyed all our aircraft." Warner, finding communications so snarled by the bombing of both Eastern and Sand Islands, thought he could do more by returning to Oahu and reporting directly to BGEN Hale, took passage in one of the returning B-17s.

Enterprise's SBDs, meanwhile, were encountering troubles of their own. His fuel tanks holed in the battle over the Mobile Force, Norman Vandivier was the first to ditch, only 10 minutes after the last of the

"Zeroes" had departed. Goldsmith's radio-gunner, Patterson, felt empty as he watched Vandivier's plane descend, for Lee Keaney, Vandivier's rear seat man, was one of his best friends. All Patterson could do was pray that Keaney and his pilot would survive. Five minutes later, John Van Buren followed; Patterson saw the pilot and his radio-gunner, Harry W. Nelson Jr., ARM1c, extract their raft from the sinking SBD and get into it. Damaged fuel tanks accounted for the loss of "Andy" Anderson's wingman, ENS Bertram Varian, some 50 miles northeast of the Japanese fleet. Anderson saw Varian and his radio-gunner, Charles R. Young, ARM3c, clamber into their raft.

A much more serious problem than lack of fuel loomed for Ware's makeshift division. They had finally managed to circle to the northeast of the *Kido Butai* and set a homeward course when Ware sighted a large formation of planes—what soon proved to be Kobayashi's attack group from *Hiryu*—closing rapidly from 8 o'clock, about 1,000 feet above; he immediately nosed over and led his division down to the "deck."

Shigematsu, incorrectly identifying the planes below as American torpedo bombers, sought, and received, Kobayashi's permission to attack. Expecting to make short work of them, Shigematsu separated his six *kansen* and descended to take them on.

Bruno Peter Gaido, AMM1c, on board *Enterprise* circa March 1942. He had been one of the "Big E's" early war heroes, during the raid on the Marshall Islands, 1 February 1942. Lundstrom

At that moment, even before the approaching fighters got to them, ENS O'Flaherty, his gasoline tanks holed in the earlier air battle, had to "ditch" his SBD. Both the pilot and his radio-gunner, Bruno Gaido, got out of the sinking SBD and got out the raft; after inflating it, they climbed in. McCarthy's radioman, Howell, saw that they appeared to be in good shape. They would be the last Americans to see the two men alive, for the destroyer *Makigumo* retrieved the two men and took them prisoner. Perishing at sea would have been preferable to what ultimately became of them; after they were interrogated, they were weighted, thrown over the side, and drowned.

Moments later, "with fresh belly tanks and red hot to fight," Shigematsu's "Zeroes" set upon Ware's little band, who countered by turning into each attack with a delayed slide to the outside of the turn by McCarthy's section, allowing the five radio-gunners to converge their fire on the attacking *kansen*. For 20 minutes, Shigematsu's pilots did their best, but their prey proved tougher than anticipated; and the Japanese broke off the engagement. Two damaged *kansen* headed back to *Hiryu*.

After the Japanese had gone, Ware and McCarthy "discussed" by hand signals which course would take them home. McCarthy felt that Ware was too far north, and although the former tried to convince him otherwise, the latter was determined that he was correct. Even so, Ware allowed McCarthy to go his own way, signalling that he was free to try his own course. McCarthy broke off, as did Lough, but Shelton and Peiffer remained with Ware. The five were in sight of each other for 15 to 20 minutes, after which time McCarthy found himself alone. No one ever saw Ware, Lough, Shelton and Peiffer, nor their radio-gunners, again.

Wade McClusky had reached the expected rendezvous point at 1120 only to find empty ocean. After radioing *Enterprise* to ask if she'd changed position, he received the information he sought and headed that direction. He entered the landing circle of the first flattop he saw, but soon discovered that it was *Yorktown*, not *Enterprise*. Wanting to report personally to Spruance, however, he headed for his own ship. Ignoring a wave-off, normally a cardinal sin in the carrier fraternity, McClusky landed at 1150, and immediately

climbed to the flag shelter. He had barely begun his report, however, when the "Big E's" XO, CDR Thomas P. Jeter, seeing CEAG's injuries, exclaimed, "My God, Mac, you've been shot!" McClusky's report of a fourth, undamaged carrier, went unnoted in the resultant concern over his wound.

Earl Gallaher soon returned, leading Stone, Pittman, Jaccard and Dexter. Dick Best soon followed, along with his wingmen, Kroeger and Weber; each group having utilized the ZB to find their ship. Leaving Murray with B-1, Best immediately reported to Browning the results of his attack and that he had seen a fourth, undamaged, carrier. He recommended that another strike be launched to get her.

By 1210 the last of the SBDs had been recovered on board the "Big E," as Kleiss, West and Micheel from VS-6 came in, as well as Hopkins and Anderson of VB-6. Along the way, Greene and Ramsay of VB-6 had splashed; their shipmates had seen them, along with their respective radio-gunners, get into their rubber boats. Dickinson and his radioman, DeLuca, also failed to reach the task force, but managed to land near *Phelps*—the ship in which Dickinson had first served when he'd graduated from the Naval Academy!

By that point, Goldsmith and Roberts, unable to reach *Enterprise*, had landed on board *Yorktown*, shortly before VB-3 broke up into sections to enter *Yorktown*'s landing pattern. They were waved-off, however, instead of welcomed. The reason soon became clear, for at 1152 *Yorktown*'s radar had picked up a contact 32 miles away to the southwest and closing; instead of a high-level approach that could be detected by radar, as had happened at Coral Sea, the Japanese had come in low and then ascended to attack. *Yorktown* warned VB-3 to get out of gun range of the task force, discontinued fueling operations and dropped an 800-gallon avgas tank over

ENS George H. Goldsmith, A-V(N) and his radio-gunner, James W. Patterson, ARM3c, converse with plane handlers on board *Yorktown* shortly after they landed on board around 1340 on 4 June. Their plane was an SBD-3 (BuNo 4542), and had been damaged in the attack on *Kaga*. NH 100740

the side, aft. Men closed down and secured compartments while CO2 blanketed the drained aviation gasoline lines.

"Swede" Pederson, on the fighter director circuit, warned all *Yorktown* planes to keep a "sharp lookout" for enemy aircraft to the southwest. At 1158, he had begun vectoring them out to intercept the incoming Japanese; hearing "many bogies, angels 10" over the radio, he directed his airborne "Wildcats" to the enemy's location, urging them to "step on it."

At 1200, LT Kobayashi sighted *Yorktown* and her screen, their white wakes betraying their presence on the blue ocean. "We are attacking the enemy carrier," he radioed, at about the same time he and his formation passed over the head of LT(jg) Art Brassfield, in *Yorktown*'s CAP, who transmitted: "Bandits above me heading for ship. Appears to be 18." He tracked the Type

99s as they closed the distance between themselves and their quarry which steamed below, ready to meet them with a healthy amount of gunfire. At 1204, soon after receipt of Brassfield's noting that the formation appeared to be breaking up, Pederson radioed: "O.K., break 'em up." Brassfield soon shot down three of the Type 99s about five miles from the carrier.

"Tally ho," signalled the beginning of the CAP's onslaught against Kobayashi's carrier bombers. CAPT Buckmaster, on *Yorktown*'s bridge, watched the CAP breaking up the attack. "Planes were falling in every direction," he noted, "many . . . in flames."

Bill Esders watched from about five miles away, from the cockpit of his badly damaged TBD. As the dying Mike Brazier doggedly worked the radio and homed onto *Yorktown*'s "hayrake," Esders kept an eye on the fuel gauge as he neared TF 17. The sighting of

Bel Geddes' reconstruction of the CAP action near TF 17 as Kobayashi's men meet resistance on their way to attack *Yorktown*. 80-G-701874

Splendid action sequence taken by a photographer on board *Astoria* as the brief but intense attack by LT Kobayashi's men unfolds. At top, *Yorktown*, F4F-4s from VF-3 parked forward, steams at full speed while a tail-less *kanbaku*, shot down, plummets toward the sea ahead of the ship...
80-G-32355

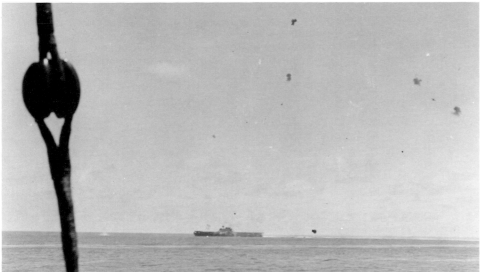

... in the middle photo, WO Iwao Nakazawa, with ENS Shimematsu Nakayama as observer, of *Hiryu*'s second *shotai*, dives on his target (his plane barely visible beneath the flak burst at the top, middle, of this view).
80-G-32310

...at bottom, fires are consuming the interior of the uptakes after Nakazawa's bomb penetrated deep into the ship. 80-G-32394

Portland's photographer, meanwhile, caught the attack from the other side, from a vantage point near the ship's Curtiss SOC floatplanes. Note the size of the U.S. ensign being flown at *Yorktown*'s fore, in the upper view; in the lower, the fires have taken hold below decks on board the stricken carrier. 80-G-21641

LT Michio Kobayashi, seen here in a prewar view by a Sasebo photographer, led *Hiryu*'s first strike against *Yorktown* on the afternoon of 4 June, and apparently survived the attack against the ship, only to be shot down soon afterward. NH 81650

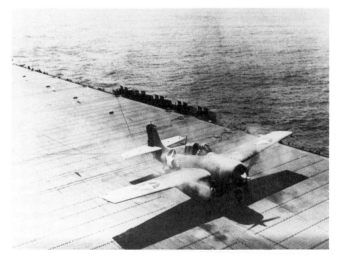

Grumman F4F-4 (BuNo 5167), flown on 4 June by LT(jg) Arthur Brassfield, a former Missouri schoolteacher, landing on board *Hornet*. Lawson

LT William N. Leonard, USNA Class of 1938, XO of Fighting THREE in the Battle of Midway, in flight gear at NAS Kaneohe, May 1942. Leonard

Kobayashi's Type 99s, however, tempered his joy at having reached friendly forces and as he headed for the clouds he noted at least three ash-gray dive bombers go down in flames—undoubtedly Brassfield's victims.

A bitter dogfight flashed and swirled ever closer to *Yorktown*, that, screened by her attendant cruisers and destroyers, steamed ready to meet Kobayashi and his brave fliers; her largest ensign snapping from her foremast truck, the carrier prepared to do battle. Informed of the imminent Japanese strike, Frank Jack Fletcher replied with characteristic amiability, "Well, I've got on my tin hat. There's nothing else *I* can do now." Down on the flight deck, LT Bill Leonard, caught on board with his plane spotted forward; frustrated at being ship-bound with *Yorktown* facing an aerial onslaught, drew his .45-caliber pistol and prepared to meet the attack in his own way. The ship's navigator, CDR Wiltsie, meanwhile gulped down the last of his lunch—a sardine sandwich.

Kobayashi's men fought their way through the CAP: two divisions from Fighting THREE, one from VF-6 and one from VF-8. The Japanese emerged with at least seven (of 11) which got close enough to *Yorktown* to push over and attack. The first Type 99s came under fire from all automatic weapons on the starboard side: 10 20-mm. Oerlikons, the four 1.1-inch quads, a dozen .50-caliber machine guns and two .30-calibers; one Aichi exploded into three distinct pieces. His bomb, though, a 242-kg. "land bomb" (high explosive) tumbled, and exploded on contact with the flight deck at about frame 132, just abaft number two elevator, blowing a 12-foot hole in the deck; shrapnel decimated the crews at 1.1-inch mounts III and IV.

On the hanger deck, shrapnel started fires among the planes parked there—one of which, from "Scouting" FIVE, sat fully gassed with a 1,000-pound bomb beneath its belly. A standout on the gridiron and diamond at the University of Maine, LT Alberto C. Emerson, the hangar deck officer, reacted quickly and averted a major conflagration by activating the hangar deck water curtains and sprinklers, extinguishing the flames immediately.

Antiaircraft fire cut a second plane to pieces, too, as it reached its drop point. The bomb tumbled in flight and splashed close astern, as did the wreckage of the aircraft and its crew. Splinters from the bomb, though, cut down men from the crews of the .50-caliber battery on the port side of the superstructure deck, aft, as well as on the port quarter of the flight deck, and touched off several fires.

Relentlessly, the attack continued. WO Iwao Nakazawa, WO Shizuo Nakagawa, and PO1c Tetsuo Seo pushed over, and lined up *Yorktown* in their telescopic sights. All dropped and claimed hits, but it appears that only Nakazawa actually scored; his 250-kg. armor-piercing bomb penetrated the flight deck 10 feet inboard of the island, and continued downward, outward and to starboard, piercing the port side of the uptakes in the hangar, hit the second deck in the vicinity of a passage inboard of the XO's office and the C&R office, and exploded in a "high order" detonation that wrecked the latter and blew a 15-foot hole in the deck, as well as in the intakes and uptakes to five firerooms. Rupturing the comparatively thin sheet steel of the uptakes, disabling two of the ship's six boilers and extinguishing the fires in five, the bomb hit released smoke and gasses into the firerooms.

Two fire parties from Repair II and III hastened to the blaze on the second deck and laundry; those from Repairs I and VII to the photo lab on the first deck. In the latter place, the raging fires, fed by film and chemicals, blazed fiercely, confronting the men with a difficult task. CDR Dixie Kiefer, *Yorktown*'s XO, led the firefighting efforts in that area, despite the infernal heat. Paint on the inside of the stack, meanwhile, caught fire and flaked off in patches, starting fires wherever it fell.

Meanwhile, the six men at number one boiler, under Charles Kleinsmith, CWT, remained at their stations, despite the broken, red-hot boiler casing and fumes from the ruptured uptakes from their boiler. By closing the throttle, the men at boiler number one were able to maintain steam pressure at 180 pounds, enabling it to carry the auxiliary load. Topside, heavy black smoke soon obscured the after main battery director, the

CDR Dixie Kiefer (seen here as a CAPT), *Yorktown*'s XO, had been characterized as "The Naval Academy Peter Pan—The Little Boy Who Never Grew Up." He would be awarded the DSM for elevating *Yorktown*'s morale and fighting spirit that allowed the ship to perform with distinction at Coral Sea, and a Navy Cross for his heroism at Midway. Later, Kiefer, as CO of *Ticonderoga* (CV-14), would be awarded the Silver Star for bravery after his ship had been crashed by kamikazes off Formosa on 21 January 1945. He remained on his bridge, wounded, for 12 hours, until he deemed his ship out of danger. Attaining flag rank in May 1945, he would die in a plane crash in the Fishkill (N.Y.) mountains on 11 November 1945. NH 100259

Sailors work to repair *Yorktown*'s flight deck, aft, after it had been damaged by a 242-kg. bomb during the attack by *Hiryu*'s Type 99 carrier bombers, 4 June. Note old- and new-style helmets in use, and the 20-mm. and .50-caliber gun galleries in background. 80-G-312020

automatic gun batteries, and the 5-inch guns on the starboard side, aft.

At about the same time, a sixth Type 99, flown by WO Shizuo Nakagawa, circled forward and dove from ahead of the ship, facing "considerably lessened fire" than those who had gone before. Nakagawa's bomb pierced number one elevator, about 17 feet to the right of the centerline, continued forward and to port, penetrating the elevator pit, some seven feet from the centerline, where it exploded in a high-order detonation in a rag and cleaning gear stowage compartment. The blast blew a four-foot hole in the deck, ruptured bulkheads within a compartment one deck below, and even pierced the overhead of compartments on the fifth deck, and plunged all compartments deep within the ship forward of frame 60 briefly into darkness, before the emergency lighting came on. Fire broke out immediately among the rags and cleaning gear and in the stores below, and it emitted a heavy volume of smoke while the heat from the blaze blistered and baked paint on the surrounding bulkheads. The blast also ruptured a fire main riser, flooding three compartments through the transverse bulkheads, as well as blew the forward magazine group sprinkling and flooding control panels from the bulkhead. A damaged circuit rendered inoperative the remote control for sprinkling the forward magazine, located just aft of the blaze.

Two repair parties hastened to the scene, one using CO_2 and a fire hose, and the other, attacking the blaze from the elevator pit, using water and foam. One group used an oxy-acetylene torch and cut through the deck beneath their feet in the elevator pit, and aimed fire nozzles down on the flames. To avert a magazine explosion, the spaces directly abaft the burning storerooms were flooded.

Although the seventh and last *kanbaku* jettisoned his bomb and it splashed into the sea off the carrier's starboard beam, the damage had already been done. Three of the seven bombs dropped against *Yorktown* had hit. Thirteen of the 18 attacking *kanbaku*, however, had fallen to either antiaircraft fire or the fighters of the CAP. The returning Japanese pilots claimed six direct hits that set their target afire, and caused her to explode. As *Yorktown* slowed and the fire took hold in the uptakes, billowing black smoke nearly obscured her; to the retiring Japanese, it looked as if the American carrier had taken mortal damage.

*Yorktown*ers, though, were not about to give up. Sailors from Repair I and the flight deck repair crew scrambled to the damaged flight deck even before the last bomb had fallen. LT Albert H. Wilson Jr., and his men, unprotected, "very expeditiously" secured wooden beams to the steel transverse ones bordering the 12-foot square hole, and then laid quarter-inch steel plate over the beams. They then dragged "five large, square, 10-pound steel plates" into place over the gap, driving spikes into the wooden flight deck bordering it, to hold them in place. While Wilson's men had finished the task in about 25 minutes, restoring use of the flight deck, *Yorktown* could not recover aircraft, as she went dead in the water because of the casualty to the boilers.

Thick, choking black smoke billowed from the stack fire, rendered the communication office and flag plot untenable, and forced RADM Fletcher and his staff to assemble on the flight deck. With *Yorktown*'s radar inoperative, with the difficulty in communicating with other ships in the task force, and with *Yorktown* immobile, Fletcher decided to shift his flag to *Astoria*. A motor whaleboat soon arrived alongside the carrier and the admiral and his staff prepared to disembark. Hesitating just as he was about to go over the side, Fletcher, who had bumped his head during the attack, claimed that he was "too damned old" for that sort of thing; he was thus lowered to the waiting boat and was soon on his way with the initial increment of his staff, clambering up a Jacob's ladder to board *Astoria* at 1324. The boat then shoved off for a second trip to get the rest of the admiral's staff.

Bombing THREE, meanwhile, having been waved off from *Yorktown*, found *Enterprise*, which had already recovered her own SBDs by 1210, open for business. The surviving TBDs of VT-6 came in soon thereafter; CHMACH Smith, flying the charmed "Scat Cat," found that his approach coincided with the end of Kobayashi's attack on *Yorktown*, and found himself the object of attention by one CAP pilot from VF-6, who fortunately recognized the TBD's friendly character and held his fire. By 1220, all four of VT-6's TBDs had reached their home deck. ENS Paul Schlegel and LT(jg) Ozzie Wiseman were the first *Yorktown* pilots to land on board "The Big E," at 1237 and 1238. One recounted that *Yorktown* was "in bad shape."

Spruance, from *Enterprise*'s flag shelter, judged "from the heavy smoke that appeared . . . that she [*Yorktown*] had been hit." Others saw it, too. Correspondent Casey, on board *Northampton*, later reported: "The black puffs attenuate and lose color and mingle with the stratus clouds in the low distance. The fires of the burning planes are quickly out. The carrier has gone over the horizon again and the ocean is as it was before save for one strange and terrifying thing—a column of smoke . . . is rising straight into the air. . . . Something is afire over there. . . . We cross our fingers and hope it wasn't the carrier. . ."

Over the next several minutes, *Enterprise*'s LSO brought in seven more SBDs, followed by four VF-3

F4F-4s, six more SBDs, and two more F4Fs—all *Yorktown* planes. Spruance, to aid Fletcher, dispatched four ships—heavy cruisers *Vincennes* and *Pensacola*, and the destroyers *Balch* and *Benham*—to help.

Some *Yorktown* planes tried unsuccessfully to reach the ship but the appearance of Kobayashi's men had compelled them to go elsewhere. The wounded ENS Sheedy managed to reach *Hornet*, but his battered mount came down hard at 1229 and slewed to starboard; his guns discharged from the shock of the landing. A six-gun burst raked the after end of *Hornet*'s island for only two seconds—long enough, though, for the slugs to kill three Marines and a sailor from VB-8,

as well as the after 5-inch gun control officer, LT Royal Rodney Ingersoll, the son of ADM Royal E. Ingersoll, CINCLANT, and a promising young officer. The other six airborne VF-6 pilots chose to land on board *Hornet*, as did three from VF-8; one of the latter's number, ENS Stephen W. Groves, A-V(N), had gone down near TF 17, probably the victim of friendly antiaircraft fire.

MACH Corl and his radio-gunner, Lloyd Childers, ditched at 1305, close enough to *Monaghan*, in TF 16's screen, to be picked up by her. CAP Esders, who had ducked his TBD-1 into the clouds when he saw Kobayashi's attack force nearing TF 17, ran out of fuel. He radioed *Yorktown* of his intention to ditch 10 miles due

Panoramic view taken by William G. Roy on 4 June showing *Astoria* hurrying up to assist *Yorktown* (L) while men go about their business of repairing the carrier's damage (R). Note details of *Yorktown*'s bridge, CXAM radar, and her largest ensign at the fore.
80-G-312019 (L) and 80-G-312018 (R)

Astoria's no. 2 motor whaleboat comes alongside that ship on the afternoon of 4 June, as RADM Fletcher and the first increment of his staff transfer to the heavy cruiser after heavy black smoke from the burning up-takes on board *Yorktown* had rendered flag plot untenable. Fletcher is wearing a windbreaker beneath his life jacket; his binoculars have white straps. CAPT Spencer S. Lewis, the admiral's chief of staff, starts up the Jacob's ladder to the well-deck. *Astoria*'s XO, CDR Chauncey Crutcher, watches the proceedings (upper left). Note mixture of helmets in use by those in the boat. 80-G-32350

As seen from *Astoria,*
Yorktown loses way, smoke
issuing from her stack. Note
F4F-4s spotted forward; at
least two SBDs can be seen
on the hangar deck. A
Curtiss SOC can be seen on
Astoria's starboard catapult
(L). USN

The fire in the uptakes gains
ground while flight deck
crews have moved all of the
F4Fs that had been at the
bow during the attack by
Kobayashi's planes, aft. In
the background can be seen
Balch (DD-363), sent by
Spruance from TF 16 (L)
and *Portland* (R). 80-G-32301

A bearded chief petty officer trudges past corpsmen treating the casualties around 1.1 inch/.75-caliber Mt. IV, as damage control efforts proceed apace after *Yorktown* had been hit by three bombs from *Hiryu*'s Aichi Type 99s. 80-G-312021

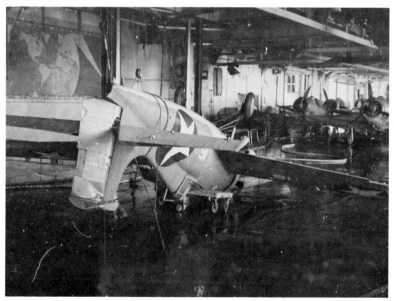

MACH Tom F. Cheek's Grumman F4F-4 (BuNo 5143) rests upside-down on *Yorktown*'s hangar deck, with at least four SBDs in the background. Cheek's plane had been damaged in landing, and had fouled the barrier for a time. It carries the standard blue gray/light gray paint scheme in use at the time, with the individual plane number, 16, on the wing root and on the fuselage, just ahead and below the windshield. 80-G-23979

Benham (DD-397), Mts. I and II trained to starboard, steams to join TF 17 at around 1436 on 4 June, as seen from *Pensacola*. 80-G-34222

-124-

Looking aft on board *Pensacola* (CA-24), this view shows *Yorktown* burning after the dive bombing attack on 4 June, with her screen (which includes *Portland*) standing by. *Pensacola* heels slightly to port as she turns to join TF 17. Note 1.1-inch mount on the fantail, near the stacked rafts; a 20-mm. mount is near the top of the picture.
80-G-21649

Monaghan (DD-354) off Mare Island, 17 February 1942. In the period before and during the Battle of Midway, this ship rescued one VT-6 crew (Lindsey's), one VT-3 crew (Corl's), and a PBY crew (ENS Ted Thueson's). 19-N-28346

west of her, then lowered his flaps and made a full stall landing. As the "Devastator" settled, nose-down, Esders tripped the flotation gear.

Hearing "Mike" Brazier calling for him, Esders climbed out of the cockpit and headed back to help his dying radioman. Gently assisting Brazier out of the cockpit and onto the wing, Esders then broke out the rubber boat and began to inflate it. Despite the fact that Japanese bullets had holed it, the raft retained enough buoyancy to support Brazier as the pilot laid him in it. After giving Brazier a drink of water, Esders attempted to patch the hole.

Suddenly, the sound of airplane engines caught his attention. Looking up, Esders saw two SBDs approach, circling TF 17 out of gun range—one he recognized as Max Leslie's B-1. The other, B-2, flown by LT(jg) Holmberg, flew low overhead and dropped a float light to mark the spot for the rescuing ship. Both SBDs, their fuel gauges showing nearly empty tanks, then hastened off to return to the task force. At about that time, Mike Brazier, bleeding profusely from wounds in his

back and both legs between knee and ankle, died. Esders, now alone, then prayed, committing the brave boy and his family to the Lord's care.

Soon afterward, however, one of the surviving *kanbaku* from *Hiryu*'s decimated attack group circled, ominously, overhead and astern. The Japanese pilot, bringing his plane around, lower, compelled Esders to dive into the water and submerge beside the still floating TBD. The enemy pilot's move, however, for whatever reason he had made it (either to strafe the TBD or merely curiosity), proved his undoing. Apparently preoccupied with the downed torpedo plane, the Japanese failed to notice the approach of Art Brassfield, who thus splashed his fourth Type 99 of the day.

Charlie McCarthy, meanwhile, after losing sight of Ware and his three companions, had climbed slowly to 3,500 feet to try and pick up *Enterprise*'s YE signal, but to no avail. Then, his two inboard fuel tanks virtually empty, and the outboard ones dry, McCarthy instructed his radio-gunner to try and pick up *Yorktown*'s frequency. Reading her YE signal "loud and clear,"

Harry Corl's TBD-1, sinking after landing alongside *Monaghan*, with the wounded Lloyd Childers, ARM3c, emerging from the rear cockpit. The photograph was taken by LT(jg) H.H. Kait. Childers via Horan

McCarthy soon sighted TF 17 dead ahead and after passing over a downed TBD—Esders'—had to make a water landing as his engine quit. Although McCarthy's SBD dropped a wing and cartwheeled into the ocean, he and his radio-gunner survived the mishap, although the pilot suffered a nasty gash on his forehead and a broken nose.

Hammann, searching for downed pilots, recovered the two soon thereafter, and then set course for Esders' position. She stopped at 1325 and brought Esders, and the body of Mike Brazier, on board, before she sank the badly damaged TBD-1 (BuN0 0286) by piercing the flotation bags with rifle fire. The "Devastator" then sank by the nose. The next day, Brazier was buried at sea and Esders, as well as the VS-6 crew, transferred to a cruiser.

There was also one VT-6 plane that could not make it home. Winchell had managed to nurse T-8 along until its fuel finally ran out. He ditched the TBD and he and his radio-gunner, Douglas Cossitt, saved their raft, their first aid kit, rations (four cans of pemmican, two packages of malted milk tablets) and both parachutes.

After leaving Esders, Leslie and Holmberg, returned to the skies over TF 17—hoping that by the time they came back *Yorktown* would be underway and able to bring them in. Sadly, the carrier's remaining temporarily *hors de combat* compelled the two to ditch. Leslie directed Holmberg to land first; at 1342, the junior pilot put B-2 within a veritable stone's throw of *Astoria*, whose number two motor whaleboat (the same one that had transferred RADM Fletcher and his staff to the cruiser) picked up the pilot and his radio-gunner. At 1348, Max Leslie brought B-1 in for a water landing; once more the no. 2 motor whaleboat effected another rescue.

A short time before, *Enterprise*'s radar picked up a bogey 45 miles to the south of TF 16, and LCDR "Ham" Dow, the fighter director, vectored a section from her fourth CAP over to intercept. At 1409, LT(jg) Rhonald J. Hoyle and MACH William H. Warden (NAP), spotted a twin-float "seaplane fighter" headed in their direction but 300 feet below them. Hoyle shot up the plane and set it on fire; as he approached for a second pass he saw one man bail out—a small uninflated life raft attached to the parachute shrouds—as the floatplane exploded. Their quarry turned out to be *Chikuma*'s no. 5 plane, an Aichi E13A1 Type 00 reconnaissance floatplane ("Jake") flown by PO3c Hisashi Hara, who had been shadowing the American carriers for over three hours.

The aviators having done their part in the battle, crippling three of the four carriers of the *Kido Butai*, the submariners were next to try to do theirs. *Grouper* crept in toward the two burning carriers she had sighted until 1314, when heavy explosions above prompted Duke to change course to the west northwest; as he explained later, he thought that he had underestimated the distance to the nearest of the two ships, and, not wanting the "first burning ship . . . to blow up and sink on top of us" moved out of harm's way. Duke decided not to come up to periscope depth to check *Grouper*'s position, as he did not desire "to attract more bombs" (she had already logged over a dozen separate bombings or depth-chargings during her approach). He also hoped to arrive at a position between the two burning carriers so that *Grouper* could sink both "with one trip to periscope depth . . ." Coming up for a look through his periscope at 1420, Duke spotted only one destroyer, which soon spotted *Grouper* and closed to attack. More depth charges forced Duke's boat deep once more, and effectively drove her out of the battle.

Nautilus, meanwhile, continued stalking *Kaga*—although Brockman, his XO, LT Roy S. "Ensign" Benson, and other officers, after having scrutinized their quarry carefully and compared her silhouette with those affixed to a conning tower bulkhead, during the hour-long approach, had identified her as *Soryu*. The carrier lay dead in the water, listing; her fires appeared to have been brought under control while two escorts—which the Americans identified as cruisers or destroyers—stood by; Brockman could see men working on the carrier's forecastle, perhaps readying a towing hawser. He decided "to complete the destruction

While LT(jg) Fisler circles the scene (L), LCDR Max Leslie (center) prepares to ditch. Astern of *Astoria*, LT(jg) Holmberg's plane sinks as he and his radio-gunner are picked up by the cruiser's no. 2 motor whaleboat. USN

LT(jg) Holmberg and his gunner, LaPlant, watch from the roof of *Astoria*'s hangar (lower right) while the ship's no. 2 motor whaleboat goes out again, this time to rescue LCDR Max Leslie and his radio-gunner, Gallagher. *Astoria*'s XO, CDR Crutcher, can be seen in front of Holmberg. Note Curtiss SOC on the catapult (R). 80-G-32305

Bel Geddes' representation of *Nautilus'* torpedoing the damaged *Kaga*. 80-G-701871

of the carrier before she could be repaired or taken in tow." Brockman's men readied four torpedo tubes, and between 1359 and 1405, three "fish" sped toward the motionless *Kaga*; one failed to leave the tube. Shortly after he and his officers observed what they believed to be the effects of their torpedoes, the escorting ships—the destroyers *Hagikaze* and *Maikaze*—depth-charged *Nautilus* again, forcing Brockman to take his boat deep.

Nautilus' attack had caught the Japanese by surprise, and the first inkling the enemy had of the attack was the wakes of three torpedoes reaching toward them. LCDR Yoshio Kunisada, one of *Kaga*'s damage control officers, saw the telltale wakes and, closing his eyes, began to pray. Two of the "fish," however, missed, while one struck amidships where it broke into two sections. The warhead sank, but the air flask did not, and it kept several of *Kaga*'s sailors afloat until their rescue by a screening destroyer.[1]

Meanwhile, for over an hour, *Yorktown*'s "black gang" toiled tirelessly to light off the fires in the carrier's boilers, while the ships Spruance had sent over took up stations in the defensive screen. To everyone's relief, success crowned the "black gang's" efforts; at 1350, the engine room reported to CAPT Buckmaster that *Yorktown* could make 20 knots or more, if required. On board the recently arrived *Pensacola*, a gunner next to correspondent Wendell Webb burst out, "Look, the *Yorktown*'s moving!" From the carrier's yards, the breakdown flag descended, replaced with "My speed five." On board every ship in the screen, all who saw the sight cheered spontaneously.

On board the carrier, the urgent business of fueling the fighters on deck proceeded apace. When asked if he could take off with a 13-knot wind over the deck (the best the engineering force reported they could do at the outset), Jimmy Thach said yes, he could. Frustrated at having had to watch *Hiryu*'s attacking planes, VF-3's skipper said "that he would be damned if he would ever be aboard ship again when the other fellow was attacking!" He much preferred the shoe to be on the other foot.

His opportunity would come soon enough, for at 1355, radar plot reported a group of planes closing roughly from the north-northwest, 35 miles away. These would proved to be the last-ditch strike from the once mighty *Kido Butai*—10 B5N2s led by LT Tomonaga, who had retained the colorfully marked *kanko* in which he had ridden that morning when Marine fighters had damaged it, escorted by six "Zeroes" under LT Mori. This small attack group had taken off from *Hiryu* at

LT Joichi Tomonaga, leader of *Hiryu*'s Air Unit in the Battle of Midway. He led the morning attack on Midway, and, flying a plane damaged by VMF-221 gunfire that morning, the torpedo attack against *Yorktown* that afternoon. He was among those shot down, probably by LCDR John S. Thach, the skipper of VF-3, in the CAP action at that time. NH 81559

1331, and like the American groups operating from the carriers that opposed them, was a composite: one of the carrier attack planes bore the *Akagi*'s markings; two *kansen*, *Kaga*'s. Each of the Nakajimas carried beneath it a type 91, modification 3 torpedo, like those that had crippled the Pacific Fleet's battle line at Pearl Harbor and had stopped *Lexington* at Coral Sea. Only a short time after they had left *Hiryu*, *Soryu*'s Type 13, now without a ship, landed, Iida reporting what he had seen and confirming the presence of three American carriers.

As she had before, *Yorktown* shut down fueling operations—none of the 10 planes spotted on the flight deck had more than 23 gallons on board, two (the ones used that morning by Thach and Macomber in escorting VT-3) had so little that they would have to be left behind. LCDR Pederson, meanwhile, vectored four of the six already airborne F4F-4s—the two sections under VF-3's LT(jg) E.S. "Doc" McCuskey, who had three VF-6 pilots in his division—toward the incoming strike, retaining two (flown by LT(jg) William S. Woollen, A-V(N) and ENS Harry B. Gibbs, A-V(N) directly above the ship to cover the launch of Thach's eight Grummans. TF 16 sent eight "Wildcats" over to help, retaining seven over that task force; on board *Yorktown*, CO_2 again purged her gasoline lines.

---

1. Fuchida and Okumiya later commented, in *Midway: The Battle That Doomed Japan*: "Thus did a weapon of death become instead a life-saver in one of the curious twists of war . . ."

LT(jg) E.S. "Doc" McCuskey, one of the VF-3 pilots engaged in the defense of TF 17 on 4 June.
NH 90482, cropped

Five B5N2s, torpedoes slung menacingly beneath their bellies, approach TF 17. These are perhaps from LT Hashimoto's 2d *chutai*, which passed astern of *Pensacola* (from which this picture was taken), and continued on toward *Yorktown*.
80-G-32248

Two B5N2s pass between *Pensacola* and *Yorktown*, in this view taken from the former, while *Morris* (DD-417) can be seen in the background, beyond the carrier's bow. Note flak bursts.
80-G-32241

Like a groggy prizefighter getting up from the canvas, *Yorktown* moved forward. She seemed to strain for every knot: 12 at 1420, 15 by 1422, and 18 by 1428, as she and her screen deployed in antiaircraft formation to meet the latest onslaught. Fletcher, in *Astoria*, then signalled: "Prepare to repel air attack." Four minutes later, lookouts on board the cruiser reported "about 16 enemy planes . . ." 15 miles out and closing.

"Willo" Woollen and Harry Gibbs were the first to tackle Tomonaga's torpedo planes, with Woollen sending one into the sea in flames before one of the escorting "Zeroes" jumped him and shot up his left wing. He managed to "ditch" his battered F4F ahead of TF 17 and broke out his rubber boat. Gibbs followed his section leader in the dive on the Nakajimas, but a "Zero" got him, too. Only 10 miles from TF 17, he tried to glide toward friendly hands until the shot-up Grumman lost altitude quickly, compelling Gibbs, too, to ditch.

While Tomonaga deployed his formation into four sections to divide the CAP and the antiaircraft fire, *Yorktown* began launching her F4F-4s at 1440. Led by Jimmy Thach, the last of VF-3 wobbled skyward while all the carrier's guns that could be brought to bear trained to port. The carrier's forward gun director had picked up five of the incoming Type 97s about 19,000 yards away, and as LT(jg) John Adams cleared the bow ramp, the ship's port 5-inch battery opened fire at 15,000 yards.

Black bursts smudged the sky ahead of the charging Nakajimas, but as CAPT Buckmaster could see, his guns, and those of his ship's screen, did not seem to be scoring any hits. Tomonaga's formation pressed on in a loose "V," some of his aircraft a scant 50 feet above the water; all jinking and changing course to avoid the barrage being hurled at them. From on board *Pensacola*, Wendell Webb could see that *Yorktown* was "putting up a scrap if any ship ever did." Correspondent William F. Tyree, on board *Vincennes*, thought that the enemy's determination to score hits on the carrier "bordered on the fanatical."

Yorktown's just-launched planes, with young ENS George A. Hopper, A-V(N), bringing up the rear, soon tangled with the B5N2s, matching the enemy's fanatical determination with their own brand of resolve. Each side's pilots braved the intense barrage from the ships. ENS Dibb, who had been Thach's wingman that morning, followed his skipper and ignored the antiaircraft to press home attacks on two Nakajimas.

ENS Milton C. Tootle, IV, A-V(N), a tall, athletic young pilot, the son of a St. Louis, Mo., banker, took off into "every bit of antiaircraft fire from our whole force." Proceeding out about a mile, he spotted an in-coming *kanko* and chased it. Closing, Tootle opened fire at short range, and saw his tracers hitting home. Down below, "Beany" Jarrett, on *Morris'* bridge, noticed an enemy plane with an F4F close on its tail, no more than 25 yards astern, saw that his own ship's 20-mm. fire seemed to be striking home, too.

Tootle, oblivious to the antiaircraft fire at the outset, had been flying through a hail of it; even as he was trying to shoot the *kanko* from the sky, his own aircraft was taking hits, too, perhaps from *Morris*. Alarmed by gathering smoke in his cockpit, he flew alongside another F4F, whose pilot told him: "When it gets bad go down and land beside the destroyer." Afraid to be trapped in a burning plane, too low to jump, Tootle climbed to 1,500 feet and bailed out. The last man off *Yorktown*'s deck, ENS Hopper, did not fare so well. One of the escorting "Zeroes" splashed him soon after he took off.

Nearly obscured by a flak burst to the left of the aiming cross in the center of the picture, a Grumman F4F-4 banks away after having just shot down a Japanese plane, as seen from *Pensacola*. 80-G-32250

Despite a heavy antiaircraft barrage, *Yorktown* is hit by a torpedo during the attack by LT Hashimoto's second *chutai* on the afternoon of 4 June. *Morris* is at left, and *Astoria*, partially obscured by smoke, is at right. Photograph was taken by William Smistik, in *Pensacola*. 80-G-414423

Enterprise's fighters—from her fourth CAP—joined in the fray. LT(jg) W.E. Rawie, and ENSs Ralph M. Rich and W.C. Presley, A-V(N), spotted one *kanko* approaching *Yorktown* and dove from 6,000 feet. Each pilot made one firing run; ENS Rich then made a second, his .50-caliber fire killing the plane's gunner on that pass. Closing to point-blank range, he then shot down the Nakajima in flames.

RE E.H. Bayers (NAP) and MACH Beverly W. Reid (NAP) sighted two "Zeroes" about 7,000 feet below them, and Bayers attacked, claiming the section leader. Escaping from the wingman of the plane he had just shot down, Bayers spotted a retreating *kanko* and claimed shooting it down in one short burst. "Frenchy" Reid engaged two *kanko* while his wingman was dueling with the "Zero," and claimed to splash both.

Enterprise's pilots in the mixed VF-3/VF-6 patrol (*Enterprise*'s fifth CAP, launched at 1340 under VF-3's "Doc" McCuskey) did not fare as well. ENSs Melvin C. Roach and Mortimer V. Kleinmann, A-V(N), and AP1c Howard S. Packard (NAP) attacked some of the escorting "Zeroes" but found themselves soon entangled in a dogfight from which they could not extricate themselves. "They were saved from embarrassment," wrote VF-6's diarist later, "by help from friendly planes with an altitude advantage who shot all of them down on their first run."

On board *Yorktown*, CAPT Buckmaster saw one *kanko* splash off the port bow, and the tracks of several torpedoes. Only making 19 knots, his ship could not comb the wakes as she had done at Coral Sea, her comparatively low speed limiting Buckmaster's excellent shiphandling abilities. One torpedo barrelled into *Yorktown*'s port side at frame 80, 15 feet below the waterline, at about 1445; a heavy explosion shook her, and she listed six degrees to port. Still underway with the damage initially confined to flooding in the forward generator room, it looked for an instant that *Yorktown* would make it through the attack. Then, however, as the column of water thrown up by the explosion of the first torpedo subsided, another towering geyser shot up alongside, disfiguring the gallery walkway above it, as a second torpedo hit the ship. Plunged into darkness below decks, *Yorktown* lost way, her list increasing to port. Her rudder jammed, the carrier went dead in the water, her radios fell silent.

Yorktown's engineering officer, LT John F. Delaney, reported that the shock of the two hits had snuffed out the fires in six boilers and that the ship had lost power. The damage control officer, LCDR Clarence C. Aldrich, told CAPT Buckmaster that without power, he could not control the flooding. The torpedo hits had also severed communication with the main engine control, both forward and after generator compartments, repair parties, and pump control stations. A quick check of the forward generator room through the door leading to central station showed that that compartment was flooded, preventing the forward damage control pumps from either draining or counterflooding the affected areas of the ship. The total loss of steam and electric power also meant that pumping fuel from the tanks on one side of the ship to the other to correct the list was out of the question. A grim possibility confronted CAPT Buckmaster at that moment; with *Yorktown* unable to correct her list, she could turn turtle, trapping almost the entire crew. He ordered Delaney and Aldrich to secure their respective departments and direct their men to come topside and don lifejackets.

Since the list had increased steadily, CAPT Buckmaster and CDR Aldrich agreed that it looked as if *Yorktown* would capsize, soon, perhaps in a "few minutes." For 16 months, Elliott Buckmaster had been in command; he had taken her through part of the Battle of the Atlantic, and the first few months of the war in

CAPT Elliott Buckmaster (seen here in 1940 at NAS Pearl Harbor), his USNA classmates said, combined the "amiable characteristics of the Southerner" with the "shrewdness of the Yankee." Designated a naval aviator in 1936, Buckmaster commanded NAS Pearl Harbor and served as XO of *Lexington* before he assumed command of *Yorktown* in February 1941. "From my intimate association with him in times of battle and stress," wrote Frank Jack Fletcher after Midway, "I know him [Buckmaster] to be an outstanding leader of men, an exceptional ship handler during times of great excitement, a rugged and fearless sailor and aviator, with unlimited nerve, but never nervous. It is a privilege to serve with such a man in time of war..." NH 57377, cropped

the Pacific. His men would have followed him anywhere; loyal to their skipper, they had cheered him at Tongatabu, after the Battle of the Coral Sea, where his shiphandling had been superb. Undoubtedly, the ship had become a part of him. No captain relishes the thought of losing his ship; no captain could relish the thought of losing men's lives when a chance existed to save them. Also, no one knew if the Japanese would be back again with *Yorktown* a sitting duck.

The captain of a ship is a lonely figure, carrying a heavy burden; at a moment such as that faced by Buckmaster shortly before 1500 on 4 June 1942, while he had the advice and counsel of his junior officers, the decision to abandon ship rested, solely, with him. With a heavy heart, and "in order to save as many of the ship's company as possible," he wrote later, "I ordered the ship abandoned."

Men brought up wounded and injured shipmates in the glare of battle lanterns. One ladder leading up from the sick bay hung crazily at an angle, loose on one side, adding to the difficulty of getting men topside. Slippery decks and the steep list rendered carrying stretchers impossible; some men had to be dragged across the deck, others carried bodily.

During the abandonment, the four *Enterprise* aircrew became separated. ENS Roberts went back to his aircraft to extract the camera with which his radio-gunner had taken pictures of the burning Japanese carriers, as well as his life raft. A *Yorktown* sailor proposed that they abandon ship together, using the pilot's raft. The sailor went over the side first and Roberts followed after throwing the raft down, but soon lost his grip on the rope and splashed into the water far below. Encumbered by his leather flight jacket, shoes, camera and his .45-caliber pistol, Roberts saw no sign of his would-be raftmate and swam to a nearby life raft to hang on.

Thrice air raids interrupted the work of the screen in picking up *Yorktown*'s men, but it proceeded apace. On board the carrier, her gregarious and energetic XO, CDR Kiefer, far from being a sidewalk superintendent, had directed the abandonment and pitched in to help wherever possible. Helping to lower a man over the side, Kiefer had lost his grip on the rope and burned his hands severely. Ignoring his own discomfort, he continued going about the business of directing the abandonment until all hands, including sick bay patients, were reportedly over the side. Telling this to the captain, who told him to go ahead and leave, Kiefer started down a rope. His hands, however, already seared by a rope burn, failed to get a good grip on the line, and he fell, caroming off the armor belt and suffering a painful compound fracture of the foot and ankle. It would take much more that that to stop Kiefer, however, for he came

Men on board *Yorktown* gather on the starboard side of the ship as the carrier lists after she was torpedoed. Note fire extinguishers on deck, and the knotted line hanging down in the foreground, evidently used by men to reach safety on the flight deck. 80-G-21603

Balancing themselves to keep their footing on the steeply canting deck, *Yorktown*'s men prepare to abandon ship. The plane visible in the background, on the "high" side of the ship, is a Grumman F4F-4 (BuNo 5165) that had been flown by LT(jg) Brainard T. Macomber, A-V(N), on the escort mission that morning. It did not have enough fuel to enable it to be launched as *Hiryu*'s second strike developed that afternoon. 80-G-14384

As seen from *Pensacola*, *Yorktown*'s people abandon ship, while destroyers stand in to rescue them. From left to right are *Benham, Russell, Balch* and *Anderson*. Three different camouflage schemes can be seen on the ships in this view: *Benham* and *Balch* in what appears to be sea blue (Measure 11); *Russell* and *Anderson* in two variants of the sea blue/ocean gray (Measure 12, mod.), and *Yorktown* in her original Measure 12 graded system paint scheme (lower color sea blue, upper ocean gray). 80-G-21694

Balch stands by at right, her main battery trained to port, while *Yorktown* sailors continue to abandon ship. Note rafts at the stern and mattresses (part of the jury-rigged splinter protection rigged around the 20-mm. guns on the stern) hanging over the fantail. 80-G-17061

Abandonment about complete, *Yorktown* lies nearly empty as two destroyers (one of which is *Balch*) stand by (R). A motor whaleboat bobs in the foreground (center) of this panorama taken from one of the screening ships. USN

to the surface after his fall and doggedly struck out for a nearby destroyer, helping to push a loaded life raft en route.

Moments later, CAPT Buckmaster started his last tour of the ship. Starting from the catwalk along the starboard side of the flight deck, the captain checked the 5-inch gun platforms, then returned to the flight deck abreast the number one crane, before he proceeded down through number one dressing station and forward, going through "flag country" and his own cabin, to the port side and down a ladder to the hangar deck. He checked that area, and, finding no one, saw the water lapping at the port side of the hangar deck. He then went aft, and, satisfied that no one remained alive on board, finally abandoned ship. As he swam away from the ship, he heard someone in trouble; he turned and saw William Fentress, one of *Yorktown*'s mess cooks; foundering in the oily sea. Swimming over to the young man, Buckmaster kept him afloat and got him to a raft.

MACH Lewis N. Williams joined a young sailor in towing a raft away from the carrier. Suddenly, the man began swearing a blue streak, prompting Williams to ask him "what was eating him so much that he cussed." "That damn recruiting officer," the sailor blurted out, "didn't tell me about this."

Gradually, *Yorktown*'s sailors, Marines, and air group men reached safety on board the nearby destroyers. *Benham* picked up 721 men; *Balch* 544, with two of her men, H.E. Prideaux, F2c and A.E. Lewis, Sea1c, distinguishing themselves by taking buoyed lines to struggling men as far as 300/400 yards away. Other *Balch* sailors had dove in to help the carrier's men, knowing full well that if an air raid materialized and forced

the ships to get underway, they diminished their own chances of survival. *Russell* rescued 499 and *Anderson* 204 (including ENS Tootle of VF-3); *Morris* pulled out 193, *Hammann* 85 (including CAPT Buckmaster) and *Hughes* 24.

In the meantime, *Enterprise* had put aloft her sixth CAP at 1450; they remained over TF 16 until "Ham" Dow vectored two sections to the vicinity of TF 17 to deal with "bogies" in *Yorktown*'s vicinity at about 1600. The VT-6 pilots spotted two floatplanes at 1626; both proved to be from *Tone*: one a Type 95 (her no. 3 plane); the other a Type 00 (no. 4). Flown by LT(jg) Hasegawa, the single-float, open-cockpit biplane proved a nimble and hardy antagonist, until two NAPs, MACHs Howell M. Sumrall and Julius A. Achten splashed him at 1633. Jim Gray, whose guns had malfunctioned in his initial pass on the *Tone*'s no. 3 plane, chased no. 4 for some time, using up nearly all of his fuel and ammunition, but failed to bring it down.

Benham, after rescuing well over 700 men, added one more to her "bag" before nightfall. At 1618, a lookout spotted a man in a rubber boat; altering course, *Benham* stood toward him, and came upon LT(jg) "Willo" Woollen of VF-3. As the destroyer approached the pilot, LCDR Joseph M. Worthington, *Benham*'s CO, heard Woollen call out cheerfully, "Take your time, Captain — I'm in no hurry. This raft won't run out of gas!"

At 1630, LT(jg) Harold W. Lough, A-V(N), of VP-23, returning from a nearly 700-mile patrol, sighted a rubber life boat in the open sea, 150 miles northwest of Midway. Although he and his crew were fatigued from the operations of that day and the days preceding, Lough landed the "Catalina" and taxied over to the raft, find-

ing ENS Troy Guillory and his radio-gunner, B.R. Cotrell, ARM2c, of Bombing EIGHT, who had ditched during the unsuccessful *Hornet* Air Group search for the *Kido Butai*. With the grateful pair on board, Lough took off to return to Sand Island.

"Scouting" FIVE, meanwhile, was providing the opportunity to avenge the crippling of *Yorktown*. The search she had launched at 1130 had yielded little fruit until one of the five two-plane sections sighted something on the return leg of its flight. At 1430, LT Sam Adams and LT Harlan R. Dickson spotted a formation of 10 ships—four destroyers, three heavy cruisers, and a carrier, which proved to be *Hiryu*. Immediately, Adams broke radio silence and transmitted an "exceptionally precise" plain-language dispatch giving the enemy carrier's location. After he had transmitted a coded transmission as a follow-up, Adams' radio-gunner, Joseph J. Karrol, ARM1c, joined Dickson's, J.M. Lynch, ARM2c, in driving off a "Zero" that had attacked them. In another sector, LT John Nielsen and ENS Ben Preston encountered a Type 95 floatplane from *Haruna*, one of those launched at 1300, which radioed at 1430: "I am being engaged by two enemy planes. Apparently there are carriers in the vicinity." Nielsen and Preston each made five runs on the biplane, causing heavy damage and killing the observer, but the pilot proved exceptionally skillful, avoiding even Preston's head-on passes, and escaped.

Upon completion of the search, all 10 planes returned to TF 16, with LT(jg) William F. Christie and LT(jg) H.M. McDowell landing on board *Hornet* and the rest on board *Enterprise*, which had received Adams' contact report at 1445.

Miles Browning had, earlier in the day, urged Spruance to launch an immediate strike against the fourth Japanese carrier, but the admiral had demurred, reasoning that the trail, by that point, was cold. As the attacks against *Yorktown* developed, it seemed that perhaps Browning had been right, and Spruance wrong. The arrival of Adams' contact report, however, soon vindicated the admiral's decision.

On board *Enterprise*, deck crews prepared another strike—this one to go after *Hiryu*. They readied 25 SBD-3s and -3As—15 of which came from Bombing THREE, grouped in five three-plane sections, to be flown by 14 VB-3 pilots and one from VB-6 temporarily assigned to the squadron to round out the complement. Command of VB-3 had devolved upon LT DeWitt Shumway, VB-3's XO, since Leslie was still on board *Astoria*. The rest of the attack group came from Scouting SIX (seven planes) and Bombing SIX (three). LT Earl Gallaher, Scouting SIX, would lead the mission.

In the meantime, *Hornet* had spotted "Ruff" Johnson's returning troops at 1456. Having monitored the sighting report from Adams, she expected to launch planes immediately to take part in the strike. Lack of communication between the two carriers of TF 16, however, again reared its head. CAPT Mitscher, hearing nothing from the flagship of a strike on *Hiryu*, elected to break the spot on his deck and recover VB-8. At the same time, she brought on board seven F4Fs (five from VF-8 and two from VF-3). Only at that point, around 1517, did *Hornet* receive word from *Enterprise* that she was launching a strike at 1530!

At 1525, TF 16 turned into the wind and after the relief CAP flight, Earl Gallaher led the strike group off to seek out the last Japanese carrier. After quickly forming up, the strike departed, its number lessened only by one, as LT(jg) J. Norman West had to return on board for a forced landing. *Enterprise* then recovered 15 F4Fs (VF-3 and VF-6); one VF-6 pilot, though, did not make the deck; running out of gasoline, MACH William H. Warden had to ditch and be picked up by a destroyer.

Meanwhile, a PBY lingered in the vicinity of the Japanese. ENS Ted Thueson had searched the sector assigned to him, but had found nothing. At 1405, he reported that, and his fuel state, and requested instructions. Ordered to search the sector that lay roughly north-northwest of Midway and return to base prior to 1900, Thueson reported three burning ships roughly northwest by north, 170 miles from Midway, at 1558. At 1609, he reported two cruisers on the same bearing and distance. He maintained his watch, seeking to identify the ships in view.

At about the same time, in TF 16, having belatedly received word of the strike, *Hornet* did not get her first SBD aloft until after the last one had cleared the flagship's deck. By 1600, with only 16 SBDs airborne, CAPT Mitscher signalled LT Edgar E. Stebbins, of VS-8, to take charge of *Hornet*'s planes in the air and proceed on the mission assigned. Gathering his force (nine VS-8 SBDs and seven from VB-8), Stebbins set out as directed.

On board *Hiryu*, her flight deck crew worked with the purposeful nature of desperate men. At dawn, the 1st Air Fleet had put aloft an aerial armada. By that point in the day, the spectre of disaster stalked the Japanese. By 1350, *Akagi* was a veritable flaming coffin, steaming out of control; only a short time before, the portrait of the Emperor had been transferred to *Nowaki*. By 1600, *Arashi* and *Nowaki* had taken on board most of the survivors. *Kaga* would soon be ordered abandoned, at 1700.

In the meantime, the interrogation of Osmus yielded information which explained what forces had been arrayed against the Japanese. At 1300, CAPT Kosaku

ENS James A. Riner Jr., A-V(N), and his radio-gunner, Floyd A. Kilmer, ARM2c, look over the damage to their SBD-3 (B-13)—holed by antiaircraft fire over Midway—back on board *Hornet* on 4 June 1942. Riner appears to be wearing leather jacket, flying gloves, and a "Mae West" as part of his flight gear, with a .45 strapped to his hip, and carries his chart board. Kilmer's "Mae West" carries his name and squadron designation (VB-8). Lawson

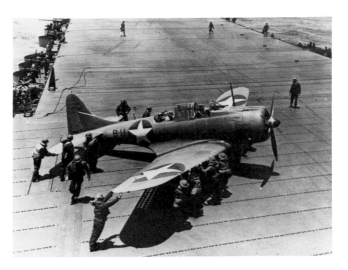

Spotting a Bombing EIGHT SBD-3 (B-11) on board *Hornet* during the Battle of Midway. Note mixture of old- and new-style helmets in use by the plane handlers. Lawson

Ariga, Commander, 4th Destroyer Division, radioed Yamamoto, Nagumo and two other fleet commanders of the results of their questioning of the American flier. They learned that there were three American carriers opposing them: *Yorktown, Enterprise* and *Hornet*; that *Yorktown*, with her screen, was operating independently of the others; that *Yorktown* had sailed from Pearl Harbor on the morning of 31 May and arrived in the vicinity of Midway the following day [ed. note: a bit of an exaggeration], and that there had been no capital ships at Pearl up to that point. Later that day, Osmus was executed and his body dumped into the sea.

The planes on *Hiryu*'s deck numbered less than two dozen; six *kansen*, five *kanbaku* and four *kanko*. Also on deck with its engine warming up was Iida's plane, which was to seek out the American task force and guide the third strike to it. Nearby steamed *Tone*, that began maneuvering to recover her aircraft when her sister ship, *Chikuma*, suddenly spotted planes over *Hiryu*. Almost simultaneously, the carrier's antiaircraft batteries opened fire.

Guided by Adams' excellent report, the *Enterprise* strike had spotted its quarry from 13,000 feet at 1645, east of the remnants of the once-powerful *Kido Butai*. Gallaher commenced climbing to 19,000 feet, circling to the southwest to gain a position up-sun of the enemy; while doing so, he ordered VB-6 to follow VS-6 in attacking the carrier, and VB-3 to attack a nearby "battleship." At 1658, Gallaher nosed into a shallow descent, turned toward the Japanese, and commenced his high-speed run to the push-over point.

Gallaher led the attack into the teeth of a heavy anti-aircraft barrage, diving on *Hiryu* as she swung to the southeast, taking evasive action. The ship's movements served her well, as both Gallaher and one of his wingmen, ENS Reid Stone, missed with their bombs.

Shumway pushed over at 19,000 feet, from out of the sun, at 1710. From where he sat, though, it looked as if none of Scouting SIX's bombs had hit; seeing this, he abruptly switched VB-3's target to the still-unhit carrier, a move that put Dick Best and his VB-6 section at risk. Seeing VB-3's first division approaching on a collision course, Best snapped into a sharp climbing turn to avoid Shumway's oncoming troops. The abrupt move

AVCDT Wesley Frank Osmus, USNR, circa 1940. Designated a naval aviator 25 March 1941, he was appointed ensign, A-V(N), 22 April 1941, and joined VT-3 on 15 August 1941. USN

caught ENS Fred Weber on the inside of the turn; compelled to flatten out to avoid stalling, he straggled several hundred yards away. A "Zero," however, flashed in and riddled Weber's plane in two passes; B-3 slanted downward in flames; neither the pilot nor his radio-gunner got out.

Shumway's assessment that none of Scouting SIX's bombs struck home was not completely accurate, as ENS Jaccard, who followed Gallaher and Stone, had laid his bomb squarely into *Hiryu*'s forward elevator. His 500-pounder penetrated the flight deck and exploded below, the force of the blast hurling the elevator platform against the forward part of the island. The other three planes to follow Jaccard, however, did miss.

The *Yorktown*ers pushed over, leaving Dick Best and "Bud" Kroeger no choice but to follow, while the remaining "Zeroes," estimated at about a dozen, swarmed over the SBDs. Three swept in astern of Shumway's "Dauntless," B-13; others attacked "Randy" Cooner's B-15, Sid Bottomley's B-10; and ENS H.A. Merrill's B-17. Two SBDs slanted into the sea in the melee — gone were LT(jg) "Ozzie" Wiseman (who had gone to the Naval Academy expressly to realize his goal of being a naval aviator) and his radio-gunner, Grant Ulysses Dawn, ARM2c, and ENS John C. Butler, A-V(N), and his radioman, D.D. Berg, ARM3c. Shumway's men and Best, however, had dropped nine 1,000-pounders on *Hiryu*, two on a nearby ship; they claimed four direct hits that turned the Japanese carrier into a floating cauldron of exploding, gasoline and ordnance.

The "Zero" pilots, however, proved a determined bunch. One stayed with Shumway as he attempted to disengage; 20-mm. shells damaged the right diving and landing flap, perforated and drained the right main gas tank, holed the right elevator and stabilizer; exploded in the baggage compartment, the fragments injuring the radio-gunner, R.E. Coons, ARM1c. Further, 7.7-mm. slugs holed the fuselage and nose section. Shumway dove steeply toward the water to escape, feigning destruction.

A trio of "Zeroes" bedevilled Randy Cooner and his radio-gunner, Clifton R. Bassett, AOM2c. One 20-mm. shell exploded in B-15's radio transmitter, fragments peppering Bassett's right knee and giving Cooner a slight leg wound. One 20-mm. shell penetrated the base of the fin, exploding in the baggage compartment and shredding the life raft stowed there. Bassett, fighting to stay conscious because of the pain and the loss of blood, claimed one "Zero" in return, however, and drove off a prowling floatplane that attacked them after the fighters had disappeared.

ENS Merrill found himself, too, the object of a "Zero's" attention. Two 20-mm. shells penetrated aft of the cockpit and exploded, temporarily freezing control cables and slightly injuring Dallas J. Bergeron, ARM3c, in both feet. Another "Zero" attacked LT(jg) Sherwood in similar fashion, but caused little damage. An enemy fighter dove on Sid Bottomley, who opened his dive flaps; the "Zero" overshot him. Pulling up, his adversary thus spoiled the aim of two more Mitsubishi s queuing up astern. Another fighter appeared during Bottomley's dive, but his radio-gunner, Johnson, drove him off with fire from his free guns. Merrill spotted a single-float floatplane—perhaps the same one which had sniped at Cooner—heading for the clouds that hung scattered to the east, but wisely decided against pur-

Bel Geddes diorama depicting the attack on *Hiryu* by planes from *Enterprise*.
80-G-701885

suit due to the proximity of the still deadly "Zeroes."

Hiryu, though, lay behind them, burning. Flames and smoke rendered accounting for the damage impossible. *Hornet*'s attack group, arriving soon after *Enterprise*'s, at 1700, found that there was nothing they could do, so went after the heavy cruiser *Tone*. Misfortune continued to dog *Hornet*'s pilots, though, for none of the 14 bombs dropped hit the target!

ENS Thueson's persistence, meanwhile, paid off, as he radioed at 1745 that the three burning ships he had spotted at 1558 were Japanese carriers—the first confirmation obtained by the Americans of the damage inflicted on the enemy. A short time later, a "Zero," probably one of the surviving CAP with no deck to land on, attacked the PBY. Thueson maneuvered the big flying boat so well that none of his crew suffered any injuries. He did, however, have to dump some fuel to avoid a fire in the air. His mission accomplished, though, he set course for Midway.

While *Hornet*'s bombers had been unsuccessful, so, too, were groups of B-17s vectored to the vicinity of the burning *Hiryu*. The first, consisting of six "Flying Fortresses" sent by Bellinger to Barking Sands early that morning, had been ordered at 1620 to proceed on to bomb the enemy and then continue on to Midway. Those B-17s, under MAJ George Blakey, each with half a bomb load (four 500-pound bombs) and a bomb bay fuel tank to extend their range, found *Hiryu* at 1830. They claimed one hit and two near-misses on the carrier and that they sank a nearby destroyer with one bomb. The Army pilots claimed that they encountered heavy antiaircraft, and that eight "Zeroes" intercepted them; four, the Army claimed, were shot down and one damaged in the battle that followed, while receiving only damage to two B-17s. Nine bombs hung in their racks, and the two damaged "Flying Fortresses" were unable to drop any of their ordnance.

About the same time, the four B-17s that had taken off from Midway shortly after 1500, under the command of LTCOL Sweeney, found the same force attacked by Blakey's bombers from Barking Sands, as did two additional B-17s from Midway whose takeoff had been delayed until 1620 with engine trouble. Four of the bombers, unhampered by fighters, attacked a "cruiser," dropping 28 500-pounders on her; the Army pilots claimed one hit, one probable hit, and two near-misses, leaving her "smoking heavily and aflame . . ." Their quarry may have been *Chikuma*, which reported an attack by three B-17s but was undamaged, that ship making note of the fact that "several bombs . . ." dropped in the water "100 meters to starboard." The other B-17s attacked a "battleship" and "burning carriers," claiming one hit and two near-misses on the former and two

hits and three near-misses on the latter, out of 16 500-pounders dropped. The Army pilots further reported that "Zeroes" intercepted them, and that three were shot down and one damaged.

The Army planes returned to Midway after sundown. Learning that there were only enough bombs for eight planes for a dawn mission, and that six B-17s had arrived as reinforcements that afternoon, Sweeney decided to return his squadron's planes to Oahu. He reasoned that the remaining airplanes under his command were unfit for combat, citing damaged wings, bomb bay doors, engines, and that his crews were exhausted.

The composite *Enterprise* group, meanwhile, returned in triumph, and reached the ship at 1808, having lost three planes: two from VB-3 (Wiseman and Butler) and one from VB-6 (Weber). By 1834, the "Big E" had recovered the last of the SBDs, even three (Shumway's, Cooner's and Merrill's) deemed "inoperative for future combat." In less than 30 minutes, *Hornet* had recovered the last of her strike group, and by 1920, the last plane of *Enterprise*'s tenth and final CAP had been brought on board, bringing to a close the day's air activity in TF 16.

Clifton R. Bassett, AOM2c, of VB-3, ENS "Randy" Cooner's radio-gunner, suffering a painful leg wound, is borne off in a Stokes stretcher on board *Enterprise* after they had returned from the strike on *Hiryu*. Cooner follows. Note pile of wheel chocks at upper right. 80-G-7746

Almost at the same time Shumway's SBDs were opening their dive flaps, Frank Jack Fletcher had decided to take TF 17 clear of the abandoned carrier and join TF 16. Consequently, his ships, augmented by the ones Spruance had sent over in mid-afternoon, formed a column and moved off. Correspondent Webb, on board *Pensacola*, later wrote: "The aircraft carrier *Yorktown* is a lonely blotch on the western sun tonight and there is a lump in many a throat. The fleet is moving on."

The fast-paced nature of modern war seldom permits much time for sentimentality. Fletcher knew that his most powerful concentration of ships, formed around his two intact carriers, lay to the east, perhaps too far away to provide adequate protection for TF 17. Enemy "snoopers" lurked about and prompted concern that the Japanese would launch a third air attack on his force (only four carriers had been accounted for of what was perhaps five in the intelligence estimates), as well as the possibility that the enemy would hurl a night surface attack to try and destroy *Yorktown*. Survivors crowded four of his destroyers; how those ships could take part in a night action with so many excess men on board was problematical.

Fletcher decided to clear the area to redistribute survivors and send back a salvage party the next day to try and save *Yorktown*. In the meantime, he radioed for assistance, requesting that a salvage tug be sent out immediately.

At 1800, as Fletcher, in *Astoria*, drew away from his former flagship, he directed COMDESRON SIX, CAPT E.P. Sauer, to detach *Hughes* to stand by *Yorktown* with instructions to prevent anyone from boarding her, or to destroy her to prevent capture or if serious fires should break out afresh on board. *Hughes* cleared TF 17 to commence her vigil, 15 minutes later.

As TF 17 steamed eastward, RADM Spruance radioed Fletcher, telling him of the attacks on *Hiryu*, and then asked if he had any instructions for him. "Negative," Fletcher responded, "Will conform to your movements." TF 17 then drew away from TF 16, around midnight, steering east.

As 4 June ended, the U.S. Navy had gained "incontestible mastery of the air." TF 16, air groups recovered (both carriers had *Yorktown* aircraft on board), then stood eastward, southward, and back to the westward, as time went on. Spruance, to whom Fletcher had passed tactical command, did not feel "justified in risking a night encounter with possibly superior enemy forces." On the other hand, if the Japanese were continuing toward Midway, he wanted to be in a position to either "follow up retreating enemy forces or to break up a landing attack . . ." The presence of that fifth carrier reported in the pre-battle intelligence reports, too, weighed heavily on the admiral's mind. With the day waning, he decided that TF 16 would move eastward until midnight, at which point it would turn north. It would proceed northward for an hour, at which time, it would head westward to be able to support Midway in the morning.

While there had been emotion shown as *Yorktown* was left behind, no less emotional were those who witnessed the agony of *Hiryu*, *Yorktown*'s antagonist,

which had been so gallantly fought. On board the destroyer *Yugumo*, Kyoichi Furuya later wrote in his diary: "As the sun went down, the *Hiryu* was burning fiercely, and seemed to scorch the heavens. The sound of explosions in the powder magazines and the fuel tanks were heard. Our aircraft, having no place to land and with their fuel and ammunition exhausted, went down tragically beside destroyers and cruisers. There was not a single friendly aircraft left. Our fate," he lamented, "is a matter of time. We resolved to do our utmost and await the orders of God. . . ."

Keenly aware of the frightful toll of men and machines that the day's operations had exacted, RADM Spruance, via CAPT Murray, while commending *Enterprise*'s ship's company and air group for their "splendid performance of duty," regretted the high cost in men—something reflected by the empty places in the wardroom and enlisted mess. Spruance felt, though, that those gallant men had "contributed materially in striking a decisive blow against the enemy."

Murray's fervent hope, as he expressed to his men, was "that many of our gallant and heroic shipmates in the Air Group who are now unaccounted for will be rescued by our own forces. Those who are not, and who have made the supreme sacrifice have done so [so] that our country may live. We salute our honored dead and are determined to exterminate the enemy and drive him from the seas. To all hands 'Well done.'"

Back at Pearl, CINCPAC's war diarist noted the start "of what may be the greatest sea battle since Jutland. Its outcome, if as unfavorable to the Japs as seems indicated, will virtually end their expansion. We lost a large percentage of highly trained pilots," he wrote, "who will be difficult to replace."

With 720 *Yorktown* men on board, *Benham* approaches *Portland* around 1900 on 4 June. Momentarily, the report of an incoming air raid (later proved false) compelled the destroyer to cast off with the carrier's men still on board. The next morning, she transferred some to *Portland* and some to *Astoria*. NH 95574

CHAPTER TWELVE

....

"I Will Do What You Pilots Want"

Although the carrier action was over for the day, the battle did not end as darkness descended. At 1700 on the 4th, a PBY had reported the presence of a "burning carrier," prompting CAPT Simard to direct LTCOL Kimes to send a strike out to finish her off. MAJ Norris, who had assumed command of VMSB-241 after Lofton Henderson's death, and mindful of what "Zeroes" had done to the squadron that morning, insisted that the attack be delayed until after dark, in order to "minimize . . . fighter opposition."

The ship in question may have been *Kaga*, which had been abandoned by that time, with the destroyers *Maikaze* and *Hagikaze* taking on board her surviving crew within an hour of her abandonment at 1700. Unchecked fires, however, reached her forward fuel bunkers at 1825, and two violent explosions ripped through the ship. Bill Brockman, with *Nautilus* still operating submerged, heard "heavy subsurface explosions" and had his ship rigged for depth-charging; when he ultimately took his boat up to periscope depth, no carrier could be seen. *Kaga* sank by 1925, taking down 800 men with her, and a periscope search revealed no sign of the ship. *Nautilus* ultimately surfaced at 1941, her batteries exhausted; she had expended five torpedoes and had taken 45 depth charges in return. Her men could see no sign of the carrier they had torpedoed.

Akagi, also doomed, lingered in her death throes. By 1920, further firefighting efforts on board the erstwhile flagship of the *Kido Butai* were regarded as useless, and CAPT Taijiro Aoki ordered all hands to abandon ship.

Getting the strike ready to go after the "burning carrier" reported by the PBY would take some doing, however, particularly since the reservicing of the B-17s had taken priority. Nearly two hours elapsed before the attack units of the remaining operational SBD-2s and SB2U-3s could be armed and bombed-up. By 1915, the squadron, divided into two units (six SBD-2s under

CAPT Marshall A. "Zack" Tyler and six SB2U-3s under MAJ Norris) had taken off, to proceed out 200 miles into the black night.

At about 1730, about a half hour after he had told LTCOL Kimes to send out the strike, CAPT Simard ordered LT McKellar's MTBRON ONE to fuel to capacity and proceed to a point 170 miles to the north-northwest of Midway—the approximate position of the "burning carrier." All boats, including *PT-29* and *PT-30* that had been at Kure Island, took on fuel (including 200 extra gallons stored in drums on deck) and got underway at 2115. Heading for the scene at 30 knots, the ELCOs sped out into the darkness.

Upon arriving at the place where the "burning Japanese carrier" had been reported, however, the Marines found no signs of the enemy. Norris' and Tyler's flights then turned and headed back to Midway through heavy squalls and beneath a low cloud ceiling. Tyler's returned as a group "without incident and without having sighted the objective." The SB2Us had remained together, too, until about 40 miles from Midway, when MAJ Norris suddenly went into a steep right bank from 10,000 feet; as he lost altitude, the group followed him until their altimeters read 500 feet. Neither he nor his radio-gunner, PFC Arthur B. Whittington, was ever seen again, as the lights of their plane disappeared a few moments after the rest of the unit broke away. Perhaps Norris experienced vertigo and lost control of his aircraft.

2dLT Whitten had been in Norris' group; on the way out he noticed the poor weather conditions, with clouds extending from 500 feet above the ocean and towering up to 6,500 feet. He became separated from the flight at about 2130 when the formation went into a descending turn to the right. Trying to follow, he pulled up at 500 feet; he tried climbing through the overcast but soon found that his turn-and-bank indicator was not functioning properly, neither could he pick up the homing signal. He spun down slowly, coming out below the overcast; twice he tried searching a square before heading roughly south-southeast. Holding that for nearly a half hour, Whitten passed over Pearl and Hermes Reef; heading west by south for the next 25 minutes, then another five, he tried another square system. Still unable to see Midway, he started back toward Pearl and Hermes Reef; after holding that course for a minute, Whitten heard his gunner report that he saw lights astern. Coming about, he flew toward what proved to be the flames from the still-burning oil tanks on Sand Island. He landed at 0145 on the 5th—the last Marine to land that day—with only 30 minutes of gasoline left.

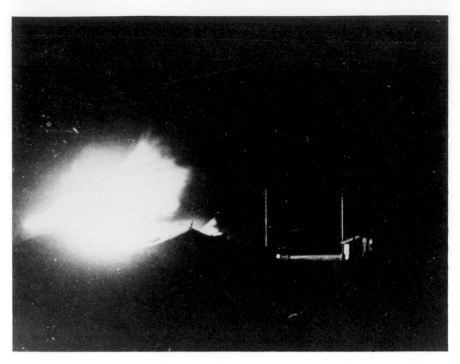

The fires from the burning fuel tanks on Sand Island continue to blaze after nightfall, providing illumination that helped at least one Marine pilot and his radio-gunner home on the night of 4 June/early morning of 5 June. 80-G-17053

Plagued by considerable quantities of salt spray that contaminated their fuel (with the consequent failure of main engines, generators and, in some instances, radios) because of their high-speed run towards the enemy, Clint McKellar's boats nevertheless pressed on, as conditions favored a night torpedo attack—intermittent rain squalls, low clouds and a smooth sea. *PT-29* and *PT-30*, having come from Kure, reached the reported position first, at about 2315. They saw no signs of enemy ships, and joined by the other boats soon thereafter, commenced a search of the vicinity.

In the meantime, Nagumo, compelled by the disaster that had befallen him on the 4th, cancelled RADM Kurita's mission of bombarding Midway at 0200 on 5 June when the four heavy cruisers were some 90 miles west of Midway and perhaps the most exposed of any Japanese fleet units at that point in the battle. The four turned, steering to the north-northwestward, and slowed to 28 knots. The interval between them lessened to 800 meters.

At 0118 on 5 June, lookouts on board *Kumano* spotted a surfaced submarine, which proved to be *Tambor* (SS-198). The flagship ordered an immediate turn to port to avoid her, but *Mikuma* turned 90 degrees instead of 45, and blundered directly across *Mogami*'s path. *Mogami*'s bow cut into *Mikuma*'s port side below the bridge, tearing a 20-by-6-meter hole in her fuel tanks. The latter could still maneuver, but her ruptured tanks leaked oil, leaving a trail easily followed. The collision left *Mogami*'s bow buckled at almost a 90-degree angle to port, back to her number one turret; flooding of the damaged section all but halted the ship. After damage control parties had detached the crumpled bow,

Mogami forged ahead, but only at 12 knots. By dawn, she could make 14.

LCDR John W. Murphy, *Tambor*'s captain, "ignorant of the location and exact composition of our own surface forces and forewarned that they might cross the submarine area during the night," had spotted four large ships on the horizon, three miles away. What appeared to be three other ships appeared soon thereafter. *Tambor* began shadowing the first group, in hopes of identifying them, steaming on a parallel course. Having transmitted a report of "many unidentified ships" at 0215, and received a receipt from Midway at 0306, the submarine was in the dark as to the identity of her quarry; ultimately, dawn revealed the enemy character of the vessels, and that one of the ships had "about 40 feet of her bow missing." When one of the ships turned toward her, *Tambor* went deep and rigged for depth-charging. At 0437, no depth-charging having occurred, the submarine came back up to periscope depth and identified two *Mogami*-class cruisers; she made her last observation of the enemy ships at 0602 as they headed westward. She did not spot them again, but passed through an oil slick at 0740 that extended from east to west—most probably fuel from *Mikuma*'s ruptured tanks.

Meanwhile, throughout the night, the rearming and servicing of the B-17s, PBYs, SBDs and SB2Us, continued, activities only briefly interrupted by *I-168*'s shelling Midway around 0130 on 5 June. Verne McCaul, MAG-22's XO, later estimated that ordnance and refueling crews hung 85 500 pounds and pumped—by hand—nearly 45,000 gallons of gasoline from 55-gallon drums. Men from MAG-22, VP-44 and from Company "C," 2d

Raider Battalion, toiled tirelessly in the darkness to accomplish the task. Ten minutes after the shelling by *I-168*, four B-17s—"no longer fit for combat duty due to damage or engineering difficulties"—took off for Oahu. Upon Sweeney's departure, command of the remaining B-17s devolved upon LTCOL Brooke E. Allen. At 0300, all hands went on alert again.

The PT-boats carried out their search in the squalls until about 0300 on 5 June. They sought signs of the enemy until daylight, but, empty-handed, started home at about 0430 on the 5th, the boats proceeding independently. En route back, *PT-20* and *PT-21* sighted a column of smoke about 15 miles to the west. The two PTs closed at 40 knots but could find no source for the smoke, which had disappeared. They found only large oil slicks and wreckage, "apparently Japanese."

Back at the atoll, at 0415 on 5 June, as the first rays of sunlight reached out from the eastern horizon, the 10 PBYs of Midway's dawn search started taking off, to search the sector to the west-southwest out to a distance of 250 miles, which would be more than adequate to pick up any invasion force if it were still pressing toward Midway. Fifteen minutes later the eight B-17s still on the atoll took off, led by LTCOL Allen, in accordance with NAS Midway's standard practice of getting the bombers airborne at dawn so that an enemy air attack would not catch them on the ground. Once airborne, they were ordered to attack the enemy force reported by *Tambor* at 0215. ENS Auman of VB-8 rode in Allen's B-17 to help the airmen tell friend from foe. After reporting unfavorable weather at 0615, and that he was unable to locate the target, Allen was ordered to return to Kure to await further instructions.

While all of the air activity was going on from Midway, *Hughes* had maintained her vigil in *Yorktown's* vicinity. Daylight on 5 June brought the ubiquitous enemy search planes: at 0626, *Hughes* picked up one on her radar, roughly west by northwest, 20 miles distant. The ship went to general quarters and increased speed, but *Chikuma's* no. 4 plane, which had been launched on a search at 0441, lurked well out of gun range.

At 0652, this plane sent off a contact report telling of an "enemy *Yorktown* class carrier listing to starboard and drifting" and of the solitary destroyer in company.

A similar vigil had been stood in the vicinity of *Akagi*. At 2225 on the 4th, CAPT Aoki's orders to sink the hulk were countermanded by ADM Yamamoto. If he had done that out of sentiment for his former command, wanting more done to save her, there is no way of telling; ultimately, though, at 0430 on 5 June, Yamamoto ordered *Akagi* scuttled. Destroyers fired torpedoes into the tortured hulk, and she sank at 0500, entombing 220 men with her.

One of the patrolling PBYs, flown by LT(jg) Shelby O. Cole, soon spotted three men—probably LCDR Mitchell, LT Ruehlow and LT(jg) Gray of Fighting EIGHT—in a rubber boat, but, unable to land and pick them up at that juncture, reported their position back to Midway at 0600. Rescue would have to wait—searching for the Japanese took priority.

In another sector, while enemy scout planes were keeping tabs on the drifting *Yorktown*, American search planes found *Mogami* and *Mikuma*. At 0630, a PBY transmitted a report of "two battleships bearing 264 distant 125 miles course 268 speed 15." Shortly thereafter, LT(jg) Norman K. Brady of VP-23, who had spotted an oil slick and followed it into an adjacent patrol sector, finding two "large capital ships" there, sent an amplifying report of the two large ships reported by the other PBY, both damaged and one streaming oil. CAPT Simard ordered VMSB-241 to attack.

The Marines took off at 0700, six SBD-2s led by "Zack" Tyler (the third VMSB-241 CO in two days), and six SB2U-3s led by Dick Fleming, who, like his shipmates in the squadron, had had less than four hours'

CAPT Marshall A. "Zack" Tyler, USMC, 8 August 1939. Tyler arrived on Midway to join VMSB-241 on 28 May 1942 and became XO on 4 June; CO later the same night upon the loss of MAJ Ben Norris. USMC

2dLT Richard E. "Dick" Fleming, circa 1941. A bright, thoughtful and talented young man killed in action in the attack on *Mikuma* on 5 June. USMC Photo 310567

PFC George A. Toms, USMC, Dick Fleming's radio-gunner, who perished along with his pilot in the attack on *Mikuma*. USMC

sleep. His plane, no. 2, was a familiar one (BuNo 2088)—he had flown it often since his arrival on Midway in December.

Approximately 40 miles from the target, the Marines picked up the trail, sighting an oil slick that served as an unerring course to the enemy. To one of the attacking pilots, Bob Vaupell, the slick looked "30 miles or more long." Tyler's unit commenced the attack at 0805 with dive-bombing runs on the two ships, pushing over from 10,000 feet in the face of heavy antiaircraft fire; Fleming's began a glide-bombing run out of the sun, from 4,000.

CAPT Leon Williamson, USMCR, in Fleming's flight, saw smoke issuing from the leader's engine throughout the glide as he kept his "Vindicator" steady and then released his bomb. Then, shortly before Williamson maneuvered his plane by a small cloud to interpose it between himself and his target as he made his approach, he saw Fleming's SB2U-3 burst into flames as the pilot tried to pull out of his dive. PVT Gene Webb, 2dLT Ringblom's radio-gunner swore that he saw two parachutes soon thereafter; if Fleming and his radio-gunner, Toms, did bail out, they were never recovered. George Koutelas, too, noted Dick Fleming's last dive; as he recounted later: "Captain Fleming was leading the attack and was hit by [antiaircraft] fire and went down in flames. He stayed in his dive even though he was in flames and dropped his bomb at 500 feet. He got a near miss on the stern of the ship."

The Marines had not scored any hits; the little group of Japanese warships continued steaming to the northwestward. Norm Brady of VP-23 maintained his watch in the vicinity, keeping close to the water to remain out of sight of the ships; pulling up periodically to observe enemy activity, he had seen antiaircraft fire in the distance but was too far away to observe results of the attack.

Soon thereafter, Brooke Allen's B-17s found what appeared to be a battleship and a cruiser—actually *Mogami* and *Mikuma*—130 miles west of Midway, at 0830. The first group of four dropped 19 500-pounders, observing two probable hits and three near-misses from 20,000 feet; the second dropped 20 500-pounders, claiming one hit on the stern of one ship and four near-misses. They encountered no fighters. In reality, none had scored direct hits, and the Japanese maintained their course to the northwest.

The 0630 contact report, meanwhile, had been followed by three reports between 0700 and 0735 of two other groups of ships also retiring to the northwest. At 0800, a PBY reported "Two battleships and one carrier afire three heavy cruisers bearing 324 distant 240 course 310 speed 12." An update at 0815 from the same PBY reported that the carrier was screened by cruisers

RADM Tamon Yamaguchi, a courageous and able officer, and an inspirational leader, commanded the 2d Carrier Division (*Hiryu* and *Soryu*). Deemed far-sighted, considerate, and unafraid of making decisions, Yamaguchi was, some said, the logical successor to Yamamoto as CinC, Combined Fleet. USNI

Having rejected his staff's entreaties that they remain with him on board his doomed flagship, *Hiryu,* RADM Yamaguchi prepares to drink a silent farewell toast, with water from a beaker held by one of his officers (L), while the destroyer *Kazagumo* stands by (background). Moments later, he removed his cap and gave it to his senior staff officer, CDR Ito, to keep as a souvenir. This painting was done in 1942 by war artist Kita Kenzo. SC 301067

Although lacking in quality this photo showing *Hiryu* burning, as seen from a plane from *Hosho* on 5 June, shows the massive damage which prompted her abandonment. Violent explosions have literally hurled the number one elevator ahead of the bridge structure, and bombs have rendered the forward part of the flight deck an unrecognizable mass. NH 73065

and destroyers. These were followed at 0820 by a report of a carrier "bearing 335 distance 250," on "course 245."

The "carrier" in question was *Hiryu*. Shortly before midnight on 4 June, when it seemed as if the Herculean efforts of the firefighters had gotten the flames under control, an explosion rekindled the blaze afresh. Further firefighting efforts seemed useless, and at 0250 CAPT Kaku ordered all hands to prepare to "abandon ship." RADM Yamaguchi and his flag captain spoke to the crew for the last time, and announced their intention to accompany *Hiryu* to the end. At 0315, CAPT Kaku ordered the crew—along with the Emperor's portrait—over the side, to be picked up by *Makigumo* and *Kazagumo*. After all survivors had been transferred to the waiting destroyers at 0430, RADM Yamaguchi and CAPT Kaku waved to their men "and with complete composure joined their fate with that of their ship." At 0510, *Makigumo* fired one torpedo into the proud carrier and then stood off, accompanying *Kazagumo* in her retirement westward. Everyone apparently thought that *Hiryu* would sink soon thereafter.

These widely diverse contacts seemed to confirm Spruance's staff estimates that the Japanese were retiring, but left a very confusing picture as to what Japanese carriers might be left. The staff was convinced that *Akagi*, *Kaga* and *Soryu* had been sunk, but that *Hiryu* had only been crippled; no one seemed ready to discount the possibility that a fifth carrier lurked out there, too, undamaged. Concerned, too, that the enemy might still be in an offensive frame of mind, Spruance continued to head southeast toward Midway. By 1100, however, convinced that the Japanese no longer posed a threat to the atoll, he changed course to one heading roughly west-northwest, to close the crippled carrier reported earlier. Unbeknownst to the Americans, *Hiryu* remained afloat until around 0900, when she finally did sink.

Meanwhile, during *Hughes'* watch on *Yorktown*, on board the latter, 18-year-old Norman M. Pichette, SEA1c, USNR, critically wounded in the abdomen by shrapnel while manning one of the Oerlikons on the fantail on 4 June, wrapped himself in a sheet. After groping across the battle dressing station where he and George K. Wiese, SEA1c, had been left for dead in the abandonment the previous day, Pichette painfully dragged himself up three ladders to reach the hangar deck. There he found a .50-caliber machine gun jury-rigged in the boat pocket aft on the low (port) side of the ship.

At 0741, he fired that gun into the water, naturally attracting the attention of *Hughes*, which drew alongside to investigate. The destroyermen saw Pichette, waving. *Hughes* stopped, lowered a boat, and then got under-

way to circle the ship while the whaleboat chugged across to the carrier. The destroyer's boarding party found Pichette, unconscious, next to the weapon he had used to call attention to his plight, and gently placed him on board the whaleboat for the trip over to *Hughes*. Bringing Pichette on board the destroyer at 0835, those who attended him heard him, when he regained consciousness briefly, mention that another man was alive on board the carrier. LCDR D.J. Ramsey, *Hughes'* captain, then sent his ship's whaleboat back on her second mercy mission. The boat crew clambered on board and down into the battle dressing station where they soon found Wiese, who was suffering from a fractured skull and other injuries. In the meantime, a PBY circled overhead, and blinkered a message that no ships lay in the area to the north or west of their position.

LCDR Ramsey sent back the ship's motor whaleboat a third time, to see if anyone else was still alive on board the carrier. At about the same time, lookouts spotted a man gamely rowing a rubber boat toward them. At 0938, *Hughes* picked up ENS Harry Gibbs, one of the four VF-3 pilots shot down the previous afternoon; he had rowed six miles toward his old ship. *Hughes* searched the waters nearby for others, but found no one.

At 0544 on 5 June, TF 17 had reversed course and reduced speed; by 0600, it was steaming some 240 miles from Midway, which lay roughly to the west-southwest. By that time, CAPT Buckmaster had been transferred on board *Astoria* from *Hammann*, and had spoken with RADM Fletcher about the possibility of saving *Yorktown*. Buckmaster wanted to return to his ship with volunteers drawn from the various divisions and departments. To obtain such a party, however, required the time-consuming process of gathering it on one ship.

Between 0604 and 0929, *Benham, Anderson, Hammann* and *Balch* transferred all of the carrier's survivors (and, from *Hammann*, the two pilots and one radio-gunner that she had rescued) to *Portland*—except the salvage party, which was gathered on board *Astoria*. At 1035, *Hammann* came alongside *Astoria* and began bringing on board Buckmaster's hand-picked salvage team—29 officers and 141 enlisted men—an evolution that consumed almost an hour. *Hammann* cleared the cruiser's side at 1127.

After the high-speed steaming of the day before, Fletcher deemed it wise to fuel his destroyers from *Portland*, an operation that commenced at 1230 and ceased at 1800. The admiral then ordered *Hammann, Balch* and *Benham*—all three ships placed under CAPT Buckmaster—to proceed toward *Yorktown* and make an attempt to save her.

As Buckmaster was gathering his salvage party, the *Vireo*, at Pearl and Hermes Reef during the opening

Taking up what appears to be almost every available deck space on board *Benham*, *Yorktown*'s men await transfer to *Portland* on 5 June. USN

Yorktown survivors gather on board *Portland*. One of the cruiser's SOC floatplanes, wings folded back, sits in the hangar (background, left). 80-G-32387

phase of the battle, guarding *Kaloli*, was proceeding toward *Yorktown*, having been detached from escort duty to lend a hand in getting the damaged carrier out of harm's way.[1] *Hughes* sighted *Vireo* approaching at 0944 on the 5th, 10 miles away, shortly before the destroyer's motor whaleboat returned to the ship with three coding machines and secret and confidential publications that had been found in two safes or loose in the coderoom. *Hughes'* boat officer reported that the destroyermen could not find any more living men on board the carrier, and that the ship did not appear to be sinking. He also said that the smoke seen forward was apparently only a waste fire, and was confined.

Vireo soon joined *Hughes*, and the former's captain, LT James C. Legg, an experienced sailor who had come up through the ranks, agreed to try and take the carrier in tow. *Hughes* contributed men to assist *Vireo's* in rigging the necessary tow line. This done, the tug started ahead at 1436, but Legg soon discovered that the best his ship could do was two or three knots. Lacking power and having a small rudder, all *Vireo* could do was keep holding *Yorktown* into the wind. A heavy sea then making up, together with the load imposed on the tug's engines, however, meant slow going. *Hughes*, meanwhile, monitoring TF 16's fighter direction circuit, learned of "enemy" planes in the vicinity. While *Vireo* had been preparing to take *Yorktown* in tow, *Monaghan*, from TF 16, and *Gwin* (DD-433), arrived on the scene.

Spruance had detached the former to pick up the crew of a PBY reported down on the water about 10 miles southwest by west of TF 16. The rescued "Catalina" turned out to be ENS Ted Thueson's. Having dumped part of his fuel to avoid a fire in the air when attacked by the "Zero" in the vicinity of the *Kido Butai*, Thueson had run out of gas on the return flight that night and landed in the open sea. He remained on the water giving bearing and distance of his position until TF 16 had neared him and Spruance sent *Monaghan* to effect the rescue. In accordance with Spruance's orders, the destroyer had left 23-P-2 intact and sped off to rejoin TF 16. Signalling later that due to an oversight the Norden bombsight had been left in the plane, Spruance ordered the destroyer to return to take that important item of equipment out of the PBY and then report to the senior officer present in *Yorktown's* vicinity. Mission accomplished, *Monaghan* headed for the damaged carrier to lend a hand. The PBY remained adrift.

Gwin, on the other hand, had departed Pearl on the morning of 3 June to join Spruance, but had been diverted en route. At 1330 on 5 June, she spotted *Yorktown* 12 miles away, and closed. LCDR John M. Higgins, *Gwin's* CO, could see that the carrier seemed in a bad way. Not content to be a bystander, Higgins ordered a salvage party to board the carrier. *Gwin's* men, assisted by some from *Hughes* and some from *Monaghan*, then boarded *Yorktown*; they jettisoned the carrier's port anchor and the 50-foot motor launch from the skids in the after boat pocket before they returned to their own ships before night fell.

At 1250 on 5 June, LT(jg) Cole, who had spotted and reported what was probably the three VF-8 pilots (Mitchell, Ruehlow and Gray) in a rubber boat at 0600, rescued ENS Gay, the only survivor of VT-8's *Hornet*-based contingent. Gay had witnessed the destruction of three Japanese carriers at close hand on 4 June.

In the meantime, CAPT Simard, having heard nothing further from the PBYs nor from TF 16's searches

ENS George H. Gay Jr., A-V(N), recuperating at Pearl Harbor, reads the "extra" edition of the *Honolulu Star-Bulletin* telling of the Japanese defeat at Midway. He was the sole survivor of the 30 men who had set out from *Hornet* in VT-8 on 4 June. USN

---

1. *Kaloli's* war diary noted *Vireo's* departure, observing that she had been left "to take care of itself [sic]." She passed through several rain squalls at nine knots, "a factor greatly in our favor . . ."

about the carrier last reported at 0815—which was, of course, *Hiryu*—sent out a strike composed of seven B-17s under CAPT Donald E. Ridings. One of the "Flying Fortresses" had a naval observer—ENS Troy Guillory of Bombing EIGHT, who had been rescued late the previous afternoon—on board, drafted into service by Simard to assist in identifying ship types. Those planes took off at 1320, and sighted TF 16 at 1430. They proceeded onward, flying roughly northwest by west.

Throughout the morning, meanwhile, as efforts to save *Yorktown* were gathering momentum, and PBYs were out searching for the Japanese or for survivors of downed planes in the wake of the action of the 4th, in TF 16, *Enterprise* and *Hornet* had maintained a CAP, the first of 12 planes to facilitate the movement of VF-3 to *Hornet* to replace the decimated VF-8 and evenly apportion the F4F-4s between the two carriers. By early afternoon, when no further contact reports came in concerning the "burning CV," Browning drew up an attack plan calling for the launch of all available SBDs at 1400 with 1,000-pound bombs. Although the admiral later admitted that the trail of the Japanese ships was "rather cold," it was "the best we had." Spruance approved the strike. The attack plan, however, drafted by Browning, mystified the CO of "Bombing 63" (the amalgamation of VB-6 and VB-3), LT DeWitt W. Shumway. First, an SBD did not possess a range of 240 miles with a 1,000-pound bomb. Secondly, since Browning's plan had not allowed for the distance the Japanese ships would cover while the attack group was enroute, the actual distance came out closer to 275 miles! Shumway conferred quickly with LT Wallace C. Short, and they, in turn, sought the advice of the wounded CEAG, McClusky, who, when he saw the order, was flabbergasted! Enlisting the injured Earl Gallaher for support, McClusky, along with *Enterprise*'s CO, CAPT George D. Murray, confronted Browning in the flag shelter.

To McClusky's contention that the mission could not be carried out as ordered, Browning responded that it could, and arbitrarily ordered the pilots to do what they were told. McClusky then asked Browning if he had ever flown an SBD, to which the chief of staff responded in the affirmative. To McClusky's question if the captain had ever flown an SBD with self-sealing tanks (which reduced the fuel carried), armored seats (which increased weight), a 1,000-pound bomb, and a full load of gas, Browning said "No." McClusky then recommended that they delay take off one hour and take only 500-pound bombs. Tempers grew more heated, and a shouting match—McClusky versus Browning—ensued.

Spruance, to Browning's astonishment, then anger, sided with McClusky. "I will do what you pilots want," he said. Browning stormed out of the shelter and down to the bridge, where he "wept and raged and screamed," and thence to his cabin, where, like Homer's Achilles, he sulked until COL Julian P. Brown, USMC, the staff intelligence officer, persuaded him to return to duty.

Spruance's siding with the aviators reflected what was apparently his increasing disillusionment with Browning. It was obvious that the results achieved the previous day had been attained through the bravery and dedication of the pilots and radio-gunners—not the plan by which they had been sent out. A new attack order was drafted and blinkered to *Hornet*. At 1500, TF 16 turned into the wind and, at 1512, commenced launch. *Enterprise*'s strike consisted of 32 SBDs, seven from "Scouting" Five and nine from VS-6 under LT Short, 10 from VB-3 and six from VB-6 under LT Shumway. All planes, each carrying a 500-pound bomb, were aloft within 30 minutes.

On board *Hornet*, however, things did not go nearly as well. Because the original intention had been to launch with 1,000-pound bombs and a full load of fuel, it had not been possible to spot the entire attack group. When the flagship directed the strike to depart at 1530, only CHAG and 10 SBDs of VB-8 stood ready. Ring departed with the planes he had—each armed with a 500-pound bomb—leaving the rest of the group to follow when ready. The remaining SBDs took their departure at 1543—15 SBDs of VS-8, five of VB-8, and one from "Scouting" Five, all under LCDR Rodee. The seven planes of VS-8's second division still carried 1,000-pound bombs in defiance of Spruance's orders. After departure, Ring's group climbed to 18,000 feet and headed to the northwest.

At 1630 the CHAG spotted five B-17's apparently returning to Midway, and, at 1715, what appeared to be a Japanese cruiser—actually *Tanikaze*—heading southwest. She had been detached to determine *Hiryu*'s status after reconnaissance planes from the light carrier *Hosho* had reported her still adrift at dawn, with men still on board. Briefed to attack the crippled carrier, though, Ring continued to search for bigger game, leading his planes out to 315 miles.

Making no further contacts, he took his men back toward the "cruiser" and ordered the attack at 1810. Using the clouds for concealment in the approach, the Bombing EIGHT pilots tried their best, but only LT Abbie Tucker came close—his bomb splashed some 25 feet directly ahead of the ship. ENS Don D. Adams, A-V(N), managed to land one some 50 feet close astern, but the rest ranged from 100 feet to "wide." "Ruff" Johnson, however, credited the Japanese with "extreme skill in maneuvering . . . to avoid being hit," and

LT Samuel Adams of "Scouting" (Bombing) FIVE, (seen here as an ENS at NAS Pensacola on 31 January 1938), "the type of man and pilot who gives strength to a squadron..." 80-PA-1A-32

Joseph J. Karrol, ARM2c, who had just turned 27 years old a month before the Battle of Midway, perished with his pilot, LT Adams, during the attack on *Tanikaze*. USN

in fighting his ship. *Tanikaze*'s captain, CDR Motoi Katsumi, showed the Americans splendid shiphandling.

The second group of *Hornet* planes, under Rodee, searched for the enemy until 1720. Then, running low on fuel because of the weight imposed by the 1,000-pound bombs, the VS-8 CO had to cut the mission short. After a brief, unsuccessful, detour to look for *Tanikaze*, Rodee and his men set course to return home.

Departing the same time as Ring, LT Shumway had led the *Enterprise* group out on a course of 324. En route, half of Shumway's group (VS-6 and V"S"-5) formed a scouting line, staying at low altitude under the 13,000 foot ceiling and heavy overcast, and the remainder (VB-3 and VB-6) climbed to 18,000 feet. By 1730, after flying the assigned 265-mile distance without a contact, Shumway changed course to roughly southwest by west for 33 miles, and then to the southsouthwest by east bearing. At 1810, he picked up Ring's order to attack the lone "cruiser."

Bombing THREE led, followed by VB-6, VS-6 and, finally, "Scouting" FIVE. CDR Katsumi again outmaneuvered the Americans, though, and none of the 32 SBDs obtained a hit as *Tanikaze* maneuvered radically and put up what VB-6's pilots described as "unusually heavy small caliber antiaircraft fire," that claimed the SBD-3 flown by Sam Adams. Both Adams and his radio-gunner, James J. Karrol, ARM1c, were killed. Later, "Dusty" Kleiss reflected in his diary: "The little devil [*Tanikaze*] fired everything he had at us, put on full speed . . . zig-zagged nicely, and was most dif-

ficult to hit. I saw several close misses, but no hits...One plane, LT Adams. . . shot down. This flight not worth the gas, bombs, and loss of a plane. . ."

The B-17s sent out from Midway at 1320 had been unable to sight their objective, and set course to return to the atoll, passing over TF 16 around 1700. On the return leg of their flight back to Midway, however, the group spotted a "large cruiser" at 1815. Four B-17s attacked from 16,000 feet; the others from 14,500. Between them, they dropped 56 500-pounders, claiming three hits and four near-misses, claiming to have neither encountered any fighters nor to have suffered any damage from antiaircraft. The ship the B-17s had attacked proved to be the destroyer *Tanikaze*.

Tanikaze would undergo more trials, though, before the day would end. At 1545, still unaware of the fact that the carrier being sought was already sunk, CAPT Simard had sent another formation of B-17s lumbering skyward with bombs and bomb-bay gasoline tanks, headed northwest. And, like the preceding group of B-17s, they, too, did not find what they were looking for. Finding *Tanikaze* instead, the five B-17s attacked her—with the same result. The destroyer maneuvered to avoid the sticks of bombs, and put up a heavy barrage of antiaircraft fire. Only one near-miss caused any damage, when a fragment penetrated the gunhouse of the no. 3 5-inch mount and the resulting explosion killed six men. She eventually reached friendly forces after sunset.

None of the 15 600-pound bombs or the eight 300-pounders, dropped by the last group from between

9,000 and 12,500 feet, hit the target! Antiaircraft fire may have hit one of the B-17s, though, the "City of San Francisco," that had been a gift of the city to the Army Air Corps, for it dropped its bomb bay gasoline tank and failed to return from the mission. Another B-17—that flown by CAPT G.H. Kramer and his crew of eight—ditched on the way back to Midway due to a fuel shortage; one man died in the landing.

Launched late in the afternoon, the SBDs, meanwhile, began returning after dark. Many of the pilots had never made a night carrier landing, and in the gathering gloom even the most experienced pilots were having trouble finding their home decks. *Enterprise*'s changing their YE set-up (her equipment outranged *Hornet*'s) and not promulgating this word to *Hornet* did not help, either; five *Hornet* planes had great difficulty finding TF-16. Spruance accordingly ordered the task force to turn on their lights to help the planes get home. *Enterprise* turned on her sidelights at 1933; her 36-inch searchlights seven minutes later. For almost 20 minutes, the carrier kept her big searchlights on, switching them off at 1958; she kept her sidelights burning until 2023. On board *Northampton*, observing the lights, correspondent Robert J. Casey heard a Marine officer near him mutter: "We may complete this recovery right square in the middle of the Japanese fleet."

Spruance had weighed the risks, however, before the launch. "If planes are to be flown so late in the day that a night recovery is likely," he reasoned, "and if the tactical situation is such that the commander is unwilling to do what is required to get the planes back safely, then he has no business launching the attack in the first place . . ." The LSOs in both carriers proved their worth that evening, bringing in 63 planes without a deck crash. Only one incident marred an otherwise perfect recovery: LT Ray Davis, VS-8's flight officer, ran out of gasoline "in the groove" and splashed astern of *Enterprise* at 2006. The destroyer *Aylwin* (DD-355), however, quickly rescued Davis and his radio-gunner, Ralph Phillips, ARM1c, "in a fine manner."

Since both carriers looked alike in the dark, several SBDs landed on the wrong ship. *Hornet* brought on board 27 of her own plus ENS Clarence E. Vammen Jr., A-V(N), of VS-6. *Enterprise*'s LSO, LT Robin Lindsey, knew that his ship had launched 32 planes; after having landed "quite a few," he asked the assistant LSO, LT(jg) Cleo Dobson, "how many more . . . we had to go before we had a complete group." "I'll be damned if I know," Dobson responded, "we've got . . . more than we are supposed to have already." *Enterprise*

recovered 30 of her own, as well as three VB-8 SBDs and two from VS-8. Six of the nine VS-6 pilots made their first night carrier landings that evening (including Vammen, on board *Hornet*). They had never flown an SBD before at night, nor had they had any nocturnal field carrier landing practice! Two VB-6 pilots found themselves in the same situation. One stranger on board *Enterprise*, LT James E. Vose Jr., VB-8's flight officer, clambered out of his SBD to encounter a crew chief whom he knew to be serving in *Enterprise*. Vose, puzzled, asked, "What the hell are you doing on *Hornet*?" Not until everyone around him burst out laughing did he realize what ship he had reached. As "Dusty" Kleiss recounted it: "Moe Vose came visiting, among others, and Vammen of our squadron repaid the visit." Kleiss had landed on the right ship by the expedient of checking the YE signal versus the bearing!

While Spruance had been intensely relieved that everyone (except the plane lost to antiaircraft fire) had landed safely, his irritation with *Hornet* mounted. Puzzled at why some planes from that ship returned before others, he discovered that they had carried 1,000-pound bombs which had reduced their airborne time. He considered *Hornet*'s performance the day before as dismal, and that day's activities had not enhanced Marc Mitscher's stock with Spruance.

As the day waned, Spruance considered his options. The Japanese could head to the northwest, where bad weather would cloak their movements, or westward to elude the American force. He thought they would move west, reasoning that a chance still existed that he could find them. By that point, Miles Browning had recovered from his pique and returned to duty; soon after TF 16 changed course to the west, the heavy cruiser *Northampton* reported sighting a submarine. Browning alertly ordered an emergency turn over the voice radio (TBS). Thirty minutes later, TF 16 resumed moving westward into the night at 15 knots; as Spruance later explained it: "That night the undesirability of running down any enemy BBs in the dark presented itself as a reason for slowing, as did the growing shortage of fuel in [TF 16's] DDs." He also decided to launch his own search planes at daybreak on 6 June. That planned out, he turned in.

As the day's action closed, ADM Nimitz sent a message to his task force commanders: "You who participated in the Battle of Midway today have written a glorious page in our history. I am proud to be associated with you. I estimate that another day of all out effort on your part will complete the defeat of the enemy."

Pilots and radio-gunners of VB-3 on board *Enterprise*, 12 June 1942. Front (L-R): ENS Robert H. Benson, A-V(N); ENS Alden W. Hansen, A-V(N); ENS Charles S. Lane, A-V(N); ENS Robert K. Campbell, A-V(N); LT(jg) Gordon A. Sherwood; LT DeWitt W. Shumway (Acting CO); LT Harold S. Bottomley; ENS Roy M. Isaman, A-V(N); ENS Paul W. Schlegel, A-V(N); ENS Philip W. Cobb, A-V(N). Rear (L-R): ENS Milford A. Merrill, A-V(N); Frederick P. Bergeron, ARM3c; Horace H. Craig, AMM1c; Harmon D. Bennett, ARM2c; Ray E. Coons, ARM1c; David F. Johnson, AMM2c; Sidney K. Weaver, ARM3c; Leslie A. Till, RM3c; Jack A. Shropshire, ARM3c; Clarence E. Zimmershead, ARM2c; ENS Bunyan R. "Randy" Cooner, A-V(N). NH 95556

CHAPTER THIRTEEN

....

"As Easy As Shooting Ducks in a Rainbarrel..."

*A*t 0350 on 6 June, *I-168*—directed to sink the crippled carrier—neared *Yorktown*, acting on the information provided by *Chikuma*'s no. 4 plane. Traveling on the surface to make better time, *I-168* spotted her quarry in the first wash of day, and then submerged.

In the meantime, *Hammann*, accompanied by *Benham* and *Balch*, neared *Yorktown*, too. At 0415, the salvage party began clambering on board the carrier with a predetermined plan of attack that called for the damage control party to extinguish the fire in A-305-A and determine the extent of the damage by inspecting the lower deck spaces; reduce topside weight on the port side and implement counter-flooding and pumping, with pumps provided by *Hammann*, which would moor alongside. The gunnery department would prepare machine guns in case of air attack, and would assist the damage control people in cutting loose and jettisoning the five-inch guns on the port side, as well as anything else movable. Likewise, men from the air department were to jettison the planes that remained on board, and any other "removable weights" that could be let go. Men from the engineering division were to inspect the lower decks and assist the damage control party in correcting the list. Navigation department people would try to bring the jammed rudder to the amidships position, communications men would maintain contact with the ships surrounding *Yorktown*, supply department people were to prepare to feed the salvage party while the medical people were to collect and identify the dead.

"*Yorktown* was dark and dead and silent," wrote MACH Williams later of the experience of boarding the carrier, "Darkness isn't black enough for the void that was in her. The silence was overwhelming. You got an eerie, unearthly dream-like feeling when you walked her decks and went below. I can't quite put into words the lonesome, dead feeling that was in her . . ."

While the salvage party began its work, *Hammann* stood away from the carrier's side and took a screening station until CAPT Buckmaster summoned her back alongside *Yorktown*'s starboard bow to provide hoses and water for the men attacking the persistent fire in the rag stowage, forward. True, finding it "impossible to lie clear of *Yorktown* and maintain position accurately enough to permit effective assistance," brought *Hammann* alongside, splinter mattresses and cane fenders hung between the two ships. *Hammann* then led out two foamite hoses to the carrier and a water hose to her flight deck, to hook up with her own foamite system. She also rigged a hose aft to pump seawater for counterflooding, and an oil suction hose to take oil from the carrier's port tanks to correct the list. *Hammann*'s cooks and mess stewards, meanwhile, began providing coffee and food for the salvage party.

Throughout the night, meanwhile, TF 16 had steamed roughly west by north so that by dawn on 6 June, it lay 340 miles northwest of Midway. As Spruance had planned, at 0500 *Enterprise* commenced launching 18 SBDs, including the five *Hornet* planes which had landed on board the night before, to search the western semicircle to a distance of 200 miles.

At 0645, ENS William D. Carter, A-V(N), in 8-B-2, radioed that he had spotted one battleship, one cruiser, and three destroyers steaming due west at 10 knots. Unfortunately garbled in transmission, the message yielded the finding of one carrier and five destroyers. The position placed the Japanese 128 miles roughly southwest by west of TF 16.

Over the previous two days, reports of sightings had proved a problem. Once one had been made and a report transmitted, contact would be lost and the admiral plunged into the proverbial "fog of war." Reacting to the report of a carrier, Spruance immediately ordered a search by cruiser-based float planes (Curtiss SOCs) to locate and trail the enemy ships.

At 0746, *Minneapolis* launched LT(jg) Larry L.

Booda, A-V(N), and J.W. Jarvis, ARM2c, in 6-CS-3; a minute later *New Orleans* catapulted off 6-CS-12, piloted by LT Samuel R. Brown Jr., with W.R. Haynes, CRM, in the after cockpit; at 0746, each cruiser launched an additional SOC: 6-CS-2, LT Lloyd F. Jakeman, pilot, and V.L. Lesh, ARM2c, passenger, from *Minneapolis*, and 6-CS-11 from *New Orleans*, LT(jg) Wilfred H. Genest, A-V(N), pilot, and H.F. Shaffer, RM1c, passenger. The "Seagulls" were to search a sector roughly south-southwest by west to due west, to a distance of 150 miles. With a 98-knot cruising speed, an SOC could linger at low level in the vicinity of the enemy for up to 10.4 hours.

Meanwhile, at 0730, ENS Roy P. Gee, A-V(N), in 8-B-8, overflew *Enterprise* and dropped a message on deck reporting the sighting of two cruisers and two destroyers steaming southwest by south at 15 knots. The position placed the enemy ships 133 miles to the south-southwest by west of TF 16. Based on the reports he had received to that point, Spruance believed he was dealing with two groups of ships, one of which included a carrier. Turning to the southwest, he increased speed to 25 knots, and ordered *Hornet* to launch her attack group.

At 0757, *Hornet* put aloft the CHAG (CDR Ring), 11 VB-8 SBDs under Abbie Tucker, and 14 VS-8 SBDs under LT "Gus" Widhelm, covered by eight F4F-4s from VF-8 under LT Warren W. Ford. Included in Widhelm's group was LT(jg) William F. Christie of "Scouting" FIVE, and ENS Vammen—ordered to return to his own ship after the mission—of "Scouting" SIX. Eight of these aircraft carried 500-pound bombs; the rest carried the more lethal 1,000-pounders. The *Hornet* planes set out

using "deferred departure."

At 0815, *Enterprise* began recovering the search planes. Two of the *Hornet* pilots who had flown from her deck that morning returned to their own ship—ENS Carter and LT(jg) Jimmy M. Forbes, A-V(N). Once on board, Carter corrected his contact report, and *Hornet* immediately blinkered the information to Spruance. At 0850, *Enterprise* radioed Ring: "Target may be battleship instead of carrier. Attack!"

Even with the corrected report, however, Spruance still believed that his planes had found two separate groups of ships. In actuality, there was only one—the heavy cruisers *Mogami* and *Mikuma* (much larger than American heavy cruisers) and the destroyers *Asashio* and *Arashio*. *Mogami*, with her crumpled bow, looked, from a distance, much smaller than her sistership, thus leading to the report of *Mikuma* as a "battleship."

LT Brown and LT(jg) Genest located the Japanese ships 150 miles from the task force. Unhindered by enemy fighters but kept at a respectful distance by antiaircraft fire, *New Orleans'* two SOCs remained in close contact with the four Japanese ships, directing the carrier planes to their targets. Over the hours that followed, until their recall, they provided a running account of what followed. LT(jg) Booda and LT Jakeman, from *Minneapolis*, ultimately confirmed that the "carrier" being sought had, in fact, sunk.

Guided by Brown and Genest, Ring spotted the Japanese ships at 0930, but, unsure that a "battleship" lay among them, passed them by. By the time he decided that these were his targets, his planes had flown past the push-over point and had to circle around to make a second approach out of the sun. At 0950, they com-

ENS Don "T" Griswold, A-V(N), the only *Hornet* pilot killed in action on 6 June, during the attacks on *Mogami* and *Mikuma*. USN

Kenneth C. Bunch, ARM1c, killed along with his pilot, ENS Griswold, when their SBD was shot down on 6 June. USN

menced the attack. Upon receiving Ring's report, *Enterprise* radioed: "This is Red Base. Blue attack group report position and results [of] your attack. Go ahead."

Scouting EIGHT obtained two hits on *Mogami*: one bomb penetrated the roof of number five turret, killing the crew inside; a second hit amidships on the aircraft deck, starting fires in the torpedo room. *Mogami*'s having jettisoned her torpedoes following her collision with *Mikuma* lessened the damage, however, and her men quelled the blaze within an hour. Bombing EIGHT—its numbers lessened by one (ENS Philip F. Grant, A-V(N), dropped his bomb accidentally prior to the dive)—concentrated mainly on the "battleship" (*Mikuma*). LCDR Johnson claimed a "paint scraper" (a very near miss), as did one other pilot. None managed a direct hit. ENS Adams, who had missed *Tanikaze*'s stern by 50 feet the previous afternoon, scored a hit on *Asashio*'s stern with his 500-pound bomb. Fighting EIGHT's F4Fs contributed to the destruction by carrying out strafing sweeps four abreast, Ford's division tackling one of the destroyers, LT(jg) Sutherland's one of the cruisers. Intense antiaircraft fire damaged several SBDs and downed two: ENS Don Griswold's 8-S-12 and ENS Vammen's 6-S-1. Griswold's SBD, trailing smoke, splashed; both Griswold and his radio-gunner, Kenneth C. Bunch, ARM1c, were killed. Vammen's plane disintegrated to a direct hit; both Vammen and his radioman, Milton W. Clark, AMM1c, died instantly.

While *Hornet*'s planes cleared the area to return to their carrier, the Japanese ships were ordered south to enable them to come under air cover from Wake Island. In response to *Enterprise*'s asking for the bearing and distance of the target and the results of the attack, Ring,

obviously thinking *Mikuma* to be a heavy cruiser and lumping the crippled *Mogami* and the two destroyers together as "three destroyers," reported: "No CV sighted. Attacked CA supported by 3 DD. One hit. Enemy course 270 speed 25. No Air Opposition." Meanwhile, TF 16 continued to close while *Enterprise* readied another strike. Spruance then believed he was chasing several damaged ships, including a cruiser that was stubbornly staying afloat.

At 1035, *Hornet* began recovering her aircraft. On board *Enterprise*, plane handlers were busily spotting the deck for launch of her strike when Spruance asked his chief of staff how many torpedo planes remained. Browning answered four, of which three were operational. The admiral sent for McClusky and LT(jg) Robert Laub, the senior surviving pilot of Torpedo SIX. "Now listen carefully," Spruance began, "I want to put that cruiser down, and the surest way to do it is to put some torpedoes into her. I want the bombers to silence their guns before you make your run. But," he added, "if there is one single gun firing out there, under no circumstances are you to attack. Turn around and bring your torpedoes home. I am not going to lose another torpedo plane if I can help it. Do you understand?"

At 1045, *Enterprise* commenced launching planes, with Wally Short in the lead, briefed to attack the same ships *Hornet*'s planes had gone after. However, at 1057, *Enterprise* informed Short, who was now airborne and on his way: "BB is your target. May be further along on course." Soon thereafter, the flagship radioed Short that three torpedo planes (Laub's VT-6 remnant) would be "coming up behind you." After taking departure, Short led his men on a slow climb to 22,500 feet, flying S-turns to allow the slower TBDs to catch up. Jim Gray, leading the fighter escort, noticed that the TBDs were lagging far behind, and attempted to alert Short to that fact.

At noon, Short spotted *Mogami* and *Mikuma* and their consorts, but, seeing no "battleship" present, passed them by. Gray, seeing the ships below, dove down to look them over, fearing that the TBDs would tackle them themselves. Studying the two cruisers, Gray concluded that these were, in fact, their quarry, and radioed Short to that effect.

Short had carried his search for the missing "battleship" 30 miles beyond the first group of ships he had sighted, but turned around to take a crack at the two crippled cruisers. Short made a high-speed approach from out of the sun and downwind from his target, and pushed over at 21,000 feet. Once the SBDs were in their dives, LT Gray and LT(jg) "Buster" Hoyle led their divisions down to strafe the two accompanying destroyers.

On board *Enterprise*, pilots' voices came over the radio in the flag shelter, as the ship's planes neared their objective, triggering a rush to be the closest to the crackling speaker. Spruance was not immune to the excitement: he adroitly "forced his way into the middle of the pack."

At 1150, an unidentified voice began: "I have the enemy in sight. I am going to attack. I am going down." Wally Short's voice was next: "Do you have them in sight?" "No," was the response, "I don't have them in sight." "They are over here," came another voice. "1 CA 1 CL 2 DD in the same position we thought he was," came the next voice, "I am going over and take the south one. You ease over and get the close one. Make one attack: that is all you have to do. We will rendezvous about 20 miles astern." Short came on at 1210: "Target is BB," and continued: "This is Wally. Target is 1 BB . . . BB ahead about 40 miles." Then, a succession of transmissions ensued as the planes found their target:

"There is BB over there!"

"Let's go! The BB is in the rear of the formation."

"This is Wally. Watch out on this attack."

Enterprise broke in at 1235, urging the attack group to "expedite attack and return."

Jim Gray, nearby, radioed: "Last ship is BB, I believe."

"Where is the remainder of our attack group?"

"We are right behind you, get going!"

"Smith from Wally. What the hell are you doing over here?"

Finally, Short radioed: "Pushing over on rear ship now." His impatience mounted as some pilots apparently tarried in pushing over: "Entering dive. Our objective is rear ship. Step on it! Are we going to attack or not?"

Mogami took two more hits: one amidships on the

aircraft deck and one forward of the bridge, which caused "medium" damage. *Mikuma*, however, fared far worse. At least five bombs struck the ship: the first exploded atop number three turret, shrapnel tearing into the bridge and killing or wounding several men—including *Mikuma*'s captain, CAPT Shakao Sakiyama; two bombs penetrated the starboard forward engine room, two into the port after engine room. *Mikuma* slowed to a halt. Heavy fires in the torpedo room ignited warheads stored there; explosions convulsed the ship. CDR Takashima, the cruiser's XO, gave orders to abandon; *Arashio* attempted to close and take off the crew. Antiaircraft fire damaged several attacking SBDs but did not bring any down. The transmissions continued to crackle out of the speaker on *Enterprise*'s flag shelter, reflecting the intoxication of attack:

"Look at that son-of-a-bitch burn!"

"Hit the son-of-a-bitch again!"

"That scared hell out of me," blurted out ENS Charles Lane of VB-3, who pressed home his attack to very low level, "I thought we weren't going to pull out!"

"Let's hit them again. Let's hit them all."

"You are going to hit them right on the fantail."

"Your bomb really hit them on the fantail, Boy, that's swell!"

"Let's get a couple of those destroyers."

"These Japs are as easy as shooting ducks in a rain-barrel."

"Gee, I wish I had just one more bomb."

"These Japs couldn't hit you with a sling-shot."

"Tojo, you son-of-a-bitch, send out the rest and we'll get those, too."

Throughout the attack, meanwhile, LT(jg) Laub had circled, out of range, with his trio of TBDs. The looked-for opening never came; every time he would take his section in, the ships would lower their guns and open fire. Unable to get in for the attack, Laub took his section home—the last combat sortie for the TBD. He transmitted a message from 6-T-4: "Cruiser is damaged. On course 240, speed 15. Other ship is still stationed in lat[itude]-long[itude] given."

At 1330, *Hornet* commenced launching another strike—12 SBDs from VS-8 under Walt Rodee, and 12 from VB-8 under Abbie Tucker—all planes armed with 1,000-pound bombs. At 1345 the group took its departure, losing one of their number soon thereafter as one plane had to abort the mission. Shortly after *Hornet*'s planes departed, *Enterprise*'s returned and, at 1415, began coming on board. The "Big E" recovered all but four of the planes she had launched—three *Hornet* SBDs that returned to their own carrier, and LT Lloyd A. Smith of VB-6. Antiaircraft fire had damaged Smith's hydraulic system, and he could only coax one gear leg down as he approached his ship. For the better part of an hour he flew around TF 16 trying to get the other gear down; by the time he finally succeeded in doing so, *Enterprise* had respotted her deck; only *Hornet*'s lay open for business.

While planes from TF 16 were out settling accounts with the Japanese, *Vireo* was still laboring ahead with *Yorktown* in tow, five destroyers steaming at 14 knots in an antisubmarine and antiaircraft screen, 2,000 yards away. Sound conditions, though, were poor, and the maximum echo range was only 900 yards at best. "Submarine propeller noises," LCDR Higgins of *Gwin* lamented, "could not be heard at any range." During the forenoon and afternoon watches, meanwhile, *Yorktown*'s men had considerably reduced the list, working despite the hazardous footing conditions imposed by the canted decks and, below decks, by the "stale and foul air." The fire in the rag stowage had been finally extinguished, while LCDR Davis, the gunnery officer, supervised the cutting away of the guns on the port side. One five-inch gun had already splashed into the depths, and work on a second was going well; five 20-mm. mount foundations had also been dropped over the side, too. The aviation department men had lowered spares from the overheads and began pushing them over the side.

All the while, CDR Tanabe was taking sightings at intervals, patiently stalking his quarry. Poor sound conditions concealed her approach, and *I-168* penetrated the carrier's screen undetected. Too close the first time, he opened out and penetrated it a second time. Tanabe determined that four torpedoes, fired with a minimal spread, would be sufficient for the job. He did not have to "lead" his target since she had so little way on. Tanabe was incredulous about his good fortune: "Either they [the escorts] were poor sailors, had poor equipment, or *I-168* was a charmed vessel." When 1,200 yards away, he ordered four torpedoes fired.

Up to that moment, *Yorktown*'s salvage party had done very well. Three submersible pumps on the "low" side of the ship, on the third deck, had transferred water from that area to the fourth deck on the starboard side, counterflooding into empty starboard fuel tanks. One submersible pump in the after engine room was pulling water overboard, while others had transferred water from *Hammann*'s bilges into the empty starboard tanks as well. The reduction of topside weight—chiefly in guns and airplanes—had reduced the water level on the third deck, aft, by three feet. No further flooding was occurring, and the list had decreased at least two degrees. The inclinometer read 22 degrees.

Lookouts on board *Balch*, though, spotted a disturbance in the water 2,500 yards beyond *Yorktown*, at

Bel Geddes' depiction of the strike on *Mogami* and *Mikuma* on 6 June. 80-G-701897

1334. A minute later, *Monaghan* radioed *Yorktown* on the voice radio circuit (TBS), "Torpedoes headed your way." Around 1336, *Hammann*'s lookouts picked up emergency signals from the screen, while almost simultaneously, that ship spotted four torpedo wakes about 600 yards away on the starboard beam. *Yorktown* sounded the alarm by firing 20-mm. guns while on board, the word "torpedo attack" spread rapidly by word of mouth. On board *Hammann*, LCDR True rang down "full speed astern" on the inboard engine, hoping to pull clear. Gunners on the starboard side Oerlikons—Willie V. Allison, GM3c, forward, and Roy T. Nelson, SEA2c, aft—opened fire in hopes of exploding the onrushing torpedoes.

As general quarters sounded, *Hammann*'s sailors rushed to their battle stations; most reached them only moments before one torpedo exploded and broke the ship's back abreast the number two fireroom. The explosion carried away the forward bulkhead of the forward engine room; oil, water, and debris cascaded into the air as two more torpedoes barreled into *Yorktown* at frame 84 and frame 95. A fourth passed astern. Men on board *Balch* noted "three huge columns of water" reaching upward alongside the carrier.

Hammann sagged, drifted aft, and began to sink, hoses and mooring lines parting. LCDR True, hurled against a desk in the pilot house, could neither speak

One of the few photos known to have been taken during the salvage operations on 6 June shows members of the air department preparing a TBD-1 (BuNo 0333) to be jettisoned over the side. 80-G-32323

a last glimpse of the ship that he had put into commission—and saw E.W. Raby, StM1c, emerging on deck without a lifejacket; seeing him, True pointed him out, and Hartigan swam back to help him. Just as he reached him, however, a "terrific explosion" rumbled up from the depths—probably *Hammann*'s depth charges going off at a pre-set depth. *Yorktown*'s communications officer, LCDR C.C. Ray, saw the heads of *Hammann*'s men as they struggled in the water until, as easily as a "windshield wiper erases the droplets from your windshield" they disappeared after the explosion.

Yorktown had trembled as if struck in the solar plexus. LCDR Davis, close to the side of the ship, overseeing the operation of cutting loose the second five-inch gun, fell overboard. He had just reached a line dangling over the side when the explosion of *Hammann*'s depth charges doubled him up. LT Wilson, whose men had expeditiously repaired the flight deck under fire on the 4th, had just about gained the hangar deck after inspecting fire damage below when a heavy hatch, jarred loose by the force of the torpedo explosions, fell on his head and arm.

The combination of torpedo hits and the explosion of the destroyer's depth charges jostled *Yorktown* violently, carrying away an auxiliary generator, shaking numerous fittings loose from the hangar deck overhead and sending them crashing to the deck below, collapsing the landing gear on two planes left on board, shearing rivets on the starboard leg of the foremast tripod, and throwing men in every direction, causing injuries and breaking bones.

LCDR Tanabe, reasoning that the last place the screening destroyers would look for him was under a sinking ship, set course to pass beneath *Yorktown* at the outset, while *Gwin, Monaghan* and *Hughes* aggressively hunted the I-boat, and *Balch* and *Benham* commenced rescue operations.[1] CAPT Buckmaster decided to suspend salvage operations and remove the salvage

nor draw a breath, temporarily; having suffered a broken rib, he paused to recover his wind. *Hammann*'s XO, LT Ralph W. Elden, seeing the skipper momentarily incapacitated and the ship doomed, passed the word for all hands to abandon ship. LT(jg) C.C. Hartigan, the gunnery officer, had been blown from the gun director to the lookout platform; regaining his senses a few seconds later, he saw *Hammann*'s forecastle awash. Making sure the director crew and lookouts had all donned lifejackets and laid below, Hartigan followed, gaining the bridge to find LT Elden climbing down the ladder parallel to the foremast. True, the last man on the bridge, inspected the pilot house, chart house and radar room, and, having found no one, joined Elden and Hartigan in jumping into the water. As True struck out from the sinking ship to avoid the suction as she sank, he paused and turned—perhaps compelled to take

---

1. The depth charge barrage from the destroyers knocked out the electric lighting in *I-168*, as well as cracked the outer casing of a storage battery, releasing chlorine gas within the submarine.

I-168 (seen here in March 1934 as I-68—she would be redesignated on 20 May 1942) achieved the biggest success of any submarine at Midway (American or Japanese) when her captain, LCDR Yudachi Tanabe, skillfully penetrated *Yorktown*'s screen on 6 June to torpedo *Yorktown* and *Hammann* and escape. NH 73054

Hammann at the Charleston (S.C.) Navy Yard, January 1942, shortly before she sailed for the Pacific theater. By the time of her loss, she had not changed from how she looked in this view. She is painted in Measure 12 (mod.) camouflage, and has just had fire control and air-search radar installed. 19-N-26593

party to the accompanying destroyers, and to return to *Yorktown* the next morning. He then directed *Vireo* to come alongside.

The tug's captain, however, had needed no such orders. Looking aft from his bridge, Legg thought that *Yorktown* might sink immediately, and ordered the tow line cut. An acetylene torch soon severed the wire linking the two ships; the tug turned back toward the carrier, and soon began hauling up *Hammann* survivors, as did *Benham*, the latter rescuing three officers and 163 enlisted men (as well as recovering 16 bodies) from *Hammann* and three officers and 19 men from *Yorktown*.

While those operations proceeded apace, the salvage party closed all watertight doors below the main deck that they could reach. Those inspecting the lower decks noted "a heavy pounding of water . . . apparently through the torpedo hole on the starboard side and against the centerline bulkhead," prompting those who heard this ominous sound to feel a "very pronounced shock" each time the sea surged through. All hands then

lay topside and began going over the side a second time, transferring to the tug that lay alongside.

Legg, in an impressive example of "seamanship of the highest order" brought *Vireo* alongside smartly, closing from astern and then shifting to the same spot where *Hammann* lay only a few minutes before, plucking destroyermen and carrier sailors from the water alike. *Yorktown*, as if resentful of the rough treatment being handed her, rolled considerably, giving *Vireo* a "terrific pounding" for the 40 minutes she lay alongside. Then, after having brought on board the last of *Yorktown*'s men, CAPT Buckmaster among them, *Vireo* moved away from the carrier's side. As she did so, LT Legg noted no appreciable change in her list and trim; CAPT Buckmaster noted it, too, but felt that the torpedo hits had counterflooded the ship, reducing the list to 17 degrees, but had caused her to settle deeper in the water.

Still optimistic, Buckmaster sent an urgent dispatch to CTF 17 and CINCPAC; telling of the two torpedo hits on *Yorktown* and the sinking of *Hammann*, *Yorktown*'s captain declared "with help [we] will bring

Bel Geddes diorama depicting the torpedoing of *Yorktown* and *Hammann* by *I-168* on 6 June. 80-G-701900

Top: Dramatic sequence of three photographs taken by William G. Roy from *Yorktown*'s forecastle, showing *Hammann*'s last moments. In the upper picture, *Yorktown* sailors crane their necks to watch as *Hammann* sinks, her back broken. Knotted lines used earlier in abandoning the carrier can be seen dangling in the foreground. 80-G-32297

In the middle view, *Hammann*'s stern slides deeper into the Pacific. 80-G-32320

In the lower view, *Hammann* has disappeared beneath the waves. The sailor who had been watching the destroyer sinking has turned to face the camera in lower foreground (R). 80-G-32322

Bel Geddes' depiction of the explosion of *Hammann*'s depth charges, which killed or maimed many survivors in the water; the concussion further strained *Yorktown*'s already "tender" hull; *Vireo* (L), having cut her tow line, doubles back to pick up survivors and take off the salvage crew. 80-G-701902

LCDR Arnold E. True, *Hammann*'s former CO (he had been her only one, since he had placed *Hammann* in com mission in 1939), is awarded the Navy Cross for his heroism in command of that ship; he is being decorated by VADM William F. Halsey, Jr., in October 1942.
80-G-40170

her [*Yorktown*] in..." After giving the position, Buckmaster requested air cover.

At 1515, Buckmaster conducted a burial service for the three bodies of the *Hammann* men whom *Vireo* had received from a destroyer's boat over an hour before—Steward's Mate Raby (whom LT(jg) Hartigan had attempted to save before the depth charge explosions) and two officers, one of whom whose only identification was his lieutenant's bars (making it either LT Elden or LT M.H. Ray Jr.). The other body committed to the deep had been identified by a laundry mark and the initials "R.P.F.E." on a USNR midshipman's ring, making it ENS Robert P.F. Enright, who had gallantly commanded *Hammann*'s motor whaleboat in the rescue of two *Yorktown* aviators from the shores of Guadalcanal on 4 May.

Balch closed *Vireo* at 1538 and transferred her medical officer and two pharmacist's mates to the tug to help treat the wounded before she resumed the search for more survivors. At 1628, *Balch* rescued LCDR True who, although "semi-conscious" was supporting two men: Robert J. Ballard, SEA1c, and George W. Kapp Jr., COX, the latter, like ENS Enright, one of the ship's heroes from the Battle of the Coral Sea.[2] While True survived the ordeal, neither Ballard nor Kapp could be revived.

Balch altered course to close the tug but, while approaching at 1737 to transfer *Yorktown* survivors, latched onto a submarine contact and laid down a depth charge barrage—six from the tracks at her stern and four from her "K" guns—the shock waves straining

2. They had figured prominently in the rescue of two *Yorktown* pilots, McCusky and Adams, from Guadalcanal. See *That Gallant Ship* for details.

Vireo's hull further, only 400 yards away. *Benham* picked up a contact at 1756 and attacked, without results. *Balch* returned alongside *Vireo* at 1846 and took on board all but eight *Yorktown* men who had been on board the tug—those eight deemed too badly hurt to be put through the ordeal of another transfer at sea—including CAPT Buckmaster. A minute later, *Monaghan* and *Hughes* sighted smoke on the horizon—*I-168*'s starting her engines—and sped toward it. Although the destroyers set off in hot pursuit, Tanabe made good his escape—his ship's engine exhaust serving as an effective, even if impromptu, smoke screen.

Less than an hour after *I-168*'s torpedoes had set back the arduous work of CAPT Buckmaster's salvage party, at 1430, *Hornet*'s planes sighted *Mogami* and *Mikuma* and their escorts, and commenced the attack 15 minutes later. In *Enterprise*'s flag shelter, pilots' voices began crackling through the static again:

"Antiaircraft fire is very heavy."

"Very good. My God, what a smoke."

"Look at that smoke, flame of that battleship."

"Got another hit on the cruiser."

"Look at that battleship burn."

Then, Walt Rodee's voice: "This is Walter One. Rendezvous with me on the right."

"Attack completed."

Near-misses damaged both destroyers, while one bomb hit *Mogami*'s aircraft deck, damaging the escape hatches for the engine room and killing men fighting fires inside. The planes encountered light antiaircraft fire, and lost none of their number to it; eventually, all planes returned safely to their carrier, beginning coming on board at 1530.

Meanwhile, *Mogami* and the two destroyers picked up 240 of *Mikuma*'s survivors, and abandoned the drifting wreck. More than 650 of her complement of officers and men were killed or died of their wounds. CAPT Sakiyama, who had commanded *Mikuma* since 1 November 1940, ultimately died of his wounds on board *Suzuya* on 13 June. The identity of the ships remained a mystery throughout the afternoon. Post-mission interrogations had yielded only the information that some pilots felt they had attacked a cruiser; others a battleship. COL Julian Brown suggested that a photo reconnaissance flight be sent out to take photographs to verify just what ship they had attacked. *Enterprise* launched two aircraft at 1553: one, flown by LT(jg) Kroeger of VB-6, carried Al Brick, a veteran movie cameraman from Movietone News; the other, flown by LT(jg) Dobson, *Enterprise*'s assistant LSO and a former member of Scouting SIX, carried J.A. Mihalovic, CP, from *Enterprise*.

Soon after the two SBDs returned on board at 1907,

Spruance ordered the two pilots to the bridge, where he questioned them personally. Kroeger, known for his sense of humor, told the admiral when he was asked what kind of a ship he had seen, responded: "Sir, I don't know, but," he brightened, "it was a hell of a big one." Spruance, a man not known for his sense of humor, did not find the young pilot's comment funny. Dobson had not taken his ship recognition cards, further arousing Spruance's ire. Mihalovic's reporting that he had snapped some excellent photographs, though, saved the day. Once those emerged from *Enterprise*'s photo lab, they yielded evidence that the afternoon's victim had not been a battleship, but a *Mogami*-class cruiser. The pictures of *Mikuma* in her death throes showed vividly the devastation wreaked by the SBDs, and one became one of the most famous war photographs to emerge from World War II.

Just over the horizon, the two Japanese destroyers and the crippled *Mogami* limped westward having had a harrowing day at the hands of TF 16's pilots. His destroyers low on fuel, his pilots and radio-gunners exhausted by three days of ceaseless battle, and his force nearing the range of Japanese land-based aircraft at Wake Island, Raymond Ames Spruance decided that the Battle of Midway was over. TF 16 swung to the northwest to replenish its depleted fuel bunkers, and the tempo of operations relaxed.

In his room later, Cleo Dobson described what he had seen on his "photo hop," revealing in his diary the sensitive nature of a man called upon to be a warrior: "We arrived there & found it [*Mikuma*] in a very bad condition. It was burning badly, most of the people had abanded [sic] it. About 400 to 500 saliors [sic] were in the water all around the ship. We took some very close & good pictures & if possible will try to get a copy of them. Before I took off I though [sic] if I saw anyone in the water I would strafe them as the Japs did when the *Langley* in the Coral Sea. [ed. note: he may have been referring to the loss of that ship in the Java campaign]. After flying over those poor devils in the water I was chicken hearted & couldn't make myself open up on them. I flew about 100 feet from the ship & could see lots of bodies lying on the deck lots more were lying on the stern of the ship & they didn't even move. They were probably injured. 5 life boats were about 300 yards from the sinking CA but they were empty. They proably [sic] got aboard one of the other ships. 2 DD & 1 CA were about 30 miles west of the burning ship trying to get away. We went over to get pictures of them but they started shooting at us so we didn't get close to them. Boy I sure would hate to be in the shoes of those fellows in the water. I shouldn't feel so sorry for them because I might be in their shoes some day. I pray

A pair of VS-8 SBDs head toward the burning *Mikuma* during Scouting EIGHT's second strike on the crippled cruisers on the afternoon of 6 June 1942. Note prominent white side-number codes S-9 (foreground) and S-13 (background). 80-G-17054

to God I'm not." In closing, he added, "I'll enjoy reading this when I'm sitting by the fire side & haven't enough ambition to go out & repeat the performance. . . ."

Mikuma, meanwhile, turned over and sank within two hours of *Enterprise*'s photographic flight having taken pictures of her. Among the flotsam in the water was a raft containing 19 men; of that group, only two would survive the ordeal. The others died of their wounds or slipped off in their sleep.

"You can easily imagine," Robin Lindsey said later, "that we were glad that the battle was over. We'd lost lots of our good friends but there is a sense of elation after a battle that comes to one just to realize that he is still alive and that he'll still be around for awhile and have a few drinks with the boys. Along the drinking line, much to our amazement on our way home the head doctor brought out in the wardroom, of all places, about four gallons of good old Ten-High bourbon, and the pilots turned to that night, and a few of us were pretty high by the time we hit the old sack. It was a welcome relief to see that in war time the old Naval Regulations go by the board in favor of a little human good sense."

There was rejoicing elsewhere, too: a PBY had picked up ENS Tony Schneider of VB-6 and his radio-gunner, G.L. Holden, ARM2c, who had had to ditch on the 4th. LT Samuel I. Ogden, A-V(N), landed his PBY and rescued CAPT Dick Blain and his radio-gunner, McFeely, of VMSB-241, who had gone down the same day on the way back from attacking *Hiryu*—interestingly, Ogden had been Blain's instructor during flight training!

LT(jg) Norman Brady, who had tracked *Mogami* and *Mikuma* the previous day, figured prominently in the third PBY rescue of the day. In the course of his search, he spotted an empty life raft 94 miles to the southwest of Midway; he proceeded on, having been ordered to locate and rescue survivors from a plane shot down 350 miles from Midway. Like the other men flying and manning the PBYs, Brady had slept little over the preceding few days. Finding nothing at the point to which he had been vectored, Brady studied the weather conditions and estimated the drift of the current.

Nearly 100 miles away, at 1445 on 6 June, he spotted a rubber boat containing the crew of LT(jg) Whitman's PBY that had been shot down near the Occupation Force on 4 June. Braving the high sea running at that time, Brady landed his heavily loaded plane. He struggled to get the PBY aloft; the waves bashed in the plane's nose and smashed the bombing window, but he persevered and took off, reporting the rescue at 1525. Safe were ENSs McCleary and Camp, the latter badly injured, and the three petty officers—Fulghum, Marsh and Weeks. Camp, sadly, died the following morning of his wounds.

Elsewhere that day, other PBY pilots were finding another of their own: ENS Robert T. Lampshire Jr., A-V(N), in 44-P-7, and ENS Richard V. Umphrey, A-V(N), in 24-P-9, spotted ENS Propst's 24-P-11, it having drifted since 4 June when it had run out of gasoline en route to Laysan Island. Despite a heavy fuel load and treacherous winds, Umphrey landed and brought Propst and his eight-man crew on board and took off for Midway, despite the hazardous addition of extra weight. Behind them, the battered 24-P-11 sank, destroyed by its crew because of its damaged condition.

For RADM Spruance and his staff, meanwhile, the

strain of combat had been reflected in their neither shaving nor showering for three days. Stubbled faces (Halsey, apparently, had been superstitious about shaving before battle, thinking it bad luck to do so) and sweat-stained khakis, however, soon disappeared. In the staff wardroom, some caught up on the news that they had ignored since 3 June. Some members of his staff, sitting near the admiral, discussed a murder case back in the 'States; one officer opined that only a man with a deranged mind could commit murder. Hearing that, Spruance lowered the paper he had been reading and said, "What do you think I have been doing all afternoon?"

Back at Pearl, ADM Nimitz's war diarist wrote on 6 June: "This was a great day for the American Navy. . . ."

Throughout the ships assembled in *Yorktown*'s vicinity, meanwhile, all hands awaited the dawn, to see if it would yield another chance to try and save her. Given the "recognized inadequacy of the torpedo protection system," it was amazing that she had remained afloat as long as she had. As if clinging tenaciously to life, *Yorktown* remained stubbornly afloat during the first and mid-watches. At 2000 on 6 June, *Balch, Benham,* and *Gwin*, with *Vireo* nearby, had begun circling the carrier at 14 knots, 4,000 yards from the ship. *Monaghan* and *Hughes*, fresh from the unsuccessful hunt for *I-168*, rejoined shortly after midnight. All hands awaited the dawn, and what it would bring.

Four views of the crippled *Mikuma*, taken by J.A. Mikalovic, CP, from LT(jg) Cleo Dobson's SBD-3 on the afternoon of 6 June.

During memorial services at Midway, 6 June, helmeted Marines stand at attention before the flag-draped remains of 11 Americans who are prepared for burial at sea from the decks of the boats of MTBRON 1. The honored dead included the posthumously promoted Jay D. Manning, ARM3c, of VT-8; 2dLT J.D. Nave, USA; MSGT F. Peoples, USA; MAJ William W. Benson, USMC; CPL Frank L. Dupes, USMC and USMC PVTs Maurice A. Belanger, William A. Burke, Robert L. Holsbro, Robert E. Mowrey, G.E. Reed and Abraham Zuckerman. USN

Showing the signs of the modernization that had followed her torpedoing off Oahu the previous January, *Saratoga* (CV-3) lies at Pearl Harbor, 6 June 1942, her deck loaded with aircraft (SBD-3s, F4F-4s, TBF-1s) that she would ferry to *Enterprise* and *Hornet* to replenish their depleted air groups. 80-G-10121

Two views showing *York-town*'s last moments on 7 June, as seen from an accompanying destroyer. USN

Portland (R) transfers *Yorktown* survivors, riding two at a time in coal bags, to *Fulton* (L) at sea on 7 June. Note the 5-inch guns atop the cruiser's hangar (lower R), and details of bridge, including the Mk. 33 gun directors and the FD and SC radar antennae. 80-G-31202

CHAPTER FOURTEEN

. . . .

"A Grim and Terrible Business..."

*B*y the dawn of 7 June, those who watched *Yorktown* from the ships nearby could detect an increasing list to port. By 0435, to watchers on board *Benham*, the carrier appeared to be listing heavily and sinking. When the end appeared to be inevitable, the men topside on the ships nearby came to attention and removed their caps or helmets; all ships half-masted colors. Then, at 0458, *Yorktown* "turned over on her port side and sank in about 3,000 fathoms of water with all battle flags flying." Many of the men who witnessed her end wept unashamedly.

Enterprise's war diary, on the other hand, reflects the considerable lessening of tensions by that point, as TF 16 retired toward a fueling rendezvous. Out of range of shore-based planes from Wake, and in an area found to be clear of enemy ships by a four-plane search, Spruance's cruisers maintained the necessary inner air patrol; the carrier air groups, *Enterprise*'s war diarist writes: "Enjoyed a much needed and well earned rest." Tempering that rest, however, was the sadness over the men who did not come back, both in "officer's country" and in the crew's quarters. The grim task of inventorying the effects of lost shipmates would soon begin, as would the business of informing the loved ones of the loss of a valued friend and shipmate.

After *Yorktown* had sunk, the ships that had been with her then set course for Pearl Harbor, *Benham* carrying *Hammann*'s survivors and *Vireo* steaming for Midway. The American ability to appraise confidently the enemy's whereabouts allowed ADM Nimitz to take another gamble. Knowing that the presence of so many survivors on board hindered a combatant ship's effectiveness, Nimitz ordered the submarine tender *Fulton* (AS-11) to sail from Pearl and rendezvous with *Portland* at sea to take the *Yorktown*ers off her hands.

Normally, a ship like *Fulton* seldom ventures forth from her home port; knowing that no I-boats posed a threat to the evolution, however, Nimitz sent the tender to bring *Yorktown*'s people home. On 7 June, the transfer took place at sea, and *Fulton* reached Pearl the following day, ADM Nimitz and RADM English among those assembled awaiting her arrival. Nearby, *Benham* tied up at the fuel dock at Merry's Point and began transferring *Hammann*'s wounded ashore.

Saratoga arrived in the vicinity of TF 16 on the 10th, but heavy fog prevented the transfer of planes from "Sara" to *Enterprise* and *Hornet* — an evolution that had to wait until the following day. RADM Fletcher broke his flag in *Saratoga*.

After the battle, meanwhile, COL Larkin flew in one of the two VMJ-252 R4D-1s out to Midway on 7 June with a 300-gallon water cart and .30-caliber incendiary ammunition; all hands eagerly greeted them — especially glad to see the water carts in view of the damage to the physical plant at Midway. Larkin carried out an informal tour of the damage and talked with the men of MAG-22 before leaving on the morning of 9 June to return to Oahu. MAJ James Roosevelt, XO of the 2d Marine Raider battalion, rode back with Larkin and listened intently to the colonel's lengthy tale of woe about the poor aircraft the Marines had been cursed with. "He [Roosevelt] has a very good picture of our deficiencies," Larkin wrote to MGEN Rowell on 10 June, "and I am sure he will tell the President the whole story of the Battle of Midway."

Ira Kimes presented Larkin with a report on the status of aircraft in MAG-22: the number of operational aircraft stood at an even dozen. As Kimes noted, however, the three remaining SBD-2s had been operated "at full power for long periods in escaping Zero fighters," and of the five SB2U-3s, only one had an engine that was not considered "overtime." In addition, Kimes considered the condition of the fabric covering of each Vought "poor," and that they had been operated "at full power many times for much longer than allowable time." Three "Buffaloes" were in commission, but all power plants had been operated "at maximum horsepower regardless of allowable limits, and [were] therefore in questionable

Her decks crowded with *Yorktown* survivors, *Fulton* (AS-11) prepares to moor at Pearl Harbor on 8 June, assisted by tugs, while waiting ambulances (background, right, on pier) stand ready for the wounded. *Hoga* and *Nokomis* (YT-142) are among the tugs involved. *YT-150* is at right. 80-G-312058

Wounded *Hammann* and *Yorktown* survivors are brought ashore from *Benham* at Merry's Point, Pearl Harbor, 8 June 1942. *Benham*'s medical officer, LT(jg) Seymour Brown, MC, USNR, attended 82 wounded men and 153 seriously wounded for the first two hours on 6 June. 80-G-312062

ADM Nimitz and members of his staff watch as *Fulton* ties up at the Sub Base upon her return on 8 June. 80-G-312025

One of the Douglas R4D-1s (BuNo 3143) from VMJ-252 flown in after the battle with water carts and other supplies is parked beyond debris from the destroyed mess hall and post exchange buildings on Eastern Island, 7 June 1942. USMC

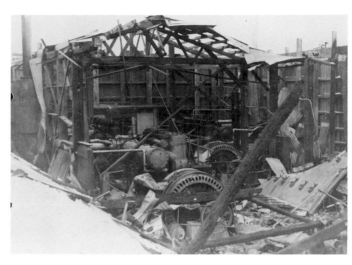

Wrecked power house on Eastern Island, 7 June 1942. USMC

On 7 June, a Marine pilot, perhaps CAPT Marion Carl, of VMF-221, stands near the crater made by an 805-kg. "No. 80 land bomb" dropped by a *Soryu* carrier attack plane. The second squadron of *Soryu*'s air unit reported damaging a runway on 4 June. USMC

Small crater on runway number one, Eastern Island, 7 June 1942, the handiwork of one of *Soryu*'s *kanko*. Visible in the background are two B-17s, one of VMF-221's two operational F4F-3s, and an SBD. USMC

View of damage to the Eastern Island camp compound, as seen on 7 June. In the background can be seen the tails of two of the four LB-30 bombers that were to bomb Wake Island. One of the four, containing LGEN Tinker, crashed, killing all on board, en route to the target. USMC

View taken 7 June 1942 showing VMSB-241 engineering tent and nose hangar on Eastern Island. USMC

Since a Japanese bomb demolished the old one, a new galley takes shape on Eastern Island; note the mixture of helmets worn. USMC

Alfresco dining on Eastern Island, 7 June 1942. Note both old- and new-style helmets. USMC

condition," while only one F4F-3, whose "power plant [had been] operated for a long period well over allowable limits." Kimes opined that the F4F-3 was "hardly better in combat than is the F2A-3 . . ." the combat performance of which he condemned as "well below that necessary for first line fighters."

Despite the heavy losses sustained by the Marines, though, Larkin felt that "Everyone out there [Midway] did one of the grandest jobs in the history of our country. Our losses were high," he continued, "but we took the initial shock and were out numbered [sic] many times on every mission. The Navy did a wonderful job as their part. The Army," he observed, "with one or two exceptions, were [sic] putrid."[1] Ironically, the Army accounts of the battle, with the overblown claims for damage inflicted on the Japanese by the B-17s, preceded the Navy's, and caused a good deal of commotion, as soldiers and airmen taunted sailors with: "Where was the Navy?" at Midway!

In the meantime, efforts to find the officers and men down at sea on 4 June continued, as PBYs, representing several different squadrons, ranged out of Midway as they shuttled in and out over the days that followed. While searching ships and patrol planes alike saw the flotsam and jetsam of war, occasionally someone was found clinging gamely to life in the trackless ocean, supported by a life raft, as those who survived the battle clung to the hope that a lost shipmate would be found. In some instances, rescues did occur.

On 8 June, LT(jg) Frank M. Fisler, A-V(N), flying a VP-51 PBY-5B, rescued ENS Johnny Talbot of VF-8, who had had to ditch on 4 June. That same day, four other Fighting EIGHT pilots, who, like Talbot, had had

to make water landings on the 4th, were plucked out of the sea: ENS Thomas Seabrook, A-V(N), of VP-72, rescued ENSs Magda and McInerney while ENS Robert E. Slater, A-V(N), of VP-23, rescued LT(jg) Jennings and Seabrook's Jacksonville flight school classmate, ENS Tallman.

That afternoon, *Cuttlefish* passed through "several square miles of wreckage and debris including almost anything that would float." That consisted of bedding, furniture, lockers, floor boards, cans, timbers, burned fragments of wood, benches, buoys, doors and life rings. *Cuttlefish*'s captain, deeming the weather too rough to send men out on deck "except for something vital," contented himself with "cruising through the stuff . . . changing course to look at likely objects." The only markings seen on anything were "Japanese characters on a broken soap box . . ." *Cuttlefish*'s captain estimated that the wreckage had been spread over an area about a mile wide and up to 10 miles long. "It was too concentrated," he wrote, "to have been discarded by a ship underway."

The following day, 9 June, on another patrol, Frank Fisler landed again and picked up Pat Mitchell, Stan Ruehlow, and Dick Gray, also of VF-8.[2] That same day (9 June), the fleet submarine *Trout* (SS-202), rescued two *Mikuma* survivors she found: Chief Radioman Katsuichi Yoshida and 3d Class Fireman Kenichi Ishikawa.

While those two Japanese may have felt some measure of relief that the sea had not claimed them, other enemy

---

1. As if to underscore Larkin's conclusion, B-17s bombed *Tambor*, causing considerable damage and necessitating an immediate return to Pearl, and *Grayling* (SS-209).

---

2. In John Ford's documentary, "The Battle of Midway," Fisler is shown (wearing a non-regulation red baseball cap) after his rescue of the three VF-8 pilots. The narrator (Henry Fonda) says: "That makes 13 for Frank." The other nine men rescued by Fisler comprised the crew of an Army B-17 that had had to ditch off Oahu on the day after Christmas of 1941. Despite a heavy sea, Fisler landed his PBY and made the rescue. Tragically, Fisler failed to return from a raid on Japanese shipping, while flying with VB-101 on 5 March 1943.

sailors expressed different emotions: a member of the Kure SNLF, Hisaichi Kawashima, wrote in his diary on 10 June (9 June east of the IDL), recounting the official imperial communique which in effect announced a great victory. He exclaimed: "What a difference from what we know!" After describing the crippling of four Japanese carriers, Kawashima lamented: "It is a great tragedy, because warships and a few thousand trained men cannot be obtained in a day . . ."

Among the ships searching for more survivors was *Ballard*, that had been dispatched from Pearl Harbor to French Frigate Shoals on 3 June to patrol that area "to deny its use by enemy submarines and/or aircraft." She had carried out that mission late on 4 June and through the 5th; ordered to Midway on the latter date to deliver what aviation bombs she carried, she also fueled four PBYs at sea, and arrived the following day. Departing Midway at 1026 on the 7th, and, aided by another PBY, located 23-P-2 (Thueson's PBY, left intact by *Monaghan* on 6 June) at 1708 and took her in tow, eventually turning her over to a tug at Midway at 1000 on the 8th. She then patrolled off the channel entrance to Midway before being ordered out again.

Ballard sailed at 0400 on 10 June to search the waters 160 miles to the northeast of the atoll, seeking "a life raft with one survivor." Arriving on station at 1424, the seaplane tender continued her search the next day (11 June) and the day following. She recovered a 60-man balsa life raft that contained an unidentified body at 1600 on the 12th, a 25-man balsa life raft an hour later, and a deflated rubber life raft in its container at 2035.

The six-plane search on 12 June, however, augmented by the Coast Guard Cutter *Taney* (WPG-37), which had arrived at Midway the previous afternoon, enjoyed considerably more success than had *Ballard* in her search, when it yielded another Bombing SIX crew. LT(jg) August A. Barthes, A-V(N), landed his heavily loaded PBY in the open sea and rescued ENS Tom Ramsey and his radio-gunner, S.L. Duncan, AMM2c.

On 14 June, though, ENS Jack L. Poteat, A-V(N), of VF 71, flying 12-P-9, while flying low over the leaden Pacific in bad weather, reported sighting a small boat with men on board roughly 410 miles west by south of Midway. The moment the "Catalina" crew spotted the boat and its occupants, however, Poteat's PBY lost contact.

The spotting of that small boat, however, prompted much interest. *Ballard* returned to Midway at 1115 that morning, off-loaded the rafts she had picked up, fueled, and then at 2118 took departure, setting course west by south, having been ordered by CAPT Simard to look for the boat that Poteat had spotted earlier that day. After another PBY had reported spotting the wing panel

from a Japanese aircraft floating in the water, she received orders to steam roughly west by north, to search for "anything of value for identification or display purposes..."

While *Ballard* carried out her search, PBYs continued to range to the west on 600 mile searches over the next few days, with five planes on the 16th, six on the 17th, five on the 18th, and six on the 19th. On the last date, LT(jg) Stuart T. Cooper, A-V(N), in 51-P-12, reported firing on a "landplane bomber" 500 miles roughly west by south of Midway—an Army B-17 "75 miles out of its assigned sector" that suffered "numerous minor material casualties..." in the encounter between "friends."

Ballard, meanwhile, searched her last assigned sector without result until ordered to a point bearing roughly northwest of Midway, where a "life raft" with 10 survivors had been spotted. Arriving at that point at 0745 on the 19th, she searched that sector, too, without success.

At 1115 on the 19th, however, LT Don Camp of VP-11 reported that he was circling over a boat. *Ballard* set out in that direction five minutes later, and at 1600, spotted a cutter—from the sunken *Hiryu*—containing 35 Japanese, who began throwing articles into the water as she approached, so that by the time the ship drew alongside, the cutter had been "stripped of anything that might be of military value to the Navy."

Ballard took 35 Japanese on board, stripped them, searched them, and then confined them in a "bull pen" on the quarter-deck.[3] The sailors proved to be a portion of *Hiryu*'s engineering force, although some men who had been stationed in a boiler room, and an electrician, had been among the rescued. They had steadfastly remained at their posts, even after the equipment in their charge had ceased running and men topside had written them off as lost.[4] When the smoke became intolerable in those spaces, they managed to break through a deck to get clear. Finding no one else on board, the men jumped over the side and swam to a lifeboat. The stopped watches among the men confirmed the fact that they had entered the water around 0900 on 5 June. One man reported hearing a loud explosion around 0600 on the 5th—perhaps *Makigumo*'s torpedo striking home to hasten *Hiryu*'s end.

For two weeks, they had subsisted on hardtack, tallow, water and beer, and CDR Eiso, the chief engineer, apparently consumed more than his share of

3. In the process, the ship's XO found himself a souvenir—a Japanese flag—only to have it disappear from his room. "Someone," *Ballard*'s historian wrote, "evidently wanted it worse than the Exec . . ."

4. In fact, Nagumo, in his battle report, wrote that "the manner in which the engine room personnel from [the chief engineer] down to the last man, carried on in the face of death which finally overtook them, can only be described as heroic . . ."

Panoramic view of *Ballard* at Mare Island Navy Yard, 6 January 1942, five months before Midway. Note her main battery of two 3-inch/50 dual purpose guns, and four .50-caliber Browning machine guns amidships on the deckhouse roof, external degaussing cable and depth charge rack at the fantail. USN

The Coast Guard cutter *Taney* (WPG-37), as she appeared after her May 1942 refit at the Pearl Harbor Navy Yard. This ship escorted *Regulus* (AK-14) to Midway, arriving on 11 June. *Taney* then participated in searches for survivors of downed planes on 12 and 13 June. USCG via Scheina

Trout (SS-202) returns to Pearl Harbor, 14 June 1942, with Chief Radioman Hatsuichi Yoshida and 3d Class Fireman Kenichi Ishikawa embarked; they'd been rescued on 9 June, survivors from the heavy cruiser *Mikuma*. *Trout*, which had brought out a cargo of gold from the Philippines in February (as ballast), had been at sea 80 out of the previous 83 days. Among the men awaiting her arrival is RADM English and ADM Nimitz. Note *Trout*'s large pre-war conning tower and sail. Two .30-caliber Lewis machine guns flank the periscope sheers. 80-G-32217

Some of the 35 Japanese—survivors of the aircraft carrier *Hiryu*—rescued and captured by the seaplane tender *Ballard* (AVD-10) between 1600 and 1630, 19 June 1942, along with their cutter. One man died that night, and was buried at sea at 0825 the next morning. 80-G-79974-1

As interested sailors and Marines watch, *Hiryu*'s men are shepherded onto trucks at Midway soon after their arrival in *Ballard*. USN

The cutter from *Hiryu* that had been captured, along with its 35 occupants, by *Ballard*, on 19 June. In the background (L&R) are nests of PT-boats *Ballard* had escorted out to Midway before the battle. Identifiable are *PT-25* and *PT-30* (upper left). 80-G-79981-21 via Wenger

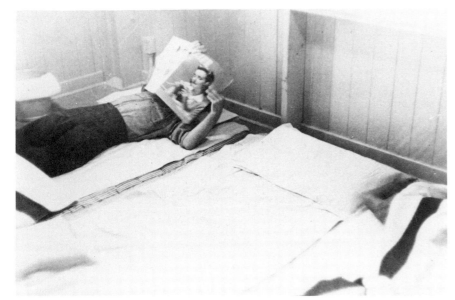

A Japanese POW adjusts to his captivity by leafing through the 24 November 1941 issue of *Life*, which included among its articles pieces on "How to Knit" and on ADM Ernest J. King.
80-G-79979-15

Hiryu survivors under guard and awaiting transportation to Hawaii. Man in foreground may be CDR Eiso, *Hiryu*'s chief engineer. Ship in background, *Sirius* (AK-15), transported the POWs to Pearl Harbor between 23 June and 1 July.
80-G-79984-28 via Wenger

the last-named commodity and caused some of the men to consider throwing him overboard. Their number shrank from 39 to 35; four died prior to the seaplane tender's arrival on 19 June. One of the 35 rescued died during the night on the 19th; he was buried at sea the next morning. At 1000 on 20 June, *Ballard* reached Midway and disembarked her prisoners, transferring custody of the 34 Japanese—three officers (including the chief engineer), one warrant officer, and 30 enlisted men—to the Marines upon arrival.

Interrogation commenced immediately, as ADM Nimitz had two Japanese language officers flown to Midway to speak to the POWs and learn as much as possible from them before they were brought back to Pearl Harbor. The interrogators found that most, including the officers, willingly talked of any subject in which they were knowledgeable. Their stories of the Battle of Midway, however, were strongly influenced by what they could observe from their battle stations below decks.[5]

On 21 June, the PBYs were out in the sector that extended from the northwest by north to the northnortheast, to 400 miles. North of Midway, 300 miles, searching planes found much wreckage; 360 miles out, LT(jg) John E. White, A-V(N), in 24-P-10, spotted two men in a rubber boat, and landed. MACH Winchell and Douglas Cossitt, ARM3c, who had been adrift in their rubber boat since their TBD-1 had gone down on 4 June, were the last downed aviators from the Battle of Midway to be picked up.

The searching PBYs, however, continued to log the presence of wreckage—mute reminder of the battle that had taken place there—on the surface of the ocean

5. After their interrogation at Midway, the *Hiryu* survivors embarked in *Sirius* and sailed for Pearl Harbor at 0900 on 23 June, in company with *Gamble* (DM-15), *Kaloli*, and seven boats from MTBRON 1.

below. They had found some on 16 June to the west of Midway, 300 miles to the north on the 21st; to the north-northwest on 23 June, aircrew spotted empty life rafts and wreckage, and a capsized boat; the next day, between 185 and 350 miles from Midway, searchers found "many empty life rafts." Some 275 miles north-northeast of Midway, an "empty, cutter-type life boat, believed to be foreign" turned up on the 25th. No more men, however, would be found; the sea had swallowed them up.

TF 16 had returned to Pearl on 13 June. Soon thereafter, *Enterprise*'s CAPT Murray wrote to his wife and described the battle. "Let no one tell you or let you believe that this war is other than a grim, terrible business. In going over the records [of the men who had died], it shocks me to find so many mothers who are the next of kin of so many of those wonderful lads. All that we can hope," Murray concluded, "is that these sacrifices will more quickly aid in crushing the forces of evil that threaten the world..."

Flag officers on board *Enterprise*, 17 June 1942, (L-R): VADM William L. Calhoun, RADM Frank Jack Fletcher, RADM Thomas C. Kincaid, RADM William W. Smith, RADM Marc A. Mitscher, and RADM Robert H. English.
80-G-10403

"EQUALITY FOR ALL"
EXCEPT THE FIGHTIN LEATHERNECKS.

Cartoon by Detling which features the Army and Navy, eating heartily of the cake labeled "plane production," while the little brother, given the appellation "marine aviation," stands off to one side, apparently elbowed out of the way by his bigger siblings. The mother, meanwhile, urges wistfully, "Now boys—couldn't you share it equally with the little feller?" USMC

Another Detling cartoon mirroring the Marines' frustration at having to do battle with old and inadequate aircraft. At top is an Army bomber, whose pilot, looking down, calls out: "Hey Marine— You go ahead and engage the enemy. We'll only be about a thousand miles behind ya." In the middle is a Navy PBY, whose crew is saying: "Yeah— You go ahead an' start shootin down the Japs then we'll drift in and mop up the survivors!" The anxious Marine pilot in his battered aircraft is followed by a seabird who says: "Say, Doc— Where'd you get the flying fortress?" USMC

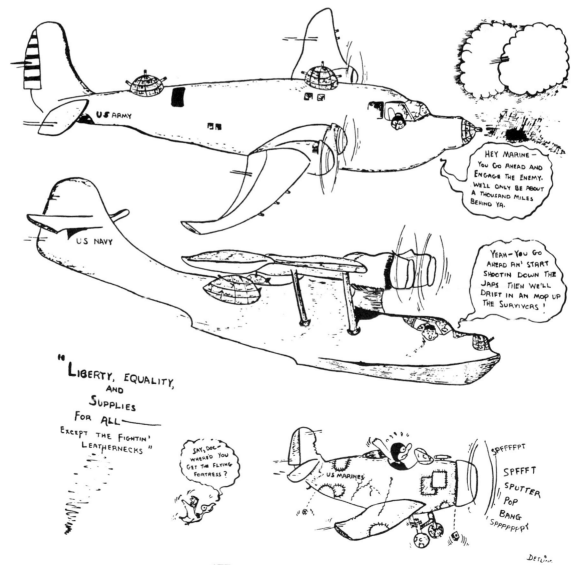

"Jap Loses Pants trying to Save Face." A cartoon by an anonymous artist from the 6th Defense Battalion shows a harried Japanese gathering up his ships to beat a hasty retreat from a USMC bulldog; the beehive represents Eastern Island's airfields. COL Shannon presented the original to ADM Nimitz in a frame made from a portion of the wing of one of the Japanese planes shot down on 4 June. NH 63438-KN

CHAPTER FIFTEEN

. . . .

"A More Pleasant Place..."

Midway's strategic location assured its continued importance to the war effort. About a month after the battle, on 5 July 1942, RADM English outlined a plan to develop a submarine base at the atoll, to service the boats being deployed to the waters off the Japanese homeland. Knowing that dredging operations in the lagoon were

continuing, English specified the *Fulton*, with an embarked Submarine Repair Unit, be sent to Midway to establish a five-point mooring buoy in the middle of the existing turning basin, to be used until dredging was completed. *Fulton* would then provide services, supplies, and repairs to submarines returning from war patrols, obviating their need to return to Pearl except in cases where their repairs were beyond the capabilities of Midway to perform. Making full use of Midway, COM-SUBPAC declared, would shorten the turn-around cycle—the interval between departure from, and arrival in, a patrol area—for each submarine by 10 days. *Fulton* arrived at Midway soon thereafter, and would remain there until October, when she sailed for Brisbane to service submarines there.[1] The submarine base was placed in commission without ceremony on 15 July 1942. At the Cable Company's suggestion, since some of the Navy's facilities had suffered damage in the battle, the Navy leased all of the company's buildings except the superintendent's residence and the Cable Office building. On 17 July 1942, four officers and 225 men of the 5th Construction Battalion (CB, or "Seabees")

1. Other tenders to provide tender service for submarines at Midway during the war included *Sperry* (AS-12), *Proteus* (AS-17) and *Aegir* (AS-23).

Pensacola at Midway, bringing in more Marines, 24 June 1942. In background (R) is *Ballard*, and in the right foreground is the tail of ENS Earnest's TBF-1 (BuNo 00380). 80-G-12147

arrived, and after preparing quarters for themselves and the remainder of the CB that followed in August, commenced construction of an airfield and a reinforced-concrete and steel hospital on Sand Island. Also in August, the NAS field was named in honor of Lofton Henderson.[2] Meanwhile, in order to head-off any command problems that would arise with the various facilities and commands, the Naval Operating Base (NOB), Midway, had been established on 29 July 1942. This new organization—encompassing the NAS, the incipient Submarine Base, Base Defense Ground Forces, and Base Defense Air Forces—would operate under the command of the senior line officer present in command of one of those aforementioned activities.

During September 1942—the same month in which John Ford's documentary "The Battle of Midway" was released to critical and popular acclaim (it would win an Academy Award, or "Oscar")—two companies of the 10th CB arrived, and work commenced on the submarine base on the northern tip of Sand Island. The following month, with Sand Island being used almost exclusively by large planes and transient aircraft, a Naval Air Transport Service (NATS) unit was sent to Midway. Initially, seaplanes carried out bi-weekly NATS runs to Honolulu, until Douglas R5Ds supplanted them two years later.

The "Seabees" completed the three strips on Sand Island by New Year's Day 1943, the longest of which was 5,300 feet long, as well as revetments, magazines, lighting for the airfield, and quarters and messing facilities. On 4 April 1943, the 50th Construction Bat-

Submarine tender *Sperry* (AS-12) lies alongside a pier at the submarine base at Midway on 5 July 1943; the five boats visible alongside the other piers include *Salmon* (SS-182), *Sailfish* (ex-*Squalus*) (SS-192), *Tinosa* (SS-281), *Sawfish* (SS-276) and *Sculpin* (SS-191); the last-named sub had just returned from a war patrol in which she had torpedoed and damaged the Japanese light carrier *Hiyo*.
80-G-103188

talion relieved the 5th, and began work on building a major submarine base. The 50th and 10th CBs together lengthened and paved two Sand Island strips to 7,500 feet and the third to 8,600; built four 13,500-barrel underground steel tanks for diesel oil and a like number of 27,000-barrel tanks for fuel oil, along with the requisite piping and pumping facilities; six finger piers at the submarine base, and installed 2,900 feet of piling.

Late in April 1943, contractors' workmen returned to Midway and commenced an enlarged dredging program in the lagoon. They widened the ship channel from 300 to 400 feet, and deepened it to 35, and increased the anchorage area to moor six cruisers, five destroyers or submarines, and a repair ship. In October 1943, CBMU-524 arrived to maintain the facilities at Midway, in addition to completing the underground hospital and setting up a recreation and recuperation center at the Submarine Base. With the arrival of CBMU-531 in November 1943, the 10th CB departed for Pearl Harbor; soon thereafter, the two maintenance units at Midway were combined into one.

Also starting in October 1943, as the result of the problems presented by drifting coral sand—bad for both equipment and people—in intensive program to decrease erosion and "stabilize" the sand was inaugurated. The NOB took over the Cable Company nursery

2. A little over 14 years later, Midway's dependent school would be named in honor of the late 1stLT George H. Cannon, USMC.

and gardens, and enlarged them; soon, ironwood trees, shrubs, Bermuda and buffalo grass had been planted. "When (the) authorities change the name of Sand Island to Green Island as a more descriptive name," the NAS Midway historian wrote hopefully, "the work of sand stabilization will be complete." The Navy had made a serious effort to tame "raw nature," and thus allow Midway to become "a more pleasant place for man to live."

Such was needed, for with the emphasis on construction of new facilities, maintenance of existing equipment and material had suffered, and anyone visiting the atoll in early 1944 would have seen a sorry jumble of broken-down vehicles, scrap building materials and some of the waste that still remained from the Battle of Midway in 1942. The green oasis of the Cable Station contrasted markedly with the littered sandy wasteland that the rest of Midway had become as the atoll went through a transitional phase in its development.

Midway's function as a defensive base went on uninterrupted for the rest of the war, but it served as the jumping-off point for a series of four night bombing raids (utilizing PB2Y-3 "Coronado" flying boats) on Japanese-held Wake Island between 25 January and 13 February 1944, to support the invasion of the Marshall Islands. It marked the first time that "a formation of heavy seaplanes had been used by the U.S. Navy in a concentrated bombing attack against enemy objectives at extreme long range . . . " Eighteen PB2Y-3s from VP-13 flew four of these 2,100-mile missions and dropped 60 tons of bombs on or near the Wake Island airfield in 50 sorties without incurring any losses. The only other air operations conducted from Midway during this period were routine air and surface security patrols and NATS flights.

Work on the submarine base, meanwhile, proceeded

An SBD-3 in a revetment, Eastern Island, July 1943.
80-G-103182

Proteus (AS-19), tending *Bang* (SS-385), *Pintado* (SS-387) and *Pilotfish* (SS-386), in a view taken between 14 and 28 May 1944, at Midway. NH 93848

apace. Between January and March of 1944, the 50th CB built three 471-foot piers at the submarine base, in addition to a 769-foot tender pier, a repair drydock (ARD) wharf, and a power plant, in addition to electrical and fuel lines connecting Eastern and Sand Island. Action of wind and wave had eroded much of the shoreline, requiring the installation of 1,200 feet of sheet piling bulkhead on Sand and 300 on Eastern.

In April 1944, the 123d CB and the 10th Special Battalion arrived on Midway, and continued work on the waterfront projects, in addition to enlarging the fuel storage capacity of the atoll. In addition, they constructed an additional two piers to berth tenders at the submarine base, four additional piers for submarines, and seven shop buildings. In December 1944, the 50th CB brought its work to a close, and CBMU-534 was assigned to handle the maintenance work.

By March 1945, the need to operate motor torpedo boats at Midway had decreased; four PT-boats of MTBRON 26 had relieved those from MTBRON ONE (that had fought at Midway) in April 1943; while initially used in anti-submarine patrols, the PTs were used eventually in searches for downed aircrew—a function of the crash boats which had been sent to the island.

Likewise, by April 1945, with practically no need to maintain Eastern Island as anything but an emergency landing field, air operations were shifted to Sand Island, retaining the mission of NAS Midway to support USMC or Navy single-engined aircraft, patrol and bomber squadrons, and to maintain a sufficient supply of fuel on hand.

The submariners who utilized the Midway base during the war enjoyed "nearly every recreational advantage provided at larger bases . . . " such as tennis and handball courts, bowling alleys, baseball diamonds, good swimming beaches, recreation halls, picnic grounds, and the opportunity to fish. The enlisted men were assigned to Camp Berry, while the officers utilized the "Gooneyville Hotel," which had formerly been the old PAA hotel. The NOB theater, constructed by the "Seabees," hosted such stars as Joe E. Brown, Betty Hutton and Boris Karloff.

Japan's surrender in August 1945 brought an end to World War II, and within a year's time, demobilization had reduced Midway to caretaker status. Military dependents arrived on the atoll, and notable "firsts" occurred over the next two years: the first male child was born on 13 August 1946; the first female child on 17 September of the same year; and the first graduation from Midway's elementary school took place on 29 May 1947.

On 21 July 1947, VMF-322, the last formal defensive unit, was detached from Midway. The outbreak of the Korean War in June 1950, however, marked the atoll's resumption of importance to the Navy, and NAS Midway, ordered reactivated in August 1950, began handling air traffic the following month. While PAA shifted the terminus of its transpacific operations to Wake in 1952, the Navy maintained its operation at Midway. Its own radio station, KMTH, began broadcasting in April 1953.

In late August 1954, John Ford returned to Midway

As the war progressed, USO tours brightened the lives of officers and men assigned to Midway; here on 21 November 1944, comedienne Betty Hutton visits the "Gooneyville Tavern," flanked by CDR Vernon L. Lowrance (L) and CDR Arthur C. House (R). Lowrance had command of an attack group with his command pennant in *Sea Dog* (SS-401) at that time. 80-G-288282

Midway, April 1945. Sand Island (bottom) sports a major landplane base, with three airstrips. The submarine base is visible in the center of the photo; Eastern Island lies at top right. 80-G-345542.

to film a movie, and found that despite the more modern aviation facilities, the atoll appeared to look much the same as it did 12 years earlier. The motion picture, "Mister Roberts," in which one can see some Midway scenery in the background, starred Henry Fonda (who had spoken a portion of the narration of Ford's World War II documentary, "The Battle of Midway"), James Cagney, William Powell and Ward Bond. Both critics and the movie-going public acclaimed the picture, and Jack Lemmon won an Academy Award as best supporting actor. Incidentally, the ship which appeared in the movie as *The Reluctant* or "The Bucket," was the small cargo ship *Hewell* (AKL-14). Filming was conducted at Midway between 1 and 24 September 1954; additional scenes were filmed at Marine Corps Air Station, Kaneohe Bay, T.H.

In January 1956, initial action on extending the United States' Distant Early Warning (DEW) Line into mid-Pacific came about, with the establishment of the Airborne Early Warning Wing, Pacific, which consisted of three squadrons of radar-equipped Lockheed EC-121 "Constellations." These, operating alongside radar-equipped destroyer escorts (DER) made up the Pacific Barrier, which went into operation on 1 July 1958. On 1 February 1960, the three-squadron wing was consolidated into Airborne Early Warning Barrier Squadron, Pacific, and homebased at Barbers Point, on Oahu.

With the coming of the Vietnam War in the mid-1960s, Midway remained active as a port-of-call and air traffic center; during 1968, 313 ships touched there, as did 11,077 aircraft (4,261 of them Military Airlift Command planes). As the war wound down, the numbers of ships and planes dwindled accordingly; by 1972, only 2,279 flights passed through; 5,018 passengers and 170 ships.

The original cable station buildings, dating from about 1905, are all that is left of the early days on the island.

Present-day barracks at Midway. The island is now a Naval Air Station with a small contingent of military personnel and several hundred civilians to service the base.

The wind that whispers through the trees at Midway, and ruffles the feathers of the "goonies" that still inhabit the place in large numbers, and the surf that pounds the jagged coral reef that surrounds the atoll like a sparkling necklace, are timeless. While those physical characteristics of Midway exist today much as they did forty years ago, memory of what occurred in the skies above it and across, over, and beneath the waters that surround it linger long as stories of heroism and devotion to duty are likely to be recounted.

Like Miltonic winged hosts, aviators from the United States and Japan met over and near a tiny speck of land in the middle of the Pacific. They attacked each other's carriers. One Japanese objective was capture of the atoll; the American objective was to deny it to them. The Japanese wanted to lure the American fleet into a trap; the former fell, instead, into a snare far more deadly than they could have imagined. The United States scored a decisive victory in soundly defeating the Japanese *Kido Butai*.

The Battle of Midway found the United States victorious because it had applied accurate intelligence boldly. Both sides fought with skill and acts of heroism by occidental and oriental abounded on both sides. The cost in terms of men and machines was high, but the Japanese never again ventured into those waters in such force, saving Hawaii from whatever chance of invasion—even if such would have only been for a short duration—existed.

Midway can still be studied for the lessons to be learned in gaging an enemy's intentions and then moving sufficient force to counter those intentions. Although the United States Navy may have had advance knowledge of when and where the enemy was picking the place of engagement, its sailors and aviators, along with Marines and Army airmen, had to prove equal to the task of meeting, and turning aside, the Japanese blow. This they did with dogged determination.

Outcomes of conflicts, it can be argued, are never certain things. The United States needed a victory in June 1942. The Japanese, at that time, were still arbiters of Asia and of the Pacific, pushing out the boundaries of their Greater East Asia Co-Prosperity Sphere. The outcome of the Battle of the Coral Sea had suggested that the oriental enemy was, perhaps, not invincible. The Battle of Midway proved it. Although the war was far from over in the Pacific—the conflict would not end until over three hard-fought years later—Midway served as an important milestone on the road to victory.

A memorial to the Battle of Midway with the ever-present "Gooney" birds.

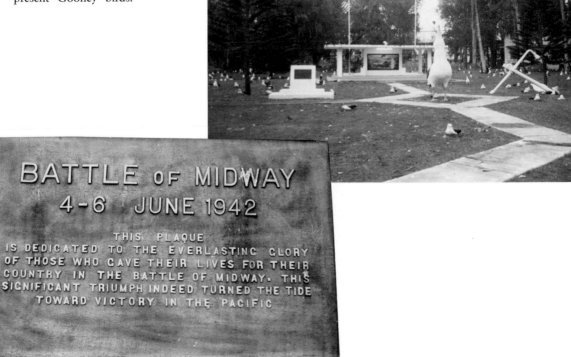

The island is famous for the
thousands of "Gooney"
birds that inhabit it.

Anchors in front of the
Navy's hangar.

APPENDIX ONE

. . . .

Personalities and Perspectives

BY STEVE EWING

Although previously mentioned in the Introduction, it is necessary to note again that, due to the tremendous scope of the engagement, there has been no definitive history of the Battle of Midway. Samuel Eliot Morison's *Coral Sea, Midway, and Submarine Actions*, Walter Lord's *Incredible Victory*, Mitsuo Fuchida and Masatake Okumiya's *Midway: The Battle That Doomed Japan*; Gordon W. Prange's *Miracle at Midway* and John Lundstrom's *The First Team* present the reader with accounts of the battle that, when taken as a whole, come close to being as "definitive" as is humanly possible.

Despite Morison's contention that his efforts and that of his staff should not be accepted as the Navy's "official" history, his 15-volume *History of United States Naval Operations in World War II* will probably be regarded popularly as about as official as any work could be. President Roosevelt had authorized Morison's travel to the various theaters of war to collect impressions and information; Morison saw active service in 11 ships and was entitled to wear seven battle stars on his campaign ribbons. Following the war, he returned to Harvard to complete research and write the 15 volumes that have been regarded as the starting point for every student of World War II naval operations. His fast-paced, colorful writing style still commands attention of not only the serious scholar but the casual reader or history "buff" as well.

Walter Lord traveled over 30,000 miles to interview participants on both sides of the Pacific who took part in Midway. Gordon W. Prange interrupted his academic career to serve as a commissioned officer in the Navy during World War II, and following hostilities served in Japan as chief of General MacArthur's G-2 Historical Section. Lord and Prange, like Morison, possessed the advantage of knowing many of the pertinent men involved, and of having access to primary sources. Researchers looking into the Battle of Midway owe a debt of gratitude for the solid scholarly foundations laid by these men.

Fuchida (who was present at Midway, in *Akagi*) and Okumiya (who was not) were among the first to present the Japanese perspective to English-speaking readers, and scholars of Midway were treated to a lesson in objectivity: Morison (and others) believed that the submarine *Nautilus* (SS-168) had torpedoed *Soryu* at Midway, on the strength of that ship's action report. After the publication of the Fuchida and Okumiya volume, which contented it was *Kaga*, not *Soryu*, that came under attack by *Nautilus*, Morison clung to his original interpretation. Lord and Prange, however, after evaluation of the evidence, reached the verdict that it was indeed *Kaga*. As more intrepid western scholars tackle the intricacies of the Japanese language and translate their sources, an even more balanced account of the Battle of Midway may yet come to light.

Japanese Personalities and Perspectives

Although many Japanese were responsible for tactical decisions at Midway, the strategic decisions rested with two men: ADM Isoroku Yamamoto and VADM Chuichi Nagumo. As time goes forward, nearly all other Japanese participants, save perhaps the indefatigable RADM Yamaguchi, may fade from commentaries, but never Yamamoto and Nagumo.

Architect of the surprise attack on Pearl Harbor, Yamamoto no doubt drew inspiration for it from Japanese history. Although the tactical commander in that instance, Nagumo, failed to press home his advantage at Pearl Harbor in going back and destroying the navy yard and other fleet support facilities—a move which would have incalculably damaged the U.S. Navy's capacity to wage war from its Hawaiian base—the Japanese public hailed the devastating surprise attack as a great victory. Yamamoto's reputation soared to heights almost equal to that of the revered naval hero of the war with Russia, ADM Heihachiro Togo. Continuing success in the Pacific in the months that followed Pearl Harbor strengthened Yamamoto's ability to influence the Naval General Staff, and despite opposition within that body, it approved, in principle, Yamamoto's projected plan to attack Midway. As we have seen, the Halsey-Doolittle Raid in April 1942, however, ended the debate between Yamamoto and the Naval General Staff, and established as a reality the fear among Japanese planners that American carriers posed a threat to the sacred soil of Nippon.

Despite its offensive nature, Yamamoto's Midway campaign was essentially defensive, as the Japanese determined that the U.S. Navy would move across the Pacific via the Aleutians, Australia, or the central Pacific. Although the Naval General Staff primarily suspected the southern route, Yamamoto believed that opportunity existed to draw the relatively weak American carrier forces into a decisive battle near Midway as the loss of that atoll would jeopardize the security of Hawaii. The

VADM Chuichi Nagumo, Commander of the *Kido Butai* from Pearl Harbor to Midway. NH 83423 via Wenger

ADM Isoroku Yamamoto, CNC, Combined Fleet, in a view probably taken early in World War II.

Aleutians campaign was to be conducted concurrently, and if all went according to plan, the Japanese would follow up success in the Aleutians and Midway by cutting the lifeline to Australia and thereby secure Japan's defensive perimeter. With interior lines of communication thus established, Japan believed that then the United States would deem the effort too costly to fight on to the Japanese homeland. The final goal was a negotiated peace: no Japanese leader, even in his most euphoric moment, envisioned an invasion of the United States mainland.

In the years since the Battle of Midway, American and Japanese historians have agreed on several criticisms of Yamamoto's grand plan, citing Japanese overconfidence at nearly all levels of command (manifestations of "Victory Disease"), the inherent problem of the dual objectives of occupying Midway and being ready to meet the American carriers, dispersion of Japanese forces, and Yamamoto not remaining in Japan where he could have been free to communicate with his dispersed forces instead of being muted by radio silence.

Yamamoto's decision to accompany the fleet, in his flagship *Yamato*, and his dispersion of forces, may have been the weakest part of the plan. Overconfidence was understandable—even if unwise—and the decision to occupy Midway was probably necessary in order to bait the trap to lure the American carriers toward the atoll. To the greatest degree possible, a historian must attempt to place his thinking in the frame of reference of the times in which the events transpired. That being the case, it is doubtful that any Japanese commander would have made decisions much different than Yamamoto in the spring of 1942. Time was running out for Japan to fully exploit her relative naval strength. If American cryptanalysts had not cracked the Japanese code, Yamamoto would have had time to occupy Midway and then be ready to devote all attention to the expected American counterattack. Time was also critical for such factors as moonlight for night operations.

The man primarily responsible for the implementation of Yamamoto's plan was VADM Nagumo. It fell to him to deal with all of the ramifications of the broken code, not the least of which was the fact that he was steaming into an ambush. Advance knowledge of Japanese intentions also tipped the balance of tactical strength in favor of the Americans, who could bring three mobile carriers and one unsinkable one (Midway) to bear against Nagumo's four flattops.

Students of naval history have often criticized Nagumo (who had been criticized earlier for his decision to limit the time he lingered in Hawaiian waters in December 1941) for overconfidence—never acceptable at high command level—and poor direction of aerial reconnaissance. Other critics focus on the fact that Nagumo was not an aviator.[1] During the Battle of Midway Symposium at Pensacola on 6 May 1988, CDR Izuyo Fujita, who had flown a "Zero" at Pearl Harbor and at Midway, who had 42 confirmed "kills" to his credit, and was then President of the "Zero" Fighter Pilots Association, defended Nagumo on that point. While noting that there had been "many criticisms" of the admiral's assignment to command the *Kido Butai*, Fujita stated: "I don't think things would have been that different, no matter who was placed as commander . . . as long as that commander is surrounded by competent staff. . . ."

Among the men upon whom Nagumo depended was CDR Minoru Genda, his air officers. Although suffering from pneumonia during the battle, he was nonetheless present on the bridge to assist Nagumo in making one of the most critical decisions for which the admiral has been most often criticized. Although there were oral instructions for Nagumo's force to hold planes in reserve for a strike against American ships, should any have been spotted in the area, Nagumo launched the first strike against Midway with planes from all four carriers. The belated spotting of American carriers by one of *Tone*'s planes forced Nagumo into deciding whether or not to strike immediately with ordnance more suited for land bases than ships, and without fighter cover. RADM Yamaguchi, Commander of the 2d Carrier Division, in *Hiryu*, recommended an immediate strike. Nagumo's chief of staff, RADM Ryunosuke Kusaka, and Genda counseled against it. Three factors swayed their decision: a desire to recover returning planes low on fuel from the Midway strike; the desire to rearm planes with torpedoes and armor-piercing bombs to attack ships rather than land targets; and having seen how vulnerable the American planes had been attacking without fighter protection. Studies have seemed to indicate that the first consideration motivated Genda, saving lives, while the latter two appeared to have motivated Kusaka.

In retrospect, Genda has indicated that he should have been more objective by being willing to lose a few to save many. Interestingly, RADM Spruance had to overrule CDR Miles Browning who at one point was willing to send off planes to attack *Hiryu* seemingly aware that the combination of fuel and bomb load would have prevented many from ever returning! As noted earlier, Yamamoto and Nagumo will always be central to any discussion of Midway; Genda and Kusaka deserve inclusion for their influence upon Nagumo. Yamaguchi's recommendation to attack without proper ordnance and fighter protection is, too, worthy of mention in even brief

retellings of the battle. To a lesser degree, historians will remember LT Joichi Tomonaga, who led the strike on Midway in place of the ailing CDR Mitsuo Fuchida (who had been incapacitated by appendicitis) and radioed the fateful call for a second strike against the well-fortified atoll, as well as LT Kobayashi, who led *Hiryu*'s dive bombers through flak and fighters to attack *Yorktown*.

Fuchida and Genda both enjoyed excellent eyewitness vantage points from which they could comment on Japanese perspectives on the battle. Minoru Genda served his country after the war in the Japanese Self Defense Air Force and in the national government; Mitsuo Fuchida became a Christian and, as an evangelist and Protestant minister, visited many of his former enemies—as did Genda—before he died in 1976. Yamamoto died when the "Betty" bomber in which he was riding as a passenger was ambushed by Army Air Force P-38s over Bougainville—again the victim of American cryptanalysts, and Nagumo committed suicide as the forces he was leading in the defense of Saipan were defeated. Yamaguchi, as we have seen, went down with his flagship, *Hiryu*, as did her CO, CAPT Tomeo Kaku. CAPT Ryusaku Yanigamoto chose to go down with his ship, *Soryu*, while CAPT Jisaku Okada of *Kaga* died early in the battle when a bomb blew up the fuel truck parked ahead of *Kaga*'s bridge, thus leaving only CAPT Tiajiro Aoki of *Akagi* as the sole survivor of Japanese carrier commanding officers; Aoki died after the war. Recent scholarship on the battle (*The First Team*) indicates that Kobayashi may have survived the attack on *Yorktown* but was shot down while attempting to ascertain the results of his unit's attack; Tomonaga perished in the torpedo attack on *Yorktown*, most likely the victim of LCDR "Jimmy" Thach.

Fuchida and Okumiya, as well as Prange, devoted considerable space at the end of their books to an analysis of the battle. Both are interesting, thought-provoking, and similar in concluding that the Japanese made many mistakes. Still one cannot help but note that Walter Lord used "incredible" and Gordon Prange used "miracle" in their respective book titles. Had it not been for several significant mistakes, Japan could have won at Midway.

American Personalities and Perspectives

The United States Navy won the Battle of Midway as the result of breaking the Japanese code and the fortuitous arrival of SBDs from *Enterprise* and *Yorktown* arriving over the Japanese carriers while the enemy's attention was still directed at the gallant torpedo plane attacks. With the former, the surprise factor shifted from the Japanese to the United States. Admittedly, all would have been for naught had not the SBD pilots been able

---

1. Neither were Frank Jack Fletcher nor Raymond A. Spruance.

to place a sufficient number of bombs into four Japanese carriers, but, prior to the destruction wrought by the planes from *Enterprise* and *Yorktown*, the actions of several men established the foundation for the opportunities of 4-6 June 1942.

If the victory of Midway was one of possessing the right intelligence, the men who labored at Station "Hypo" at Pearl Harbor, seeking to break the Japanese JN-25 naval code, deserved the most significant laurels for achieving it. CDR Joseph J. Rochefort, LCDR Thomas H. Dyer, LCDR Joseph Finnegan, "Ham" Wright, and others working under the fleet intelligence officer, CDR Edwin T. Layton, all brought not only ability but dedication to their endeavor.

At the top level of command in the Pacific sat ADM Chester W. Nimitz, a quiet and gentle man who could exhibit toughness when the situation demanded it. Although not an aviator, he fully appreciated the potential of naval air power, and enjoyed the advice and counsel of men who were aviators: RADM Patrick N. L. Bellinger (COMPATWING TWO) and CAPT Arthur C. Davis, his aviation officer. The major decisions which Nimitz reached included his acceptance of an ailing VADM Halsey's recommendation that RADM Raymond A. Spruance assume command of TF 16; his acceptance of Layton's and Rochefort's intelligence estimates, and his decision to take the calculated risk in meeting the oncoming Japanese with the three carriers he had available to him in Hawaiian waters. Rather than assume a strict defensive posture, he had the vision to practice Confederate General Nathan Bedford Forrest's getting there first with the most. Although the Japanese outnumbered his forces, Nimitz entered the Battle of Midway with the element of surprise backed up by three flattops and patrol planes and bombers operating from Midway itself.

Nimitz enjoined Fletcher and Spruance to "inflict maximum damage . . . by employing strong attrition tactics." In the context of the time (May-June 1942), it could be surmised that Nimitz was thinking more toward preventing a defeat than scoring a victory. An economist would have particularly enjoyed Nimitz' applying the principle of "point of diminishing return" to the science of war.

In contrast to his counterpart, Yamamoto, Nimitz (probably because of his smaller forces) adopted a much less complex plan—something of little comfort to Fletcher and Spruance, who would have to carry out the "strong attrition tactics" Nimitz decreed. Some historians view Midway as the high point of Fletcher's career. As we have seen, ADM King's questioning Fletcher's fitness to remain in the command of TF 17 prompted Nimitz to interrogate the admiral upon his return to Pearl Harbor from the Coral Sea on 27 May; again in August and September 1942, after the Battle of the Eastern Solomons, his conduct of the battles that he had fought came into question again. While he never again held a sea command, he did contribute to the prosecution of the war with Japan.

At Midway, Fletcher demonstrated ability and personal character by separating TF 16 and TF 17 approximately 20 miles apart—which proved to be close enough to allow returning planes to find a clear flight deck but far enough apart to keep an enemy strike from hitting all three carriers at once, and, after *Yorktown* had been crippled and he had shifted his flag to a heavy cruiser, unselfishly transferred tactical command to Spruance, his junior, when he found himself not in a position to continue direction of the battle.

Spruance's star was on the rise at the Battle of Midway; judiciously considering his staff's advice (most importantly that of CDR Browning) in accepting some suggestions and rejecting others, as we have seen, Spruance made the decisions that put American naval aviators in a position to win the battle. Although criticized for it at the time, Spruance's decision to turn away from the Japanese on the night of 4-5 June, thus minimizing the chance of his force running into an enemy surface force that heavily outgunned him, was correct, as post-war examination of enemy records showed. Spruance was, after all, totally in his element as a surface warfare specialist.

None of the American carrier commanders—*Yorktown*'s CAPT Buckmaster, *Enterprise*'s CAPT Murray, or *Hornet*'s newly promoted RADM Mitscher—were lost at Midway, although circumstances compelled *Yorktown*'s commander to swim to safety twice! All would later rise to flag rank, as did the two captains peripherally involved at Midway: Mitscher's relief, CAPT Charles P. Mason, who was embarked during the battle, and Nimitz's aviation officer, CAPT Arthur C. Davis, who was slated to relieve Buckmaster in *Yorktown*. Each of the three captains suffered disappointment and loss: Buckmaster the loss of his ship, Mitscher the loss of VT-8 and his other pilots and aircrew, Murray the delay in sending off the morning strike on 4 June.

While the junior officers of the Imperial Japanese Navy exhibited bravery and skill in pressing home their attacks, so, too, did their U.S. Navy counterparts. Generally accepted as an outstanding act of initiative on the part of a junior officer was that of LCDR C. Wade McClusky's extending his search beyond the expected point of interception. Discarding an expanding box search due to dwindling fuel, McClusky also decided not to give up and return to the ship to refuel. *Yorktown*'s Air Group Commander, CDR Oscar Pederson (retained on board ship as fighter director) and the air officer, CDR Murr Arnold, sent their people off with instructions to fly north, away from Midway, if they did not spot the Japanese as anticipated. Circumstances forced McClusky to act on the spot, resulting in his bringing the *Enterprise* SBDs over the Japanese carriers at nearly the same time as *Yorktown's*.

Ultimately attaining flag rank, Wade McClusky would live out the remainder of his days until his death in 1976 secure in the knowledge that he had served his country well. McClusky received the Navy Cross for his stalwart leadership.[2] LCDR Maxwell F. Leslie, who would replace McClusky as *Enterprise's* air group commander, enjoyed the same professional satisfaction as he did. Even after losing his bomb en route to the target, Max Leslie defined devotion to duty in remaining in the lead of his squadron and taking it down to the attack, for which he, too, was awarded the Navy Cross. Despite evidence to the contrary, however, Max Leslie maintained until his death in 1985 that VB-3 had put *Kaga*—not *Soryu*—out of action.

Stanhope Ring, *Hornet's* Air Group Commander, for his part, is perhaps remembered as the epitome of the naval officer in intelligence, industry, bearing, and ability. Some of his men, though, remembered him as formal, rigid, and overbearing; to what degree these attributes influenced his decision-making at Midway may never be known, as he declined to comment on why his SBDs and F4Fs failed to find the Japanese on the morning of 4 June. It is believed that Ring simply could not exert control over his pilots as fuel became critical and the realization set in that perhaps the CHAG— who was apparently taken to task by VT-8's skipper for taking the wrong route—had chosen the wrong course. So strong is the feeling in some quarters that George Gay, in *Sole Survivor*, does not mention Ring by name.

Pilots whose planes carried torpedoes against Japanese carriers on the morning of 4 June did not fare well by any standard, although without fighter cover no reasonable individual could have expected any other result. As we have seen, four Army B-26s went out from Midway—only two returned; six new TBFs went out— only one came back: 41 TBDs took off from the three American carriers involved—four got back to *Enterprise*, two from *Yorktown* survived the attack on the *Kido Butai* but had to ditch near TF 17, and none from *Hornet* survived. Of the officers who led the torpedo attacks, only the Army's B-26 unit commander survived. All four Navy unit commanders (the three carrier-based squadrons and the Midway-based VT-8 detachment)

died.

Lack of fighter cover doomed the torpedo planes to terrible losses. Scrambled without any fighters to protect them, the Midway-based units suffered heavily; the carrier squadrons were to have received help from their respective F4F-equipped units, but circumstances dictated otherwise. Other contributing factors to the bloody demise of the torpedo squadrons were the comparative slowness of the TBD and the slow speed required for release of their "fish" (which were slow and unreliable as well) and the lack of coordination with the dive bombers. While they reckoned the American pilots and aircrew as heroic, the Japanese evaluated the performance of their materiel with contempt.

As we have seen, *Hornet's* fighters became separated from VT-8, *Enterprise* picked up the wrong squadron during the movement to the target; only *Yorktown's* VF-3 accompanied the TBDs they were supposed to protect, but did well to defend themselves against the onslaught of "Zeroes." After returning to *Enterprise*, one of the surviving VT-6 pilots, who believed LT Gray was responsible for the frightful losses suffered by Lindsey's men that morning, had to by physically restrained from attacking the fighter squadron skipper. Bob Laub, one of the other survivors, however, is more charitable: "He couldn't see us; there was cloud cover between us. . .

If he had come down, he and his few fighters would have also been shot down because the F4F . . . was no match for the 'Zero' at low altitude."[3]

A number of the pilots and radio-gunners of the SBDs from *Yorktown* and *Enterprise* have openly wondered why their units did not receive unit awards such as that given VT-8. Although the valor of Torpedo EIGHT is not debated, the question remains why the units that actually placed the bombs on the four enemy carriers were not similarly recognized. Individual awards of the Navy Cross abounded: LT(jg) Paul Holmberg, LT W. Earl Gallaher, LT Dick Best, LT DeWitt Shumway and LT Sam Adams; each pilot of VT-8 was awarded one (all, except George Gay's, posthumously).[4] No awards, though, could either ease the pain of friends lost, or could repay the debt owed by the country to those men who died.

---

3. At the Battle of Midway symposium on 6 May 1988, retired CAPT Jim Gray rose to request an opportunity to explain what happened that morning VF-6's escort used up much gasoline during the flight to the target and, reasoning that "only an idiot runs out of gas in an airplane," elected to return to *Enterprise*. VF-6 "went back, and lived to fight another day," VF-8, on the other hand, "landed the whole outfit in the water." Up at altitude, Gray explained, VF-6 simply "ran ourselves out of gas getting up there . . ."

4. CAPT Mitscher recommended that each pilot in VT-8 be awarded the Medal of Honor.

2. Contrary to what is apparently popular belief, Wade McClusky was never formally recommended for the Medal of Honor.

Lingering Debates?

A number of questions pertinent to certain aspects of the Battle of Midway continue to interest students of naval history. Some are still being asked after 48 years and several were addressed during the Battle of Midway symposium in May 1988.

(1) *What was the Japanese Intent If They Had Succeeded at Midway?*

Just as disagreement existed within the Japanese high command concerning an attack on Midway, there were questions as to what action *would* follow success in the Midway operation. The Naval General Staff favored heading toward Fiji and Samoa and severing the southern lifeline to Australia. The Combined Fleet favored a move toward Hawaii, and could foresee the possibility that occupation of that place might be achieved by default after the destruction of American carriers.

(2) *Did the Battle of Midway Cost the Japanese the Cream of Their Naval Pilots?*

During the May 1988 Symposium, Walter Lord, Bill Esders, and Dick Best all stated the significance of Japanese pilot losses at Midway. However, one of the Japanese panelists disagreed and stated that over half of the Japanese pilots engaged at Midway survived. The generally held belief that Japan suffered grievously in pilot loss at Midway has merit but more so along the lines of thinking offered by Fuchida and Okumiya. The Japanese policy of keeping combat experienced pilots at the front rather than rotating them back to training commands would signal the greatest loss for Japan at Midway. In conclusion, the loss of Japanese pilots was not so much in quantity as it was in quality no longer available for training others, and the loss of key components from well-organized teams: the air groups from four veteran flattops.

(3) *How Significant Was the Capture of a Japanese "Zero" Fighter to the Development of the F6F "Hellcat?"*

Zero (published in 1956) by Masatake Okumiya and Jiro Horikoshi, edited by Martin Caidin, claimed that the "Hellcat" was designed as a specific response to the "Zero," following the Americans' thorough study of a Mitsubishi captured after the raid on Dutch Harbor on 4 June 1942. Incredible as it may seem, some still believe that this is true! The Navy ordered the first prototype XF6F-1 on 30 June 1941, and the second example flew on 30 July 1942, less than three weeks after a PBY crew spotted the nearly intact "Zero" upside down in a bog on Akutan Island. It is correct, though, to credit evaluation of the "Aleutian Zero" in influencing the overall optimum utilization of the "Hellcat" in the Pacific War.

(4) *Was Midway the "Turning Point of the Pacific?"*

Midway was the turning point in the Pacific if the major consideration of the question is directed to when the United States was able to turn from a defensive strategy to an offensive one. If the question is directed in the perspective of the turn toward victory for the United States and defeat for Japan, then Guadalcanal was the turning point.

(5) *Was the Aleutian Operation a Diversion with Regard to Midway?*

No. The Japanese move into the Aleutians possessed a purpose separate from the primary goals of the Midway operation. The two Japanese goals for Midway were (1) occupation of the atoll and (2) to lure the American fleet into a decisive battle where it could be annihilated. The Japanese believed that they would have two days to defeat the Midway garrison and then have use of the island—an unsinkable aircraft carrier—to meet the expected American counterattack. If all was accomplished on the Japanese timetable, the simultaneous thrust into the Aleutians might divert American forces for a day, but in the broad scheme of planning, it was not critical for American carriers to move north. The Japanese believed that they had sufficient time to attack and occupy Midway before American naval units could move into the Midway area. The Japanese purpose of the Aleutian thrust was to deny the United States its forward bases in its northern outposts from which long-range bombers might attack the Japanese homeland. The move was defensive in strategic planning, not offensive.

(6) *Was Yorktown Abandoned Prematurely?*

After having taken three bombs and two torpedoes on the afternoon of 4 June, *Yorktown* quickly rolled to 26 degrees and was ordered abandoned. She remained afloat for two days, however, leading some to charge that she was abandoned prematurely. Careful investigation, however, reveals that all of the evidence available at that time support CAPT Buckmaster's decision.

Essex (CV-9)-class aircraft carriers had been designed to incorporate the lessons learned from the operations of the two *Yorktown*-class ships, most importantly changing the arrangement of the boiler and engine rooms so that a single torpedo hit could not stop the ship dead in the water.[5] CAPT Buckmaster knew that the loss of power would not permit his men to

---

5. *Essex*, the class leader, was not launched until July 1942; *Yorktown* (CV-10), named to honor the carrier lost at Midway and the second ship of the class, until January 1943.

counterflood, and that flooding in the engineering spaces would be almost impossible to repair rapidly even if all back-up generators were operational. Advised that power was not available from the damaged generators, Buckmaster could only conclude that the combination of no power and an increasing list could spell disaster; despite the *Yorktown* class's extensive compartmentation, it was logical to deduce that the concussion of bomb and torpedo explosions would have compromised the ship's watertight integrity. If the ship continued to fill with water, she would sink quickly, trapping over 2,000 trained men on board. Ships could, to some extent, be replaced; trained men, however, were much harder to come by. CAPT Buckmaster, given the situation as it existed at the moment he ordered "abandon ship," could not have acted otherwise.

The experiences of *Yorktown, Enterprise* and *Hornet* demonstrated those ships' capacity to absorb heavy damage. *Yorktown*'s experience — the lengthy process of gathering a salvage party to go back and attempt to save the ship — proved the most significant lesson learned, as ADM Nimitz ordered that such a salvage party be organized as standard procedure. The *Essex*-class *Franklin* (CV-13) and *Bunker Hill* (CV-17) proved that that class was just as tough, although even though those two heavily hit ships returned home under their own power, they never again saw active service.

(7) What Were the Major Reasons for the Relatively Poor Performance of the American Planes Based on Midway That Were Used in Defending the Atoll and in Attacking the Kido Butai?

Inexperience of the pilots, obsolete aircraft, and a decision to use the fighters for the defense of Midway instead of accompanying the strike group on its flight to the Japanese fleet (which left the strike planes bereft of cover) all contributed to the heavy losses and disappointing results achieved by the units operating from Midway. Those three things, combined with the quality of the enemy fighter pilots and their planes, spelled disaster, particularly for the marines. However, their sacrifice was not in vain, for their exertions kept the Japanese off-balance and preoccupied, thus interfering with their carrier operations.

(8) Was the Grumman "Avenger" Given its Name to Commemorate Torpedo EIGHT's Losses in the Battle of Midway?

In October 1941, Secretary of the Navy Frank Knox promulgated popular names for naval aircraft, and "Avenger" for Grumman's TBF-1 was among them — long before either Pearl Harbor or Midway had occurred to give the airplane something to "avenge."

(9) Who Sank Hiryu: Pilots from Yorktown or Enterprise?

Research has shown somewhat conclusively that *Yorktown*'s VB-3 sank *Soryu* while *Enterprise*'s VB-6 and VS-6 sank *Akagi* and *Kaga*. As we have seen, *Yorktown* planes landed on board "The Big E" after *Yorktown* had been stopped dead in the water by Kobayashi's dive bombers on 4 June. LT Earl Gallaher of VS-6 led a strike, composed of 14 ex-*Yorktown* SBDs and 10 *Enterprise* planes, against *Hiryu* later that afternoon, assigning his own ship's troops the carrier and *Yorktown*'s the screening "battleships" (actually cruisers).

Historians generally agree that Gallaher and the next two *Enterprise* pilots missed their target, and that LT D. W. Shumway of VB-3, forsaking the "battleship," went after *Hiryu* instead. The debate on the subject begins at this point and agreement ends — the victim of unit pride.   While Morison, Prange and Lundstrom do not specifically address the "who-hit-*Hiryu*" debate, Walter Lord, however, whose meticulous research on what squadrons hit what ships that morning has withstood the test of time, concluded that "Scouting SIX probably got one . . . Bombing THREE certainly two . . . Bombing SIX another — but it was hard to tell. . . ." In short, it was at the very least a shared "kill."

This debate, lingering if even in the minds of the dwindling number of participants in the event, draws attention to the loyalties held to units and shipmates of long ago. It is no easy task to interview veterans of the battle, some of whom defend their perspective as gospel and any variance with it as blasphemy.[6] One may find few veterans of *Yorktown*'s VB-3 who will credit hits on *Hiryu* to anyone other than themselves. Veterans of VB-6 and VS-6 acknowledge two hits by pilots from *Yorktown* but insist that they achieved at least two themselves![7]

Lying within this minor debate on who deserves credit for who inflicted what damage is the fundamental thing exhibited by each pilot at Midway — his skill at what he was trained to do. Frederick Mears, at the time of the Battle of Midway, was a new pilot in *Hornet*'s Torpedo EIGHT, and as such would not fly that morning. He would, however, fly in combat at Guadalcanal soon thereafter, and would die in action. "If there is any one trait that carrier pilots have in common," he wrote,

---

6. In doing research on a book about *Enterprise*, I interviewed a fighter pilot who insisted that Japanese planes had followed the returning strike groups back to *Yorktown* and thus learned her location in that fashion. One would think he *had* to know — after all, he was there and in the air at the time. Note, *Soryu*'s "Judy" did just that, as recorded earlier in the book.

7. Although some veterans of that attack decline to say anything negative about that attack on *Hiryu*, Jim Murray, a radio-gunner in VB-6, claimed that *Yorktown*'s diving SBDs posed nearly as much danger to the *Enterprise* planes as they did to *Hiryu*!

"it is matter-of-factness. . . . In the Navy, and especially in wartime, you do what you are told to do, and if some of your comrades are killed in the process it's tough to take but it doesn't change you into a wrathful avenger. Eventually, if it happens too many times, it leads to a dull despair at thoughts of so many good men dead, and to a steadying, cold determination to beat the Japs and win the war. But fancy words don't help. Any time a pilot says, 'Thoughts of Jack or Joe will be riding with the next torpedo,' he is just blowing or else he is emotionally unfit to be a combat aviator. The only thoughts which should be riding with a torpedo to make it hit are those of entry and departure from the target, target angle, target speed, dropping point, avoidance of AA fire, and other matter-of-fact considerations. . . ."

Also lying within is evidence that unit loyalties instilled during training reflect a solid educational strategy. The men who flew their planes against the Japanese, no less than the men who manned the ships on TF 16 and 17 and manned defense positions on Midway proper, all were conscious of who they were and what was expected of them. Are unit rivalries important? Absolutely, and for the sake of the security and welfare of our nation, may that never change.

The men who flew their slow TBDs into the teeth of the flak and fighters defending the *Kido Butai*, the men who rode their SBDs down toward their targets, or fought their F4Fs or F2As in action with "Zeroes," were most likely thinking of those "matter-of-fact" things that Frederick Mears so eloquently expressed, doing that for which they were trained. They did their duty the best they could with the tools they had, and gave ample evidence of heroism and devotion to duty; they each in a very special way wrote a unique portion of what ADM Nimitz called: "A glorious page in our history." May they be ever so remembered.

APPENDIX TWO

·················

Tribute

BY STEVE EWING

How best to honor the memories of brave men and momentous events is an elusive thing. An exhibit is erected, deteriorates in time, and then is dismantled or stored away. A speech may survive as long as the listener, or the medium upon which it is recorded; a ship named for one lost in battle may usually serve actively for 20 or 30 years, or much less. While a film record has possibilities, a book may be the best form, a veritable traveling exhibit.

Midway—no matter in what form the story is recorded—continues to capture the imagination of all interested in naval history. The elements of any good story—suspense, underdogs, courage, providence, secrecy (and secrecy revealed), failure and success—are all part of the Midway story. Within the confines of this battle are thousands of individual trials and tribulations; victories and defeats. As intriguing as the individual stories are, the most compelling episodes will most likely continue to be the torpedo plane attacks. The heroic charge of these planes has established itself as a part of American folklore equivalent to the British "Charge of the Light Brigade"—an aerial Balaklava.

The pilots and radio-gunners who remain forever young from that day forward are remembered for demonstrating duty, courage, and sacrifice. Enemy fighters flying much faster planes confronted the TBD pilots, forcing them to abandon the coordinated attack called for by doctrine. Even had their planes possessed more speed, the practice of going "low and slow" to drop a slow, unreliable torpedo made them sitting ducks. They attacked, however, without hesitation. Sacrifice is a term used so often that sometimes its meaning is lost on generations that have enjoyed the fruits of victory; peace, security, order and stability. The sense of loss by family and friends runs very deep for those who fell at Midway.

Commemorating those gallant men who their shipmates who flew into battle beside them. On 11 October 1987, CAPT Albert K. "Bert" Earnest, USN(Ret), joined LT George Gay, USN(Ret), CDR Wilhelm G. "Bill" Esders, USN(Ret) and RADM Robert Laub, USN(Ret) for dedication ceremonies of the largest permanent memorial exhibit honoring the officers and men of the torpedo squadrons lost at Midway. In a moving speech, Esders, the only survivor of the 12 VT-3 pilots who took off from *Yorktown* on 4 June (another surviving pilot, then-MACH Harry L. Corl—like Esders, an NAP—was lost in the Battle of the Eastern Solomons on 24 August 1942), paid homage to the pilots and gunners of his squadron, but rather than relate how he assumed command when "Lem" Massey, the squadron CO, was shot down, he offered special thanks to the memory of then-LCDR John S. "Jimmy" Thach, for the latter's advice on how to defend against the "Zeroes": "Fly low against the water, fly as slow as possible, let them shoot at you, and then turn just before the projectiles hit you." Esders had heeded Thach's ad-

President Franklin D. Roosevlet presents CAPT Richard E. Fleming's posthumous Medal of Honor to his mother, Mrs. Michael E. Fleming, in a White House ceremony, 24 November 1942, as GEN Thomas Holcomb, USMC, Commandant of the Marine Corps, looks on. Fleming

monition, his skill rewarded by the sight of an adversary, flying his "Zero" parallel to the shot-up TBD-1, waving at him. Esders interpreted the wave as meaning: "You live . . . because you've earned it."

Following Bill Esders, Robert Laub paid tribute to his fallen shipmates from Torpedo SIX in *Enterprise*. One of five VT-6 pilots to survive the battle (four returned to the "Big E," while one had had to "ditch," remaining in a rubber boat, along with his radioman, for 17 days before rescue), Laub is often invited to speak at observances of Midway, to represent not only himself but the squadron and all others who fought there. Most often at his own expense he accepts these invitations, rises to speak, but gets halfway through and then has to pause as old emotional scars reopen.

All of these men attempt to find words adequate to honor their friends, but such words are beyond human capacity. Nonetheless, they try, as they did at the Navy Museum at the Washington Navy Yard, in the summer of 1987, on board the memorialized *Yorktown* at Patriot's Point, in October 1987, at Pensacola in May 1988, and in all of the other places to which they have traveled to speak, their presence an eloquent testimonial.

The exhibit which Earnest, Gay, Esders and Laub dedicated on 11 October 1987 on board *Yorktown* at Patriot's Point, focuses on the men of the torpedo squadrons who died at Midway. A framed picture and engraved plate identify each man, and serve to remind visitors of how young and full of life each once was. An intensive search yielded individual photographs from family, friends, reunion groups, and Navy records; where photos could not be located, a photograph of a print by artist Joe Cason, depicting a flight helmet, with goggles, floating on the water, its lenses mirroring Japanese carriers aflame on the horizon, is in its stead. Resting in one of the display cases alongside the original Cason rendering is a letter written by VT-8's LDCR John Waldron to his wife Adelaide, optimistically assuring her that "It will all come out well—I am sure."

Several other artifacts and displays in the exhibit have drawn considerable attention from the visitors. When Stephen B. Smith, an NAP in VT-6, brought his badly shot-up TBD-1 back to *Enterprise*, his plane was consigned to the ocean. Before it went over the side, though, while others were counting the holes, Smith was busy cutting off a small painting of a black cat, his back arched, with the word "Scat," from the "Devastator's" fuselage. The 18-inch by 24-inch "Scat" rests in a display case, the only known part of a TBD-1 that flew at Midway.

Other items of special interest include the Navy Crosses awarded Esders and Laub, a large scratch-built model of a TBD-1 by John Ficklen, and dioramas,

crafted by James Grigerick and Tom Arusiewicz, of the American and Japanese carrier task forces at Midway. While nearly all of the children are drawn immediately to the models, the adults walk to the pictures of Waldron, Lindsey, Massey, and the others, and pause and reflect.

Within the National Air and Space Museum in Washington, D.C., one finds an exhibit on the Battle of Midway, while the Midway exhibit that opened in May 1987 at the Navy Museum, in the Washington Navy Yard, was constructed as a traveling one (it was viewed at the Midway Symposium at Pensacola in May 1988), work on a permanent exhibit on the battle, to be placed in the World War II portion of the museum, was brought to completion in June 1989. Among items of interest relating to the battle which are exhibited in the Nimitz Museum at Fredericksburg, Texas, is the flight suit worn by LT Wilmer E. Gallaher, skipper of Scouting SIX.

Paintings and photographs are central to any museum exhibit, and few exhibits which commemorate the battle exist without a print of one of R. G. Smith's paintings of the action. Smith, a long-time employee of McDonnell-Douglas—which, in 1940-1942, built the "Dauntless"—has painted a number of views which dramatically convey the few minutes which changed the fortunes of war for the United States and Japan. Several of Smith's paintings are displayed at the Naval Aviation Museum at Pensacola.

For those interested in "moving pictures," only one movie has done justice to the battle—"Task Force" (1949) starring Gary Cooper, Wayne Morris and Walter Brennan (playing the fictional character patterned on Frank Jack Fletcher). Skillfully blending actual footage with scenes played by the actors, "Task Force" captured the drama of the successful wait for word announcing the discovery of the Japanese carriers, and featured TBDs and footage of *Enterprise*. Some felt that "Midway" (1976) got too bogged down in peripheral themes ("a silly soap opera," one critic declared) to be effective, and borrowed scenes from "Tora, Tora, Tora" and "Thirty Seconds Over Tokyo." One segment of the TV mini-series, "War and Remembrance," captured some of the drama of the battle.

In a class by itself is John Ford's "Midway" (1942). Filmed, as we have seen, by Ford himself, with additional footage obtained by his assistant, Jack MacKenzie, and with narration written by Ford, Dudley Nichols and James K. McGuinness, "Midway," filmed in color, was released in September 1942, and won an Oscar for being the first documentary of the war. The narration was spoken by part of the cast of the movie "The Ox-Bow Incident," and included Henry Fonda, Jane Darwell, and Donald Crisp. While some of the footage (of the "Vindicators" taking off, for example) was shot before

The large aircraft carrier *Midway* (CVB-41), *circa* 1947, near the Norfolk Naval Shipyard. Note peace-time haze gray paint scheme with unshadowed white hull number (41) on her stack, as well as the large number of 5-inch/54 caliber and 40-mm. guns along her side.

LT George Gay stands beside *Midway*'s sponsor, Mrs. Bradford W. Ripley, II, just before the ship is launched at Newport News Shipbuilding and Dry Dock Co., 20 March 1945.

80-G-K-3516

Midway (CVB-41) awaits her launching at Newport News. Sign at right reads: "U.S.S. MIDWAY, *Queen of the Seven Seas,* Commemor-ative War Bonds *Sold Here.*

80-G-K-3515.

Wiseman (DE-667), named for the VB-3 pilot killed at Midway, stands out of San Diego in this 1960's vintage photograph, one of the many ships which honor the men who fell in battle at Midway or exercised leadership.

Mrs. Robert S. Whitman (R), widow of the only patrol plane commander killed at Midway, stands beside her matron of honor, Mrs. J.M. Andress, shortly before Mrs. Whitman would smash the bottle of ceremonial champagne on the bow of the ship named for her late husband, at the Mare Island Navy Yard on 19 January 1943.
NH 96610

the battle, the exploding bombs and scenes of destruction are real, shot by Ford from his position atop the Power House on Sand Island. Less well-known is "Torpedo Squadron 8," filmed on board *Hornet* in late May 1942 and on 4 June. This showed VT-8's men and machines up to the day of the battle, and included scenes of the TBD-1s taxiing past *Hornet*'s island to fly against the Japanese carriers. This limited-edition film (only the families of the men lost in VT-8 received copies) was never released theatrically.

While the public remembered Midway in this fashion, the Navy, in particular, remembered the battle. It is a long-standing tradition in the Navy to name appropriate ships for naval heroes and leaders. Many destroyers and destroyer escorts honored men who were killed in action at Midway: Sam Adams, Lofton Henderson, Fred Weber, Robert Brazier, Langdon Fieberling, Ben Norris, John C. Butler, Edgar Bassett, Gene Lindsey, John Waldron, and others. As the leaders at Midway passed on, they, too, received appropriate recognition as ships were named for them: Chester Nimitz, Raymond A. Spruance, and Frank Jack Fletcher. The battle itself was commemorated in an escort carrier (CVE-63), that was renamed to clear the name for one of the three large carriers (CVB-41) built toward the end of World War II. This ship is at the time of this writing (1990) still in commission.

Midway, indeed, and the men who fought there, will not be forgotten—neither in the United States nor in Japan. The Battle of Midway symposium in May 1988 featured, among its guests, three Japanese: CDR Masatake Chihaya, CDR Hitoshi Tsunoda, and CDR Izuyo Fujita. While few Americans approached them at the initial events of the symposium, few could get close toward the end, as all three, with Fujita in particular, had destroyed cultural barriers and historical prejudices with their courtesy, wit, and humor. These who had once been enemies now appeared to be just men who did their duty for the country in which they were born. Indeed, these were people with the same capacity for joy and sorrow as all the Americans noted in the pages of this book. In retrospect, the Symposium seemed to demonstrate that men could be friends to the degree that they were once enemies.

Burning Japanese aircraft carriers are reflected in the lens attached to a flight helmet of a fallen TBD pilot in this rendering by Joe Cason. Original art work is on display within the Battle of Midway Carrier Torpedo Squadrons Memorial at Patriots Point Museum.

In October 1987 only five torpedo plane pilots who flew in the Battle of Midway still survived. Four of the five were present for the dedication of the Battle of Midway Torpedo Squadrons Memorial aboard *Yorktown*. From left are George Gay (VT-8, USS *Hornet*); CAPT Bert Earnest (VT-8, Detached to Midway); CDR W. G. Esders (VT-3, USS *Yorktown* CV-5); and RADM R. E. Laub (VT-6, USS *Enterprise*). At the podium is Dr. Steve Ewing, Patriots Point Museum Senior Curator. Patriots Point

CDR W. G. Esders photographed during WWII and in 1987 with his wife beside his enshrined Navy Cross in the "Midway" exhibit aboard the second carrier *Yorktown*. Patriots Point

Uniform of LT Earl Gallaher of *Enterprise*'s Scouting Six in the Fredericksburg, Texas, Nimitz Museum's Battle of Midway display. Ewing

For many second generation WWII historians, images of the Battle of Midway are those painted by the eminent naval aviation artist, R.G. Smith. One of Smith's memorable paintings of Douglas SBDs destroying Japanese carriers at Midway is seen in this photograph among several of his other works on display within the National Museum of Naval Aviation, Pensacola, Florida. Ewing

In the mini-series "War and Remembrance," this large SBD model was featured in the Battle of Midway sequence. After filming, ABC Circle Films donated the model to Patriots Point Museum where it is suspended from the overhead within *Yorktown*'s hangar deck. Patriots Point

APPENDIX THREE

....

American & Japanese Carriers at Midway

BY STEVE EWING AND ROBERT CRESSMAN

The principal weapon in the hands of each fleet commander at Midway was the aircraft carrier. The three American fleet carriers all shared the same birthplace: Newport News, Va., and *Yorktown* (CV-5) and *Enterprise* (CV-6)—both authorized on 16 June 1933—rose, side by side, on the building ways. Laid down on 21 May 1934, *Yorktown* was launched on 4 April 1936 and christened by Mrs. Franklin D. Roosevelt, wife of the President of the United States; she was commissioned at NOB Norfolk on 30 October 1937. *Enterprise* was laid down on 16 June 1934, and launched on 3 October 1936. She was christened by Mrs. Claude A. Swanson, wife of the Secretary of the Navy, who, in quoting from Shakespeare's *Othello* waxed more ironic than she could know in foreshadowing this ship's career: "May she also say with just pride: I have done the state some service." She was commissioned on 12 May 1938. *Hornet* (CV-8), authorized on 27 March 1934, was laid down on 25 September 1939 and launched on 14 December 1940, christened by Mrs. Frank Knox, wife of the Secretary of the Navy. Built with a number of improvements in the original *Yorktown*-class design, she was commissioned on 20 October 1941. Each of these ships possessed a main battery of eight 5-inch/38 caliber dual purpose guns, and four quadruple-mount 1.1-inch/75 caliber antiaircraft machine guns and (when commissioned) eight .50-caliber machine guns. Wartime requirements dictated a replacement of the .50-calibers with the more effective 20-mm. Oerlikons.

Yorktown, the first of the class to be fitted with radar (a CXAM antenna, fitted in October 1940)—pioneered the use of that vital detection device in the U.S. Navy's carriers. Her being the first modernized flattop resulted in her being sent to augment the Atlantic Fleet in the spring of 1941 in the as-yet undeclared Battle of the Atlantic. She conducted neutrality patrols and escorted convoys before Pearl Harbor. Unable to undergo further needed modernization due to the exigencies of war, *Yorktown* left Norfolk for the last time on 16 December 1941. The first Atlantic Fleet carrier to be deployed to the Pacific, she reached San Diego on the last day of the year. She teamed with *Enterprise* to cover the movement of Marines to Samoa, and then in raids on Japanese installations in the Marshalls and Gilberts. Her air group suffered losses in that action, due primarily to the weather, while targets proved sparse. While her sister ship went on to conduct raids on Wake and Marcus, *Yorktown* was sent to the South Pacific, where she joined *Lexington* (CV-2). Together with "Lady Lex," *Yorktown* carried out a devastatingly successful raid on Japanese shipping at Lae and Salamaua, New Guinea, causing serious disruption to the southern movements of the Japanese and resulting in the dispatch of enemy aircraft carriers into the region to protect the nascent operations there. At Coral Sea, *Yorktown* and *Lexington* air groups sank the light carrier *Shoho*, damaged *Shokaku*, and decimated *Zuikaku*'s air group. Returning to Pearl Harbor, via Tongatabu, after the Battle of the Coral Sea, *Yorktown* underwent a quick repair job that enabled her to stand out to meet the Japanese at Midway. Her name, however, was not forgotten, for as soon as her loss was announced (for security reasons) in September 1942, the name was reassigned to a new *Essex* (CV-9)-class carrier. This ship, now memorialized after her decommissioning and striking, now lies at Patriot's Point. In the current (1990) fleet, yet another *Yorktown*—a *Ticonderoga* (CG-47)-class guided missile cruiser—still serves proudly.

Enterprise entered the fleet in 1938, and, with *Yorktown*, comprised Carrier Division (CARDIV) TWO (CARDIV ONE consisting of *Lexington* and *Saratoga*). Modernized and fitted with radar in early 1941 (she received a CXAM-1 radar, *vice* CXAM as fitted in her sister ship) she operated in the Pacific. She ferried USAAC fighter planes to Oahu in early 1941. The Japanese attack on Pearl Harbor found *Enterprise* returning from Wake Island. On 7 December, 18 of her aircraft (predominantly from Scouting SIX but with Bombing SIX aircraft as well), returning from scouting ahead of the ship, ran into Japanese aircraft over or near Oahu. Several were shot down by Japanese planes (one by American antiaircraft); that night, an unsuccessful search for the Japanese carriers ended tragically when one flight of six fighters from VF-6 was fired upon in the uneasy night skies over Pearl.

In the months prior to Midway, *Enterprise* proved a busy ship; after working with *Yorktown* to cover the movement of troops to Samoa, *Enterprise*—as the nucleus of TF 8—steamed to the Marshalls and Gilberts, where, along with *Yorktown*, she attacked enemy positions in those Japanese possessions. She received her first battle scars when a Japanese plane nearly crashed the ship on 1 February 1942. Then, she and her air group attacked Japanese-held Wake, and Marcus; she provided cover for *Hornet* as she delivered

LTCOL James H. Doolittle's B-25s within range of the Japanese homeland for the raid on Tokyo. *Enterprise*, along with *Hornet*, then steamed south to the Coral Sea, their presence in that region alarming the Japanese. Her large role in turning the tide of war at Midway has been recounted elsewhere in this book. Following Midway, *Enterprise* joined the modernized *Saratoga* and *Wasp* in providing cover for the invasion of Guadalcanal. By the end of the Guadalcanal campaign, however, *Enterprise* was the only fleet carrier the Navy possessed in that theater: *Saratoga* had been torpedoed a second time (Battle of the Eastern Solomons); *Wasp* had been lost covering a reinforcement convoy to Guadalcanal; and *Hornet* had been lost at Santa Cruz. *Enterprise*, herself, had been damaged at Eastern Solomons, and again at Santa Cruz.

By the end of the war, *Enterprise* had earned the Presidential Unit Citation and the Navy Unit Commendation, in addition to 20 engagement (or "battle") stars on the Asiatic-Pacific Campaign ribbon authorized for her crew. This represents the highest total of such awards given a U.S. Navy ship during World War II. In late 1945, Secretary of the Navy James Forrestal, calling *Enterprise* "the one ship that most nearly symbolizes the history of the United States Navy in World War Two," recommended to President Harry Truman that the carrier, which had seen action in nearly every major action from Pearl Harbor to Okinawa, be preserved as a national memorial. Twelve years later, Congress approved a resolution to memorialize "The Big E," and President Dwight D. Eisenhower approved it. Lack of funding, however, did what Japanese bombs and *kamikazes* could not do: spelled her doom. She was broken up for scrap. Like *Yorktown*, however, her name, too, was perpetuated, in the nuclear aircraft carrier *Enterprise* (CVN-65), which, as of this writing, is still active.

The third of the Newport News-built ships, *Hornet*, had the shortest life; commissioned on 20 October 1941, she sank exactly one year and one week later (27 October 1942), after having taken heavy damage the day before in the Battle of Santa Cruz. Not allowed the comparative luxury of a full "shaking down," due to the war, *Hornet* took 16 B-25s to the veritable doorstep of the Japanese empire; her participation in the "Halsey-Doolittle Raid" of April 1942 provided President Roosevelt with a bit of whimsy in a press conference soon thereafter, as he told the press the bombers had come from "our new secret base at Shangri-La." After participating in the Battle of Midway, *Hornet* spent some time in Hawaiian waters, training, until she sailed for the Solomons. She covered a reinforcement convoy to Guadalcanal (the same one in which *Wasp* met her doom at the hands of *I-19*) and subsequently carried out air strikes on Japanese shipping and installations in the northern Solomons. She then participated in the Battle of Santa Cruz (26 October 1942). She proved a tough ship to sink; "friendly" fire (shells and torpedoes) failed to sink her; that task fell to the Japanese destroyers, which torpedoed her and sank her the following morning. She was the last of the Navy's pre-war fleet carriers lost in World War II.

Enterprise at Pearl Harbor, March 1942. Early war and modifications have been carried out: 20mm Oerlikons, with light splinter shielding, have replaced the .50-caliber batteries; two 20mm Oerlikons in a tub at the bow have been added as well. Visible at her foremost is a CXAM-1 radar; atop her foremast truck is her YE "hayrake."

Hiryu, underway circa 1939.

Of the four Japanese fleet carriers which opposed the three American, *Kaga* was the oldest. Laid down under the 1918 building program as an "improved *Nagato*-type" battleship—which would have mounted a formidable main battery of 10 16-inch guns—she was launched at Kobe on 17 November 1921. Stricken, however, in 1922 to comply with the Washington Treaty limiting naval armaments, *Kaga* would have been scrapped had it not been for the earthquake which hit the Tokyo area in 1923; its devastation extended to the Yokosuku naval dockyard, where the incomplete *Amagi*, which had been earmarked for conversion to an aircraft carrier under the Washington Treaty, was lying. Substituting *Kaga* for *Amagi* on 19 November 1923, the former was soon taken in hand for completion as an aircraft carrier, the work being performed at Yokosuka, where she was completed on 31 March 1926. Between 25 June 1934 and 25 June 1935, *Kaga* was modernized, fitted with a full-length flight deck (817-1/2 feet long, 100 feet wide) and a small island structure on her starboard side. *Kaga* participated in the Sino-Japanese War, and took part in raids on Pearl Harbor, Rabaul, Port Darwin, and Java, prior to Midway.

Akagi, flagship of the 1st Air Fleet at the time of the Pearl Harbor attack, was the next oldest Japanese carrier. Laid down as a battlecruiser (like *Lexington* and *Saratoga*), *Akagi* was launched on 22 April 1925 and was completed (on 25 March 1927) as an aircraft carrier. As completed, her main battery included two twin 8-inch single-purpose turrets; others in casemate mounts brought the total to 10 guns of that caliber; secondary antiaircraft batteries consisted of 4.7-inch high-angle guns and 22 machine guns. She could carry 60 aircraft.

Between 24 October 1935 and 31 August 1938, *Akagi* underwent modernization, wherein a flight deck,

extending the length of the ship, was constructed and a small island structure added on her starboard side. Her 8-inch armament was reduced to six casemate mounts; the 4.7-inch battery remained constant, with 28 25-mm. antiaircraft guns. She could, however, then carry 91 aircraft. Her pre-World War II battle experience included the Sino-Japanese War; she participated (as VADM Nagumo's flagship) in the Pearl Harbor attack; raided Rabaul, Port Darwin, Java, and Ceylon before she sailed to support the projected occupation of Midway.

Although nominally regarded as "sisterships," *Soryu* and *Hiryu*—comprising Carrier Division 2—had been both laid down under the 1931-1932 "supplementary program." *Soryu* was launched at Kure on 23 December 1935 and completed on 29 December 1937. *Hiryu*—launched at Yokosuka on 16 November 1937 and completed on 5 July 1939—had, however, been built to a slightly different design than *Soryu*, with *Hiryu* possessing a deeper draft, fuller beam, greater radius of action, and displacing 1,400 tons more. Both ships were capable of attaining 34-1/2 knots, top speed, and had a main battery of 12 5-inch/40 caliber dual-purpose guns. Secondary antiaircraft armament comprised 28 25-mm. guns in *Soryu*, 31 in *Hiryu*. Aircraft complements were very similar: *Soryu* carried 71 planes, *Hiryu* 73. The two ships differed in external appearance, too, with *Hiryu*'s island, built on the port side, being situated almost amidships; *Soryu*'s was more forward, on the starboard side. Both ships had seen action in the war with China, and, besides Pearl Harbor, had covered the final operations which led to the capture of Wake Island, as well as Rabaul, Ambon Island, Timor, Port Darwin, Java, and Ceylon.

Akagi, seen here in the summer of 1941, served as the flagship for VADM Nagumo until massive damage forced her abandonment. She is shown here with three Mitsubishi A6M2 Type 00 carrier fighters parked forward on her flight deck. NH73059

Kaga, underway *circa* 1939.

Soryu, underway, *circa* 1938. NH 73061

-205-

APPENDIX FOUR

. . . .

American & Japanese Aircraft at Midway

BY BARRETT TILLMAN

Some 600 aircraft, flown by aviators of the Imperial Japanese Navy and the United States Navy, Marine Corps, and Army Air Corps, fought the Battle of Midway. The diversity of these planes included almost every configuration found in the respective services engaged: carrier-based tactical aircraft, observation floatplanes, twin-engined amphibians, flying boats, and multi-engined bombers.

An airplane—like any other machine—is a compromise. It is designed with a specific purpose in mind, and the engineering dilemma is timeless; the careful balancing of weight versus available power, of maximum speed versus landing speed, of altitude and range. This is especially true of carrier-based aircraft, which need to perform the same combat chores as their land-based counterparts, but must routinely operate from the narrow confines of a flight deck.

In 1942, carrier aviation was 20 years old in both the U.S. and Japanese navies. Both had evolved essentially the same three classes of aircraft types since *Langley* (CV-1) and *Hosho* began their initial trials two decades previously; single-seat fighters, two-seat dive bombers, and three-seat torpedo planes. Though tactical doctrine and technological progress differed to varying degrees, the six primary combatants at Midway shared a similar heritage.

On the American side, the Grumman F4F-4 "Wildcat," Douglas SBD-2/SBD-3 "Dauntless," and Douglas TBD-1 "Devastator" were original or derivative designs from the 1935-1938 period in which each made its first flight. Their counterparts—the Mitsubishi A6M2 Type 00 carrier fighter ("Zero"), Aichi D3A1 Type 99 carrier bomber ("Val") and Nakajima B5N2 Type 97 carrier attack plane ("Kate")—were of slightly later development, having first flown between 1937 and 1939. Aside from the generally superior performance of the Japanese types, an institutional advantage fell to the Imperial Navy since all three had been combat-proven in China prior to December 1941.

Though much maligned, the TBD-1 should be placed in context. When it entered squadron service in 1937, it was the first all-metal monoplane ever deployed on board a U.S. aircraft carrier, in short, the "state of the art." Merely five years later, competitors had passed the "Devastator" in the ceaseless race for aviation progress. While the TBD-1 sustained a 95 percent loss rate at Midway, this was not terribly worse than the 83 percent loss rate sustained by the vastly superior Grumman TBF-1 "Avenger" that flew from the island during the battle.

By way of comparison, the Nakajima B5N2 that equipped all four Japanese carrier attack squadrons at Midway enjoyed significant advantages. It carried a greater payload farther and faster; a 1,760-pound torpedo or equivalent bomb load at speeds exceeding 200 knots. Therein probably lay the Nakajima's greater combat success, for even though antiaircraft fire and CAP fighters shot down five of the 10 B5Ns that attacked *Yorktown* on the afternoon of 4 June, they obtained two hits and left their victim dead in the water and listing heavily. Japan's torpedoes possessed those attributes of a desirable weapon—reliability and accuracy—which the American Mk. XIII did not. It may never be known how many TBD pilots got close enough to launch their "fish," but it is known that none scored hits.

The two navies were much more evenly matched in dive bombers (or, as the Japanese termed them, "carrier bombers") than torpedo planes. In fact, during the four carrier battles of 1942 (Coral Sea, Midway, Eastern Solomons and Santa Cruz), both sides achieved about 70 percent of their hits on flattops with bombs rather than torpedoes. The reasons, primarily, were intrinsic. Because of its steep overhead attack, the dive bomber presented a more difficult target than a low-flying "torpecker" and concluded its attack much quicker. Thus, shipboard gunners proved less able to engage dive-bombing attacks, and frequently, fighter pilots found it difficult to stay with a bomber after it had extended its speed brakes and nosed over.

In the "Dauntless," the U.S. Navy possessed one of the finest antiship aircraft of World War II. Evolved from the Northrop BT-1 of 1935, the Douglas-built SBD series joined its first squadrons in 1940 and equipped half of the embarked carrier squadrons in TF 16 and TF 17. Each bombing and scouting squadron possessed 16 to 18 SBD-2s and SBD-3s, the latter by far the most numerous. The "Speedy Three" (sardonically named for its laconic 217-knot top speed) possessed the best range of any U.S. carrier-based aircraft at Midway. Only the strike composition of accompanying fighters and torpedo planes limited its tactical radius.

With a crew consisting of a pilot and radio-gunner, the SBD usually flew search missions with a 500-pound bomb on the centerline rack and strikes with a 1,000-pounder, plus two 100-pounders under the wings. It was capable of defending itself against fighters in some

U. S. AIRCRAFT—ACTION WITH ENEMY

INSTRUCTIONS

(a) To be filled out by unit commander immediately upon landing after each action or operation in contact with the enemy.

(b) Do not "gun deck" this report—if data can not be estimated with reasonable accuracy enter a dash in space for which no data is available.

1942 JUN 23   12   56

---

1. Date..June 4.............. 194.2. Lat.30-40N... Long.179-35W. Time.1220.. Zn..#10.

2. Weather Unlimited - Scattered Clouds 1500 - 2000 feet.................

3. Unit Reporting Torpedo Squadron Six.......... Type Planes....TBD-1...........

---

4. Nature of Operation:

   Torpedo Attack delivered against Japanese CV's accompanied
   by BB's, CA's, CL's and DD'S.

5. Specific Objective:

   CV of the KAGA type.

6. Forces Engaged (include models and markings):

   Own | Enemy
   14 TBD-1 | Numerous Type "O" Fighters.
   | Fighters painted a greenish brown with red
   | circles on wings and fuselage. One plane was
   | observed to have a red stripe around fuselage.

7. Type of Attack (Own/Enemy) (scratch one):
   All fighter attacks were from overhead and rear but were not pressed
   home in face of free gun fire.

8. Enemy Tactics: (ship's) CV's turned continuously to place VTB on
   quarter, other ships maneuvered independently, at times becoming
   widely seperated.

9. Brief Description of Action (include altitudes and range of contact. Altitudes and directions
   of release and withdrawal).

   See attached statement.

---

10. Weapons Employed:

   Own | Enemy
   Torpedoes-free guns(twin.30Cal.) | Many fighter planes & concentrated
   | light and heavy A.A. fire.

11. Evasive Action Employed:
   Variations in altitude & direction of approach, variations in range for
   opposing "AA" guns seemed to be most effective avoiding action.

12. Ammunition Expended (include types and fuse settings. Indicate number of duds.)

   14 Torpedoes - set at twelve (12) feet depth.
   .30 Cal. AAMG. No known duds.

13. Results (certain):

   None (Certain) Estimated two (2) torpedo hits.

DAMAGE TO OWN AIRCRAFT: 10 planes shot down by either AA or fighter fire,
   probably the latter, no leak proofing, installed armor effective
   (against 7.7 hits) (no hits from 20 MM.)

6

Two VF-3 Grumman F4F-4 "Wildcats" at NAS Kaneohe, 29 May 1942. At left is BuNo 5167 (no. 5) and BuNo 5149 (no. 10). 80-G-61533

Douglas TBD-1 (BuNo 1505), coded 6-T-13, in flight circa late 1941, was flown on 4 June 1942 by LT Paul J. Riley; his radio-gunner was E.J. Mushinski, ARM2c.

"Scouting" FIVE (the temporarily redesignated VB-5) Douglas SBD-3, no. 17, piloted by ENS Leif Larsen, A-V(N), prepares to launch for the afternoon search, 4 June. 80-G-312000

situations, as was proved at Midway, but its crews much preferred evasion of interception to a shoot-out. The "Dauntless" meat was dive-bombing, and anything that interfered with that objective was counterproductive.

With beautifully balanced controls, the SBD was splendid in a dive. By extending the perforated dive brakes at the trailing edge of the wing, an SBD pilot could maintain a dive angle of 70 degrees or more, retaining excellent control to make necessary corrections during a typical 40-second attack from 15,000 feet. At Midway, the carrier-based "Dauntlesses" achieved a 30 percent hit ratio against the four Japanese flattops. By comparison, the less experienced Marine pilots from Midway itself (who, in all fairness, had just received the aircraft about a week before) attacked in shallower (and, hence, longer) glide-bombing runs. As we have seen, the Marines suffered heavy casualties without compensating damage on the enemy. The lesson is clear: technology is less important than training and experience.

The Japanese Aichi D3A1 Type 99 came off a relatively poor second to the SBD-3, yet it had still proved effective. First flown in January 1938, it was introduced to combat over China during 1941 and had sunk Allied warships at Pearl Harbor, at Port Darwin, in the Indian Ocean and at Coral Sea. Its fixed landing gear made for a distinctive recognition feature in combat, but limited the dive bomber to barely 200 knots top speed. Possessing a shorter range than the "Dauntless," the "Val" (as it came to be known) also carried a smaller payload—usually a single 550-pound bomb under the fuselage and two 60-pounders under the wings. It proved surprisingly agile, however, with its large elliptical wing and a highly accurate dive-bombing platform. Eighteen D3A1s from *Hiryu* attacked *Yorktown* on 4 June, and although seven survived the CAP and antiaircraft fire to dive on her, five scored direct hits or damaging near-misses.

The Aichi, however, was extremely vulnerable to fighters. The rearseat man (often a warrant or commissioned officer, as opposed to the U.S. Navy practice which found an enlisted man in the back seat) had only a single 7.7-mm. machine gun, which proved inadequate for close-in defense. Grumman "Wildcats," primarily from *Yorktown's* VF-3, got among the Japanese formation during its approach to TF 17 and shot down 11 despite the presence of escorting "Zeroes."

The fighter portion of the battle has become part of Midway's enduring legend. Introduction of the "Thach Weave," as well as the spectacular losses among the Brewster F2A-3s are featured in most accounts. But here, as well as with the saga of the torpedo planes, there is room for examination and, perhaps, a bit of revisionism.

Mitsubishi's astonishing A6M2 was not the only surprise the Japanese sprung upon the often-complacent U.S. Navy, but surely it remains the most enduring. The prototype first flew in April 1939 and a preproduction batch achieved spectacular success over China during 1940-41. Today, it is easy to forget that the *Zero-Sen* was the first carrier fighter superior to all of its land-based opponents, and with a 500-mile tactical radius there was nothing else on the planet that matched its potential.

With a typical mixed armament of two 20-mm. machine guns and two 7.7-mm., the A6M2 reflected Japanese design philosophy under European influence. The 7.7s were often used as ranging reference, with tracers indicating when close enough to engage with the 20-mm. guns. Some later "Zero" models replaced the 7.7s with one or two 13.2-mm. guns, apparently in deference to the effectiveness of American .50-caliber weapons.

Regardless of armament, however, the "Zero" proved a potent adversary in the traditional dogfight. Light and extremely maneuverable, it could out-turn and out-climb any of its 1942 adversaries. Also, it was some 20 knots faster than its chief rival at Midway, the Grumman F4F-4 "Wildcat."

One month prior to Midway, in the Battle of the Coral Sea, F4F-3s had come out poorly in the scoring column against "Zeroes." "Wildcats" splashed three A6M2s in exchange for six of their number lost to enemy fighters, and the U.S. Navy squadrons quickly tried to adapt to the situation. It was no easy task, given not only the press of time but a change of equipment. The F4F-4 replaced the "dash 3" in Pacific Fleet fighter squadrons a short time before Midway, and not every aviator considered it a change for the better. Several hundred pounds heavier with no increase in power over the previous model, the new "Wildcat" possessed two perceived advantages. The first was indisputable, since the folding wing F4F-4 allowed a 50 percent increase in fighter strength on board each carrier, from 18 to 27. Secondly, armament was increased from four .50-caliber guns to six.

The "more is better" philosophy did not always find favor among F4F pilots. The six-gun configuration was the result of a British request to BuAer, as Grumman was building "Martlet" versions of the "Wildcat" for export. While the Royal Navy was more than pleased with its Grummans, American pilots noted that internal room in the folding wings reduced total ammunition capacity by 360 rounds. Four guns had proved sufficient to destroy Japanese aircraft, as the Browning .50-calibers were potent weapons, and, as LCDR "Jimmy" Thach noted: "A pilot who can't hit with four guns will miss with eight." Reduced firing time in the F4F-4, however, would prove hurtful throughout the rest of the year. The F4F-4's self-sealing fuel tanks and extra armor plate added to its survivability but also impaired performance, especially the climb rate. The newer-model "Wildcat" still could not dogfight with the "Zero" so the answer to reversing the fighter exchange lay in new tactics, and Thach's squadron (VF-3) led the way. Fighting THREE at Midway was *Yorktown*'s resident VF-42 under Thach, reinforced with some of his VF-3 pilots. On 4 June, however, they inaugurated the scissoring, mutual-defense pattern in combat and proved its effectiveness. "Wildcat" pilots now realized that fast, diving attacks were a means of negating the "Zero's" superior turn and climb. When the Battle of Midway was concluded, the three F4F-4 squadrons engaged had outfought the Mitsubishis by a margin of better than two to one.

The other fighter engaged at Midway was the much-maligned Brewster F2A-3, of which 20 equipped VMF-221 based on the atoll. First flown in December 1937, the "Buffalo" became the first U.S. Navy fighter monoplane to enter fleet service in mid-1940. Pilots, who found the plane generally faster than the "Wildcat," basically liked the F2A-3 but found it troublesome to land on board a carrier because of its somewhat awkward landing gear. This, with its lack of "stretch" in the basic design led to an early retirement while the contemporary F4F soldiered on.

Of 19 Brewsters that took off from Midway early that morning, only four returned. Similarly, only one of the six Marine F2A-3s remained combat-ready after contesting the Japanese raid. But as poor as the F2A-3's limited combat record may have been (in American hands), the conditions of that combat militated against success. Committed piecemeal by sections and divisions, attacked at an altitude disadvantage by superior numbers of better fighters flown by more experienced pilots, the fight could only have gone one way. Not even those aviators who enjoyed flying the F2A-3 relished the idea of taking it into combat, but it entered the arena anyway, with every possible disadvantage.

Midway's hodge-podge garrison air force included several other types as well. Numerically the most important were the Consolidated PBY "Catalinas" that operated from Midway, the PBY-5As from Eastern Island and the -5s from Sand. Used for long-range patrols, the "Catalinas" flew 700-mile search legs in pie-shaped wedge patterns from Midway and succeeded in locating both the Japanese transport force and the carrier striking force. A nocturnal torpedo attack conducted by four PBYs in the wee hours of 4 June gained one hit that slightly damaged a tanker. Reconnaissance was the "Catalinas" primary contribution before the battle, and rescue, afterwards. In each role they performed splendidly.

The 7th Army Air Force was represented at Midway with 19 B-17Es and four B-26s. Contemporary reports accorded significant combat results to the "Flying Fortresses" and "Marauders," but postwar evaluation of Japanese records forced a revision of wartime claims. The four-engined Boeings, designed and flown in accordance with USAAC doctrine of high-altitude bombardment, were intrinsically unsuited for attacking fast warships maneuvering in the open sea. The B-17s dropped some 320 bombs in several attacks and failed to score a single hit. However, they did help disrupt the Japanese operating cycle and provided Midway with a long-range search-strike potential that otherwise would have been unavailable.

Fast, well-armed Martin "Marauders" took torpedoes modified for high-speed drops into the teeth of the Japanese carrier force with some prospects of getting hits. They could make nearly 300 mph at sea level, which vastly reduced their exposure to enemy flak and fighters, but they were too few and could not fully coordinate with other aircraft for maximum tactical flexibility. Only two of the four engaged returned to base.

A similar fate befell the six Grumman TBF-1s of VT-8's land-based detachment. *Hornet* had left the east coast in February 1942, before the planes had been delivered to the squadron. Half of Torpedo EIGHT traveled to Bethpage, where they took delivery of the new Grummans in March. Delivered by ship to Pearl Harbor on board *Kitty Hawk* (APV-1), they trained out of Ford Island while their ship operated at sea, until the six-plane detachment was formed on 31 May and dispatched to Midway the following day. The TBFs should have done better than the TBDs, since they were 60 knots faster, but they were armed with the same marginal torpedoes and faced heavy odds against an alerted enemy task force. Only one of the six planes returned.

The Marine SBD-2s differed little from the SBD-3s flown by Navy pilots. They were, however, a considerable improvement over the Vought SB2U-3 "Vindicators"—fabric-covered monoplanes whose prototype had first flown six-and-a-half years before. Built expressly for the Marines (as opposed to "hand-me-downs" from the Navy), production problems delayed the arrival of these planes into USMC hands until early 1941. By 1942, the "Vindicator," left a great deal to be desired. Aviators termed it the "Wind Indicator" and lamented its poor performance with a 1,000-pound bomb while bemoaning its lack of dive brakes. The

Consolidated PBY-5A "Catalina" flying boat (dropping a depth bomb) circa 1942. 80-G-40467

Brewster F2A-3 "Buffalo" fighter at Eva Mooring Mast Field, early 1942. Note nearly full-chord wing insignia visible beneath the left wing. USMC photo 145220

Grumman TBF-1 "Avenger" from VT-8, at NAS Norfolk, 26 March 1942, coded 8-T-1. 80-G-12232

designers had intended that altering the propeller pitch would retard the SB2U's diving speed, but the concept proved a failure. This technical lapse, combined with the relative inexperience of most of its pilots, limited the SB2U-3 to a shallow-angle glide-bomber, and its losses proved prohibitive. The Vought was never committed to combat again.

One more class of aircraft needs consideration to round out the Midway combatants. While scout observation floatplanes flew from U.S. and Japanese warships, the Imperial Navy made wider use of them—a move dictated largely by geography and doctrine. Lacking the long-range search capability of land-based air, the Japanese Navy, preferring to retain its carrier aircraft for the attack role, utilized floatplanes in the scouting and search function. The heavy cruiser *Tone*'s floatplanes—Aichi E13A1 Type 00s ("Jake")—performed significant service in locating the American task force.

Another reconnaissance aircraft involved at Midway was the Yokosuka D4Y1 "Suisei" ("Comet"). Two had been embarked in *Soryu* before she sailed for Midway. One was an operational casualty en route, the other made two reconnaissance flights. Radio malfunction drastically limited the role the intelligence gathered by the crew could play, but the one operational plane— which ultimately sank with *Hiryu*—had functioned well. American pilots would later know this plane as the "Judy," the fastest dive-bomber of World War II.

American cruisers usually embarked four to five Curtiss SOC-3 "Seagull" floatplanes; these saw limited employment from the heavy cruisers of TF 16 and TF 17 during the battle. The "Seagull" was a popular, reliable biplane whose crews insisted that SOC stood for "Scout on Catapult." The last U.S. Navy biplane in fleet service and capable of service on floats or on wheels, only disappeared from land-based units in 1946-1947.

Most of the other American aircraft engaged at Midway were long gone by the time the last SOCs were stricken from the Navy inventory. On V-J day only the "Avenger" remained a significant weapon in U.S. naval aviation, as the General Motors-produced TBM-3. The much-improved General Motors FM-2 remained in service on escort carriers but had been replaced by the Grumman F6F-3/5 "Hellcat" and the Vought F4U-1 "Corsair," and, later, by the Grumman F8F-1/2 "Bearcat."

"Dauntlesses"—the primary victors of the carrier battle of Midway-completed their fast carrier service in July 1944. Their one-time stablemates both ashore and afloat had faded into oblivion and even extinction by that time as TBDs, SB2Us and F2As dropped far astern in naval aviation's headlong rush toward the jet age. Perhaps the most enduring of all Midway aircraft was the ungainly, but supremely utilitarian, PBY. The "Catalina" remained in Navy service until 1949, and even longer with the U.S. Coast Guard.

Of the Army Air Corps aircraft that fought at Midway, both the B-17 and B-26 gained superior reputations in other theaters—in roles for which they were designed. The four-engined Boeing, of course, became the very symbol of daylight high-altitude bombardment over Nazi-occupied Europe while the "Marauder" proved effective as a low- and medium-level tactical bomber in a variety of theaters.

The Japanese Navy provided a marked contrast in longevity to its American counterparts. All three main types that fought at Midway were still in front-line service in 1945, particularly the "Zero," which found its ultimate expression in the A6M7 variant. "Kates" and "Vals" (as the Nakajimas and Aichis had been dubbed), were still encountered by Allied fighter pilots three years after Midway, and were usually shot down with little effort. Therein lies a lesson: the process that began at Midway was completed by a new generation of American naval aircraft that exceeded Japan's technological quality, and then smothered it under a depth of quantity that previously had been unimaginable.

From four decades later, the end result seems to have been inevitably certain. But at the time, no such certainty existed. That, too, may be a lesson worth pondering today.

The only known part of a TBD that flew at Midway is this small section removed from Stephen B. Smith's badly shot-up Devastator before it was pushed off the deck of *Enterprise*. "Scat" is currently on display in the "Midway" exhibit aboard *Yorktown* CV-10. Patriots Point

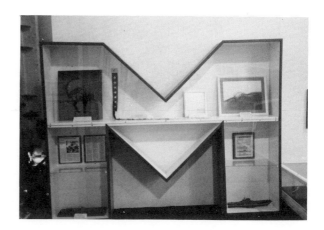

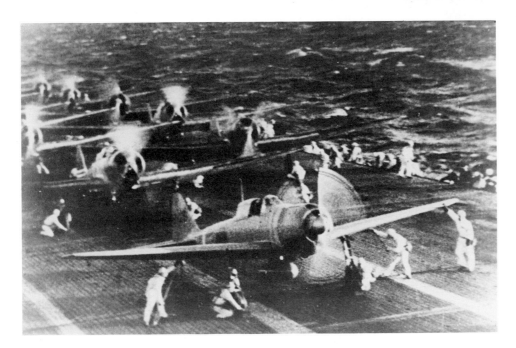

Mitsubishi A6M2 Type 00 carrier fighter ("Zero") warms up on board *Shokaku*, 7 December 1941.
80-G-71198

Aichi D3A1 Type 99 carrier bomber ("Val") over Pearl Harbor, 7 December 1941.
80-G-32908

A captured Nakajima B5N2 carrier attack plane ("Kate") in flight. USN

APPENDIX FIVE

....

The Truth about Miles Browning

BY CLARK G. REYNOLDS

CDR Miles R. Browning, as Chief of Staff for COMAIRBATFOR, VADM Halsey, on 1 February 1942.

CDR Miles Browning was one of the unsung heroes of the Battle of Midway—partly because of an unpleasant and then unsavory personal reputation within the professional naval community. As acting chief of staff to RADM Raymond A. Spruance during late May and early June 1942, Browning received high praise with a Distinguished Service Medal that cited his "judicious planning and brilliant execution" as being "largely responsible for the rout of the . . . Japanese fleet in the Battle of Midway."

By any measure, Browning was one of the most brilliant tacticians of carrier air warfare before and during World War II, making his professional demise one of the great wastes to the American prosecution of the war in the Pacific. Born Miles Rutherford Browning in New Jersey on 10 April 1897, he had graduated 53rd among the 199 members of the Class of 1918, behind such future wartime naval aviation luminaries as Forrest P. Sherman, Thomas L. Sprague, John J. Ballen-

tine, Clifton A. F. Sprague, and J. J. "Jocko" Clark.[1]

Earning his wings at Pensacola in 1924, he soon exhibited great skill in the cockpit but also a wild streak that did not endear him to his ship- and squadron mates. His quick, incisive mind apparently contributed to a cold but temperamental personality—the latter overlooked by his superiors, however, as he advanced in the relatively small peacetime naval aviation community.[2]

An example of his tactical genius was a 13-page, single-spaced typewritten memorandum on carrier operations that he prepared in 1936 while in VF-3B. In one important respect, it anticipated the fatal flaw in the Japanese carrier performance at Midway: "Every carrier captain has known the bitter experience of rushing his aircraft up and down the deck to meet changing probabilities in the situation and to care for the impending return of a scouting flight, just as the situation was becoming crucial. Every carrier we have has known what it means to be 'bopped' with all planes on deck, because her hands were tied by uncertainty as to her next move . . ."[3]

It was such insights that led to his assignment as a student to the Naval War College during 1936-1937, and his attracting the attention of RADM William F. Halsey, Jr., who became COMCARDIV TWO in the spring of 1938, and who soon appointed Browning to his staff in the new billet of air tactical officer. Despite Browning's "aloof and condescending manner," he so excelled that two years later, when Halsey relieved VADM Charles A. Blakely as COMAIRBATFOR, Browning remained as operations and war plans officer.[4]

Curiously, the affable Halsey seemed to utilize men of personalities opposite to his own, perhaps to act as foils or counterweights. His chief of staff, for example, was CAPT John H. Hoover, so dour an individual that his peers cynically dubbed him "Genial John." When Hoover was detached in June 1941, Browning relieved him.

With his flag in *Enterprise*, Halsey—provided sage counsel by Browning—conducted several successful raids against Japanese island outposts in February and

1. Who graduated 2d, 19th, 32d, 43d, and 47th, respectively.

2. J. J. Clark, with Clark G. Reynolds, *Carrier Admiral* (New York: David McKay, 1967) p. 22.

3. Browning to ADM J. M. Reeves, "A Short Discussion of Shipbased Aircraft Operation in the Fleet," 1 June 1936. Robert P. Molten Papers, Patriot's Point Naval and Maritime Museum, Patriot's Point, S.C.

4. E. B. Potter, *Bull Halsey*, (Annapolis: Naval Institute Press, 1985), pp. 64-65, 139-140.

March of 1942. Halsey rewarded Browning by recommending to ADM Chester W. Nimitz, CINCPAC, that his chief of staff be selected for promotion to captain, a recommendation that Nimitz approved. Just prior to Midway, when Halsey fell ill, RADM Spruance, Halsey's hand-picked successor, inherited Browning and the rest of the staff. Browning gave Spruance the crucial advice that led to Spruance's success at Midway, as anticipated in his 1936 memo quoted above. Two weeks after the battle, Browning received his promotion.[5]

At that moment of triumph in the summer of 1942, however, Browning committed the sin of having an affair with the wife of a brother officer. The incident could hardly be kept quiet, and it created a feeling of deep resentment of the already unpopular Browning within the naval aviation fraternity. While the wronged man instituted divorce proceedings, VADM Halsey set out to salvage Browning's career, for the captain was still assigned as his chief of staff. Back in Hawaii in October 1942 to resume his duties as COMCARPAC, Halsey recommended the DSM for Browning, as well as promotion to flag rank. On 14 October, Halsey and Browning departed Pearl Harbor to inspect the South Pacific theater, where Allied fortunes were flagging. Upon their arrival on the 18th, the admiral received orders from ADM Nimitz appointing him to command the South Pacific area.

The same day, Nimitz penned a long handwritten note to "Bill" Halsey: "While I share your high opinion of Browning as an operating and planning for operations-officer [sic], I do not think I could ever lend support to any proposal looking to his promotion to rear admiral, primarily because of the circumstances which recently lead [sic] to his bodily punishment by an irate brother officer [the officer whose wife Browning had been romancing caught the pair in the act and, being a former middleweight boxer at the Naval Academy, beat the proverbial living daylights out of Browning—Ed.] . . ." However, "only yesterday I heartily endorsed for approval your recommendation that he be awarded the DSM. With no desire whatever to interfere in your staff set-up, nor to disparage Browning, I suggest that you give consideration to selecting a rear admiral as a chief of staff . . ."[6]

With Browning at his side, Halsey performed the command miracle that reversed the declining Allied fortunes in the theater, and waited until New Year's Day 1943 to reply to Nimitz's letter. He judged a man by his professional, rather than personal, actions. Halsey observed: "Miles . . . has an uncanny knack of sizing up a situation and coming out with an answer." Admitting that Browning was "decidedly temperamental," Halsey begged "Chester" not to break up "this partnership" between himself and his chief of staff: ". . . I am almost superstitious about it." Nor did Halsey believe Browning ought to be demoted to be operations officer to a new rear admiral chief of staff, an action he felt would adversely affect staff morale.[7]

Days later, however, Browning antagonized visiting Secretary of the Navy Frank Knox, who then urged that Browning be replaced. ADM Ernest J. King, COMINCH, concurred.[8] King got word to Halsey, as well as to Nimitz, that if Halsey did not relieve Browning, "I would have to do it myself . . ." Nimitz, King believed, "is very slow about making changes like that, but when he understood that something had to be done, he sent word to Halsey."[9]

Nimitz "understood" from Halsey's increasingly sloppy staff organization and many questionable decisions that Nimitz and King attributed to Browning. Still, however, Halsey defended Browning, and urged that he at least be promoted to commodore. Finally, apparently figuring that Browning would retrieve his personal honor by marrying the woman with whom he had had the affair, Halsey sent his chief of staff home to marry her—which he did on 30 March 1943. Halsey had done this, however, without having issued Browning official orders, which drew Nimitz's wrath. To lure Browning away from Halsey, King's staff offered the newlywed his own command—a new carrier—something that even Halsey could not protest. In July 1943, Browning was detached from Halsey's staff with orders as prospective commanding officer of *Hornet* (CV-12), still under construction.[10]

5. Edwin P. Hoyt, *How They Won the War in the Pacific: Nimitz and His Admirals* (New York: Weybright and Talley, 1970), pp. 64, 99-100; Samuel Eliot Morison, *Coral Sea, Midway, and Submarine Actions* (Boston: Little, Brown, 1974), pp. 131-132; Nimitz to Halsey, 18 October 1942 (#14, Series XIII, Nimitz Papers, Operational Archives Branch, Naval Historical Center).

6. Walter Lord, *Incredible Victory*, pp. 65, 78. The story of Browning's beating was recounted to the author by ADM George W. Anderson, Jr., in 1964 and by VADM Herbert D. Riley in 1966.

7. Nimitz to Halsey, 18 October 1942. Nimitz suggested that Halsey select either RADM W. L. "Pug" Ainsworth or RADM R. C. "Ike" Giffen, neither of whom were aviators.

8. After the war, King recalled that Browning was "no damn good at all." He rated Browning as handsome, an adequate pilot, but lacking brains and understanding, a judgment not shared by many officers before the unhappy sexual encounter.

9. Halsey to Nimitz, 1 January 1943 (#14, Series XIII, Nimitz Papers, AR, NHC)

10. *ibid.*; Hoyt, *op. cit.*, pp. 208, 242, 245, 249; Potter, pp. 242-244. Browning's relief was a man of far milder temperament, RADM Robert B. Carney.

Sadly, Browning remained his own worst enemy. He brought *Hornet* out to the Pacific in March 1944 and immediately reported that his ship was not ready for combat operations because of an abbreviated shakedown cruise and that the ship's air group possessed insufficient training, as evidenced by high operational casualties. Since *Hornet* was the only one of the new flattops in TF 58, the fast carrier task force, to be so ill-prepared for battle, VADM Marc Mitscher, Commander TF 58, assigned his newest carrier division commander, RADM J. J. "Jocko" Clark to break his flag in Browning's ship. Mitscher had instructed Clark, whom he had considered "one of the best carrier captains that it has ever been my pleasure to serve with," and who had commanded one of Mitscher's flagships, *Yorktown* (CV-10) earlier that year, to "advise [Browning] and assist in straightening matters out in so far as he could . . ."[11]

At the very outset, Browning exhibited poor seamanship. On entering Majuro lagoon, he nearly ran *Hornet* aground. During air strikes on the Palau Islands, Browning was about to send an insubordinate message to the task group commander, RADM Alfred E. Montgomery, before Clark talked him out of it. Clark, utilizing *Hornet* as his flagship, then took command of TG 58.1 for the Hollandia operation in April 1944, and witnessed the spectacle of Browning nearly ramming *Hornet* into a tanker during flight operations. Browning also chagrined Clark by berating his ship's department heads "like a wild man," and blaming his troubles on *Hornet*'s air officer, whom he wanted transferred.[12]

Mitscher and Clark agreed that Browning should be replaced, for, as the former observed, "All things add up to the fact that the *Hornet* is a jittery ship . . ." The overt act they needed as a pretext for the relief occurred late in May 1944, while TF 58 lay anchored at Majuro, prior to the invasion of the Marianas. During the showing of a movie on the hangar deck, someone discharged a CO_2 bottle, letting off a whistle that triggered a stampede. Two men fell overboard and 32 others went to sick bay with minor injuries. Browning rejected Clark's advice to take a muster, and two days later the body of one of the two sailors floated to the surface. The board of investigation, ordered by Clark as the result of the incident, criticized Browning, whereupon Clark recommended Browning's detachment. Mitscher concurred and relieved him.[13]

To insure that Browning never returned to an operational post, ADM King had him "banished" to the Army's Command and General Staff College at Ft. Leavenworth, Kansas, for the duration of the war. Retiring from active duty on 1 January 1947, he died seven years later.

The name of Miles Browning, however, deserves a place among the list of heroes of the Battle of Midway. Unfortunately, his personal behavior compromised his reputation and his ability, and eventually led to his demise. One might even argue that ADM Halsey most keenly felt Browning's subsequent absence from the Pacific war. Upon taking command of the carrier-oriented 3d Fleet during 1944-1945, Halsey made grave mistakes that might very well have been averted had the old "partnership" continued, for it had been much more than a "superstitious" combination. Halsey's real expertise in carrier tactics had been provided by Browning, just as it was for Spruance at the Battle of Midway.

---

11. Mitscher to Nimitz, 24 May 1944 (Nimitz Personal Correspondence, AR, NHC); Clark, p. 149.

12. Mitscher to Nimitz, *op. cit.*; Clark, pp. 149-150, 154, 157.

---

13. Mitscher to Nimitz, *op. cit.*; Clark, pp. 157-157. CAPT William D. Sample relieved Browning and turned *Hornet* into an effective ship immediately. CDR Roy L. Johnson, destined for flag rank, relieved the air officer.

AUTHORS' BIOGRAPHIES

EDITOR AND PRINCIPAL AUTHOR

Robert J. Cressman holds BA and MA degrees in history from the University of Maryland, College Park, where he studied under the late Dr. Gordon W. Prange and is currently employed at the Ships Histories' Branch of the Naval Historical Center. A contributor to historical journals and carrier editor for *The Hook*, he has published two books: as sole author of *That Gallant Ship, USS Yorktown (CV-5)* and as co-author, with J. Michael Wenger, of *Steady Nerves and Stout Hearts: The USS Enterprise Air Group and Pearl Harbor, 7 December 1941.*

PROJECT COORDINATOR

Dr. Steve Ewing, Senior Curator and Director of Exhibits for Patriots Point Naval and Maritime Museum, was for 16 years a college and university professor. After four years of military service he earned two degrees from Marshall University and two from the University of Southern Mississippi. He is the author of several books on naval history including *Memories and Memorials: The World War II U.S. Navy 40 Years After Victory; American Cruisers of World War II; The Lady Lex and the Blue Ghost;* and *USS Enterprise CV-6: The Most Decorated Ship of World War II.* Among the exhibits Dr. Ewing has designed aboard the memorialized carrier *Yorktown* in Charleston Harbor is the Battle of Midway Torpedo Squadrons Memorial.

CONTRIBUTORS

Barrett Tillman, formerly managing editor of *The Hook*, holds a journalism degree from the University of Oregon and has been published in a great number of periodicals in both the United States and in Europe. Having learned to fly at age 16, he has flown a variety of vintage and military aircraft, including an SBD he and his father have restored. His first book, *The Dauntless Dive Bomber in World War II*, has gone through five printings since its publication in 1976, and he has written five other aircraft histories, contributed heavily to two others, and has completed his first novel.

Dr. Clark G. Reynolds, currently chairman of the History Department at the College of Charleston, is a former professor of history at the U.S. Naval Academy, the University of Maine, and the U.S. Merchant Marine Academy. Formerly historian and curator of the Patriots Point Naval and Maritime Museum, he has authored *The Fast Carriers, Command of the Sea: The History and Strategy of Maritime Empires, Famous American Admirals, The Fighting Lady* and *The Carrier War* in Time-Life Books "Epic of Flight" series.

Stan Cohen founded Pictorial Histories Publishing Company in 1976 and since then has authored or co-authored 38 books and published over 120. He has traveled extensively to Pacific battlefields including two trips to Midway Island.

Mark E. Horan is 34 years old and resides in Windsor Locks, Connecticut. He is an avid researcher of WWII carrier battles and the Civil War. He first became interested in the Battle of Midway after reading Walter Lord's book, *Incredible Victory*, and has spent 10 years researching the air actions that occurred during the battle.

The cover for this book was painted by Capt. Bob Rasmussen, USN (Ret). After a distinguished career including assignment to the Blue Angels and combat duty in Viet Nam, Captain Rasmussen retired from active duty, first joining the Naval Aviation Museum Foundation and then was named Director of the National Museum of Naval Aviation at Pensacola, Florida.

Barrett Tillman, Stan Cohen, Dr. Clark G. Reynolds and Dr. Steve Ewing at Pensacola, May 1988.

BIBLIOGRAPHY

· · · · · · · · · · ·

Primary Sources

I. DOCUMENTS:

A. ACTION REPORTS, ETC.:

CINCPAC to COMAIRBATFOR and COMPATWING TWO, "Naval Air Station Wake and Naval Air Station Midway—Basing of Aircraft at," (10 November 1941) in CINCPAC files Jul-Dec 1941, NHC/AR

CINCPAC to COMINCH, "Battle of Midway" (28 June 1942)

CINCPAC to CNO(DNI), "Interrogation of Japanese Prisoners Taken After Midway Action 9 June 1942" Ser 01753. (21 June 1942)

COMCURPAC (RADM F.J. Fletcher) to CINCPAC, "Action Report, Battle of Midway" (14 June 1942)

CO USS *Yorktown* to CINCPAC, "Report of Action for June 4, 1942 and 6 June, 1942" (18 June 1942) (encl., Executive Officer's Report, War Damage Report)

COMCRU TF17 (RADM W. W. Smith), "Report of Action, 4 June 1942" (12 June 1942) (encl., reports of *Astoria* and *Portland*)

CTG 17.4 (Capt. A. R. Early) to COMINCH, "Report of Action, June 4, 1942" (4 June 1942) (encl., reports of DESDIV FOUR, *Morris, Russell, Anderson, Hughes*)

CO USS *Hughes* to CINCPAC, "Operations in Conjunction with U.S.S. *Yorktown* from time of abandonment until sinking" (11 June 1942)

CO USS *Hammann* to CINCPAC, "Action Report 46 June 1942" (16 June 1942)

LT P. H. Hart, VT-3 OpOrder, "Tactical Organization, 1 June 1942"

LT(jg). C.N. Conatser, VB-5 Op Order, "Operation Schedule Wednesday 3 June 1942"

LT(jg). C.N. Conatser, VB-5 Op Order, "Operation Schedule Thursday 4 June 1942"

CO VB-3(LCDR M. F. Leslie) to CYAG, "Attack Conducted 4 June 1942 on Japanese Carriers located 156 miles NW Midway Island, Narrative Concerning" (7 June 1942)

MACH Harry L. Corl to CYAG, "Report of Action 4 June 1942" (6 June 1942) Wilhelm G. Esders, CAP, to CYAG, "Report of Action 4 June 1942" (6 June 1942)

LT Arthur J. Brassfield to CO VF-3, "Report of Action 4 June 1942" CTF 16 (RADM R. A. Spruance) to CINCPAC, "Battle of Midway" (16 June 1942)

Personal Ltr. RADM Raymond A. Spruance to ADM Chester W. Nimitz (8 June 1942)

CO USS *Hornet* to CinCPac, "Report of Action" (13 June 1942) (encl., "VF-3 partial Bag")

Air Ops. Officer (LCDR J. G. Foster) to CO, USS Hornet, "Defects Observed During the Action off Midway, June 4, 1942" (12 June 1942)

CO VB8 to CO USS *Hornet*, "Action Report 5-6 June 1942" (7 June 1942)

CO VS-8 to Judge Advocate General of the Navy, "Administrative Report on Crash of SBD3 Airplane, Bureau No. 4664, Ens.Richard B. Milliman, USNR, pilot, Tony R. PLETO, ARM3c, USN, Passenger During Operations 29 May 1942" (14 June 1942)

CO USS *Enterprise* to CINCPAC, "Battle of Midway Island, June 4-6, 1942, Report of" (8 June 1942) "Air Battle of the Pacific, June 4-6, 1942, Report of" (13 June 1942)

CO VB-5 (Temporarily Designated VS-5) to CO USS Enterprise, "Report of Action June 4-6, 1942" (7 June 1942)

LT Sam Adams, "Aircraft Action Report, 1615 4 June 1942"

LT John Nielsen, "Aircraft Action Report, 1615 4 June 1942"

CO VB-5, "Aircraft Action Report, 2000 5 June 1942"

CO VB-5, "Aircraft Action Report, 1445 6 June 1942"

CO VB-6 to CO USS *Enterprise*, "Report of Action June 4-6, 1942" (10 June 1942)

CO [Acting] VB-3 (LT D. W. Shumway) to CO USS *Enterprise*, "Report of Action June 4-6, 1942" (10 June 1942)

CO VS-6 to CO USS *Enterprise*, "Report of Action June 4-6, 1942" (20 June 1942)

CO VS-6, "Aircraft Action Report, 1205 4 June 1942"

CO VS-6, "Aircraft Action Report, 1905 4 June 1942"

CO VS-6, "Aircraft Action Report, 1915 5 June 1942"

CO VS-6 (LT F. A. Patriarca), "Aircraft Action Report, 1430 6 June 1942"

CO VF-6 to CEAG, "Narrative of Events 4-6 June 1942" (10 June 1942)

Acting CO VT-6 (LT(jg) R. E. Laub), "Report of Action 4 June 1942"

Acting CO VT-6 (LT(jg) R. E. Laub) to COMINCH, "Torpedo Plane Operations in the Battle of Midway, June 4, 1942" (21 June 1942) (encl., lst endorsement by CAPT G. D. Murray, CO USS *Enterprise*)

CTF 16 (RADM T. C. Kincaid) to COMINCH, "Torpedo Plane Operations in the Battle of Midway, June 4 1942" (12 July 1942) (2nd endorsement of LT(jg) Laub's Report and letter)

COMCRU TF 16 (RADM T. C. Kincaid) to CTF 16, "Report of Action June 4, 1942" (11 June 1942) (encl., reports of *Pensacola* and *Vincennes*)

CTG 17.4 (CAPT A. R. Early) to CTF 17, "Japanese Torpedo Plane Attack on U.S.S. *Yorktown* during the Battle of Midway, June 4, 1942, Report of" (12 June 1942) (encl., reports of *Benham* and *Balch*)

CO NAS Midway to CINCPAC, "Report of Engagement with the Enemy, Battle of Midway, 30 May-7 June 1942" (18 June 1942)

COMPATWING TWO (RADM P. N. L. Bellinger) to COMINCH, "Employment of Aircraft in Connection with Enemy Attack on Midway" (23 May 1942)

CO MAG-22 to CINCPAC, "Battle of Midway Islands, Report of" (7 June 1942)

XO MAG-22 to CO MAG-22, "Executive Officer's Report of the Battle of Midway, June 3, 4, 5, 6, 1942 with Preliminary Phase from May 22, 1942" (7 June 1942)

CO VMF-221 to CO MAG-22, "Enemy Contact, Report on" (6 June 1942) (encl., pilot statements of Carey, Canfield, Carl, Hughes, Irwin, White, Merrill, Armistead, Humberd, Brooks, Kunz, Corry, Musselman)

CO VMSB-241 to CO MAG-22, "Report of Activities of VMSB-241 during June 4 and June 5, 1942. (12 June 1942) (encl., pilot statements of Blain, Cummings, Glidden, Iverson, Koutelas, Moore, Ringblom, Schlendering, Thompson, Vaupell, Whitten, and Williamson)

LCDR Robert C. Brixner, CO, VP-44 Op Order 13-44M, "Search Employment 4 June 1942"

LT W. L. Richards to COMPATWING TWO, "Night Torpedo Attack, 3-4 June 1942, Report of" (18 June 1942)

CAPT Logan C. Ramsey to ADM Chester W. Nimitz, "Army Participation in the Battle of Midway, 30 May to 6 June 1942" (15 June 1942)

CO Naval Base [Pearl Harbor] Air Defense (COMPATWING

TWO) to Secretary of the Navy, "Participation of Naval Base Air Defense Aircraft in the Battle of Midway, Report of" (30 June 1942)

CO NAS Pearl Harbor, T.H. to COMINCH, "TBF-1 Airplane BuNo 00380—Investigation of Gunfire Damage on, Report of" (31 July 1942)

MAJ Jo K. Warner to CG VII Bomber Command, "Liaison Journal, 26 May to 4 June" (4 June 1942)

CAPT James F. Collins to CG VII Bomber Command, "Action Report, 4 June 1942" (6 June 1942)

CAPT James P. Muri to CG VII Bomber Command, "Action Report, 4 June 1942" (6 June 1942)

CO 431st BS(H) to CO llth BG(H), "Combat Operations, Midway Area, 3-4 June 1942

CAPT Cecil F. Faulkner to CG VII Bomber Command, "Special Mission" (6 June 1942)

1stLT Edward A. Steedman to CG 7th Bomber Command, "Special Mission" (6 June 1942)

1stLT Robert B. Andrews to CG VII Bomber Command, "Special Mission" (6 June 1942)

LT W. A. Smith "Midway Mission Report" (12 June 1942)

LTCOL Brooke E. Allen, "AAC Action with the Enemy"

CAPT Charles E. Gregory, "AAC Action with the Enemy"

LT H. S. Grundman, "AAC Action with the Enemy"

CAPT O. H. Rigley, Jr., "AAC Action with the Enemy"

LTCOL Walter C. Sweeney, Jr., "AAC Action with the Enemy"

1stLT Paul I. Williams, "AAC Action with the Enemy"

CAPT Carl E. Wuertele, "AAC Action with the Enemy"

CINCPAC to COMINCH, "Personal Account of Attacks on Japanese Carriers June 4, 1942" (11 June 1942) (forwards Cdr. R. A. Ofstie Memorandum on interview with ENS George H. Gay, USNR, VT-8, 7 June 1942)

WDC 160985 "Battle Report of Battle of Midway" (includes Battle Reports of *Akagi, Kaga, Soryu,* and *Hiryu*)

B. STATEMENTS:

Statement of ENS T. J. Wood and T. T. Guillory A-V(N), USNR to RADM Leigh Noyes (8 June 1942)

Statement of VF-8 Pilots Attached to USS *Hornet* (Lt(jg). M.F. Jennings, senior officer present) to RADM Leigh Noyes (11 June 1942)

Statements to LTCOL L. B. Stedman, Jr., USMC: CPL Eugene T. Card, CPL John H. Moore, PFC Gordon R. McFeely, PVT Charles W. Huber, PVT Teman Wilhite

C. WAR DIARIES:

CINCPAC (CAPT Steele's "Running Summary...") ("GRAYBOOK") NAS Midway Island MAG-22 (May 1942)

TF 9/PATWINGSPACFLT/PATWINGTWO/Naval Base Air Defense

Enterprise (CV-6); *Hornet* (CV-8); *Kaloli* (AOG-13); *Kitty Hawk* (APV-1); *Monaghan* (DD-354); *Minneapolis* (CA-36); *New Orleans* (CA-32); Pearl Harbor Navy Yard; *Vireo* (AM-52/AT-144); VB-8 (May-June 1942); VMSB-241 (April-May 1942); VP-24 (1-25 June 1942); VT-8 (May-June 1942)

D. MISCELLANEOUS REPORTS, INTERVIEWS, AND NARRATIVES.

TF-16 Operational Orders (March 1942)

CO, VT-3 (LCDR J. E. Clark) to COMAIRBATFOR, "Aerial Torpedo Attack Tactics" (12 January 1942)

ENS Albert K. Earnest, A-V(N) to COMCARPAC, "Report of attack on Japanese Force by Six TBF-1 Airplanes," (23 June 1942)

LCDR James H. Flatley to COMCARPAC, "The Navy Fighter" (25 June 1942)

MAJ Charles F. Hurlbut, USMCR to CMC, "Comment on Historical Monograph," (n.d.) in Midway Monograph "Comment File," RG-127, Archives Section, MCHC re:

Kimes' remark about the Japanese fleet

BGEN Ira L. Kimes, USMC(Ret.) to CMC, "Return of Historical Monograph," (20 January 1948), in Midway Monograph "Comment File," RG-127, Archives Section, MCHC

LT Robin Merton Lindsey, USN, "Narrative," (17 September 1943)

Bureau of Aeronautics Interviews: LCDR John S. Thach, USN (26 August 1942); LTCOL Ira L. Kimes, USMC (31 August 1942)

LT(jg) George H. Gay, A-V(N), Narrative, 12 October 1942

E. SUBMARINE WAR PATROL REPORTS:

Argonaut (SS-166); *Cachalot* (SS-170); *Cuttlefish* (SS-171); *Flying Fish* (SS-229); *Grouper* (SS-214); *Gudgeon* (SS-211); *Nautilus* (SS-168); *Tambor* (SS-198); *Trout* (SS-202)

F. DECK LOGS:

Saratoga (CV-3); *Enterprise* (CV-6); *Hornet* (CV-8); *Minneapolis* (CA-36); *New Orleans* (CA-32); *Vincennes* (CA-44); *Pensacola* (CA-24); *Northampton* (CA-26); *Portland* (CA-33); *Astoria* (CA-34); *Monaghan* (DD-354); *Nautilus* (SS-168)

G. MUSTER ROLLS:

VB-5, VB-6, VB-8, VF-3, VF-6, VF-8, VS-8, VT-3, VT-6, VT-8 (encl., detachment), VP-12, VP-23, VP-24, VP-44, VP-72, VP-91, VMF-221, VMSB-241

H. PERSONAL PAPERS:

MGEN Claude A. Larkin, USMC, in Marine Corps Historical Center Personal Papers Collection

II. UNPUBLISHED STUDIES AND DIARIES:

A. UNPUBLISHED WORKS:

Barde, Robert E., "The Battle of Midway: A Study in Command" PhD. Dissertation, University of Maryland, 1971

Gray, Capt. James S., Jr., "Decision at Midway"

McClusky, RADM C. Wade, Jr., "The Midway Story"

Murray, CDR James F., "Bombing Six In Action: A Radio Gunner Looks Back"

Roberts, RADM Wilmer E., "The Battle of Midway"

U.S. Naval War College, "The Battle of Midway, including the Aleutian Phase, June 3 to June 14, 1942. Statistical and Tactical Analysis (NavPers 91050), Newport, 1948

U.S. Navy, Fighter Director School, Navy Yard, Pearl Harbor, "Battle of Midway Island" (3 Apr. 1943)

Weisheit, Bowen P., "What Happened to Mark Kelly"

B. PERSONAL DIARIES:

LT(jg) Cleo J. Dobson (June 1942) furnished by Mrs. Dobson.

LT Norman J. Kleiss (June 1942) furnished by CAPT Kleiss.

III. INTERVIEWS

RJC Interview with RADM William N. Leonard, USN (Ret.) Alexandria, VA, 3 June 1987.

RJC Telephone Interview with RADM Wilmer E. Gallaher, USN (Ret.) Garrett Park, MD, 1 February 1983.

Secondary Sources

IV. BOOKS AND ARTICLES

Akimoto, Minoru. "Kugisho, Carrier Dive-Bomber, 'Suisei,'" *Koku Fan*, Vol. 30, No. 7, July 1981.
_____. "Nakajima Type 97 Carrier Attacker," Pts. 1 and

2, *Koku Fan*, Vol. 31, No.9/No. 10, September/October 1982."

Barde, Robert E. "Midway: Tarnished Victory," *Military Affairs* Vol. XLVII:4 (December 1983).

Blair, Clay, Jr. *Silent Victory: The U.S. Submarine War Against Japan*. Philadelphia: J. B. Lippincott Co., 1975.

Braisted, William R. "Midway Islands, U.S. Naval Air Station and Submarine Base, 1941," in Paolo E. Coletta, Ed., *United States Navy and Marine Corps Bases, Overseas*. Westport, Connecticut: Greenwood Press, 1985.

Buell, Thomas B. *The Quiet Warrior: A Biography of Admiral Raymond A. Spruance*. Boston: Little Brown & Co., 1974.

Casey, Robert J. *Torpedo Junction: With the Pacific Fleet from Pearl Harbor to Midway*. Indianapolis: Bobbs-Merrill Co., 1942.

Coletta, Paolo E. *Patrick N.L. Bellinger and U.S. Naval Aviation*. Lanham, Maryland: University Press of America, 1987.

Cressman, Robert J. *That Gallant Ship: USS Yorktown (CV5)*. Missoula, Montana: Pictorial Histories, 1985.

Dickinson, Clarence E., Jr. with Boyden Sparks. *The Flying Guns: Cockpit Record of a Naval Pilot from Pearl Harbor Through Midway*. New York: Charles Scribner's Sons, 1943.

Dull, Paul S. *A Battle History of the Imperial Japanese Navy* Annapolis: Naval Institute Press, 1974.

Ewing, Steve. *USS Enterprise (CV6): The Most Decorated Ship of World War II: An Illustrated History*. Missoula, Montana: Pictorial Histories, 1982.

Ferrier, Harry H. "Torpedo Squadron Eight, The Other Chapter," *U.S. Naval Institute Proceedings* October 1964.

Frank, Pat and Joseph D. Harrington. *Rendezvous at Midway: USS Yorktown And the Japanese Carrier Fleet*. New York: John Day, 1967.

Fuchida, Mitsuo, and Okumiya, Masatake (Clarke Kawakami and Roger Pineau, ed.). *Midway: The Battle That Doomed Japan* Annapolis: Naval Institute Press, 1955.

Gay, George H. *Sole Survivor*. Naples, Florida: Privately Printed, 1979.

Griffin, Alexander R. *A Ship to Remember: The Saga of the Hornet* New York: Howell Soskin, 1943.

Heinl, Robert D. *Marines at Midway*. Washington, DC: GPO, 1947.

Holmes, Wilfred J. *Undersea Victory: The Influence of Submarine Operations on the War in the Pacific*. Garden City, NY: Doubleday and Co., Inc., 1966.

Hoyt, Edwin P. *How They Won the War in the Pacific: Nimitz and His Admirals*. New York: Weybright and Talley, 1970.

Japan: War History Office. *Senshi Sosho* (War History Series), Vol. 43, *Middowe Kaisen* (Midway Sea Battle). Tokyo: Asagumo Shimbunsha, 1971.

Jentschura, Hansgeorg; Jung, Dieter; and Mickel, Peter. *Warships of the Imperial Japanese Navy, 1869-1945*. Annapolis, Maryland: Naval Institute Press, 19 .

Lacroix, E. "The Development of the 'A Class' Cruisers in the Imperial Japanese Navy," Pt.VII, "The *Mogami* 'B class' Cruisers modified to 'A class' Standard." *Warship International* No.3, 1984.

Lord, Walter. *Incredible Victory*. New York: Harper & Row, 1967.

Lundstrom, John B. *The First South Pacific Campaign: Pacific Fleet Strategy, December 1941-June 1942*. Annapolis: Naval Institute Press, 1976.

_____. *The First Team: Pacific Naval Air Combat from Pearl Harbor to Midway*. Annapolis: Naval Institute Press, 1976.

McClusky, C. Wade. "Historical Commentary," in *Midway Battle Manual*. Baltimore: Avalon-Hill, 1964.

Mears, Frederick C. *Carrier Combat*. New York: Doubleday, Doran, 1944.

Mikesh, Robert C., and Rikyu Watanabe. *Zero Fighter*. New York: Crown, 1981.

Morison, Samuel Eliot. *Coral Sea, Midway, and Submarine Actions, May 1942-August 1942*, Vol. IV in *History of United States Naval Operations in World War II*. Boston: Little, Brown, 1950.

Olynyk, Frank J. *USMC Credits for the Destruction of Enemy Aircraft in AirtoAir Combat, World War II*. Aurora, Ohio: Privately Printed, 1982.

_____. *USN Credits for the Destruction of Enemy Aircraft in Air-to-Air Combat, World War II*. Aurora, Ohio: Privately Printed, 1982.

Prange, Gordon W., with Donald M. Goldstein and Katherine V. Dillon. *Miracle at Midway*. New York: McGrawHill, 1982.

Shelmidine, Lyle S. "The Early History of Midway Islands," *The American Neptune*, Vol. 8, July 1948.

Smith, William W. *Midway: Turning Point of the Pacific* (New York: Thomas Y. Crowell, 1966.

Stafford, Edward P. *The Big E*. New York: Random House, 1962.

Stephan, John J. *Hawaii Under the Rising Sun: Japan's Plans for Conquest After Pearl Harbor*. Honolulu: University of Hawaii Press, 1984.

Taylor, Theodore. *The Magnificent Mitscher*. New York: Norton, 1954.

Tillman, Barrett. *The Dauntless Dive Bomber in World War II* Annapolis: Naval Institute Press, 1976.

_____. "Where Are They Now? Bert Earnest." *The Hook*, Summer 1983.

Tuleja, Thaddeus V. *Climax at Midway*. New York: Norton, 1960.

U.S. Navy, Office of Naval Intelligence. *The Japanese Story of the Battle of Midway*. Washington, D.C.: GPO, 1947. (Translation of parts of First Air Fleet, Detailed Battle Report No. 6, Midway Operations, 27 May-9 June 1942, in the *ONI Review,* May 1947)

Wilmott, H. P. *The Barrier and the Javelin: Japanese and Allied Strategies, February to June 1942*. Annapolis: Naval Institute Press, 1983.

INDEX

10th Construction Battalion 180
123d Construction Battalion 182
3d Defense Battalion 12, 31
4th Defense Battalion 24, 25
50th Construction Battalion 180, 181
5th "Artillery Civilian Defense Organization" 23
4th Construction Battalion 179
6th Defense Battalion 15, 19, 23, 25, 31
Abe, Hiroaki, RADM, IJN 110
Achten, Julius, MACH 135
Adams, John, LT(jg) 130
Adams, James W., ACRM 73
Adams, Samuel, LT 136, 150, 191, 199
Adams, Don D., ENS 149, 155
Adkins, Floyd D., AMM2c 107, 108
Ady, Howard P. LT, USN 33, 59, 83
Aichi D3A1 Type 99 Carrier Bomber ("Val") 209, 212
Aichi E13A1 Type 00 Reconnaissance Floatplane ("Jake") 209
Akagi (Japanese Aircraft Carrier) 59, 64, 69, 72, 81, 92, 93, 97, 99, 101, 104, 107, 110, 111, 128, 136, 141, 143, 146, 189, 193, 204
Akebono Maru (Japanese Tanker) 57
Aldrich, Clarence C., LCDR 131, 132
Allen, Brooke E., LTCOL, USAAC 81, 143, 144
Allison, Willie V., GM3c 157
Anderson, Edward L., LT(jg) 110
Anderson, Edward R., RM3c 96, 109
Antares (AKS-3) 12
Arashi (Japanese Destroyer) 77, 82, 96, 101, 111, 136
Arashio (Japanese Destroyer) 154, 156
Argentina Maru (Japanese Freighter) 55
Argonaut (SS-166) 17, 19, 21, 23
Armistead, Kirk, CAPT 59, 62
Ashley, Earl D., PFC, USAAC 72
Auman, Forrester C., ENS 114, 143
Aylwin (DD-355) 86, 151
Bagley, David W., RADM USN 34, 35
Baker, Paul, TSGT, USMC 49
Balch (DD-363) 86, 122, 135, 146, 153, 157, 158, 161, 164
Ballard (AVD-10) 35, 39, 40, 41, 171, 175
Ballard, Robert J., Sea1c 161
Barchet, Stephen J., LCDR, USN 19
Barthes, August A., LT(jg) 171
Bassett, Clifton R., ADM2c 138
Bayers, E.H., RE 131
Baylor, Walter L.J., MAJ 24
Bear, Robert J. "R," 2dLT, USMCR 75
Beaver (AS-5) 9
Bellinger, Patrick N.L., RADM, USN 31, 35, 43, 48, 50, 139, 190
Benham (DD-397) 86, 122, 135, 146, 153, 158, 159, 162, 164, 167
Benson, Roy S. ("Ensign"), LT 68, 126
Bergeron, Dallas J., ARM3c, 38
Best, Richard H. Best, LCDR 86, 96, 101, 102, 104, 107, 115, 137, 138, 191, 192
Blain, Richard L., CAPT, USMC 25, 78, 163
Blakey, George, MAJ, USAAC 139
Boeing B-17E/F "Flying Fortress" 15, 210, 212
Booda, Larry L., LT(jg) 153, 154
Bottomley, Harold S., LT(jg) 105, 138
Brady, Norman K., LT(jg) 163
Brazier, Richard B., ARM2c 99, 100, 199
Brewster F2A-3 "Buffalo" 210
Brixner, Robert C., LCDR, USN 37, 48
Brock, John W., ENS 94
Brockman, William H., Jr., LCDR 60, 73, 77, 82, 110, 126, 128, 141
Brooklyn (CL-40) 12
Brooks, N.B., CAPT 1
Brown, Julian P., LTCOL, USMC 149, 162
Brown, Samuel R., Jr. LT 154
Browning, Miles R., CDR, 37, 84, 96, 115, 136, 149, 151, 155, 189, 190, 214-16
Buckmaster, Elliott, CAPT 89, 116, 128, 130-32, 135, 146, 153, 158, 159, 161, 162, 190, 193
Buckner, Jean H., CAPT, USMC 19, 20
Bunch, Kenneth C., ARM1c 155
Burch, William O., LCDR 108
Butler, John C., ENS 62, 105, 139, 199
Callaghan, D. J., ENS 68
Camp, Jack H., ENS 73, 74, 163

Camp, Don, LT 171
Campion, Kenneth O., 2dLT, USMCR 77, 79
Canfield, Clayton M., 2dLT, USMC 62
Cannon, George H., 1stLT, USMC 20
Card, Eugene T., CPL, USMC 61, 65, 74, 75, 79
Carey, John F., CAPT, USMC 59, 62
Carl, Marion, CAPT, USMC 62, 114
Carter, William D., ENS 153, 154
Casey, Robert J. (War Correspondent) 121, 151
Chappell, Clarence J., MAJ, USMC 17, 23, 25, 34
Chase, William E., LT(jg) 59, 60, 73, 83
Cheek, Tom F., MACH 97, 98, 107
Chester (CA-27) 15
Chihaya, Masatake, CDR, IJN 199
Chikuma (Japanese Heavy Cruiser) 59, 60, 92, 97, 111, 126, 137, 139, 143, 153
Childers, Lloyd F., ARM3c 97-9, 100, 122
Childs (AVD-1) 10
Chitose (Japanese Seaplane Carrier) 73
Chochalousek, Walter G., ARM1c 84, 107
Christie, William F., LT(jg) 136, 154
Clark, Milton W., AMM1c 155
Cole, Shelby O., LT(jg) 143, 148
Colley, Benjamin W., 5
Collins, William F., Jr., CAPT, USAAC 70, 72, 73, 78
COMSUBPAC (See English, RADM)
Consolidated PBY-5/-5A/-5B "Catalina" 15, 79, 210, 212
Consolidated PB2Y-2 "Coronado" 181
Cooner, Bunyan R., ENS 125, 138, 139
Cooper, Stuart T., LT(jg) 171
Coral Sea, Battle of 83, 87, 89, 108, 115, 128, 131, 132, 161, 162, 190, 202, 206, 209
Corl, Harry L., MACH 97-99, 122, 195
Corry, Roy A., 2dLT, USMCR 62, 64
Cossitt, Douglas M., ARM3c 94, 126, 175
Cottrell, B.R., ARM2c 136
Crommelin, Richard G., LT 58, 84, 89
Cummings, Daniel L., 2dLT, USMCR 78, 79, 80
Curtiss (AV-4) 28, 153
Curtiss SOC-3 "Seagull" 153, 212
Davis, Arthur C., CAPT, USN 35, 50, 190
Davis, Douglas C., LT(jg) 56
Davis, Ray, LT(jg) 151, 153
Davis, LCDR 157, 158
DeLalio, Armond, CAPT, USMCR 75
Delaney, John J., LT 131, 132
DeLuca, Joseph F., ARM1c 108, 115
Dexter, James C., ENS 102, 115
Dibb, Robert A.M., ENS 98, 130
Dickey, Robert L., MARGUN(NAP), USMC 26, 27
Dickinson, Clarence E., Jr., LT 102, 104, 115
Dickson, Harlan R., LT 136
Dobson, Cleo J., LT(jg) 151, 162
Dodson, Benjamin, ARM3c 99
Dorr, William R., Jr., 2dLT, USMC 19
Douglas SBD-2/-3 "Dauntless" 206
Douglas TBD-1 "Devastator" 206
Dow, "Ham," LCDR 126, 135
Duke, Claren E., LCDR 73, 126
Duncan, S.L., AMM2c 171
Eagle No. 40 (PE-40) 7
Earnest, Albert K., ENS 61, 78, 195, 196
Eaton, John M., LT(jg), D-V(G) 21, 23
Elden, Ralph W., LT 158, 161
Elder, Robert M., ENS 105
Ely, Arthur V., LT 84
Emerson, Alberto C., LT 119
Emmons, Delos, GEN, USA 37, 38
English, Robert H., RADM 38, 73, 167, 179
Enterprise (CV-6) 17, 29, 31, 37-40, 44, 51, 56, 58, 84, 86, 87, 93, 94-6, 101, 102, 107, 108, 113-15, 121, 125, 126, 131, 132, 135, 136, 139, 140, 149-51, 153-56, 162, 163, 167, 176, 189-91, 193, 196, 202, 214
Esders, Wilhelm G., CAP 99, 122, 125, 126, 192, 195, 196
Everton, Loren D., 2dLT, USMC 17, 23
Faulkner, Clark W., ENS 68, 81
Ferrier, Harry H., RM3c 70
Fieberling, Langdon K., LT 47, 61, 69, 73, 86, 199
Fisher, Clayton E., ENS 86, 95, 113

Fisler, Frank M., LT(jg) 170
Fleming, Richard E., CAPT, USMC 47, 61, 65, 74, 75, 79, 143, 144
Fletcher, Frank Jack, RADM, USN 12, 31, 38, 39, 44, 52, 54, 56, 58, 74, 83, 84, 87, 89, 119, 121, 122, 126, 130, 139, 140, 146, 190, 199
Forbes, Jimmy M., LT(jg) 154
Ford, Warren W., LT 86, 154, 155
Ford, John, LCDR 35, 40, 50, 51, 61, 64-66
Forrester, Charles R., LT(jg) MC 47
Fuchida, Mitsuo, CDR, IJN 187, 189, 192
Fujita, Izuzo, CDR, IJN (Ret) 189, 199
Fukuda, Minoru, LT, IJN 104
Fulghum, Philip L., AOM2c 73
Furuya, Kyoichi, IJN 140
Gaido, Bruno, AMM2c 114
Gallaher, Wilmer E., LT 101, 102, 108, 137, 138, 191, 193, 196
Gambia (Hawaiian Bark) 1
Gay, George H., ENS 86, 148, 191, 195, 196
Gaynier, Oswald J., ENS 47, 61
Gee, Roy P., ENS 154
Genda, Minoru, CDR, IJN 189
Genest, Wilfred H., LT(jg) 154
Gibbs, Harry B., ENS 128, 130, 146
Glidden, Elmer G., Jr., CAPT 75, 79
Gogoj, John J., TSGT, USAAC 72
Goldsmith, George H., ENS 110, 114, 115
"Gooneyville Hotel" 182
Grant, Philip F., ENS 155
Gratzek, Thomas, 2dLT, USMCR 75
Gray, James S., LT (VF-6) 91-94, 113, 135, 156
Gray, Richard, LT(jg) (VF-8) 86, 113, 143, 170
Greene, Eugene A., ENS 109, 115
Griffin, Raphael, COL, USMC 15
Griswold, Don "T," ENS 155
Groves, Stephen W., ENS 86, 122
Grumman TBF-1 "Avenger" 212
Grumman F4F-3/-4 "Wildcat" 17
Guillory, Troy T., ENS 95, 136, 149
Gwin (DD-433) 35, 43, 148, 157, 158, 164
Hagikaze (Japanese Destroyer) 128, 141
Hale, Willis H., BGEN, USAAC 46, 47, 50, 114
Halsey, William F., Jr., VADM, USN 12, 17, 29, 31, 35, 37, 164, 190, 214, 215, 216
Halsey, Delbert E., ENS 105, 110
Halsey-Doolittle Raid 29, 187, 203
Hamilton, John H., CAPT (PAA) 21, 23
Hammann (DD-412) 126, 135, 146, 153, 157-59, 161, 167
Hanson, William A., ENS 107
Hara, Hisashi, PO3c, IJN 126
Hartigan, C.C., LT(jg) 158, 161
Haruna (Japanese Battleship) 36, 56, 59, 72, 77, 78, 79, 136
Hasegawa, LT(jg) IJN 135
Haynes, W.R., CRM 154
Hazelwood, Harold R., CPL 20
Heard, Harold F., ARM2c 109
Heck, Edward, Jr., ENS 94
Henderson, Lofton R., MAJ, USMC 34, 35, 43, 61, 74-76, 141, 180, 199
Hepburn, Arthur J., RADM, USN 9
"Hepburn Board" 9, 10
Hewell (AKL-14) 183
Hibberd, Charles P., LT(jg) 55
Higgins, John M., LCDR 148, 157
Hiryu (Japanese Aircraft Carrier) 58, 59, 62, 64, 66, 69, 75, 76, 79, 99, 101, 110, 111, 114, 115, 125, 128, 136-40, 146, 149, 163, 171, 189, 193, 204, 209, 212
Hissem, Joseph M., ENS 47
Holden, G.L., ARM2c 163
Holmberg, Paul A., LT(jg) 105, 125, 126, 191
Hopkins, Lewis A., ENS 109, 115
Hopper, George A., ENS 130
Hornet (CV-8) 29, 31, 38, 40, 51, 84, 86, 87, 95, 96, 107, 113, 114, 122, 136, 137, 139, 148-51, 153-57, 162, 167, 190, 191, 193, 194, 199, 202, 210
Howell, Earl E., ARM2c 108, 114
Hoyle, Rhonald J., LT(jg) 126, 156
Huber, Charles W., CPL, USMC 76, 78
Hughes, F. Massie, LDCR 50
Hughes, Charles S., 2dLT, USMC 61, 64, 66
Hughes (DD-410) 162, 164

Humphrey, William C., ARM1c 94
Huntington, Robert K., ARM3c 92
I-123 (Japanese Submarine) 40
I-168 (Japanese Submarine) 47, 142, 143, 157, 162, 164
I-173 (Japanese Submarine) 26
I-69 (Japanese Submarine) 26
Ichiki Detachment 31
Iida, Masatada, PO1c, IJN 89, 111
Ingersoll, Royal R., LT 122
Isaman, Roy M., ENS 96, 107
Ishikawa, Kenichi, 3dClass Fireman, IJN 170
Ito, FP01c (*Kaga* Pilot) 66
Iverson, Daniel, Jr., 1stLT, USMCR 74, 75, 79
Jaccard, Richard A., ENS 102, 108, 115, 138
Jakeman, Lloyd F., LT 154
Jarrett, Harry B. ("Beany"), LCDR 46, 130
Jarvis, J.W., ARM2c 154
Jennings, M.F., LT(jg) 113, 170
Jeter, Thomas P., CDR 115
Johnson, Robert R., LCDR 86, 155
Johnson, Daniel F., AMM2c 105
Jorgenson, J.A. 3
Julson, Maynard E., MTSGT, USMC 49
Kaga (Japanese Aircraft Carrier) 36, 59, 64, 66, 69, 81, 92-94, 97, 101, 102, 104, 107, 109, 110, 126, 128, 136, 141, 146, 187, 189, 191, 193, 204
Kaku, Tomeo, CAPT, IJN 111, 146, 189
Kaname, Konishi, CAPT, IJN 20
Kapp, George W., Jr., COX 161
Karrol, Joseph J., ARM1c 136, 150
Kate Piper (Schooner) 2
Katsumi, Motoi, CDR, IJN 150
Kawashima, Hisaichi, IJN 171
Keaney, Lee E.J., Sea1c 109, 114
Kelley, John C., LT(jg) 91
Kiefer, Dixie, CDR 119, 132
Kikuchi, Rokoru, LT, IJN 62
Kimes, Ira L., LTCOL, USMC 34, 35, 37, 39, 47, 49, 50, 64, 141, 167, 170
Kimmel, Husband E., ADM 17
Kimmel, Theodore E., AMM2c 57
Kimura, FPO3c 66
King, Ernest J., ADM, USN 31, 33, 44, 190, 215
Kirishima (Japanese Battleship) 83
Kitty Hawk (APV-1) 35, 37, 43, 47
Kiyozumi Maru (Japanese Transport) 55, 57
Kleinmann, Mortimer V., ENS 131
Kleinsmith, Charles, CWT 119
Knight, C.E., CPL, USMC 43
Kobayashi, Michio, LT, IJN 111, 114, 116, 119, 121, 122, 189, 193
Kondo Isamu, SPO, IJN 89
Kraker, Donald A., ENS, A-V(N) 23
Kramer, George H., CAPT, USAAC 151
Kroeger, Edwin J., ENS 96, 104, 115, 162
Kumano (Japanese Heavy Cruiser) 59, 142
Kunisada, Yoshio, LCDR, IJN 128
Kunz, Charles M., 2dLT, USMCR 64
Kurita, Takao, RADM, IJN 59, 142
Kurusu, Saburu 15, 17
Kusumi, Tadashi, LCDR 104
Lackawanna 1, 2
Laing, Michael B., CDR, RN 46
Lampshire, Robert T., Jr., ENS 163
Lane, Charles S., ENS 96, 105, 156
LaPlant, George 107
Larkin, Claude A., COL, USMC 48, 50, 167, 170
Larsen, Harold H., LT 47
Laub, Robert, LT(jg) 94, 155, 156, 195, 196
Layton, Edwin T., LCDR, USN 34, 190
Legg, James C., LT 148, 159
Leonard, William N., LT, USN 89, 119
Lesh, V.L., ARM2c 154
Leslie, Maxwell F., LCDR 44, 89, 96, 97, 104, 105, 107, 125, 126, 136, 191
Lewis, A.E., Sea1c 61, 135
Lexington (CV-2) 17, 23, 29, 31, 44, 84, 128
Lindsey, Robin, LT 151, 163
Lindsey, Eugene E., LCDR, USN 40, 58, 84, 92-94, 191, 199
Lord, Walter 187, 189, 193
Lough, John C., ENS 108
Lough, Harold W., LT(jg) 135
Lowell, R.H., MM2c 68
Lumpkin, George T., 2dLT, USMCR 77, 79
Lyle, James P.O., ENS 52
Lynch, J.M., ARM2c 136

-221-

MacKenzie, John A., PhoM2c 35, 40
Magda, John J., ENS 95, 113, 170
Maikaze (Japanese Destroyer) 128, 141
Makigumo (Japanese Destroyer) 114, 146, 171
Manning, J.D., Sea1c 70
Marmande, James H., 2dLT, USMC 79
Marsh, Virgil I., AMM1c 74
Martin B-26 "Marauder" 191, 210, 212
Mason, Stuart J., Jr., ARM2c 110
Massey, Lance E., LCDR 44, 89, 97-99, 104, 195
Mattingly, Henry E., 1stLT, USA 19, 25
Maury (DD-401) 51, 86
Mayes, Herbert C., 1st LT, USAAC 72
McCarthy, John R., ENS 108
McCarthy, Francis P., 2dLT, USMCR 26, 27, 31
McCarthy, Francis P., CAPT, USMC 59, 62, 64
McCaul, Verne J., MAJ, USMC 25, 34, 37, 47, 59, 142
McCleary, Lee C., ENS 74, 163
McClusky, Clarence W., LCDR, USN 58, 86, 87, 92-96, 102, 104, 107, 113, 149, 155, 190, 191
McCuskey, Elbert S. ("Doc"), LT(jg) 128, 131
McDowell, H.M., LT(jg) 136
McFeely, Gordon R., PFC, USMC 78, 163
McInerney, John, ENS 86, 95, 113, 170
McKellar, Clinton, Jr., LT 68, 141, 142
McMillen, Hoyt D., CAPT, USMC 19
McPherson, Irvin H., ENS 94
Mehle, Roger W., LT 86
Melo, Frank L., Jr., SGT, USAAC 72
Merrill, Milford A., ENS 105, 138
Merrill, Herbert M., CAPT, USMC 64, 68, 80, 96
Miastowski, V.J. F3c, USNR 68
"Midway" (Motion Picture) 196
Midway Symposium, May 1988 189, 192
Mihalovic, J.A., CP 162
Mikami, Ryotaka, LT, IJN 104
Mikuma (Japanese Heavy Cruiser) 59, 142-44, 154-56, 162, 163, 170
Milliman, Richard D., ENS 51
"Mister Roberts" (Motion Picture) 183
Mitchell, Samuel G., LCDR 86, 143, 148
Mitscher, Marc A., CAPT 84, 136, 151, 190, 216
Mogami (Japanese Heavy Cruiser) 59, 142-44, 154-56, 162, 163
Monaghan (DD-354) 40, 86, 122, 148, 157, 158, 162, 164, 171
Moore, Thomas F., Jr., 2dLT, USMCR 76, 78, 79
Moore, William W., 2dLT, USAAC 72
Morita, Chisato, CAPT, IJN 46
Mosley, Walter H., ENS 73
Mote, J.L., ENS 66
Mott, Orville R., TM2c 66
MTBRON 26 182
MTBRON ONE 182
Mullins, Charles L., SGT, USMC 49
Mundorff, George T., LCDR 24
Munsch, Albert S., MARGUN, USMC 49, 50
Muntean, Samuel A., RM3c 109
Muri, James P., 1stLT, USAAC 72
Murphy, John W., LCDR 142
Murray, James F., ACRM 86, 96, 104, 107
Murray, George D., CAPT, USN 140, 149, 176, 190
Nagara (Japanese Light Cruiser) 83, 110, 111
Nagumo, Chuichi, VADM 27, 36, 58, 60, 69, 74, 76, 77, 81, 82, 84, 86, 89, 91, 92, 95, 96, 99, 101, 111, 137, 142, 187-89
Nakagawa, Shizuo, WO, IJN 119, 121
Nakazawa, Iwao, WO, IJN 119
Nankai Maru (Japanese Transport) 55
Nashville (CL-43) 15, 33
Nation, William M., LCDR 47
Nautilus (SS-168) 60, 69, 73, 76, 77, 80, 82, 96, 110, 111, 126, 128, 141, 187
Neefus, James L., CAPT, USMC 26, 27, 31
Nelson, Harry W., Jr., ARM1c 114
Nelson, Roy T., Sea2c 157
Nielsen, John, LT 136

Nimitz, Chester W., ADM 31-35, 37-40, 43, 44, 46, 50, 52, 56, 64, 151, 164, 167, 175, 190, 193, 194, 199, 215
Norby, Clarence J., Jr., AMM3c 73
Norris, Benjamin W., MAJ, USMCR 35, 43, 61, 74, 77-79, 141, 199
North Haven 7
O'Brien, John Murray, CRM 84
O'Farrell, William H., RM3c 73
O'Flaherty, Frank W., ENS 108, 114
O'Neill, Edward J., LT 86
Ogawa, Shoichi, LT, IJN 104
Oglala (CM-4) 9
Osmus, Wesley F., ENS 99, 101, 111, 136
Owen, Clarence S., 2dLT, USMC 6
Owens, James C., Jr., LT 91, 92
Pacific Commercial Cable Co. 4, 6, 9, 10, 17, 179, 180
Packard, Howard S., AP1c(NAP) 131
Pan American Airways 7, 9, 23
Parks, Floyd B., MAJ 34, 62, 64
Patoka (AO-9) 7
Patriarca, Frank A., LT 86
Patterson, James W., Jr., ARM3c 110, 114
Payne, Paul, CAPT, USAAC 80
Pederson, Oscar, LCDR, USN 89, 128, 190
Peiffer, Carl D., ENS 108, 115
Pelican (AM-27) 7
Penland, Joe, LT 102, 109
Perry, Leo E., ACRM 99
Peters, Dale L., CPL, USMC 21
Philadelphia (CL-41) 12
Phillips, Hyde, 2dLT USMCR 66
Pichette, Norman M., Sea1c 146
Pittman, William R., ENS 102, 107, 108, 115
Pleto, Tony, ARM3c 51
Porter (DD-356) 24, 25
Portland (CA-33) 146, 167
Poteat, Jack L., ENS 171
Prange, Gordon W. 187, 189, 193
Presley, W.C., ENS 131
Preston, Benjamin, ENS 136
Prideaux, H.E., F2c 135
Propst, Gaylord D., ENS 56, 113, 163
PT-20 68, 78, 80, 143
PT-21 66, 143
PT-22 66, 68, 114
PT-24 40, 66
PT-25 40, 65
PT-28 68, 114
PT-29 64, 141, 142
PT-30 64, 141, 142
Quady, Frank B., LT(jg) 86
Raby, E.W., StM1c 158, 161
Ramlo, Orvin H., 2dLT, USMCR 79
Ramsey, D.J., LCDR 50, 51, 146
Ramsey, Thomas W., ENS 171
Ramsey, Logan C., CAPT, USN 43, 47
Rawie, Wilmer E., LT(jg) 131
Ray, Clarence C., LCDR 89, 158
Raymond, Elza L., SGT, USMC 74
Reid, Jewell H. ("Jack"), ENS 54
Reid, Beverly W. ("Frenchy"), MACH 131
Reynolds, William R., CAPT, USN 1, 2
Rich, Ralph M., ENS 131
Richards, William L., LT 55-57
Richardson, Robert C., Jr., MGEN 37
Ring, Stanhope C., LCDR, USN 84, 86, 91, 92, 95, 113, 149, 150, 154, 155, 191
Ringblom, Allan H., 2dLT, USMCR 77, 78, 144
Roach, Melvin C., ENS 131
Roberts, Wilbur E., LT(jg) 109, 110
Roberts, MAJ Harold C., USMC 12
Roberts, John Q., ENS 102, 132
Robinson, L.D., SC2c 66
Rochefort, Joseph J., LCDR, USN 26, 33, 34, 190
Rodee, Walter F., LCDR 86, 95, 113, 149, 150, 156, 162
Rodenburg, Eldor E., ENS 96
Rodgers, J.B., S2c 68
Rodman, Hugh R., LCDR, USN 5
Roosevelt, James, MAJ, USMC 167
Rothenberg, Allan, ENS 56, 58, 113
Rowell, Ross E., MGEN, USMC 48, 167
Ruehlow, Stanley E., LT 86, 95, 113, 143, 148, 170
Saginaw (Sidewheel Gunboat) 2, 3
Sakiyama, Shakao, CAPT, IJN 156, 162

Saratoga (CV-3) 25, 29, 34, 38, 44, 167, 203
Sauer, E.P., CAPT 140
Savannah (CL-42) 12
Sazanami (Japanese Destroyer) 19, 20
Schlegel, Paul, ENS 121
Schlendering, Harold G., 2dLT, USMC 78, 80
Schneider, Tony F., ENS 96, 163
Scollin, Raymond C., MAJ, USMC 50, 66
Seabrook, Thomas, ENS 170
Seagull (AM-30) 7, 154
Seo, Tetsuo, PO1c, IJN 119
Settle, Frank E. 20, 23
Shaffer, H.F., RM1c 154
Shannon, Harold D., COL, USMC 15, 19, 20, 31, 50, 60
Sheedy, Daniel C., ENS 98, 99, 122
Shelton, James A., ENS 108, 115
Shigematsu, Yasuhiro, LT, IJN 111, 114, 115
Short, Wallace C., Jr., LT 89, 149, 155, 156
Shumway, DeWitt W., LT 105, 107, 136-39, 149, 150, 191, 193
Sicard, Montgomery, LCDR, USN 2, 3, 43
Simard, Cyril T., CAPT, USN 15, 17, 19, 23, 25, 31, 34, 35, 39, 43, 47, 50, 51, 54, 59, 60, 114, 141, 143, 148, 149, 150, 171
Sirius (AK-15) 10, 12
Slater, Robert E., ENS 170
Smith, Stephen B., CHMACH 94, 121, 196
Smith, Edward O., PFC, USMC 7, 8
Smith, Lloyd A., LT 156
Somers, Charles W., Jr., 1stLT, USMC 27
Soryu (Japanese Aircraft Carrier) 59, 62, 64, 89, 92-94, 97, 99, 101, 104, 105, 107, 110, 111, 126, 128, 146, 187, 191, 192, 204, 212
Soucek, Apollo, CDR 84
Spruance, Raymond A., RADM, USN
Stanfield, C.J., Sea2c 65
Starks, Henry I., PVT, USMC 78, 80
Stebbins, Edgar E., LT 136
Stedman, L.B., Jr., MAJ, USMC 47
Stewart, Edward J., SM3c 68
Stone, Reid W., ENS 102, 108, 115, 137, 138
Sumrall, Howell M., MACH 135
Supply 6
Suzuya (Japanese Heavy Cruiser) 59, 162
Swan (AVP-5) 10
Swansberger, Walter W., 2dLT, USMCR 59
Sweeney, Walter C., LTCOL, USAAC 46, 47, 50, 54, 55, 59, 74, 80, 81, 114, 139, 143
Swindell, Thurman R., AOM1c 102
Talbot, Johnny A., ENS 113, 170
Tallman, Humphrey L., ENS 113
Tambor (SS-198) 142, 143
Tanabe, Yudachi, LCDR, IJN 47, 157, 158
Tanager (AM-5) 7
Taney (WPG-37) 171
Tangier (AV-8) 25
Tanikaze (Japanese Destroyer) 149, 150, 155
"Task Force" (Motion Picture) 196
TF1 34, TF7 38, 39, 73
TF8 17, 34, 39
TF11 38, 39
TF12 17, 23
TF16 31, 34, 35, 37-40, 43, 50, 51, 54, 83, 84, 89, 94, 96, 108, 110, 113, 122, 126, 128, 135, 136, 139, 140, 148-51, 153-55, 157, 176, 190, 194, 206, 212
TF17 31, 32, 37, 38, 39, 44, 50, 51, 54, 56, 58, 84, 85, 89, 96, 110, 116, 122, 125, 126, 130, 135, 139, 140, 146, 190, 191, 194, 206, 209, 212
Thach, John S. ("Jimmy"), LCDR 44, 89, 96, 97, 100, 101, 107, 108, 128, 130, 189, 195, 210
"The Battle of Midway" (Ford Documentary) 180, 183, 196
Thompson, Elmer P., 2dLT, USMC 61
Throneson, H.K., CAPT, USMC 43
Thueson, Theodore S., ENS 136, 139, 148, 171
Tinker, Clarence L., MGEN, USAAC 35, 37, 46
Tomonaga, Joichi, LT, IJN 58, 62, 69, 83, 128, 130, 189
Toms, George A., PFC, USMC 77, 79, 144

Tone (Japanese Heavy Cruiser) 59, 76, 89, 91-93, 111, 113, 135, 137, 139, 189, 212
Tootle, Milton C., ENS 130, 135
Trout (SS-202) 17, 19, 21, 23, 170
"Torpedo Squadron 8" (Ford Documentary) 199
True, Arnold E., LCDR, USN 157, 158, 161
Tsunoda, Hitoshi, CDR, IJN 199
Tucker, Alfred B., LT 113, 149, 154, 156
Tweedy, Albert, 2dLT, USMCR 74, 75
Tyler, Marshall A., CAPT, USMC 141, 144
Tyree, William F., (War Correspondent) 130
Umphrey, Richard V., ENS 163
Ushio (Japanese Destroyer) 20
Utah (AG-16) 7
Vammen, Clarence E., ENS 151, 154, 155
Van Buren, John J., LT(jg) 109, 110, 114
Vandivier, Norman F., ENS 109, 110, 114
Varian, Bertram S., ENS 110, 114
Vaupell, Robert W., 2dLT, USMCR 61, 66, 144
Ventres, D.B., LT (CEC) USN 10
VMF-211 17, 60
VMF-221 15, 26, 28, 34, 35, 48, 50, 61, 64, 66, 68, 78, 79, 81, 210
VMF-322 182
VMSB-231 17, 19, 23, 24, 28
VMSB-241 28, 34, 35, 37, 43, 47, 61, 65, 74, 77, 79, 143
Vose, James E., LT(jg) 15
Vought SB2U-3 "Vindicator" 17, 210
VP-13 47
VP-23 35, 46, 50, 59, 143, 144, 170
VP-44 35, 46, 48, 50, 59, 142
VP-72 170
Wake Island 155
Waldron, John, LCDR, USN 84, 86, 91-93, 95, 196, 199
Wallace, William, MAJ, USMC 25, 26, 50
Wandering Minstrel 3
"War and Remembrance" (Television Motion Picture) 196
Ward, Maurice A., 2dLT, USMC 61, 75
Warden, William H., MACH (NAP) 126, 136
Ware, Charles R., LT 108, 109, 114, 115, 125
Warner, Jo K., MAJ, USAAC 35, 37, 47, 54, 55, 78, 114
Watanabe, FPO1c, IJN (*Kaga* Pilot) 66
Watson, William S., 1stLT, USAAC 72
Webb, Gene, PVT, USMC 79, 144
Webb, Wendell, (War Correspondent) 128
Weber, Fred T., ENS 104, 107, 115, 138, 139, 199
Weeks, John C., AMM2c 74
White, Phillip R., CAPT, USMC 64
White, John E., LT(jg) 175
Whitman, Robert S., Jr., LT(jg) 73, 163
Widhelm, William J., LT, USN 40, 154
Wiese, George K., Sea1c 146
Wilhite, Teman, PVT, USMC 79
Wilke, Jack W., ENS 47
Williams, Lewis N., MACH 81, 135, 153
Williamson, Leon, CAPT, USMCR 144
Wilson, Albert H., LT 121, 158
Winchell, A. Walt, MACH 94, 126, 175
Wiseman, Osborne B., LT(jg) 105, 121, 130
Wood, Thomas J., ENS 113
Woollen, William S., LT(jg) 128, 130, 135
Worthington, Joseph M., LCDR 135
Wright (AV-1) 17, 24, 25
Yamaguchi, Tamon, RADM 111, 146, 187, 189
Yamamoto, Isoroku, ADM, IJN 28, 31, 82, 92, 110, 111, 137, 143, 187, 188, 190
Yanigamoto, Ryusaku, CAPT, IJN 105, 189
Yokosuka D3Y1 Type 13 Experimental Carrier Bomber ("Judy") 212
Yorktown (CV-5) 31-34, 37-39, 40, 44, 46, 54, 56, 58, 84, 87, 89, 96, 97, 108, 115, 116, 119, 121, 122, 125, 126, 128, 130-32, 135-38, 140, 143, 146, 148, 149, 153, 158, 159, 161
Yoshida, Katsuichi, CR, IJN 170
Young, Charles R., ARM3c 114
YP-284 43
YP-290 43
YP-345 43
YP-350 43
Yugomo (Japanese Destroyer) 140

Admiral Ohta giving a pep talk to his troops on departure for Midway. USMC Photo

Ground forces staff for the
occupation of Midway. USMC
Photo

8th Combined SNLF staff
ready for Midway. USMC Photo

Loading a transport from a tug for the Midway operation. USMC Photo

Battle practice in Japan
before the Midway opera-
tion. USMC Photo

Kure Naval Barracks. USMC
Photo